Poetic Inquiry

My work — As Research
"Soundscape" Dancer, Andrea
P. 39 par. 1

⇒ Note: use style of
"Nissopoesis" for
Next year —

Poetic Inquiry

Vibrant Voices in the Social Sciences

Monica Prendergast
Lesley University, Cambridge, USA

Carl Leggo
University of British Columbia, Vancouver, Canada

Pauline Sameshima
Washington State University, Pullman, USA

SENSE PUBLISHERS
ROTTERDAM/BOSTON/TAIPEI

A C.I.P. record for this book is available from the Library of Congress.

ISBN 978-90-8790-949-9 (paperback)
ISBN 978-90-8790-950-5 (hardback)
ISBN 978-90-8790-951-2 (e-book)

Published by: Sense Publishers,
P.O. Box 21858, 3001 AW
Rotterdam, The Netherlands
http://www.sensepublishers.com

Printed on acid-free paper

POETIC INQUIRY:
VIBRANT VOICES IN THE SOCIAL SCIENCES

EDITED BY
MONICA PRENDERGAST, CARL LEGGO
& PAULINE SAMESHIMA

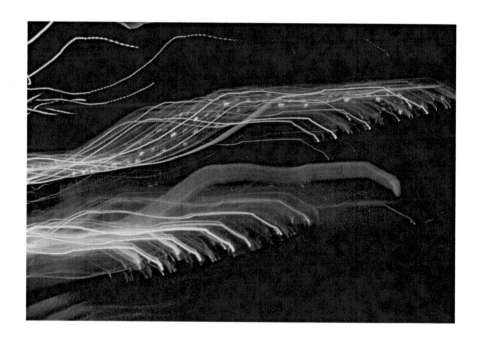

TABLE OF CONTENTS

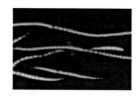

SECTION I: VOX THEORIA
Section Editor: Monica Prendergast

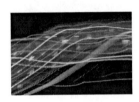

SECTION II: VOX AUTOBIOGRAPHIA/AUTOETHNOGRAPHIA
Section Editor: Carl Leggo

SECTION III: VOX PARTICIPARE
Section Editor: Pauline Sameshima

IVAN BRADY

FOREWORD

Social science methods get fuzzy on close inspection. Statistical studies are the type case for quantitative methods, of course, relying as they do on the premise that mathematical models have a "goodness of fit" with social reality. That is a challengeable assumption but nonetheless the clearest line drawn for the types of methods associated with it. Other studies show a broad mix of qualitative and quantitative methods, more or less dependent on logical-positivism and representing conventional science to that degree. Still others more qualitative in nature, but not far off the clone of conventional science platforms, leave the numbers behind and operate on the premise that their data will somehow "speak for themselves" if the research results can be laid out in a detailed descriptive account that hides the author, that is, as if things "just happen" the way they are said to happen and analytic snapshots of that appear on their own momentum in print. Those efforts always fail on one count: Nothing speaks for itself. Interpretation is as necessary to human life as breathing. Authors can be hidden but nothing in actuality can be done without them. Distancing oneself through reporting that avoids first-person constructions and other overtly personal appearances in the text usually comes with the posture of being "objective." It has a long-established place in social science research, despite its fictional nature—a useful one, to be sure, but a fiction nonetheless because all research necessarily starts with an observer moving through the world as a personally-situated sensuous and intellectual being. Distanced accounts can only be created by passing *through* that universe of everyday realities, editing out anything that appears to be extraneous to the methods and problems selected, including the author. Moreover, another pot-stirring has it that successful representation often boils down simply to picking the right vocabulary for describing the problem at hand.

There is a muddle in this picture. Every method for mapping out realistic scope and depth of information about being human has a fuzzy thin spot or a hole in it. Some of the difficulty can be alleviated with broader coverage of both what is studied and how it gets done. The need for a plurality of methods that can be applied to individual research projects on the human condition has never had a stronger calling than it does now. What follows in this remarkable book is dedicated precisely to expanding that possibility through social science poetics.

Poetic methods are qualitative and call for self-conscious participation. Instead of being inverted like a telescope for a distancing effect, poetics turns it back around for magnified encounters with life as lived, up close and personal, and sets it in a mode where everything reported is proprietary, overtly as the authors write about their presence in the research or implicitly on the strength of always claiming the representations as a personal product (interpretation) of sorts. Whether it is used or not, first–person language always (and frequently an I-Thou philosophy) fits the mode. Comparisons of such work are in fact more often tied to the creativity and skills of the authors than to the substance of their works, a lopsidedness that generally appears the other way around in quantitative studies. But this can also be carried too far. The differences are relative. They have overlapping middle ground. So the appropriate metaphor might better be shifted from telescope to teeter-totter, one of those terrific playground devices that locks the action into a zero-sum game while one person lifts the end of the board on a fulcrum as the other end sinks. Riders push up and down this way, ideally amusing each other with the exercise of being earthbound at one moment and free of it in the next. They can also try to balance it. With clever maneuvering, both ride suspended on the scale. Research methods are like that, up and down on the degree to which they rely on qualitative or quantitative principles and often ending up somewhere in a shaky middle, a continuum that prevents either extreme from being completely removed from the other. And while life itself is never absolutely a zero sum game, the teeter-totter analogy points nicely to the reality of our situatedness as actors who are always moving in Bakhtinian space, that is, always viewing, choosing, and communicating in contexts cluttered by communications, choices, and related behaviors from others. These patterns help to structure our understandings of the nature of the world and our place in it and thereby our language and associated behaviors, including picking methods and theories we think will improve our ability to represent experience.

Language is the key connector of the variable perspectives, styles, smoothings, and uncoverings of arguments in science and poetics. All language is poetic in the sense of depending on metaphors and related tropes at one level or another for communication. Poets use existing language in creative ways that differ from the special usages of chemists, historians, sociologists, and others. But even knowing the central tendencies of usage for special or heightened purposes in any language—assuming they can in fact be indexed sensibly—still doesn't solve the problem of mapping precise boundaries for the cross-traffic of transition zones in the middle. Just as science has no monopoly on rigor or a high valuation of systematic thinking, so does poetry lack a monopoly on poetic processes. We find grains of poetics in everyday speech, wherever new or in other ways conspicuous metaphors are used (e.g., "tacking into terrible winds" as one speaker said recently about John McCain's losing campaign for the U.S. presidency). Poetry makes an art form out of ordinary language use possibilities. Our lives and thoughts are shot through with poetic character. And so is science in thought and deed.

Consider cognitive scientist Raymond Gibbs, Jr., on the need to come to grips with the fundamental poetics of everyday thought:

> Figurative language is not the novel creation of unconstrained imaginative thinking, because the evidence…clearly indicates a picture of figurative imagination as a systematic and orderly part of human cognitive processes. My plea is for a greater recognition of the poet in each one of us—to recognize that *figuration is not an escape from reality but constitutes the way*

we ordinarily understand ourselves and the world in which we live (Gibbs
1994, p. 454, emphasis added)[1]

It follows as good advice to those who would judge this work exclusively in terms
of how well it conforms to conventional scientific models that they need to get
beyond that self-serving bias, as one might in trying to understand another culture.
No one is offering poetics *per se*, especially poetry, as science. Poetry is not
science, it does not aspire to be science, and it cannot be thought of rationally as a
replacement for science. That would be absurd. But neither is any of this meant to
obviate the overlap between poetics and science in cognitive and linguistic
processes. None of it is meant to say that arts-based research lacks rigor or
undervalues systematic thinking, that it cannot report accurately on the empirical
world through various means, or that an important compromise in the form of
artful-science is somehow impossible to achieve. Some middles are better served
by their respective ends than others. Locating poets in serious conversations with
scientists about plural methods for getting more than the name and address of
everything in the universe is a middle worth pursuing, especially when it holds the
promise of new and complementary information about shared objects of study.

This book shows plainly that poetic processes can be used both as tools of
discovery and a unique mode of reporting research, that there are activities and
domains of participation in life that can *only* be accounted for realistically with
qualitative methods, with poetic-mindedness, thereby further opening the door to
bricolage and a commitment by many social science and educational researchers
to plural methods as the respected wave of the future. The trick is knowing how to
read the information on its own terms. The trick is to remember that context is
practically everything for determining meaning. The trick is to remember that
sometimes it is better to have more than a hammer in your toolkit, especially if you
are, say, building a house, or, more to the point, writing a poem about life as lived.
There is more than one way to see things, to say things, and therefore to know
things, each inviting different points of entry into the research equation.

If the common goal in the social sciences is to get to know humanity in all of its
phases, foibles, tragedies, triumphs, histories, accidents, passions, enchantments,
cruelties, creations, kinships, friendships, and concrete realities running from fire
dancing in a jungle to deep breathing in outer space, a poetic mentality, and poetry
in particular, has the advantage of covering any and every subject one can think of,
literally and figuratively. Nothing is out of bounds for it. Conventional science
cannot make that claim. Practices built on logical-positivism have a long list of
things that cannot be studied in depth and for that reason are generally avoided.
The black box behind the human face in old school psychology is to poets a huge
and unending world of full-color activities—three-dimensional sights, smells,
tastes, touchings, and sounds. Bathed in the phantasmagoric and eternal spring of
salt water, the human brain is the launching pad for the passions and the prospects
of acting out the meanings of being human—and the poets want to be there when it
happens. They already have the equipment needed to share in the action. The
problem is how to assess and communicate it, how to give it agency in substantive
re-presentation and theory. No exception to that quest, one can find in this

text shades of phenomenology, hermeneutics, semiotics, and several varieties of educational, feminist, queer, and literary theory integrated with poetic concerns.

Whether posited as reading writing or speaking thinking, sung out in shamanic rhythms, or just whispered in a mirror (performance prospects abound), poetics is every bit a sensuous-intellectual activity—centering, decoding, reframing, discovering, and discoursing ourselves in ways that show us something of what we are, literally, as embodied participants and observers. When pushed through new linguistic and imagistic experiences, that same body-centered system gives us unlimited meaning-making opportunities, weighed through our existing repertoires of information, verbal and non-verbal, as stored in our cognitive and emotional memory banks. This is the universe of, in, and through which we make meanings of all kinds, scientific or otherwise. It is the nature of the environment in which we learn, think, share, emulate, communicate, and otherwise act as culturally-saturated, sentient individuals. Making science or poetry out of it requires heightened sensitivity to its properties—more language-centered behavior that can be emphasized or deemphasized according to the demands of the moment.

Unafraid of sensual immersions, subjectivities, mutual constructions of meaningful relationships, and sometimes deliberately fictionalized realities that "ring true," poetry is a way of constructing lines and meanings in spoken or written work for aesthetic results and more. The focus on composition and the conspicuous display of proprietary language used in poetics are the mainstays, not simply its forms of production (e.g., poetic prose, rich with metaphor and allegory; poetry as prose or verse; chanting, singing) or the kinds of messages sent (e.g., aesthetic, didactic, mythic, ritualized). Poets do not report their collected facts in a manner typical of the social sciences. Instead of writing or talking through abstract concepts *about* their research without ever immersing deeply in the culturally-constructed worlds of the people they study, as one might proceed in writing or applying scientific theory, poets write *in* and *with* the facts and frameworks of what they see in themselves *in relation to* Others, in particular landscapes, emotional and social situations.

Creating work in that earthy context obviously involves making choices among rules and prospects for form as well as theme. But only in the cobbler sense is the form the message. An obsession with poetic form is the equivalent of spending too much time nailing soles on shoes of known sizes and not enough time wearing them. Making poetry according to pre-existing forms is a wonderful activity. But it does not measure the uses to which poetry can be put as methods of representation *about* life. In that sense this is much less a book about words and forms than it is about the things that go with words and forms—*sharing* meanings about being human that in turn can lead to social action, in and out of the classroom.

Poets can be pushy about remedies. They know that life is more than a newspaper story, that poetry is more than an amusement, a parlor game to play when leisure comes calling. Sometimes the action sought is a profound celebration of life itself, a *re*-valuation of the ties that bind in what poet Gary Snyder has called so handsomely the Assembly of All Beings. Sometimes it is aimed as criticism about what ails us in the weak spots of a shared planet. Some of it is pointed directly at the blindness of our conventions and wants to go off like a firecracker in the brain in the quest for change. That poet asks:

> Now that you have found my unfaced place
> in the census count
>   and pulled me up as a person,
> and thus have heard my heartbeat,
> and had a glimpse of the interior of my soul,
>
> How will you deal with living a life
> that includes rape, murder, bigotry,
> bombs, beatings,
>   and the stoning to death of children,
> among other things that cannot be *re*-presented
> as numbers in a survey?
>
> And if you cannot empathize with these things
> slicked up wet by floods of blood and tears,
> how will you ever deal honestly
>   with the enthrallments
> and ecstasies of life that erase the pain
> reported so dutifully by your local poet?
>
> Am I you?
> Can you find yourself in me?
>   What is my number now?

Ensuring interpretations grounded in self-awareness and author presence, poetics is also designed to keep premature closure on thinking in check while encouraging creativity in both research and reporting. Furthermore, because poets today are generally knowingly situated, morally and ethically accountable participants and observers who respect the integrity of their subjects, they have an opportunity to better inform the gaps of certain "Othernesses" that divide us, for example, in relations sorted by ethnicity, politics, gender, and age. By accounting for life's exigencies in these personal terms, poetry forces the issue of making sense of numberless things that are instead personified, named, and filled with the rhythms of breathing, the music of life itself, albeit sometimes broken and off-key. That's where the storytellers of life live, where they have always lived, as fundamental features of the human landscape. We are storytellers all, and poetry, an equally ancient part of that toolkit, is about all of us. It always has been. Many in the one, one in the many. The particular in the universal. Missing or misunderstanding those things in attempts to study the social in the social sciences, the human in the humanities, the habitual in the habitat, makes the research unnecessarily incomplete and unrealistic. A plurality of methods can cast a wider net, catch more, put us in the web of a truly productive artful-science—into a core of thinking that promotes robust discourse from ivy-covered halls to the hinterlands of humans *being*. Like philosophy, poetry can catch us in the act of *being*. What could be more fundamental to knowing the human condition than that?

The voices raised in this work are diverse and clear about poetics as the artful assemblage of language raised to methodological strategy. Sharing these biographical and experiential spaces through heightened language and an ongoing process of resensualizing ourselves, and by aiming for representation from one self-conscious interiority to another in a manner that flags the language used as proprietary, finds the strange in the everyday, and takes us out of ourselves for a moment to show us something about ourselves in principle if not in precisely reported fact, poetics can add to the whole of our knowledge about any experience. Arguments in this collection about life as lived and how to study and represent it through poetics are organized appropriately by established principles and objectives of qualitative inquiry. The result is a primary reference work on poetics/arts-based research that will anchor related studies for a long time to come. I am honored to have had the privilege of addressing it at the outset.

Ivan Brady
Distinguished Teaching Professor Emeritus
State University of New York, Oswego
Oswego, New York, USA

NOTES

¹ Gibbs, Raymond W., Jr. (1994). *The Poetics of Mind: Figurative Thought, Language, and Understanding.* Cambridge: Cambridge University Press.

ACKNOWLEDGMENTS

Three chapters in this collection have been reprinted, with permission:
- Cahnmann, M. (2003). The craft, practice, and possibility of poetry in educational research. *Educational Researcher, 32*(3), 29–36.
- Piirto, J. (2002). The question of quality and qualifications: Writing inferior poems as qualitative research. *International Journal of Qualitative Studies in Education, 15*(4), 431–445.
- Prendergast, M. (2009). "*Poem* is what?" Poetic inquiry in qualitative social science research. *International Review of Qualitative Research, 1*(4), 541-568.

A number of these chapters were presented at the First International Symposium on Poetic Inquiry, hosted by Drs. Prendergast and Leggo of the Centre for Cross-Faculty Inquiry, Faculty of Education, University of British Columbia on October 27 to 29th, 2007. Thanks to CCFI and to the Canadian Society for the Study of Education for their support.

The research presented in the Introduction was part of a postdoctoral inquiry carried out by Dr. Monica Prendergast at the Centre for Cross-Faculty Inquiry, University of British Columbia (2006-2008) under the supervision of Dr. Carl Leggo. This research project was generously funded by the Social Science and Humanities Research Council of Canada, Postdoctoral Fellowships program.

Additional presentations and other poetic inquiry contributions may be found in the special issue of *Educational Insights* (2009) on this topic, guest edited by Monica Prendergast, Carl Leggo and Pauline Sameshima. Thanks to Lynn Fels and the staff of the journal for their kind invitation and support. www.educationalinsights. ca

Cover design courtesy of Pauline Sameshima.

MONICA PRENDERGAST

INTRODUCTION: THE PHENOMENA
OF POETRY IN RESEARCH

"Poem is What?" Poetic Inquiry in Qualitative Social Science Research

The poets march on, taking two principles of language very seriously: meaning is unlimited and everybody has some. So we say to the tinhorns: Kill and eat all the poets you want. We'll make more—in the underground, in our hearts, our thoughts, our stories, and the backrooms of our academies. And when the sun comes around again, look for us.

(Brady, 2004, p. 636)

An annotated bibliography/anthology of poetry in qualitative research that I generated as the data for a Canadian federally-funded postdoctoral research project (2006-2008) has, as of now (Spring 2008), the following:

Table 1. Statistics on Poetic Inquiry: An Annotated Bibliography
(Prendergast, 2007a)

	Bibliography	Appendix	Total
NUMBER OF CITATIONS	182	52	234
NUMBER OF PAGES	996	92	1088
NUMBER OF WORDS (Approx.)	195,000	20,000	215,000

The bibliography contains poems found in peer-reviewed social science journals, bracketing out studies that have appeared in book form, theses and dissertations or what I call "Poet's Corners"; that is, poems that appear as a regular feature within a social science journal, but not necessarily as the product of an inquiry. Examples of each of the bracketed-out poetry appear in the Appendix to the bibliography.

Poet's Corners may be found in the following journals:

- *Advanced Development*
- *Africa Today*
- *American Anthropologist*
- *American Indian Culture and Research Journal*
- *Anthropology & Humanism*
- *Educational Insights/Studio*
- *European Judaism*
- *Feminist Studies*
- *Gastronomica*
- *Journal of Family Issues*
- *Journal of Homosexuality*
- *Journal of Interdisciplinary Studies*
- *Journal of Medical Ethics*
- *Journal of Gerontological Social Work*
- *Journal of Sex Research*
- *Journal of Holistic Nursing*
- *Milbank Quarterly*
- *ReVision*
- *Rethinking History*
- *Social Alternatives*
- *Social Work*

Figure 1. List of Poet's Corners in Peer-Reviewed Social Science Journals

I am employing the term *poetic inquiry* as an umbrella to cover the multiple terminologies I have been finding in this meta-analytical study, a list of terms that in itself reveals the hybridity and heteroglossia present in this field of arts-based inquiry practice:

Multiple Terms for Poetic Inquiry

- research poetry or research poems (Cannon Poindexter, 2002; Faulkner, 2007; O'Connor, 2001)
- data poetry or data poems (Commeyras & Montsi, 2000; Ely et al., 1997; Neilsen, 2004)
- poetic representation (MacNeil, 2000; L. Richardson, 1994, 1997; Waskul & van der Riet, 2002)
- poetic transcription (Freeman, 2006; Glesne, 1997; Whitney, 2004)
- poetic narrative (Glesne, 1997)

- poetic resonance (Ward, 1986)
- found poetry/found poems (Butler-Kisber, 2002; Prendergast, 2004b, 2006; Pryer, 2005, 2007; Sullivan, 2000; Walsh, 2006)
- anthropological poetry (Brady, 2000; Brummans, 2003)
- narrative poetry (Finley, 2000; Norum, 2000; Patai, 1988; Tedlock, 1972, 1983)
- aesthetic social science (M. Richardson, 1998)
- poetic, fictional narrative (P. Smith, 1999)
- ethno-poem (W.N. Smith, 2002)
- ethnopoetry (Kendall & Murray, 2005)/ethno-poetry (Smith, W.N., 2002)
- ethnopoetics (Rothenberg, 1994)
- transcript poems (Evelyn, 2004; Luce-Kapler, 2004; Santoro & Kamler, 2001)
- interview poems (Santoro & Kamler, 2001)
- map-poems (Hurren, 1998)
- poetic condensation of oral narratives (Öhlen, 2003)
- fieldnote poems (Cahnmann, 2003)
- field poetry (Flores, 1982)
- hybrid poem (Prendergast, 2007)
- poetic portraits (Hill, 2005)
- poetic self-analysis (Black & Enos, 1981)
- poetic analysis (Butler-Kisber et al., 2003)
- poetic format (Chesler, 2001)
- prose poems (Brady, 2004; Clarke et al., 2005; Saarnivaara, 2003)
- poetic texts (Dunlop, 2003)
- poetic monologue (Durham, 2003)
- autobiographical poems (Furman, 2004)
- poetic forms (Furman, 2006)
- collective poems (Gannon, 2001)
- poetic reflection/resistance (Kinsella, 2006)
- poetic rumination (Leggo, 1999, 2002, 2004a, 2005a)
- soliloquies/choral soliloquies (Prendergast, 2001, 2003a)
- research-generated poetry (Rath, 2001)
- autoethnographic verse, autoethographic poetry (Davis, 2007; Ricci, 2003)
- performance poem (Finley, M., 2003; Richardson, L., 1999)
- verse (Simonelli, 2000)
- performative autoethnographic poetry (Spry, 2001)
- investigative poetry (Hartnett, 2003)

Poetic inquiry is an area of growing interest to arts-based qualitative researchers. This is a fairly recent phenomena in qualitative inquiry, as most citations in the bibliography I have gathered date from the past decade, with only a few stretching back to the early 80s. There are examples of poetic inquiry to be found in many areas of the social sciences: psychology, sociology, anthropology, nursing, social work, geography, women's/feminist studies and education are all fields that have published poetic representations of data. Historically, poetic inquiry has been found in discussions and practices of *autobiography* and *autoethnography* as research methods and in *narrative inquiry*, although often relatively undifferentiated from prose writing forms (see Clandinin and Connelly, 2000). The potential power of poetic inquiry is to do as poetry does, that is to synthesize experience in a direct and affective way. Although a certain amount of contextualizing may be necessary for the fullest appreciation of poetry in a research setting, it is my contention that the best examples of inquiry poems are good poems in and of themselves.

Poetic inquiry tends to belong to one of the three following categories, distinguished by the voice that is engaged:

— *VOX THEORIA* - *Literature-voiced poems* are written from or in response to works of literature/theory in a discipline or field. Or, alternately, these may be poems about poetry and/or inquiry itself. Some of these poems are overtly political and critical in their content (especially some poems written in the wake of Sept. 11th events). This voice form makes up 13% of the citations in the bibliography.

— *VOX AUTOBIOGRAPHIA/AUTOETHNOGRAPHIA* - *Researcher-voiced poems* are written from field notes, journal entries, or reflective/creative/ autobiographical/autoethnographical writing as the data source. This category is problematic in that it could conceivably encompass all poetry, if positioned as an essentially autobiographical art form, taking its data from the poet's (researcher's) life experience. Of course, poems must be framed in a research context in order to qualify here, but all poetry could also be argued to be a form of research, a re-searching of experience and sorting into expression and communication through language. This voice form makes up to half the citations in the annotated bibliography (49%).

— *VOX PARTICIPARE* - *Participant-voiced poems* are written from interview transcripts or solicited directly from participants, sometimes in an action research model where the poems are co-created with the researcher. The voices in the poems may be singular or multiple. Also, inquiry poems may blend both the researcher's and the participants' voices. This voice form makes up one-third of the entries in the bibliography (35%).

Method must lend itself to topic, as in any research design. What kind of topics are most suited to poetic forms of inquiry? The poetic inquiry bibliography I have been assimilating covers a wide range of disciplines in the social sciences and humanities, including anthropology, education, English, health (nursing and social work), women's studies, psychology, sociology, counselling and planning. Therefore, poetic inquiry – just as poetry itself – can function well within a broad range of topics. However, my sense is that the best poetic inquiry – again, as seen in poetry – will carry within it the power to move its audience affectively as well as intellectually and will deal with the kinds of topics that lead into the affective experiential domain. For example, some of the key questions answered in studies using poetry are:

— How do managers feel about losing their jobs (Brearley, 2000)?
— How do young Batswanians (sic) feel about their gender roles (Commeyras & Montsi, 2000)?
— How do primary elementary students feel about their relationship with their teacher (Butler-Kisber, 2002)?
— How do parents of autistic children feel about their interaction with the health and education systems (Beatson & Prelock, 2002)?

- How does a young homeless person feel about her life (Finley, 2000)?
- How does it feel to be a mother (Barg, 2001), an art teacher (Buttignol et al., 2001), a parent with school-aged children (Freeman, 2001), a girl (Gannon, 2001), a gay teacher (Grace, 2001; Guiney Yallop, 2005), a teacher of colour (Santoro & Kamler, 2001), a refugee (Hones, 1998), a terminal cancer patient (Kendall and Murray, 2005; Öhlen, 2003; Philip, 1995), or a couple living with HIV (Cannon Poindexter, 2002)?

This list could continue up to the many dozens of citations found in the annotated bibliography that forms the basis of the meta-analysis of poetic inquiry offered here. In almost every case, a clear affective element in the topic under investigation opens the methodological possibility of poetic transcription, representation and/or interpretation.

WRITING POETIC INQUIRY: A GUIDE

The how-to of writing poetic inquiry has been almost absent in the literature prior to the recent past (late 90's and 2000's), although anthropologists Tedlock's (1983) transcription of participant data into "narrative poetry" and Gee's (1985) method of poetic transcription – dividing interview data into quatrain stanzas – offer useful early models that pre-date the recent development of arts-based inquiry. Glesne (1997) and Richardson (1992a, 1992b, 1993, 1994, 1997) both offer some poetic inquiry-writing techniques and/or advice, taken up below. Walsh (2006) and Butler-Kisber (2002) describe their processes of creating found poems from transcripts. Piirto (2002) and Neilsen (2004) address the important issue of qualifications in arts-based research and also present their own poetry. Others offer their own varied considerations of the value of poetic approaches to inquiry that range from the most pragmatic to the most philosophic.

Sifting through data, whether researcher data from field texts of various kinds or participant data, is the process of intuitively sorting out words, phrases, sentences, passages that synthesize meaning from the prose (see Glesne, 1997, pp. 205–207). These siftings will be generally metaphorical, narrative and affective in nature. The process is reflexive in that the researcher is interconnected with the researched, that the researcher's own affective response to the process informs it. As Ely et al. (1997) state, "creating poems . . . has been an extremely successful activity for many qualitative researchers" (p. 136). They also note "one joyful thing about writing poetry is that, given the same data, different people create differing versions" (p. 136). The process is performative in nature in that poetry is originally an oral art form deeply rooted in the sense of voice. Creating poetic inquiry is a performative act, revealing researcher/participants as both masked and unmasked, costumed and bared, liars and truth-tellers, actors and audience, offstage and onstage in the creation of research.

Forging strong links to poetic practice in literature is one way to validate poetic inquiry in research that is under-examined (see Faulkner, 2007, for an exception to this rule). For example, poetic transcription mirrors the practice of *found poetry* that has an established history and practice in literature, including works by prominent poets such as Maya Angelou (1991), Annie Dillard (1995), Rick Moody (2001) and John Robert Colombo (1966). Ezra Pound included elements of found poetry in his famous work *Cantos* (1948), as did T.S. Eliot in his works. Contemporary poets such as Christian Bök and Daniel Nussbaum set themselves extremely difficult tasks to create what I call *constrained poetry*. Bök's *Eunoia* (2001) is limited by words containing only a single one of the five vowels used once or more per word. His award-winning collection is therefore divided into five sections: A, E, I, O and U. Nussbaum (1994) writes found poems using only text from Californian vanity license plates. The self-composed constraints of these poets' work can be paralleled to the constraints of working with data to create found poems in a research context. Finally, the work of poets across time who have written about themes of social injustice, poverty, war, alienation, and so on, offer strong inspiration to a social science scholar who wishes to explore poetic methods in his or her own work. An example of this is seen in the American poet Muriel Rukeyser's remarkable 1938 achievement *The Book of the Dead,* an ethnography of a West Virginia mining town where the miners were dying of lung disease due to unsafe working conditions. Rukeyser interviewed miners, their families, union officials, company officials, lawyers and many others and wrote a suite of twenty poems that has been described as, "one of the major poem sequences of American modernism" (Nelson, 2000, p. 655). To read Rukeyser, alongside other social poets such as Langston Hughes, Amiri Baraka, Richard Wright, and Carolyn Forché – to mention only a very few English-speaking poets – is to begin to understand the potential of poetry in the context of inquiry.

A comparative study between found/constrained poetry, social poetry and poetic inquiry – the focus of which would be to measure whether or not poetic inquiry succeeds *as poetry* – is another important contribution yet to be made to this debate. In a most positive development along these lines, Melisa Cahnmann's (2003) article in *Educational Researcher* considers the use of poetry in educational research practice and shares her own ethnographic research poems, one of which has been published in both research and literary journals, and also in a large daily newspaper. She writes in her abstract:

Developing a poetic voice prepares scholars to discover and communicate findings in multidimensional, penetrating, and more accessible ways. The author explores the craft, practice, and possibility for a poetic approach to inquiry among teaching and learning communities and encourages all researchers, especially those using qualitative methodologies, *to consider what poets do and learn how to incorporate rhythm, form, metaphor, and other poetic techniques to enhance their work*....[T]he use of poetry [is] a means for educational scholarship to impact the arts, influence wider audiences, and improve teacher and graduate student education. (p. 29, emphasis added)

Moving on now, from poetry in literature to poetry in inquiry, leads us to the work of Laurel Richardson (1992a, 1992b, 1993, 1994, 1997) and Corinne Glesne (1997). These two writers are most commonly cited in studies employing poetry, specifically in the poetic transcription and representation of participant interview data. Sociologist Richardson does not focus on the how-to aspects of her lyrical ethnographic research poems, preferring to tell how her work has been received. But she does make the comment that:

> By settling words together into new configurations, the relations created through echo repetition, rhythm, rhyme let us see and hear the world in a new dimension. Poetry is thus a *practical* and *powerful* means for reconstitution of worlds. It suggests a way out of the numbing and deadening, disaffective, disembodied, schizoid sensibilities characteristic of phallocentristic social science. (Richardson, 1993, p. 705)

Glesne (1997) breaks down for the reader how she goes through a sifting process (p. 206) to create two versions of poetic narratives from participant interview transcripts. The first version is "chronologically and linguistically faithful to the transcript" (p. 207), the second "draws from other sections of the interviews, takes more license with words" (p. 207). She describes how she worked from a more typical qualitative data analysis involving coding and sorting data by themes and then moved into the poetic transcription process:

> I found myself, through poetic transcription, searching for the essence conveyed, the hues, the textures, and then drawing from all portions of the interviews to juxtapose details into a somewhat abstract representation. Somewhat like a photographer, who lets us know a person in a different way, I wanted the reader to come to know Dona Juana [the participant] through very few words. (p. 206)

Glesne later attempts a definition of poetic transcription that "moves in the direction of poetry but is not necessarily poetry" (p. 213). She goes on:

> Poetic transcription approximates poetry through the concentrated language of interviewee, shaped by researcher to give pleasure and truth. But the truth may be a 'small t' truth of description, re-presenting a perspective or experience of the interviewee, filtered through the researcher. It may not reach the large "T" truth of seeing "with the eyes of the spirit" for which poetry strives. (p. 213)

This stance raises a key philosophical issue in arts-based research, that is: Is research of this kind *art* or merely "art-like"? Barone (2001) addresses this, and as with Glesne here, seems to fall on the safer side of the fence, positing arts-based research as not-quite-art: "[T]he research may be characterized as arts-*based* rather than as full-fledged art" (p. 25). My intention to articulate a methodology for poetic inquiry is to position it as an artistic practice carried out within a research framework that cannot and must not diminish the critical/aesthetic qualities of these kinds of poems *as* poetry.

Here, I am grateful for Piirto's (2002) criticism of arts-based research being carried out by unqualified or under-qualified researchers, or, I might add, by those who are insufficiently contextualizing their work within aesthetics and fine arts/humanities as well as social science. She asks questions as her criteria for conducting arts-based/arts-informed research:

- How can the artistic way of knowing be honored in education, a field of the social studies?
- How much should a person have studied or practiced an art before utilizing it in educational
- discourse, especially high-stakes discourse such as dissertations, products in peer-reviewed
- scholarly venues, or theses?
- What is the difference between accomplished art and art used for social purposes and personal expression in the field of social studies?
- In an era that cries out for interdisciplinarity, is it necessary to have studied or performed the art in order to attempt to do it, display or perform it, use it? (p. 432)

She also makes a strong call for aesthetic qualifications for arts-based researchers:

A field is transformed through individual creators pushing the boundaries of their domains. People working within the domain decide that change is called for. This is what the arts-based researchers are doing currently, in the domain of educational research. They are saying that in certain ways the social studies way of knowing is inadequate, wanting. In order to transform a field, the researcher, the creator, must have mastery of the theory, the rules, the ways of knowing of that field, and also of the domain that is being used to transform it. (p. 433)

Piirto emphatically suggests here that researchers undertaking arts-based projects have solid educational and/or practical backgrounds in the arts in order to qualify themselves for this method of inquiry.

Along these lines, Neilsen (2004) is a professor of literacy education and a published poet in her own right. She "offer[s] the following observations in the hope that they will provide support for others who are beginning to explore poetry, not only as a form of representation (data poems, for example) but, also, as a legitimate form of inquiry itself" (p. 42):

- *Poetry and inquiry ask us to listen deeply.* We must put ourselves in the context; we must feel, taste, hear what someone is saying. Sometimes we must learn to listen under the words, to hear what is not being said. We must be empathetic, aware, non-judgmental, and cautious. We owe our participants and ourselves nothing less.
- *Language is always inadequate.* We dance with impossibility each time we put words on the page. It is far better to dance with impossibility than to accept the first ordinary word that comes to mind, the easy cliché. Honouring the circumstances and the individuals by careful, hard-won description is, fundamentally, an ethical choice we make each time we approach the page.

- *There are rhythms to the inquiry process as there are rhythms in poetry.* (I refer here to rhythms – rhyming is another issue entirely). Just as a good interview is not forced, but evolves, led by the rhythm of the participants' voice and flow of ideas become a creature with its own particular rush, or sway, or meditative motion. Again, listening helps us work inside and with the process.
- *Less is more.* Always. Data poems, for example, are not just transcriptions of interviews or observations with random line breaks – they must be spare, economical, rich and resonant. An elixir. Potent. An effective data poem is no different from an effective poem – each word, right down to *the* or *and*, matters. Each line break matters; each space matters.
- *The complex and the difficult are necessary.* This is why the "less is more" truism is such a challenge. We are lured by the easy answer, the simple emotion, the tidy summary, what we think we see, the happily ever after – yet we know that life, people, emotions, and circumstances are extraordinarily complex and sometimes...not easy to face. Yet how can we turn away from each others' pain, how can we refuse to honour their winding paths, the complex journeys they have made?
- *Our apprenticeship never ends.* We can look at this prospect as a life sentence, or an opportunity. When I began to do research twenty-five years ago, I thought that very soon, I would have it right, that I could, with enough effort, know all there was to know about inquiry practices. A few years later, thankfully, I became less naïve and, I hope, more humble (there is something about education and our rapidly-changing perspectives, our search for the *all-purpose right way*, that seduces our profession). When I began to write poetry seriously a few years ago, I knew that this would be a long journey of listening. What I didn't realize was what a gift it would be when poetry and inquiry came together. (p. 42)

A few more entries in the annotated bibliography address issues of craftsmanship in poetic inquiry. Cannon Poindexter (2002) describes her method of creating research poetry as the "'diamond-cutting' activity of carving away all but the phrases and stanzas that seemed most evocative in emotion and clarity" (p. 709). She presents participant-voiced poems, taken from interviews with a couple living with HIV. Carr (2003) presents poetic transcriptions of her participants who are long-term family caregivers in a hospital setting. She says in her conclusion:

> The main goal of the experimental text is to evoke the reader's emotional response and produce a shared experience. Poetry, as an experimental text form, can be an effective way to reconstruct and confirm the lived experience of others while challenging researchers to learn about their abilities to communicate qualitative inquiry in a different way. (p. 1330)

Clarke, Febrraro, Hatzipantelis and Nelson (2005) offer poetic transcriptions of interviews with formerly homeless mentally ill participants. They say that:

> The initial report was a qualitative evaluation of the perceptions of this sample of formerly homeless mentally ill people of the benefits of the housing currently provided. It offers a categorical analysis of personal,

relationship, and resource issues across childhood, adulthood, and since supported/supportive housing. The present analysis, based on the same interviews, destabilizes the original findings and offers a different window into the lives of the study participants. It does this through prose poems that replicate the language, the central issues of the participants, and their braided logic-in-use among other things.(p. 913)

Here we can see the potentiality of revisiting data with a fresh eye that poetic transcription offers (see also Commreyas and Montsi [2000] for another example of this revisiting of data approach).

Sparkes, Nilges, Swan, & Downing (2003) consider the advantages of poetic representation:

- Since poetry embraces the notion of speech as an embodied activity, it can touch both the cognitive and the sensory in the reader and the listener. Therefore, poetic representations can touch us where we live, in our bodies. This gives it more of a chance than realist tales to vicariously experience the self-reflexive and transformational process of self-creation.
- For the researcher, producing and sharing poetic representations can make them more attuned to the lived experiences of others.
- Poetic representations can provide the researcher/reader/listener with a different lens though which to view the same scenery, and thereby understand data, and themselves, in different and more complex ways. It is, therefore, a powerful form of analysis.
- Constructing poetic representations draws upon both scientific and literary criteria and allows the researcher to satisfy the desire to integrate the scientist and poet within themselves. Thus, different aspects of the self are integrated in this form of writing.
- Writing up interviews as poems honouring the speaker's pauses, repetitions, alliterations, narrative strategies, rhythms, and so on, is a more accurate way to represent the speaker than the normal practice of quoting snippets in prose.
- Normally the orchestrations and constructions of the researcher as author are glossed over when realist tales are produced that draw upon interview data. In contrast, transforming data into poetry displays the role of the prose trope in constituting knowledge, and is a continual reminder to the reader or listener that the text has been artfully constructed. Here, the facticity of the constructedness is ever present for both the researcher and the reader. This dissolves any notion of separation between observer and observed. (p. 154)

Walsh (2006) and Butler-Kisber (2002) both write about the creation of found poems from interview data:

To create found poetry, I read and reread the transcripts, made notes, and delineated a number of recurring themes. I culled words and cut and pasted segments of conversation into specifically labelled files, then played poetically with the segments of conversation in an attempt to distil themes and write succinct versions of them. I tried to stay as true as possible to the original words of the women. I did, however, make choices that were both academic and artistic. I included only those phrases that I saw as pertinent to the theme that was emerging. I reordered phrases at times to improve clarity for the reader. I wrote, walked away, rewrote, and revised in an ongoing recursive process. The use of poetry situates me too as poet and reminds the reader through its very form that, as poet, I too am the poem. I resymbolize what occurred in the group according to my own life and experiences. I cannot do otherwise. There is no one true account of what happened and how it affected each, or any, of us. (Walsh, 2006, p. 990)

- Interview material is the easiest to work with because it most closely resembles natural, everyday talk that in turn can be portrayed in ways that evoke the reader.
- Audiotaped material to a certain extent, and definitely videotaped field texts, make the task that much easier. Audiotapes retain dimensions of the interactions that help to get at the sensory elements not apparent in prose. Videotapes preserve both the auditory and the visual, making revisiting the material even more authentic.
- Because poetry has a performance/auditory dimension, in the process of creating found poetry it is useful to read it aloud repeatedly in order to fine-tune the work. As in all qualitative work, getting a response from the participant(s) helps deal with ethical issues, but also contributes to crafting the product.
- A working collaboration between the interviewer and interviewee that is built on trust and reciprocity over time is most conducive for producing a context in which interesting and important stories will emerge. The trust and reciprocity tend to produce symmetry in the relationship between the participant and researcher. This helps balance the power differential inherent in such work and encourages researcher reflexivity.
- Whether found poetry is used as a public form of representation or as an analytic tool within the inquiry process, it will bring the researcher closer to the data in different and sometimes unusual ways that can yield new and important insights.
- Reading poetry, and reading about poetry, and attending workshops or courses all help to develop and hone artistic skills. (Butler-Kisber, 2002, p. 235)

In a variation on these themes, Furman, Langer, Davis, Gallrado & Kulkani (2007) provide a collaborative model of poetic inquiry where poetry "is used as data, as a means of data representation, and as a process of inquiry [in order to] explore the nature of poetry as a tool of qualitative research for investigating human phenomena" (p. 301). The authors describe their method:

Poetry is used in a four-step process in this research: 1) the first author created autobiographical poems as data; 2) the second author created research tankas using the first set of poems as data; 3) the third author used a variation of a grounded theory analysis to analyse the original poems and the tankas; 4) the third and fourth authors responded to the original poems and the 'findings' from the grounded theory analysis as responsive poems. (p. 301)

Furman (2006) writes another poetic inquiry employing autobiographical poetry and a detailed description of the writing process. He says that while writing autobiographically of a traumatic emergency visit to the hospital his goals were "(a) to represent faithfully the salient affective and psychosocial issues, (b) to create an aesthetically satisfying poem, and (c) as a means of self-exploration and even self-therapy" (p. 561). Furman (2004), a committed poetic inquirer, also writes that, "[t]he images inspired by a poem engage the reader in a creative relationship that moves beyond passivity to co-creation" (p. 163).

Kendall and Murray (2005) transcribe interviews with terminal cancer patients into poetic form. They reflect on this decision made "[b]ecause people often respond more directly and emotionally to poetry, a clinician interpreting a patient's 'history of the presenting complaint' in poetic form may be enabled to appreciate more of the emotional toll of the cancer journey; it also raises new challenges in the research process regarding processes of re-presentation and voice" (p. 733). Psychoanalyst Robert Lundquist also reflects on the value of the poetic process, saying "[w]hat the poetic process implies, to me, is that there is something extremely valuable about solitude, and to offer this to an analysand, to enter into solitude, paradoxically, together, is a rare opportunity within most of our culture in America" (p. 290). The potential for empathy and the value of contemplative solitude are two key elements of poetic writing, whether literary or scholarly (or both) in its intent.

To conclude this section, we can see that quite a significant number of scholars have not only made use of poetry in their work, but also have reflected on the hows and whys of this approach to arts-based inquiry. The next section of this paper moves in to a more consciously philosophical reflection on poetic inquiry that draws on a number of foundations, especially phenomenology and hermeneutics, along with key concepts such as relationality and the ever-opening question of how to live well in the world.

PHILOSOPHICAL REFLECTIONS ON POETIC INQUIRY

A number of poetic inquirers choose to speak more philosophically than practically about their use of poetry. Norum (2000, p. 249) writes reflectively about her poetic transcriptions in poetic form:

the desire
the decision

to poetically re present lives
an adventure
a foray into new genre

no innocent writing task
"messy" text
a challenge a puzzle
fraught with writerly (courageous?) judgment calls

I'm no Laurel Richardson
Can I do this? Dare I do this?
What will they think?

What do I think?
I think I like it!
this adventure
this challenge
this puzzle
this foray

O'Connor (1997) makes a strong case for not talking too much about the poetry-writing process when she says: "If the poem does not succeed without these words, these words cannot succeed even with the poem. If I were you, I wouldn't read them" (p. 20). And Rath (2001) comments: "In crafting poems from the transcriptions of interviews, I do something with data, rather than saying something about it" (p. 117). Ricci (2003) compares poetry with inquiry: "Poetry and qualitative research share in their goals of providing meaning, density, aestheticism, and reflexivity. They are also evocative" (p. 591).

From a different and more internalized perspective, Clough (2000) writes about the working of the unconscious and its connection to poetry:

> The unconscious is a turning—not so much the subject's turning in, looking at
> herself,
> but a turning around of vision so to see the other side of the scene—the other side
> of
> seeing,
> not quite seeing from another's perspective but imagining that there is another
> perspective—
> for oneself.
> Seeing another, seeing as another sees—both are impossible or impossibly so; that
> is
> to say,
> both only can be desired/desirable.
> This desire haunts. It is a ghosting of vision, a shadow at the edge of vision.
> This ghosting of vision is generations long; it is a familial unconscious.
> It is that which makes vision turn; it is that which urges poetry.
> (p. 318, formatted as in original)

In a very early entry in the bibliography, anthropologist Flores (1982) reflects on her use of "field poetry":

> In sum, it seems to me that my experiment in writing "field poetry" produced some suggestive results. I did not do the same things, investigate the same phenomena, reach the same understandings as I would have had I written in prose. The result was not ethnography chopped into short lines. I conducted my own, private psychotherapy. I paid a great deal of attention to the concrete, sensually apprehended realities of a people's existence. I paid a great deal of attention to the singular and unique, especially to the particular person, the individual. I used metaphors, images, and sensual details to analyze the problems I had set out to investigate and also to locate the problems and concerns that the Cangueses [participants] themselves deemed important. In attending to particular selves, I also had to attend to the relations between selves, to the problems of crossing cultural boundaries, and to the concerns of our common humanity. Finally, I created for myself new and deeper understandings of my own being. If I also created some decent poetry, that will be an unlooked for gift. (p. 22)

Freeman (2001) concurs with both Clough and Flores from a philosophical hermeneutic perspective, stating that, "[t]he challenge for interpretive researchers is incorporating in their understanding of a topic the physical, emotional, situational, and relational conditions within which communication and thus understanding occur" (p. 646).

Miles Richardson (1998), an anthropologist and poet, writes:

> Poetry, as a special language, is particularly suited for those special, strange, even mysterious moments when bits and pieces suddenly coalesce. These moments arrive with a sharp poignancy in the field, when the ethnographer, away from home and in a strange culture, has a heightened sense of the frailty of being human. In such a sense, poetry appears to be a way of communicating instances when we feel truth has shown its face. Finally, poetry, although a special manner of speaking, may in fact be closer to what it is to be human than more ordinary talk - given that we humans, that is, you and I, are not ordinary facts stored away in nature's warehouse. (p. 451)

Another anthropologist, and also a significant American poet, Jerome Rothenberg (1994) writes both poetically and politically about the turn to poetry in anthropology known as "ethnopoetics":

> The ethnopoetics that I knew was, first & last, the work of poets. Of a certain kind of poet.
> As such its mission was subversive, questioning the imperium even while growing out of it.
> Transforming.

It was the work of individuals who found in multiplicity the cure for that conformity of thought, of spirit, that generality that robs us of our moments. That denies them to the world at large.
A play between that otherness inside me & the identities imposed from outside.
It is not ethnopoetics as a course of study—however much we wanted it—but as a course of action.
"I" is an "other," then; becomes a *world* of others.
It is a process of becoming. A collaging self. Is infinite & contradictory. It is "I" & "not-I."
"Do I contradict myself? Very well I contradict myself. I is infinite. I contains multitudes."
Said Rimbaud/Whitman at the very start.
It is from where we are, the basis still of any ethnopoetics worth the struggle.
For those for whom it happens, the world is open, & the mind (forever empty) is forever full.
There is no turning back, I meant to say.
Here the millennium demands it. (pp. 523–524)

Yet another anthropologist and postmodern poet, Armand Schwerner (1986), reflects on his challenging and fascinating poetic translations of ancient Sumerian tablets in aphoristic writing he calls 'divagations' ("A divergence or digression from a course or subject" [www.answers.com]):

The commentator takes on a more active part. His 'notes' become 'poems.' What does that mean? What are the differences in the first place? "Poem" is what?

Poetry is the processual impulsion toward identity, an identity which is intermittently arrived at through image and through pattern. Each poem is a new start from a minutely different place.

Poetry must make us live and perceive more intensely, not by the direct use of symbols, but by a religious concern for the present real–the destruction of almost dead categories and nostalgia.

Only from such destructions will present life arise. Urban destructions. The aim of my poetry is to reduce the 'gulf between the unconscious and the ego.'

Prose is eloquence, wants to instruct, to convince; wants to produce in the soul of the reader a state of knowledge. Poetry is the producer of joy, its reader participates in the creative act.

And suppose the fear of any discovered world is so great as to make writing almost impossible?

A fish can only swim. If a poem is a fish it must discover that swimming's what it does. (pp. 357–379)

Wolff (1986) a phenomenologist and sociologist, writes:

The power of the poem's language is that it seizes the poet, and thus the listener or reader, by virtue of its sedimentedness, the poem (in contrast to the cliché) being the latest layer in a process of building it up since time immemorial. A poem thus is a palimpsest, with sedimented language shining through. (p. 357)

These metaphors of impulsion toward identity, producer of joy, swimming fish, sedimentedness and layered palimpsests may prove useful to poetic inquirers as concepts with which to talk about their work. What are the many layers in a poetic inquiry process? What is the nature of the sediment upon which the poem is written in response?

Carl Leggo, a professor of language and literacy education and published literary poet, writes about poetry as a way of living, a way of being in the world. He calls his scholarship "rumination" (2002, 2004a, 2005a) and "speculation" (2004b, 2005b) on living poetically. Much of his writing is poetic in form and autobiographical in content:

More and more I find my living and teaching and researching are poem-making—meandering, lingering, constantly surprised by twists and turns revealing views and vistas that take the breath away and then fill me with oxygen enough to explode the lungs. (Leggo, 2001, unpaginated)

And:

> Because we are constituted in language,
> because we know ourselves in language,
> because we constantly write ourselves,
> and rewrite ourselves,
> and write our relations to others,
> and seek to understand
> the loneliness alienation separateness
> we know always, we need
> frequent opportunities to engage
> in discursive practices,
> and an environment which nurtures
> desire, insatiable desire,
> to know, to quest/ion, to seek.
> So, I explore ways of writing
> that expose lies like vermilion threads
> tangled in the illusion of a linear composition

> that composes lives as lines
> by experimenting
> with composing in poetry,
> posing in poetry,
> seeking composure and repose
> without imposing, always afraid
> of disposing and decomposing,
> constantly proposing and supposing
> the fecundity of composting.
> (Leggo, 2002, unpaginated, right-formatted as in original)

This section has shared philosophical thoughts from a number of poetic inquirers who have considered the multiple meanings and values of poetry and poetry-making in general and poetic inquiry in particular. As sociologist Lemert (2002) says:

> Stand on a street corner and look. You may see, but you may not understand. Sit on a corner and listen; you may hear but not quite understand. After a while, you might ask someone, "What the hell's goin' down here?" They may lie. They may tell you a story. Do this for a long while on as many corners as you can stand. Then, you may be able to make poetry. Then, you may be able to make sociology. Then, you will be living a public life. (p. 390)

Clearly, to engage in poetic inquiry is as much a calling as it is a method; a calling between the 'I' and the 'Other', a call-and-response, a song that is sung, a voice that wills itself to be heard, in many spaces, both private and public, whispered (or shouted) into multiple ears.

CONCLUSION: TWENTY-NINE WAYS OF LOOKING AT POETIC INQUIRY

In homage to Wallace Stevens' poem "Thirteen Ways of Looking at a Blackbird" (in Nelson, 2000, pp. 127–129), and in an attempt to summarize my findings, I offer the following:

POETIC INQUIRY IS...

I

Poetic inquiry is a form of qualitative research in the social sciences that incorporates poetry in some way as a component of an investigation.

II

Poetic inquiry is found in the social science fields of anthropology, education, geography, nursing, psychology, social work, sociology, women's studies and more.

III

Poetic inquiry is rooted in the arts-based inquiry movement that has seen growing acceptance in both conferences and peer-reviewed publications over the past decade or so.

IV

Poetic inquiry is, like narrative inquiry with which it shares many characteristics, interested in drawing on the literary arts in the attempt to more authentically express human experiences.

V

Poetic inquiry is, in exemplary practices, indistinguishable from literary poetry.

VI

Poetic inquiry is, sometimes, a failed experiment that may function effectively for the purposes of the inquiry but does not sustain nor reward reader engagement as in a successful poem.

VII

Poetic inquiry is always aware of ethical practices in the use of human participants when engaged in poetic transcription and representation of the voices and stories of others.

VIII

Poetic inquiry is the attempt to work in fruitful interdisciplinary ways between the humanities [literature/aesthetic philosophy], fine arts [creative writing] and the social sciences.

IX

Poetic inquiry is a response to the crisis of representation experienced in postmodern critical perspectives on traditional approaches to ethnography and other social science research paradigms.

X

Poetic inquiry is, like all poetry, interested in creative language-based processes of constraint, synthesis, crystallization, image, and lyrical forms.

XI

Poetic inquiry is sometimes presented or published as a single poem or suite, context free.

XII

Poetic inquiry is sometimes presented as a prose-based essay that includes poetry woven throughout.

XIII

Poetic inquiry is sometimes presented and/or published with visual images or art or photography that interplay with each other.

XIV

Poetic inquiry is most often found in autobiographical, autoethnographical or self-study investigations.

XV

Poetic inquiry is also commonly seen as poetic transcription and representation of participant data.

XVI

Poetic inquiry is occasionally seen as a way to artistically present the work of theorists and/or practitioners using the technique of *found poetry*.

XVII

Poetic inquiry is sometimes a socio-political and critical act of resistance to dominant forms and an effective way to talk back to power.

XVIII

Poetic inquiry is sometimes a phenomenological and existential choice that extends beyond the use of poetic methods to a way of being in the world.

XIX

Poetic inquiry is a way of knowing though poetic language and devices; metaphor, lyric, rhythm, imagery, emotion, attention, wide-awakeness, opening to the world, self-revelation.

XX

Poetic inquiry is used by scholars to express various kinds of affective experiences such as being a girl, a student, a teacher, a social worker, a caregiver, a nurse, a cancer patient, a refugee, an immigrant, an anthropologist in an alien culture.

XXI

Poetic inquiry is called by a multiplicity of names in social science but is always interested in expressing human experience, whether that of Self or Other or both.

XXII

Poetic inquiry is practiced on the margins of qualitative research by a small number of poet/scholars, a number of whom are also literary poets.

XXIII

Poetic inquiry is very challenging to evaluate, assess and/or review as little established criteria exist.

XXIV

Poetic inquiry is often published without full peer-review, even in peer-reviewed journals; rather, it is selected by the journal's editor[s] or, in some cases, by a poetry editor.

XXV

Poetic inquiry is philosophically aligned with the work of poets through literary history who were and are committed to using poetry as a means to communicate socio-political and cultural concerns, as an act of witness.

XXVI

Poetic inquiry is philosophically aligned with the work of poets through literary history who were and are committed to using poetry as a means to communicate experiences of memory, identity, place, relationality, hope, fear and/or desire.

XXVII

Poetic inquiry is most often seen as free verse, although there are some examples that make use of particular poetic forms [haiku, tanka, pantoum, sestina etc.] or that employ some kind of rhyme.

XXVIII

Poetic inquiry is distinct from poetry therapy; that is, a field of art therapy interested in using poetry reading and writing as a therapeutic technique.

XXIX

Poetic inquiry is, along with all arts-based inquiry approaches, deeply concerned with aesthetic issues around quality, qualifications, preparedness, elitism and expertise.

REFERENCES

Angelou, M. (1991). *"Preacher don't send me." Twenty poems from voices of power* (G. Danielson, Ed.). New York: Bantam Books.

Barg, R. (2001). Rebirthing mother. In L. Neilsen, A. L. Cole, & J. G. Knowles (Eds.), *The art of writing inquiry* (pp. 115–124). Halifax, NS: Backalong Books.

Barone, T. (2001). Science, art, and the predispositions of educational researchers. *Educational Researcher, 30*(7), 24–28.

Barone, T. E., & Eisner, E. (1997). Arts-based educational research. In R. M. Jaeger (Ed.), *Complementary methods for research in education* (2nd ed., pp. 73–99). Washington, DC: American Educational Research Association.

Beatson, J. E., & Prelock, P. A. (2002). The Vermont Rural Autism Project: Sharing experiences, shifting attitudes. *Focus on Autism and Other Developmental Disabilities, 17*(1), 48–55.

Black, C., & Enos, R. (1981). Using phenomenology in clinical social work: A poetic pilgrimage. *Clinical Social Work Journal, 9*(1), 34–43.

Bök, C. (2001). *Eunoia*. Toronto: Coach House Press.

Brady, I. (2000). Three jaguar/Mayan intertexts: Poetry and prose fiction. *Qualitative Inquiry, 6*(1), 58–64.

Brady, I. (2004a). In defense of the sensual: Meaning construction in ethnography and poetics. *Qualitative Inquiry, 10*(4), 622–644.

Brady, I. (2004b). Parables and plaster hares: Two strange prose poems. *Qualitative Inquiry, 10*(6), 907–908.

Brearley, L. (2000). Exploring the creative voice in an academic context. *The Qualitative Report, 5*(3&4). Retrieved from http://www.nova.edu.ssss/QR/QR5-3/brearley.html

Brummans, B. H. J. M. (2003). Reconstructing Opa: Last meditations of a meteorologist. *Qualitative Inquiry, 9*(5), 828–842.

Butler-Kisber, L. (2002). Artful portrayals in qualitative inquiry: The road to found poetry and beyond. *The Alberta Journal of Educational Research, XLVIII*(3), 229–239.

Butler-Kisber, L., Allnutt, S., Furlini, L., Kronish, N., Markus, P., Poldma, T., et al. (2003). Insight and voice: Artful analysis in qualitative inquiry. *Arts and Learning Research Journal, 19*(1), 127–165.

Buttignol, M., Diamond, C. T. P., & "Eleanor". (2001). Longing to be free: A trilogy of arts-based self-portraits. In L. Neilsen, A. L. Cole, & J. G. Knowles (Eds.), *The art of writing inquiry* (pp. 44–55). Halifax, NS: Backalong Books.

Cahnmann, M. (2003). The craft, practice, and possibility of poetry in educational research. *Educational Researcher, 32*(3), 29–36.

Cannon Poindexter, C. (2002). Research as poetry: A couple experiences HIV. *Qualitative Inquiry, 8*(6), 707–714.

Carr, J. M. (2003). Pearls, pith, and provocation: Poetic expressions of vigilance. *Qualitative Health Research, 13*(9), 1324–1331.

Chesler, M. A. (2001). The charge to the white male brigade. *The Journal of Applied Behavioral Science, 37*(3), 299–304.

Clandinin, D. J., & Connelly, M. (2000). *Narrative inquiry: Experience and story in qualitative research*. San Francisco: Jossey-Bass.

Clarke, J., Febrraro, A., Hatzipantelis, M., & Nelson, G. (2005). Poetry and prose: Telling the stories of formerly homeless mentally ill people. *Qualitative Inquiry, 11*(6), 913–932.

Clough, P. T. (2000). A familial unconscious. *Qualitative Inquiry, 6*(3), 318–336.

Colombo, J. R. (1966). *The Mackenzie poems/William Lyon Mackenzie & John Robert Colombo*. Toronto: Swan Publishing.

Commeyras, M., & Montsi, M. (2000). What if I woke up as the other sex? Batswana youth perspectives on gender. *Gender & Education, 12*(3), 327–347.

Davis, A. M. (2007). S.I.P. (School Induced Psychosis): Poem for my daughter. *Qualitative Inquiry, 13*(7), 919–924.

Dillard, A. (1995). *Mornings like this*. New York: Harper Collins.

Dunlop, R. (2003). Lector in fabula: The poet's notebook. *Language and Literacy, 5*(2), unpaginated. Retrieved from http://www.langandlit.ualberta.ca/archivesDate.html

Durham, A. (2003). For Teri. *Qualitative Inquiry, 9*(3), 18–19.

Ely, M., Vinz, R., Downing, M., & Anzul, M. (1997). *On writing qualitative research: Living by words.* London: The Falmer Press.

Evelyn, D. (2004). Telling stories of research. *Studies in the Education of Adults, 36*(1), 86–111.

Faulkner, S. L. (2007). Concern with craft: Using ars poetica as criteria for reading research poetry. *Qualitative Inquiry, 13*(2), 218–234.

Finley, M. (2003). Fugue of the street rat: Writing research poetry. *International Journal of Qualitative Studies in Education, 16*(4), 603–604.

Finley, S. (2000). Dream child. *Qualitative Inquiry, 6*(3), 432–434.

Flores, T. (1982). Field poetry. *Anthropology and Humanism Quarterly, 7*(1), 16–22.

Freeman, M. (2001). "Between eye and eye stretches an interminable landscape": The challenge of philosophical hermeneutics. *Qualitative Inquiry, 7*(5), 646–658.

Furman, R. (2006). Poetic forms and structures in qualitative health research. *Qualitative Health Research, 16*(4), 560–566.

Furman, R. (2004). Using poetry and narrative as qualitative data: Exploring a father's cancer through poetry. *Families, Systems, & Health, 22*(2), 162–170.

Furman, R., Langer, C. L., Davis, C. S., Gallrado, H. P., & Kulkarni, S. (2007). Expressive, research and reflective poetry as qualitative inquiry: A study of adolescent identity. *Qualitative Research, 7*(3), 301–315.

Gannon, S. (2001). (Re)presenting the collective girl: A poetic approach to a methodological dilemma. *Qualitative Inquiry, 7*(6), 787–800.

Gee, J. (1985). The narrativization of experience in the oral style. *Journal of Education, 167*(1), 9–35.

Glesne, C. (1997). That rare feeling: Re-presenting research through poetic transcription. *Qualitative Inquiry, 3*(2), 202–221.

Grace, A. P. (2001). Poetry is narrative inquiry. In L. Neilsen, A. L. Cole, & J. G. Knowles (Eds.), *The art of writing inquiry* (pp. 26–31). Halifax, NS: Backalong Books.

Guiney Yallop, J. J. (2005). Exploring an emotional landscape: Becoming a researcher by reawakening the Poet. *Brock Education, 14*(2), 132–144.

Hartnett, S. (2003). *Incarceration nation: Investigative poetry in American prisons.* Walnut Creek, CA: AltaMira Press.

Hones, D. F. (1998). Known in part: The transformational power of narrative inquiry. *Qualitative Inquiry, 4*(2), 225–248.

Hill, D. A. (2005). The poetry in portraiture: Seeing subjects, hearing voices, and feeling contexts. *Qualitative Inquiry, 11*(1), 95–105.

Hurren, W. (1998). Living with/in the lines: Poetic possibilities for world writing. *Gender, Place and Culture, 5*(3), 301–304.

Kendall, M., & Murray, S. A. (2005). Tales of the unexpected: Patients'poetic accounts of the journey to a diagnosis of lung cancer: A prospective serial qualitative interview study. *Qualitative Inquiry, 11*(5), 733–751.

Kinsella, A. (2006). Poetic resistance: Juxtaposing personal and professional discursive constructions in a practice context. *Journal of the Canadian Association for Curriculum Studies, 4*(1), 35–49.

Leggo, C. (2005a). Pedagogy of the heart: Ruminations on living poetically. *The Journal of Educational Thought, 39*(2), 175–195.

Leggo, C. (2005). Autobiography and identity: Six speculations. *Vitae Scholasticae: The Journal of Educational Biography, 22*(1), 115–133.

Leggo, C. (2004a). The curriculum of joy: Six poetic ruminations. *JCACS (Journal of the Canadian Association of Curriculum Studies), 2*(2), 27–42. Retrieved from http://www.csse.ca/CACS/JCACS/V2N2.html

Leggo, C. (2004b). The poet's corpus: Nine speculations. *JCT: Journal of Curriculum Theorizing, 20*(2), 65–85.

Leggo, C. (2002). A calling of circles: Ruminations on living the research in everyday practice. *Networks: On-line Journal for Teacher Research*, 5(1). Retrieved from http://www.oise.utoronto.ca/ ~ctd/networks/journal/Vol%205(1). 2002march/ index.html

Leggo, C. (2001). Writing lives is more than writing lines: Postmodern perspectives on life writing. *Language and Literacy*, 2(2), unpaginated.

Leggo, C. (1999). Research as poetic rumination: Twenty-six ways of listening to light. In L. Neilsen, A. L. Cole, & J. G. Knowles (Eds.), *The art of writing inquiry* (pp. 173–195). Halifax, NS: Backalong Books.

Lemert, C. (2002). Poetry and public life. *Cultural Studies <=> Critical Methodologies*, 2(3), 371–394.

Luce-Kapler, R. (2004). *Writing with, through and beyond the text: An ecology of language*. Mahwah, NJ & London: Lawrence Erlbaum.

Lundquist, R. (2005). The essence of, and feeling thought: Reflections on the poetic, and the analytic process. *The American Journal of Psychoanalysis*, 65(3), 285–291.

MacNeil, C. (2000). The prose and cons of poetic representation in evaluation reporting. *American Journal of Evaluation*, 21(3), 359–368.

McCrary Sullivan, A. (2000). The necessity of art: Three found poems from John Dewey's art as experience. *International Journal of Qualitative Studies in Education*, 13(3), 325–327.

Moody, R. (2001). Three poems. *crossXconnect*, 5(2). Retrieved March 28, 2003, from http://ccat.sas.upenn.edu/xconnect/v5/i2/t/contents.html

Neilsen, L. (2004). Learning to listen: Data as poetry: Poetry as data. In L. Butler-Kisber & A. Sullivan (Eds.), *Journal of Critical Inquiry into Curriculum and Instruction*, 5(2), 40–42.

Neilsen, L., Cole, A. L., & Knowles, J. G. (Eds.). (2001). *The art of writing inquiry*. Halifax, NS: Backalong Books.

Nelson, C. (Ed.). (2000). *Anthology of modern American poetry*. New York & Oxford: Oxford University Press.

Norum, K. E. (2000). School patterns: A sextet. *International Journal of Qualitative Studies in Education*, 13(3), 239–251.

Nussbaum, D. (1994). *PL8SPK*. New York: Harper Collins.

O'Connor, K. (1997). Glossary of validities. *Journal of Contemporary Ethnography*, 25(1), 16–21.

Öhlen, J. (2003). Evocation of meaning through poetic condensation of narratives in empirical phenomenological inquiry into human suffering. *Qualitative Health Research*, 13(4), 557–566.

Patai, D. (1988). Constructing a self: A Brazilian life story. *Feminist Studies*, 1, 143–166.

Philip, C. E. (1995). Lifelines: A journal and poems. *Journal of Aging Studies*, 9, 265–322.

Piirto, J. (2002). The question of quality and qualifications: Writing inferior poems as qualitative research. *International Journal of Qualitative Studies in Education*, 15(4), 431–445.

Pound, E. (1948). *The cantos*. Norfolk, CT: New Directions.

Prendergast, M. (2007a). *Poetic inquiry: An annotated bibliography*. Vancouver, BC: Centre for Cross-Faculty Inquiry, Faculty of Education, University of British Columbia.

Prendergast, M. (2007b). Thinking narrative (on the Vancouver Island ferry): A hybrid poem. *Qualitative Inquiry*, 13(5), 743–744.

Prendergast, M. (2006). Found poetry as literature review: Research poems on audience and performance. *Qualitative Inquiry*, 12(2), 369–388.

Prendergast, M. (2004a). Inquiry and poetry: Haiku on audience and performance in education. *Language and Literacy*, 6(1), unpaginated. Retrieved from http://educ.queensu.ca/~landl/current.html

Prendergast, M. (2004b). 'Shaped like a question mark': Found poems from Herbert Blau's The Audience. *Research in Drama Education*, 9(1), 73–92.

Prendergast, M. (2003a). "I, Me, Mine": Soliloquizing as reflective practice. *International Journal of Education and the Arts*, 4(1), unpaginated. Retrieved from http://ijea.asu.edu/v4n1

Prendergast, M. (2003b). Data poetry in qualitative research: An annotated bibliography. *Arts-Informed*, 2(1), 20–24. Retrieved from http://home.oise.utoronto.ca/~aresearch/arts-informed.pdf

Prendergast, M. (2001). *"Imaginative complicity": Audience education in professional theatre*. Unpublished Master's thesis, University of Victoria, British Columbia, Canada.

Pryer, A. (2007). Two found poems. *Language and Literacy, 9*(1), unpaginated. Retrieved from http://www.langandlit.ualberta.ca/Spring2007/Pryer.htm

Pryer, A. (2005). Six found poems. *Language and Literacy, 7*(2), unpaginated. Retrieved from http://www.langandlit.ualberta.ca/archivesDate.html

Rath, J. (2001). Representing feminist educational research with/in the postmodern: Stories of rape crisis training. *Gender & Education, 13*(2), 117–136.

Ricci, R. J. (2003). Autoethnographic verse: Nicky's boy: A life in two worlds. *The Qualitative Report, 8*(4), 591–597. Retrieved October 18, 2006, from http://www.nova.edu/ssss/QR/QR8-4/ricci.pdf

Richardson, L. (2001). Alternative ethnographies, alternative criteria. In L. Neilsen, A. L. Cole, & J. G. Knowles (Eds.), *The art of writing inquiry* (pp. 250–252). Halifax, NS: Backalong Books.

Richardson, L. (1999). Dead again in Berkeley: An ethnographic happening. *Qualitative Inquiry, 5*(1), 141–144.

Richardson, L. (1997). *Fields of play: Constructing an academic life*. New Brunswick, NJ: Rutgers University Press.

Richardson, L. (1994). Nine poems. *Journal of Contemporary Ethnography, 23*(1), 3–13.

Richardson, L. (1992a). The poetic representation of lives: Writing a postmodern sociology. *Studies in Symbolic Interaction, 13*, 19–29.

Richardson, L. (1992b). The consequences of poetic representation: Writing the other, rewriting the self. In C. Ellis & M. G. Flaherty (Eds.), *Investigating subjectivity: Research on lived experience* (pp. 125–140). Newbury Park, CA: Sage Publications.

Richardson, M. (1998). Poetics in the field and on the page. *Qualitative Inquiry, 4*(4), 451–462.

Rothenberg, J. (1994). "Je est un autre": Ethnopoetics and the poet as other. *American Anthropologist, 96*(3), 523–524.

Saarnivaara, M. (2003). Art as inquiry: The autopsy of an [art] experience. *Qualitative Inquiry, 9*(4), 580–602.

Santoro, N., & Kamler, B. (2001). Teachers talking difference: Teacher education and the poetics of anti-racism. *Teaching Education, 12*(2), 191–212.

Schwerner, A. (1986). Poems. *Dialectical Anthropology, 11*(1–2), 357–380.

Simonelli, J. (2000). Field school in Chiapas. *Qualitative Inquiry, 6*(1), 104–106.

Singer Gabella, M. (1998). Formal fascinations and nagging excerpts: The challenge of the arts to curriculum and inquiry. *Curriculum Inquiry, 28*(1), 27–56.

Smith, P. (1999). Food Truck's party hat. *Qualitative Inquiry, 5*(2), 244–261.

Smith, W. N. (2002). Ethno-poetry notes. *International Journal of Qualitative Studies in Education, 15*(4).

Sparkes, A. C., Nilges, L., Swan, P., & Downing, F. (2003). Poetic representations in sport and physical education: Insider perspectives. *Sport, Education and Society, 8*(2), 153–177.

Spry, T. (2001). Performing autoethnography: An embodied methodological praxis. *Qualitative Inquiry, 7*(6), 706–732.

Sullivan, A. (2004). Poetry as research: Development of poetic craft and the relations of craft and utility. *Journal of Critical Inquiry into Curriculum and Instruction, 5*(2), 34–36.

Sullivan, A. (2000). The necessity of art: Three found poems from John Dewey's art as experience. *International Journal of Qualitative Studies in Education, 13*(3), 325–327.

Tedlock, D. (1983). *The spoken word and the work of interpretation*. Philadelphia: University of Philadelphia Press.

Tedlock, D. (1972). *Finding the center: Narrative poetry of the Zuni indians*. New York: Dial Press.

Walsh, S. (2006). An Irigarayan framework and resymbolization in an arts-informed research process. *Qualitative Inquiry, 12*(5), 976–993.

Ward, J. P. (1986). Poetry and sociology. *Human Studies, 9*, 323–345.

Waskul, D. D., & van der Riet, P. (2002). The abject embodiment of cancer patients: Dignity, selfhood, and the grotesque body. *Symbolic Interaction, 25*(4), 487–513.

Whitney, S. L. (2004). Don't you wish you had blond hair? *Qualitative Inquiry, 10*(5), 788–793.

Monica Prendergast
Graduate School of Arts and Social Sciences
Lesley University
Massachusetts, USA

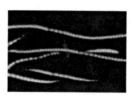

SECTION I: VOX THEORIA

LYNN BUTLER-KISBER & MARY STEWART

THE USE OF POETRY CLUSTERS IN POETIC INQUIRY

Humankind has forever been attracted to poetry because of the musicality and poignancy it portrays in the rhythms of its contracted form, and because of the mystery it suggests in the ambiguity it retains. So much can be said in so few words and in such compelling ways. Poetry is an imaginative awareness of experience expressed through meaning, sound, and rhythmic language choices so as to evoke an embodied response (Flanagan, 2007). It portrays particular qualities of being, elicits metaphorical wondering, synthesizes various modes of perception, and shows a way of paying attention (Wormser & Cappella, 2004). Poetry allows the heart to lead the mind rather than the reverse. It can be used as an analytical or reflexive approach as well as a representational form in qualitative work. It is a form of inquiry.

The use of poetry in qualitative research is not particularly new. There is evidence of poetry in anthropological research that dates back until at least 1982 (Flores, 1982). As well, there are instances of a burgeoning interest in poetry in nursing research that emerged at approximately the same time (Oiler, 1983). However, the possibility of using poetry in qualitative research became more widely known, particularly in educational circles, with advent of sociologist Laurel Richardson's work in the early 1990s. We would suggest that Miles and Huberman's second edition of their book entitled the *Handbook for Qualitative Research: An Expanded Sourcebook* (1994) raised researchers' awareness of her work beyond the confines of sociology when they devoted a section to her research on page 110. This brief overview of poetic possibilities attracted researcher interest. In 1993, Elliot Eisner initiated the first American Educational Research Association (AERA) Arts-based Winter Institute on qualitative research. It was a novel idea that brought together both artists and researchers from Canada, United States, Australia and Japan and the interest in poetic inquiry, among other art forms, expanded and grew.

It was only natural in this post-modern era that researchers who were grappling with issues around voice and representation would turn to other ways of communicating narrative work in which they were involved (Glesne, 1997). Richardson used "found" poetry, words extracted from sociological interviews and crafted into poetic form, to "re-create lived experience and evoke emotional responses" (Richardson, 1994, p. 521). Others have built on this work to counteract

M. Prendergast, C. Leggo and P. Sameshima (eds.), Poetic Inquiry: Vibrant Voices in the Social Sciences, 3–12.

the hegemony inherent in more traditional texts, to bring the reader closer to the work, and to permit silenced voices to be heard (Butler-Kisber, 2002, p. 230).

It has become apparent that since form mediates understanding (Eisner, 1991) non-traditional texts bring new and unexpected insights into the world of everyday experience. Found poetry not only mediates different kinds of understanding, but also enhances the relational dimensions of research. Because it relies on the words found in the data, found poetry is restricting. However, those limits can be comforting because the researcher is not compelled to find the "perfect word" but rather plays with the existing words in ways that most closely portray a particular story and its emotional nuances (Butler-Kisber & Stewart, 1999).

In the last decade, qualitative researchers have begun to move from found poems to more autobiographical or "generated" poetry. Generated poems are created using words that come from within to express researchers' understandings of their own and others' experiences, or to explore and reflect upon research memories, roles and assumptions (Butler-Kisber, 2005; Neilsen, 1998; Stewart, 2003; Sullivan, 2000). Unlike found poetry, generated poems have unlimited possibilities. This freedom may be exhilarating for an experienced poet, while potentially daunting for a novice. This suggests that initial forays into poetic inquiry may be made easier by starting with found poetry.

In our experience with poetic inquiry, we have become aware that creating a series or "cluster" of poems around a theme is a powerful way of expressing a range of subtle nuances about a topic while simultaneously producing a more general overview (Butler-Kisber, 2005; Butler-Kisber & Stewart, 2007). These simultaneous perspectives that are provided by poetry clusters give a richer and deeper understanding of a phenomenon.

> If a goal of ethnography is to retell 'lived experience,' to make another world accessible to the reader, then I submit that the...poem, and particularly a series of...poems...comes closer to achieving that goal than do other forms of ethnographic writing. (Richardson, 1994, p. 8)

Poetry clusters help to show the tentativeness of individual interpretations, that is, how each understanding of a theme, topic, or concept is limited by the time, place, context and stance of the researcher at the time it is written. A poetry cluster that represents different events, moods, topics etcetera, can acknowledge the "truth" of each of the poems in the series while simultaneously uncovering something more. The "something more" is the revelation that often occurs in the unveiling of a poetry cluster. The reader, and/or author(s) herself, can see for the first time dimensions of a theme that might not otherwise be revealed. The clustering of poems that are unique and at times even contradictory allows for an up-close and granular reading of a theme and a more general reading simultaneously. This simultaneous appreciation of experience removes the need to move back and forth from the particular to the general and, as mentioned earlier, provides a richer understanding of the phenomenon.

In what follows we present two types of poetry clusters. The first on "Death and Dying" is a cluster composed of each of our generated poems. The individual poems were written during times when the authors were grieving the loss of people close to them. It was a way to come to terms with emotions connected with these experiences. Each poem was created somewhat differently. In general, the process used was to free write about the remembered experience and then to highlight words and phrases from the free write that seemed to carry special significance. These highlighted bits served as a starting point to another free write, and this process continued until enough words and phrases warranted laying them out on a page. At this stage, the authors focused more closely on line breaks, rhythm, and the general structure of the poem while still attending to other poetic features.

Each poem is able to stand on its own and provides a specific viewpoint on the experience of dying. Read together, however, we would suggest that this cluster provides various nuances that point vividly to the mundane aspects of dying, the inevitable interconnectedness between the living and dying, to life's irony, and the reluctance to name death that denies the inevitable, but in so doing, protects the players. Furthermore, clusters that are generated by a number of individuals around a single theme allow for a more multi-vocal understanding of a phenomenon than single-authored clusters, and lend themselves to team inquiry.

The second cluster of poems entitled "School Days" is a single-authored series reflecting poignant and unforgettable events that occurred in elementary and high school days. It should be pointed out that the author considers her school experiences to be largely positive, but has found it noteworthy that these events remain so vivid so many years later (Butler-Kisber, 2005). To create these poems a series of words most reminiscent of both the auditory and visual contexts of each experience was generated. Then these words were worked to shape the poems by adding and subtracting using rhythm, line breaks, pauses, repetition and word play to re-create each memory.

We would suggest, again, that each poem can stand on its own, but the cluster provides the nuances and an overview that illustrate the power of intimidation both physical and verbal, and the resulting humiliation and possible guilt that produces a profound silencing. It speaks to the multilayered effects of schooling and the dark side of interactions that go on largely unnoticed, but that can have cumulative effects.

Sullivan (2007) has indicated that there is a delicate architecture in poetry that includes concreteness, voice, emotion, ambiguity, tension, and associative logic. We would contend that although these qualities are present to a greater or lesser extent in any strong poem, poetry clusters make these characteristics more robust because of the wider offering to the reader, the more complex web of connections that can be made within and among the texts and the richer rendering of meaning that results. As such, poetry clusters have value in qualitative inquiry because of the varied possibilities they afford, the simultaneous close and more distant lenses they provide, and the richer meaning they portray. We have not shown clusters using found poetry (Butler-Kisber, 2001), clusters created by multiple contributors, or how multi-authored clusters can be used as an analytic tool and/or a final representational form. These are some other possibilities that can be used by novice as well as more experienced poets/researchers. However, it is the flexibility, as well as the richer and deeper insights that can result from invoking both a close and more distant reading that make poetry clusters an appealing option in qualitative inquiry.

CLUSTER 1

Putting my father down

Propped up
in the velvet wing chair
in my parents' bedroom
my father looks like
a fevered child waiting
in the principal's office
to be taken home.

Quietly, knowing
my role I slink
to the basement
and make the call.
Bring him in
I am told
his numbers
are way off.

As if luring
a puppy into a cage
I offer half truths
and help him pack
the old razor, the one
that won't get stolen,
into his soft-sided
luggage next to
seven hundred pages of Serum
and crosswords.

He jokes about the cute nurses
at the General
And I, laughing,
follow his shortcuts there.

(Stewart, 2001)

Walking my mother

Like a large insect
moving toward its prey

the chair rolled steadily
through the bland corridor
only her small silver head
peeked above
the handles hard
between my hands.
Careening thoughts
resounded noisily
love, sorrow
fragility, finality
questions...
She said, "I used to push you."
We laughed
at life's irony.

(Butler-Kisber, 2005)

Death Eyes
They sat
silent
an invisible shroud
warding off intrusion.
Knowing pools sunken
reflecting
flickering fear
on bloated cheeks
agony of the inevitable.
They gazed
transfixed by food
slow ritual
mundane promise
frozen
amid kaleidoscope
of life.

(Butler-Kisber, 2002)

Fani

You sat
diminished
breathless on the couch.
The cough
a ripple that interrupted
erupted
wracking every sinew.

Your luminous gaze
chided my inner thoughts
bathed me in warmth.
Gently, you said,
"I thought
I would be
one of those miracles,
I won't."
Like giving birth
taking death is slow
an arduous argument
between spirit and body.

(Butler-Kisber, 2008)

CLUSTER 2: SCHOOL DAYS
(Butler-Kisber, 1999)

Miss Good

A grade one teacher
called Miss Good
at her desk
never stood.

A rule of silence reigned supreme

launched each day
by the queen.
A small black notebook
provided means
keeping track
of grand misdeeds.
Question
secret
wonder
dream
Monstrous crimes
indeed.
A twelve-inch weapon
marked the way
doling out
smacks each day
A thundrous call

strike of three
lurking demon
unleashed all.
A ruler-wielding power source
eliciting fear
not remorse
Anna
David
Paul
and Lynn
delinquents
of course.

A searing moment
acute chagrin
not what exists
deep within.
A grade one teacher
called Miss Good
pillar of pedagogy!
never
understood.

Shattered

Dancing and skipping
Whirling and squealing
over concrete
Abruptly stopped
to pluck
the pale blue oval
shimmering
in the grass,
a robin's loss.
Gingerly
slowly
fingers entwined
to the stairs
Carefully
Trembling
over the threshold.
Excitedly
Cautiously
to her spot.
Suddenly
it plopped

splattered
on the Kinder's floor

Mrs. Meekle's frown
piercing from the door
commanded
to the naughty chair
a dismal wound
most unfair.

Despicable Bill

Where are you despicable Bill?
Still
carving insults on a desk
sexist slurs
women's breasts.
Lurking, slinking
down the hall
raiding lockers
grabbing all.
Sporting leather
boots and chain
sneering threats
bully's game.
Colour yellow
underneath
running scared
of pending heat.
Leaving scars along the way
faceless wounds
etched to stay.
Where are you despicable
Bill
Oblivious
Colourless
Mindless Bill
Still?

Bus Ride

Tired but happy
the game won
she rushed
for a bus
a commuter's nightmare.

Crowded ride
coat over tunic
books askew
forced to retreat
to the stern
a pew
in the middle.
She closed her eyes...
her stop was called
she moved forward
and recoiled
then pushed past
the arm
a weapon
that groped
for her innocence.
Shaking, weeping
after the stop
fearing...
she succumbed to silence
not voice.

REFERENCES

Butler-Kisber, L. (2001). Whispering angels: Revisiting dissertation data with a new lens. *Journal of Critical Inquiry into Curriculum and Instruction*, *2*(3), 34–37.

Butler-Kisber, L. (2002). Artful portrayals in qualitative inquiry: The road to found poetry and beyond. *The Alberta Journal of Educational Research*, *XLVIII*(3), 229–239.

Butler-Kisber, L. (2005). Inquiry through poetry: The genesis of self-study. In C. Mitchell, S. Weber, & K. O'Reilly-Scanlon (Eds.), *Just who do we think we are? Methodologies for autobiography and self-study in teaching* (pp. 95–110). New York: Routledge Falmer.

Butler-Kisber, L., & Stewart, M. (1999, February). *Transforming qualitative data into poetic form*. Paper presented at the International Institute for Qualitative Methodology, Advances in Qualitative Methods, Edmonton, AB.

Butler-Kisber, L., & Stewart, M. (2007). *Poetic inquiry in qualitative research*. Paper Presented at the International symposium on poetic inquiry, University of British Columbia, Vancouver, BC.

Eisner, E. (1991). *The enlightened eye*. New York: Macmillan.

Flanagan, M. *What is poetry?* Retrieved October 1, 2007, from http://contemporarylit.about.com/cs/literaryterms/g/poetry.htm

Flores, T. (1982). Field poetry. *Anthropology and Humanism Quarterly*, *7*(1), 16–22.

Glesne, C. (1997). That rare feeling: Re-presenting research through poetic transcription. *Qualitative Inquiry*, *3*(2), 202–221.

Miles, M. B., & Huberman, A. M. (1994). *Handbook of qualitative research: An expanded sourcebook* (2nd ed.). Thousand Oaks, CA: Sage.

Neilsen, L. (1998). *Knowing her place: Research literacies and feminist occasions*. San Francisco: Caddo Gap.

Oiler, C. (1983). Nursing reality as reflected in nurses' poetry. *Perspectives in Psychiatric Care*, *21*(3), 81–89.

Richardson, L. (1994). Nine poems: Marriage and the family. *Journal of Contemporary Ethnography*, *23*(1), 125–137.

Stewart, M. (2003). *Literacy instruction in a cycle one classroom: A qualitative study*. Unpublished Doctoral Dissertation, McGill University, Montreal, QC.

Sullivan, A. M. (2000). Notes from a marine biologist's daughter. On the art and science of attention. *Harvard Educational Review, 70*(2), 211–227.

Sullivan, A. M. (2007). *Defining poetic occasion in inquiry: Concreteness, voice, ambiguity, emotion, tension and associative logic*. Paper presented at the International Symposium on Poetic Inquiry, University of British Columbia, Vancouver, BC.

Wormser, B., & Cappella, D. (2004). *A surge of language: Teaching poetry day by day*. Portsmouth, NH: Heinemann.

Lynn Butler-Kisber
Faculty of Education
McGill University
Quebec, Canada

Mary Stewart
Learn Quebec
Editor, Learning Landscapes
Quebec, Canada

MELISA CAHNMANN-TAYLOR

THE CRAFT, PRACTICE, AND POSSIBILITY OF POETRY IN EDUCATIONAL RESEARCH[1]

I dwell in Possibility—
A fairer House than Prose—
More numerous of Windows—
Superior—for Doors—

Of Chambers as the Cedars—
Impregnable of Eye—
And for an Everlasting Roof
The Gambrels of the Sky—

Of Visitors—the fairest—
For Occupation—This—
The spreading wide my narrow Hands
To gather Paradise—

—Emily Dickinson

Writing is a vital element of any research inquiry. Thus, the more varied and practiced the art of writing, the more possibilities there are "to discover new aspects of our topic and our relationship to it," (Richardson, 2000, p. 923) and the more vital our writing will be. There has been recent interest and support for alternative forms of data representation including poetry, story, and theater as means to increase attention to complexity, feeling, and new ways of seeing (Eisner, 1997).

However, accompanying the demand for alternatives has been a call for tough critics, those who advocate alternatives but will not substitute "novelty and cleverness for substance" (p. 9). To foster a tough, critical community, more arts-based educational researchers need to share the techniques and aesthetic sensibilities they use to prepare other researchers to understand, sensibly critique, and further develop arts-based approaches to scholarship. In this article, I focus on poetry as a method of discovery in educational research and examine some specific techniques of poetic craft that can help increase the value and impact of qualitative data collection, analysis, and representation.

M. Prendergast, C. Leggo and P. Sameshima (eds.), Poetic Inquiry: Vibrant Voices in the Social Sciences, 13–29.

If poetry, as others before me have argued (Richardson, 2000; Eisner, 1997), offers a means to say what might not otherwise be said, how do educational researchers with an interest in poetry develop sufficient skill in this genre to bring back its riches to qualitative inquiry? I begin by examining why poetry has been largely dismissed in educational research and argue for the value and validity of poetry in our processes and publications. Specifically, I share some elements of the craft and practice of poetry that I have found helpful in my own data collection, analysis, and publication. I conclude by discussing the possibilities poetry offers for taking risks and expanding the potential for empiricism and for educating graduate students in educational research.

WHY NOT POETRY? LET ME COUNT THE WAYS

According to 2001–2002 U.S. poet laureate, Billy Collins (2002a), high schools are places where poetry goes to die. Where Collins's (2002b) approach to poetry would be "to take a poem/and hold it up to the light/like a color slide," he believes schools are where students learn to "tie the poem to a chair with rope/and torture a confession out of it," or "beat it with a hose/to find out what it really means" (2002b). In essence, critical analysis of poetry has taken away from what might otherwise be a pleasurable experience, an unlabelled appreciation of the language, image, and music in verse. Thus, many of us are left with distaste for poetry since our own high school days of a "subsistence diet of male American poets with three names" (Collins as quoted in Stainburn, 2001).

However, many of us have questioned our high school diets and sought out our own adult varieties of poetry, only to scan literary journals filled with obscure references or attend monotone readings in a room of black turtlenecks (or at least that's what we think we'd find there if we attended poetry readings). The stereotyped image of the self-important and incomprehensible poet may not be entirely false. A modernist language and literary movement in poetry that began in the first half of this century has been alternatively described by some poets as "playfully subversive" and "freshening attention" (Hass, 1999) and by others as filled with "obscurity and self indulgence" (Naik, 1999), "high flown gibberish [and] . . . impenetrability (Kowit, 1999, p. 115). Despite the simultaneous presence of highly accessible and moving public poetry in regular newspaper columns such as the Washington Post's "Poet's Choice," on subway systems such as the New York City transit's "Poetry in Motion" series, and in oral performance venues called "Poetry Slams," many Americans have not been exposed to what Webb (2002) refers to as "Stand-up poetry," highly accessible poems filled with humor, insight, and imagination. Because of its undeserved reputation as exclusive and technical, many U.S. intellectuals pass up poetry as part of their reading lists as they would undoubtedly pass up an MRI or sophisticated triple by-pass surgery.[2]

However, even if an intellectual, as most of us would consider ourselves to be, happens to find a love of poetry (despite the plentiful deterrents), few of us would ever consider using poetry in our research. Naturally, "it's not science!" is the first accusation we hear. By mentioning the role of creative writing in an academic study, one risks the impression that one's research is less a piece of scholarship than an invented narrative (Ceglowski, 1997, pp. 193–194). In fact, this impression may be reality according to a recent report from the National Research Council (Shavelson & Towne, 2002), which explicitly distinguishes poetry from scientific inquiry. For example, in defining basic principles that differentiate educational research science from other forms of scholarship, the authors dismiss arts-based methods of inquiry such as "connoisseurship" (Eisner, 1991) or "portraiture" (Lawrence-Lightfoot & Hoffmann, 1997) as methods that are unreliable, unreplicable, or ungeneralizable in rigorously "scientific" ways (Shavelson & Towne, 2002, pp. 75–77). If researchers dared to speak of poetry in their research, they would be easy targets for dismissal from funding agencies and major research organizations under the following criteria for distinction made in this report:

> We realized for example, that empiricism, while a hallmark of science, does not uniquely define it. A poet can write from first-hand experience of the world, and in this sense is an empiricist. And making observations of the world, and reasoning about their experience, helps both literary critics and historians create the interpretive frameworks that they bring to bear in their scholarship. But empirical method in scientific inquiry has different features, like codified procedures for making observations and recognizing sources of bias associated with particular methods. (pp. 73–4)

According to the authors, poetry may be empirical but it is not science. However, the report is careful to recognize qualitative research as science and avoid distinctions between qualitative and quantitative or basic and applied research (p. 19)—all of it having the potential for rigorous, codified, and generalizable findings. Many of the report's "guiding principles" are more in line with paradigmatic traditions that exclude many examples of research in the qualitative tradition. In fact, many of the same descriptive words they use to support quality science are the same types of descriptive language that have been used in attacks from nonqualitative proponents (Peshkin, 1993) and more recently the political right (Lincoln & Cannella, 2002, p. 4).

Despite a long tradition of figurative language and poetic representation in all types of scientific research to express novelty, such as the clockwork metaphor for the solar system and the pump metaphor for the heart (Angelica, 1999–2000, p. 209), qualitative researchers in general and ethnographers in particular have been the most avid and publicly reflexive about using poetry and other expressive forms in research. Perhaps this is so because qualitative researchers are accustomed to responding to detractors, having worked hard to distinguish qualitative work (e.g. to funders, editors, the academy) as science rather than art, journalism, or other (often poorly paid) writer identities. The results of this tradition have been at least two-fold. First, qualitative researchers have strategically adopted the language and structures necessary to gain legitimacy, authority, and power (i.e., to seek funding, publish, achieve tenure, etc). This type of response has provided a 20-year foundation in qualitative inquiry, with journals, training programs, and conferences supporting this work. Second, many of these same scholars have sought to push at the edges of methodological inquiry (Eisner, 1997, p. 4; Barone & Eisner, 1997). Qualitative researchers such as Elliot Eisner, Sarah Lawrence-Lightfoot, Tom Barone, Laurel Richardson, and others—confident that alternative, arts-based methods are rigorous, relevant, and insightful—have taken risks and explored new methods for analysis and publication that experiment at the scientific perimeter to push our questions outward and enhance the field.

However, despite many qualitative researchers who are advocates and public users of arts-based research methods, little is written about how this approach takes place and the specific techniques used by artist-researchers (see Glesne, 1997, an exception). Poetry is a risky business. If poetry is to have a greater impact on research, those engaged in poetic practices need to share our processes and products with the entire research community, and the terms of its use must be clearly defined. The remainder of this article speaks most directly to those working in qualitative traditions. However, knowing that researchers continue to cross borders and collaborate across methodologies, I hope this article also informs researchers in other traditions about the possibilities of poetry in a wide-range of investigations. To quote Elizabeth Barrett Browning, let me count the ways.

WHY POETRY AND QUALITATIVE RESEARCH? COUNTING THE MANY WAYS

Gaining legitimacy, guiding traditions, and pushing at the edge of tradition—these are aspects of research with which qualitative proponents are very familiar. Good qualitative researchers know they are always proving themselves, each time, over again—proving their ideas are the most exciting, their research is worth talking about, their theory understands paradox and contradiction, their methodology is the most rigorous, their excerpts are the most memorable, their relationship with participants is the most honorable and reciprocal, their implications are most vital, and their criticism is the most astute. Most of all, qualitative researchers are long accustomed to proving through words that qualitative work is important, rigorous, and valuable as "a science." The burden of proof through language is one of many reasons that we cannot separate the form of writing from the content of our research: we have to show through writing that what we have done both builds on what has been done before and adds to it in fresh and vital ways.

However, more important than the burden of proof, a focus on language and a variety of writing styles not only enhances the presentation of ideas, but also stimulates and formulates the conception of ideas themselves (Rose & McClafferty, 2001, p. 29). The emphasis in poetry on formalist, free verse, and experimental techniques takes as a given that alternative possibilities of form imply alternative possibilities of content (Hass, 1984, p. 126). Just as the microscope and camera have allowed different ways for us to see what would otherwise be invisible, so too poetry and prose are different mediums that give rise to ways of saying what might not otherwise be expressed.

Next, I explore three of the many ways poetry can contribute to how qualitative researchers go about doing their work. First, I discuss the craft of poetry. What are some of the devices poets use that are also useful as we develop theories and heuristics for understanding education and communities of learning? Second, I explore poetic practice. What professional development practices do poets engage in that are similar to and might enhance those in qualitative research? Third, I explore the possibilities poetry offers for alternative ways to view what educational researchers do and their impact on the public and political community at large.

POETRY AND QUALITATIVE RESEARCH AS CRAFT

Poets often refer to visits from the muse and her ability to see truth before the writer sees it. However, most writers will also agree they are much more active in the creation process than this romantic image of a visiting muse suggests. Rather, poets develop craft to sustain and fortify their original impulses, moving between what former poet laureate, Stanley Kunitz, called "letting go and pulling back" (Kunitz & Moss, 1993, p. 13) using structured forms to support creative play.

Below I describe some of the devices poets use that are also useful to qualitative, and perhaps all, researchers. Though not an exhaustive list, I highlight central devices such as meter, rhyme, form, image and metaphor that make important contributions to a qualitative researcher's interpretive frame and presentation.

Rhythm and Form

First and foremost to any poet and valuable to the qualitative researcher's craft is a heightened sense of language, from the sounds of phonemes, prosody, and tone to syntactical structures of word order to the way phrases and sentences are ordered to create images, meanings, logic, and narrative. Though many poets have broken free from the strict confines of sonnets and villanelles from the past, elements of formal craft such as meter, rhyme, and repetition appear in the work of the most free verse poets from Walt Whitman to Gertrude Stein to Robert Hass. Formal elements of craft are critical to all poets because their existence offers the writer techniques to play with for greater effect.

Meter, Greek for "measure," is a term used to describe the patterns of stressed and unstressed syllables in a line (Addonizio & Laux, 1997, p. 141). For example, "cre-áte" and "in-spíre" are iambic words because they have unstressed syllables followed by stressed ones (often represented as "U /"), making up what is called a "foot." Thus, Shakespearean iambic pentameter (five iambic feet) is often rhythmically associated with the "daDum daDum daDum" we hear in a heartbeat: for example, "Or thát the Éverlásting hád not fíx'd/His cánon gáinst self-sláughter! Ó God! Gód!" (Hamlet).

Educational researchers such as discourse analysts and micro-ethnographers have a tradition of analyzing speech for its rhythm and meter, pitch and tone. For example, Erickson and Schultz's (1982) seminal study of counselor and student interactions found that distorted rhythms were heavily associated with cultural and racial differences. Different social identities and communication styles between counselor and student had the potential to adversely affect the outcome of these gatekeeping encounters (p. 169). It is no coincidence that one of the authors, Fred Erickson, has a great interest in music composition and theory. Thus, experience in the study of sound patterns in music and poetry may allow researchers to develop what poet Richard Hugo (1992) called "obsessive ears," enhancing our ability to notice, name, and make sense of both regularities and irregularities in the stress patterns of everyday speech in educational settings.

In my own work I studied the way a Puerto Rican inner-city teacher made use of "rhythm as a resource," relying on traditional African-American and Puerto Rican speech patterns such as call and response and repetition to enhance students' engagement and learning (Cahnmann, 2000a). This work is within a tradition of scholarship that recognizes the relationship between different ways of talking and social identity; equity; and access to cultural, linguistic, and educational capital (Bourdieu, 1977, 1991; Erickson, 1982; Phillips, 1983; Tharp & Gallimore, 1988).

In addition to assisting analysis, the study of written poetry forms may enhance our presentation of recorded data, building on previous transcription conventions to best represent the authenticity and dimensionality of an observed interaction (Edelsky, 1993). A researcher who is exposed to various poetic approaches to line breaks can exploit the possibilities to control representation and effect. For example, poets work alternatively with end stop lines, lines that end with a period, comma, or semicolon, or enjambment where one line runs into the next. Researchers too might use end stops, punctuation, white space, and short lines to slow down a transcript and focus visual and auditory attention. Alternatively, a researcher might enjamb lines of a transcript to convey the speed of an interlocutor's contribution and use long overlapping lines to show motion in turn-taking. Taking in the many different visual layouts of poems on the page offers researchers new ways to represent interview data that respect the tone and movement of the original conversation in ways that may not yet have been imagined in education research before. In sum, I believe it is in paying attention to the rhythms of speech in communities where we carry out research, and learning how to adapt that speech to the page that we learn to ask new questions and use poetic structure to represent and interpret complexity in educational settings.

Image and Metaphor: "No Ideas but in Things"[3]

Another shared aspect of craft in poetry and qualitative research is documentation of everyday detail to arrive at what Erickson (1986, p. 130) called "concrete universals." Images, anecdotes, phrases, or metaphors that are meaningful are those that keep coming back until the researcher-poet is sure the concrete detail means something more than itself (Wakowski, 1979, p. 114). A poetic approach to inquiry requires a keen sense of noticing from data collection and analysis to descriptive writing as foundational for an interpretive outcome that "engenders new concepts but also elaborates existing ones" (Peshkin, 1993, p. 26).

Just as William Carlos Williams wrote "So much depends upon a red wheelbarrow," so too good qualitative researchers incorporate poetic images and metaphors drawing attention to the rhythms of everyday speech and images of the ordinary, particular, and quotidian. For example, the title of Heath's (1982) seminal article, "What No Bed-Time Story Means," serves as a metaphor for middle class care-taking norms that dominate the school system and unfairly privilege communities that have middle class child-rearing practices. Another example is the play on words used in the title of Olsen's (1997) book, *Made in America*, which conjures both a stamp of national pride on U.S.-made products and stands metaphorically for how the assimilation process works in this country to "make" different kinds of first, second, and third generation "Americans" out of differently raced and classed immigrant communities. Similarly, Erickson (1996) draws on ocean metaphors such as "turn sharks" and "conversational dolphins" to interpret what he describes as an "ecosystem of relations of mutual influence between speakers who are also hearers and viewers" (p. 54).

Poet Jane Kenyon (1999, pp. 139–140) wrote that if one believed and acted on Ezra Pound's assertion "that natural object is always the adequate symbol," then poems would not fly off into abstraction. This sound poetic advice can be translated to qualitative research writing. Increasing the use of ordinary language and concrete, resonating images and decreasing the use of academic jargon and theoretical abstraction, we are more likely to communicate intellectual and emotional understanding of classroom life.

In sum, all phases of a qualitative research project can benefit from poetic sensibilities. By reading and implementing poetic craft, researchers can enhance their abilities to listen and notice in the field during data collection, creatively play with metaphor and image during analysis, and communicate with more liveliness and accuracy when representing data to larger audiences. A poetic approach to inquiry also understands that writing up research is a part of a critical iterative feedback loop that informs ongoing decision making in the field.

POETRY AND QUALITATIVE RESEARCH AS PRACTICE

Keeping a poetry journal, reading copiously and variously, taking notes on favorite lines and techniques are some of the many practices poets engage in that also serve the interest of qualitative researchers. A poetic approach to inquiry requires the careful study of our own written logic, technique, and aesthetic. This section focuses on journaling techniques that might be shared by the poet and educational researcher to enhance the quality of data collection and analysis. Just as qualitative researchers keep a field notebook on visits to research settings, so too poets keep writing notebooks, only their fields are not limited to a particular site. Qualitative researchers might enhance their fieldnotes by learning from a few practices poets use to document a wide scope of seeing.

One poetic practice to educational research includes the use of a notebook both in and out of the field setting. Having a notebook at the bedside, the office, the carwash, or the dentist's waiting room allows the possibility for researchers to write down images, metaphors, and overheard phrases that may have direct or indirect relationship to our studies in the field. A poet's pursuit is to find fresh ways of expressing themes that have undoubtedly been addressed before—themes about love, death, social justice, home. A fresh way of seeing requires the practice of noticing— whether in everyday life or from copious and varied reading—such as a Lakota-English dictionary, Aesop's fable, Emily Dickinson's verse. By drawing on the unexpected and "assuming and exploiting a common frame of reference" (Gioia, 1999, p. 31), poets achieve a concise ability to give language to the unsayable. Just as Whorf (1956) used Einstein's theory of relativity to explore his notion of linguistic relativity, and Lévi-Strauss (1962/1966) used the concept of the bricklayer to explore ingenuity within constraint, so too educational researchers might find the practice of noticing through note taking to connect common frameworks to uncommon perspectives on traditional educational themes. In other words, by keeping our notebooks with us both in and out of the field and taking notes on everyday observations and from varied academic and nonacademic reading, we are, like poets, more likely to be surprised by unexpected connections and understanding.

However, poetic practice is not just about taking notes but about how one takes and revises notes to reimagine ways of understanding the familiar (Cahnmann, 2001). One approach poets use is to write within formal constraints such as meter and rhyme. Another approach is to use the principles of formalist poetry, such as the repeating lines and words in the villanelle and sestina,[4] to highlight what stands out from the underlying repetition. A contemporary structure is often referred to as anaphora, using repeated phrases such as "if only," "because," or "I remember," to build rhythm in the exploration of a particular context. One can hear this technique in poetry as well as prose, as in the Martin Luther King's "I have a dream" speech or the repeating "we" and staccato rhythm in Gwendolyn Brooks' (1999) poem "We Real Cool":

We Real Cool

The Pool Players.
Seven at the Golden Shovel.

We real cool. We
Left school. We

Lurk late. We
Strike straight. We

Sing sin. We
Thin gin. We

Jazz June. We
Die soon.

Gathered in eight units of approximately three-beat lines, this lean poem is thick with meaning, ironically juxtaposing a playful, sing-song form with tragic content. Brooks achieves this juxtaposition when she breaks the predominant rhythm—two strong beats, one weak beat—with two strong beats that stand alone at the end. This poem leaves the reader without the identifying "we," the tragic consequence of a society divided by race, class, and education.

Just as important as what is included in the poem is what is left out. In this poem we hear the pool players' voices because of carefully selected word choice reflecting African-American dialect and experience. Formal aspects of poetry help the writer make these selections, synthesizing large transcripts from life into a block quote or a three-beat line. Rhythm, repetition, and other formal considerations offer researchers creative tools throughout the research process for identifying salient themes and capturing them in imaginative and poetic ways.

I have found the use of rhythm and repetition particularly useful when taking fieldnotes and beginning to think about analysis. Below I include an excerpt from an interview I had (personal communication, April 9, 2002) with the principal and lead English-as-a-second-language teacher of a low-performing school where they explained reasons for the school's rank of 1,052nd in the state. I am less interested in the poem-in-progress itself as a product and more interested in how the poetic device of listing helped me capture the fervor and paradox in these administrators' reflections. The poetic repetition enabled me to draw attention both to pattern and deviation from common underlying deficit theories and where the principal thought she had some power to critique and change the situation:

So Many Plates Spinning

The principal says our test scores are
   ABYSMAL.

because tests don't show progress.
because politicians aren't educators.
because everyone is not created equal.
because of IQ.
because other schools have a top that pulls up the scores.
because the school board doesn't want to hear.

because 30% have Spanish as a first language.
   (Every teacher should be able to say "zapatos")
because they don't read.
because parents are illiterate.
because Mommies can't even sign their own name.
because it takes 5 years to learn a language.
   (I have to cut that down in half).
   because the state doesn't care about the process.
because of a capital L for LAZY.
NOT because they can't.
   I don't want to hear "our kids can't."
   I can't hear it,
      I can't.
because we're left with Black and Hispanic kids.
Even our OWN students don't know how to speak English.

because of school choice.
because of white flight.
      SOMEONE should have seen THAT coming.

If you create good neighborhood schools, people won't go running.
If you stop blaming and start doing.
If you work with parents.

It's because I'm working two jobs.
You work like a dog to change a program.
I've never had so many plates spinning.

"So many plates spinning" is a synthesis of the quotes I took from a group interview with an African-American principal and White teacher that incorporates some rhythm from the mixture of African-American and Southern dialect. In my original handwritten fieldnotes, I distinguished quotations from each participant and included much more than what I include in this poem. After the field I returned to my office to write up my notes in the computer and used poetry to help me capture the essence of what was said— the feelings, contradictions, dualities, and paradoxes.[5] My identity as both a poet and researcher gave me license to adjust what was "true" (with a lower case "t") in the original and the detailed accuracy to capture "Truth" (with a capital "T"), that is, the depth of feeling and music in the original situation. All researchers, whether they adjust numbers or extract quotations from a transcript, find themselves somewhere along the continuum between what is "true" and "True." The difference may be the claims to fact or fiction that are made (Richardson, 2000, p. 926; Clifford, n.d., as cited in Van Maanen, 1988, p. 101). Once we realize that all claims to "scientific truth" are suspect, influenced by the culturally bound nature of the researcher's text, we can free ourselves to write in ways that name and claim feeling, story, and relationship. In so doing we will be better equipped to communicate findings in multidimensional, penetrating, and more accessible ways.[6]

Another example of the way poetry helped me understand contradiction in both my fieldnotes and analysis is from a previous study of bilingual schooling in inner-city Philadelphia (Cahnmann, 2001). While driving to my fieldsite I found myself musing on numerous pairs of shoes I saw hanging off an electric wire. Through a listing of images in my fieldnotes of inner-city life, I realized the deficit theories I brought with me everyday and my limitations at seeing the full scope of life in this community. The child's voice in the poem is a collection of wisdom from many children at my research site, Black and Latino. Their answers came from questions I was hesitant to ask because they seemed unrelated to my research project on bilingual education. Yet these questions were most revealing of contradictions I had otherwise been unable to see.

Driving through North Philly

I see them. The shoes
on Eighth Street—there must be
thirty pair perched upside down.
An uneven silhouette of sneakers
slung over electric wire;
the lightness soaked out of them,
except for the eager cleats,
less familiar with the whims of weather.

Here a boy doesn't give up shoes
unless they give up on him;
a face bruised with September
and measured kicks through corn chip bags
crushed in the side-pockets of this city.

I think of other reasons for these pairs in flight:
maybe a test of gravity, feet got too big,
or a protest against restrictions
on tilted chairs, names gouged on desktops,
on-time, straight lines in the yard.

For weeks I wonder until I stop
to ask a kid from the neighborhood.
We study each other: a black boy,
backpack over left shoulder, pants big enough
for two of him, and a white woman dressed like a teacher
with notepad and loopy earrings. "Because it's fun, Miss,"
he says, as if the answer were scrawled on the wall
behind me in oversized bubble letters.
And then, "So they remember you when you're gone."

I think of the thirteen apartments I've lived in
over the last nine years and how I've never left anything behind.
I look at the newest pair, think how impractical
to let color fade, perfectly good and out of reach,
an empty walk on sky.

"I done it lots a'times, Miss," he says with a grin.
I consider how little I know about joy.
What it's like to throw something up in the air
that's important, that weighs something, that takes you places—
and not wait for it to come down.

I provide these examples of fieldnote poems as one model for what is possible in ways we document and understand educational settings. The act of writing and revising "Driving Through North Philly" helped me understand and share with others the complexity of working class and inner-city life in ways that my training in largely deductive, Marxist thinking did not allow. Writing poetry and poetically inspired fieldnotes allowed me to be honest with the limitations and assumptions in my own understanding in ways that might never have been questioned otherwise. [7]

POETRY AND QUALITATIVE RESEARCH AS POSSIBILITY

Does exercising the craft and practice of poetry mean all educational researchers should become poets? My answer: God help us. As far as I'm concerned we do not need anymore struggling poets in the world.[8] However, I do advocate all researchers be exposed to what poets do and how researchers might reap the benefits of poetic craft and practice in our work. Through poetic craft and practice, we can surprise both ourselves and our audiences with new possibilities. Using elements of poetry in our data collection, analysis and write-up has the potential to make our thinking clearer, fresher, and more accessible and to render the richness and complexity of the observed world. To use a now banal, but useful metaphor, poetic craft and practice are "tools" we should not overlook in the repertoire of devices we use for conveying meaning, analyzing data, and attracting a broader readership.

Formal poetic devices give writers of all genres the tools to work at the height of convention just as researchers work within traditional forms that structure the presentation of our data. However, poetry is also about risk. Walt Whitman and Gertrude Stein are examples of poets who used surprising language and play to transform old forms and ideas and make something new. Educational researchers can benefit from arts-based approaches to research that question the limits of tradition just as an architect might question the institutional use of cinderblock walls. For example, we often instruct students to use citations rather than teaching them to explore their own words and imaginations. This reduces knowing. Rather, we need to teach students to develop their own voices. Poetry can be an important means to that end.

There are themes and patterns in human experience that can only be grasped in narrative renditions, beyond historical and anthropological nonfiction to include other verbal formats such as fiction, plays, and poetry. There is increasing recognition that researchers who develop a poetic voice are better prepared to write ethnographic prose in ways that are lyrical, engaging, and accessible to a wider audience. Thus, education and social science scholars such as JoBeth Allen at the University of Georgia, Mike Rose at the University of California, Los Angeles, and Renato Rosaldo at New York University, among others, are teaching courses that blend techniques for ethnographic and creative writing (Rose & McClafferty, 2001; Piirto, 2002). We also see scholarly journals, such as *Qualitative Inquiry, Harvard Educational Review, Anthropology and Education Quarterly*, and *Anthropology & Humanism*, publishing an increasing number of arts-based informed research and writing. Additionally, the Society for Humanist Anthropology annually awards the Victor Turner prize for the best written ethnography, hosting an annual open mike for anthropologists who are also poets and fiction writers at the annual meeting of the American Anthropological Association, promoting writing that is simultaneously engaging and scientific.

In sum, if we value engaging a diverse and wide-ranging readership, we ought to consider more "rigorous" training as writers and thinkers, beyond the inherited toolbox from the past.

CONCLUSION: THE "SO WHAT TEST"[9]

Arts-based approaches are not an either-or proposition to traditional research paradigms. We do no service to ourselves as arts-based researchers to define ourselves in opposition to traditional practices. Rather, the literary and visual arts offer ways to stretch our capacities for creativity and knowing, creating a healthy synthesis of approaches to write in ways that paint a full picture of a heterogeneous movement to improve education. In educational research and practice we are working with human beings in all their ever-changing complexity. Incorporating the craft, practice, and possibility of poetry in our research enhances our ability to understand classroom life and support students' potential to add their voices to a more socially just and democratic society. Thus, I do not suggest a poetic approach replace qualitative or quantitative study, merely that poetry enhance and add to our research.

Likewise, the work of ethnographers in education can enhance the direction of contemporary poetry. Social scientists often work from the presupposition of social responsibility. This is especially true of ethnographers of education, aiming to inform and improve education for all youth. Poetry has a lot to learn from disciplines that take on social and cultural themes, political activism, and social change. Our audiences should help dictate the kinds of genres we use but should not eliminate the possibility for mergers between the work of artists and social scientists, adding dimensionality and empowerment to both.

As mentioned earlier in this article, one can read a poem such as Brooks' (1999) "We Real Cool" over and over again, sharing it with lay and academic audiences alike and each time realizing new depths of understanding. Thus, another value of reading and writing poetry alongside fieldwork is to share it with a much larger readership than that of a typical educational study, with more immediate and lasting impact. For example, I frequently incorporate poetry with educational and cultural themes into my courses directed to teacher education and research students. I find poems and short stories profoundly influence my students' abilities to connect and transfer learning from more dense and abstract academic readings. I have also found that when luck and craft merge my poetry writing has the potential to be well received by lay and non-educational audiences. For example, the poem "Driving Through North Philly" was published in *The Philadelphia Inquirer* (Cahnmann, 1999) and *Quarterly West* (Cahnmann, 2000b), a national literary magazine, and thus the "findings" contained therein about crossing race, class, and culture boundaries were shared by large local and national communities. Educational researchers may not all write quality poems (Piirto, 2002), but we all can make greater efforts to incorporate rhythm, form, image, metaphor, and other elements of poetic craft into the ways we write through and about our investigations. Instead of "yak[ing] endlessly about the need for a more engaging, passionate social science" (Foley, 2002), let's teach ourselves and our students how to do it.

Last, my answer to the "so what test" is to answer, "why not?" The available traditions for analysis and write up of research are not fixed entities, but a dynamic enterprise that changes within and among generations of scholars and from audience to audience (Gioia, 1999, p. 32). We cannot lose by acquiring techniques employed by arts-based researchers. We must assume an audience for our work, an audience that longs for fresh language to describe the indescribable emotional and intellectual experiences in and beyond classrooms. We may not all write great popular or literary poems, but we can all draw on the craft and practice of poetry to realize its potential, challenging the academic marginality of our work. We might decide to read more poetry, take a creative writing class, and take more risks in our field notes and articles. My hope is for educational researchers to explore poetic techniques and strategies beyond those mentioned here to communicate findings in multidimensional, penetrating, and more accessible ways.

AUTHOR'S NOTE

I am grateful to my colleagues, teachers, and friends who have joined me in scholarly writing groups, helping to keep one another's writing clear and vibrant.

NOTES

[1] A similar version of this chapter first appeared in article form: Cahnmann, M. (2003). The craft, practice, and possibility of poetry in educational research. *Educational Researcher, 32* (3), 29–36.

[2] Poetry is less appreciated in the United States than it is in many other nations (e.g., Ireland where poetry is held in much higher public regard). This article is primarily addressed to an American audience and most references here are to American poets and arts-based scholars. I am hopeful that a colleague can write a piece more international in scope on the use of poetry in scholarship abroad. My advance apologies to the many scholars working in arts and poetic approaches to inquiry that I was unable to cite here.

[3] "No ideas but in things" is a line from William Carlos Williams's 1927 poem "Paterson" and can be located at www.en.utexas.edu/wcw/back/94fall/hahn.html.

[4] The villanelle has 19 lines with five tercets (three-line stanzas) and ends in a quatrain (four lines). The first and third lines of the opening stanza are repeated, as is the "aba" rhyme scheme (abaa for the quatrain). The sestina has six stanzas of six lines each (sestets) and ends with a tercet. The end word in each of the six lines gets repeated in a specific order throughout the poem and all six words are used in the final tercet. For further explanation see Addonizio and Laux (1997, pp. 138–161).

[5] This poem-draft has gone through several phases of revision and will likely not become a stand-alone poem I am satisfied with but rather serves as a part of the process of poetic scholarship. Nonetheless, it may be helpful for readers to know about the process of the data-to-poem-draft that appears here. Though my field notes began with many of these same lines, I have used poetic sensibilities to delete some words (such as excessive articles—i.e., a and the—that slow down the poem) and entire lines that were redundant and/or didn't read as powerfully as those I have selected thus far. I have also added the repetition of the word "because," emphasizing the list of disparate and often contradictory reasons given for school failure. In this piece, representation is fine-tuning a process that began in data collection.

[6]   The difference between truth and Truth is a controversial topic worthy of more discussion than space allows here. Entire articles and volumes have been written about this subject (e.g., Anderson, 1996; Barone, 2000, 2001; Eisner, 1991). I invite readers to respond in the most productive (and least confrontational) ways to further this discussion as modeled by Ellis (2002).

[7]   Two years passed from the time I wrote the first poetic observation to the time I crafted the first full draft of this poem; I have subsequently revised this poem over 8 years to the current version you see here in 2008. One major disadvantage of writing poetic representations of data is that the poet-scholar cannot rush the poem or insist the poem be "about" the subject of our research. Poems take on their own natures and timelines and when rushed can result in an aesthetic that feels forced and either over or underwritten, compromising both Truth and Beauty.

[8]   See Piirto (2002) for further discussion on how much study and practice in art is necessary before using it for various purposes in educational discourse.

[9]   Kenyon (1999) talks about the "so what test" in her collection of essays on poetry.

REFERENCES

Addonizio, K., & Laux, D. (1997). *The poet's companion: A guide to the pleasures of writing poetry.* New York: WW Norton & Company.

Anderson, T. T. (1996). Through phenomenology to sublime poetry: Martin Heidegger on the decisive relation between truth and art. *Research in Phenomenology, 26,* 198–230.

Angelica, J. C. (1999–2000). The metamorphosis of metaphor: From literary trope to conceptual key. *Lenguas modernas, 26–27,* 209–225.

Barone, T. (2000). *Aesthetics, politics, and educational inquiry.* New York: Peter Lang.

Barone, T. (2001). *Touching eternity: Life narratives and the enduring consequences of teaching.* New York: Teachers College Press.

Barone, T., & Eisner, E. W. (1997). Arts-based educational research. In R. M. Jaeger (Ed.), *Complementary methods for research in education* (2nd ed.). Washington, DC: American Educational Research Association.

Bourdieu, P. (1977). Cultural reproduction and social reproduction. In J. Karabel & A. H. Halsey (Eds.), *Power and ideology in education* (pp. 487–511). New York: Oxford University Press.

Bourdieu, P. (1991). *Language and symbolic power* (G. Raymond & M. Adamson, Trans.). Cambridge, MA: Harvard University Press.

Brooks, G. (1999). *Selected poems.* New York: Harpercollins.

Cahnmann, M. (1999, September 5). Driving through North Philly. *Philadelphia Inquirer,* p. E5.

Cahnmann, M. (2000a). Rhythm and resource: Repetition as a linguistic style in an urban elementary classroom. *Working Papers in Educational Linguistics, 16*(1), 39–52.

Cahnmann, M. (2000b). Driving through North Philly. *Quarterly West, 51,* 98–99.

Cahnmann, M. (2001). *Shifting metaphors: Of war and reimagination in the bilingual classroom.* Unpublished Doctoral Dissertation, University of Pennsylvania, Philadelphia.

Ceglowski, D. (1997). That's a good story, but is it really research? *Qualitative Inquiry, 3*(2), 188–201.

Collins, B. (2002a). The new U.S. Poet Laureate plans to bring poetry into high schools across the country. *On Poetry 180: The Osgood File.* CBS Radio Network. Retrieved July 16, 2002, from http://www.acfnewsource.org/education/poetry_180.html

Collins, B. (2002b). *Introduction to poetry.* Retrieved July 16, 2002, from http://www.poems.com/intro_lo.htm

Edelsky, C. (1993). Who's got the floor? In D. Tannen (Ed.), *Gender and conversational interaction.* New York: Oxford University Press.

Eisner, E. W. (1991). *The enlightened eye: Qualitative inquiry and the enhancement of educational practice.* New York: Macmillan.

Eisner, E. W. (1997). The promise and perils of alternative forms of data representation. *Educational Researcher, 26*(6), 4–10.

Ellis, C. (2002). Being real: Moving inward toward social change. *Qualitative Inquiry, 15*(4), 399–406.

Erickson, F. (1982). Money tree, lasagna bush, salt and pepper. Social construction of topical cohesion in a conversation among Italian-Americans. In D. Tannen (Ed.), *Analyzing discourse: Text and talk.* Washington, DC: Georgetown University Press.

Erickson, F. (1986). Qualitative methods in research on teaching. In M. C. Wittrock (Ed.), *Handbook of research in teaching* (3rd ed.). New York: Macmillan.

Erickson, F. (1996). Going for the zone: The social and cognitive ecology of teacher-student interaction in classroom conversations. In D. Hicks (Ed.), *Discourse, learning and schooling* (pp. 29–62). Cambridge, UK: Cambridge University Press.

Erickson, F., & Schultz, J. (1982). *Counselor as gatekeeper: Social interaction in interviews.* New York: Academic Press.

Foley, D. E. (2002). Writing ethnographies: Some queries and reflections. *Qualitative Inquiry, 15*(4), 383.

Gioia, D. (1999). The poet in an age of prose. In A. Finch (Ed.), *After new formalism: Poets on form, narrative, and tradition* (pp. 31–41). Ashland, OR: Story Line Press.

Glesne, C. (1997). That rare feeling: Representing research through poetic transcription. *Qualitative Inquiry, 3*(2), 202–221.

Hass, R. (1999, July 18). Poet's choice: Robert Hass reviews Lee Ann Brown. *The Washington Post,* p. X12.

Hass, R. (1984). *Twentieth century pleasures: Prose on poetry.* Hopewell, NJ: The Ecco Press.

Heath, S. B. (1982). What no bedtime story means: Narrative skills at home and at school. *Language in Society, 11*(1), 49–76.

Hugo, R. (1992). *The triggering town.* New York: WW Norton & Company.

Kenyon, J. (1999). *A hundred white daffodils: Essays, interviews, the Akhmatova translations, newspaper columns, and one poem.* Minneapolis, MN: Graywolf Press.

Kowit, S. (1999). The mystique of the difficult poem. *Poetry International, 3,* 114–131.

Kunitz, S., & Moss, S. M. (Eds.). (1993). *Interviews and encounters with Stanley Kunitz.* Hanover, NH: Sheep Meadow Press.

Lawrence-Lightfoot, S., & Hoffmann Davis, J. (1997). *The art and science of portraiture.* San Francisco: Jossey-Bass.

Lévi-Strauss, C. (1966). *The savage mind.* Chicago: The University of Chicago Press. (Original work published 1962)

Lincoln, Y., & Cannella, G. (2002). *Qualitative research and the radical right: Cats and dogs and other natural enemies.* Paper presented at the annual meeting of the American Educational Research Association, New Orleans, LA.

Naik, G. (1999). *A blue jeans kinda style. Interview with Billy Collins.* Retrieved July 16, 2002, from http://www.champignon.net/Magma/Magma14/collinsInterview.html

Olson, L. (1997). *Made in America: Immigrant students in our public schools.* New York: The New Press.

Peshkin, A. (1993). The goodness of qualitative research. *Educational Researcher, 22*(2), 24–30.

Phillips, S. U. (1983). *The invisible culture: Communication in classroom and community on the Warm Springs Indian reservation.* Prospect Heights, IL: Waveland Press.

Piirto, J. (2002). The question of quality and qualifications: Writing inferior poems as qualitative research. *International Journal of Qualitative Studies in Education, 15*(4), 431–446.

Richardson, L. (2000). Writing: A method of inquiry. In N. K. Denzin & Y. S. Lincoln (Eds.), *Handbook of qualitative research* (2nd ed., pp. 923–948). London: Sage Publications.

Rose, M., & McClafferty, K. A. (2001). A call for the teaching of writing in graduate education. *Educational Researcher, 30*(2), 27–33.

Shavelson, R. J., & Towne, L. (Eds.). (2002). *Scientific research in education.* Washington, DC: National Academy Press.

Stainburn, S. (2001). Pushing poetry (Interview with Billy Collins). *Teacher Magazine, 13*(3), 11.

Tharp, R., & Gallimore, R. (1988). *Rousing minds to life: Teaching, learning, and schooling in social context.* New York: Cambridge University Press.

Van Maanen, J. (1988). *Tales of the field: On writing ethnography.* Chicago: The University of Chicago

Press.

Wakowski, D. (1979). *Toward a new poetry.* Ann Arbor, MI: University of Michigan Press.

Webb, C. H. (2002). *Stand up poetry: An expanded anthology.* Iowa City, IA: University of Iowa Press.

Whorf, B. L. (1956). The relation of habitual thought and behavior to language. In J. B. Carroll (Ed.), *Language, thought, and reality: Selected writing of Benjamin Lee Whorf* (pp. 134–159). New York: MIT Press & John Wiley and Sons.

Melisa Cahnmann-Taylor
Faculty of Education
University of Georgia
USA

ANDREA DANCER

THE SOUNDSCAPE IN POETRY

Language is the very voice of the trees, the waves, and the forests.
Merleau-Ponty, 1968, p. 155.

DRONING

Poetry is as much an oral as written form of expression. While poetry often relies on imagistic details to convey a sense of place, an event or experience, meaning also resides in the rhythm, rhyme, and sounds that comprise a poem. In this way, poems have an acoustic aspect to them, but how does this work?

We humans are immersed in an acoustic environment that entrains our bodies towards certain rhythms and that influences life worlds (all planetary life) spatially, in addition to temporally. From a critical social-Marxist point of view, contemporary rhythms are tied to production, consumerism, and to cultivating consumers as producers (Lefebvre, 1991). It follows that human listening habits— their focus, sophistication, and rhythms—are changing and adapting to these shifting acoustic environments, narrowing our capacity to hear the diversity in sound while the soundscape itself is flattening, a phenomenon that entered soundscapes with the industrial revolution where sounds are increasingly highly redundant (drone-like), have a low information value, and an eclipsed attack and decay. When observed graphically, as R. Murray Shafer (1977) first noted about the shifting industrialized soundscape (pp. 77–82), these type of sounds show as a continuous flat line. Instead of listening to a train whistle travelling across the prairie to know about local weather systems (the classic Canadian example), we are aurally re-tuned to the mono/tones and undifferentiated rhythms of traffic, a common market-driven soundscape effect. This fits with contemporary western society's mon/ocularity, vision being selective in perception and rhythm – we can always shut our eyes to control what we are experiencing visually. In other societies and in other times, people have relied more on hearing, which tends to be polymorphous and immersive –we adapt to the sound environment as, without ear-lids, we continue to hear even when sleeping or unconscious.

The contemporary degradation of acoustic environments is leading to a degradation of our hearing capabilities, perhaps our perceptions and thought processes as well. More startling than the effects of loudness are the effects of non-discrete, non-interrupted sounds that dull our abilities to hear complexity. We are less able to distinguish between sounds, to hear over distances, hearing's tonal range is diminishing and flat-lining. The organic curvature in natural sound is

M. Prendergast, C. Leggo and P. Sameshima (eds.), Poetic Inquiry: Vibrant Voices in the Social Sciences, 31–42.

being replaced by the abruptness of digitalized sound —not to mention the impact of mono-sound on creatured worlds.

The activity of researching a soundscape re-tunes the ear and hones listening skills in order to critically analyze and develop an appreciation for ones place in its fabric. It is a practice of appreciation of Derrida's difference. First, however, the researcher engages with the soundscape experientially and aesthetically. In posing the question of what we hear when we listen in on the natural world, it becomes apparent that it is highly subjective. While music and film theorists focus on the music of nature, Fisher (1999) points out that this is part of the values we bring to nature (pure, good, rejuvenating, originary); that we ascribe music to nature whereas nature itself exceeds our definitions of music. Whether music originated in nature or whether our constructions of nature have formed music is arbitrary; nature is socially mutable and there is no one nature, static and ahistoric just as there is no one music. As a social phenomenon, I agree with Fisher that we bring our worldviews to that which we have constructed as *nature* but we are also not separate from it. There *is* music in nature but how are the values we bring to nature shaping natural acoustic soundscapes in profoundly human ways?

SOUNDS POETIC

A cultivated hyper-sensitivity to sound profoundly influences my being-in-the-world, my artistic practice, and the substance of the poetry I craft. It shapes the poem's content, melodic qualities and rhythms, sometimes to the expense of intellectual and word meaning-making, with the aim of re-creating an acoustic rather than/as well as an intellectual or imagistic experience. I refer to rhythm rather than meter because rhythm is experiential and embodied, whereas the metre of a poem is a measuring device, an applied abstracted discipline. These nuances into where the meaning of a poem resides also creates awareness of the give-and-take interrelatedness of acoustic environments, of bodies making sounds and listening within a matrix of lived experiences, natural and man-made. The natural soundscape can be understood as a tightly woven auditory fabric, where each creature occupies a locale, each locale has a unique soundscape signature, and everything occupies a *niche* that is its place, the place of its sound-making body – in order to send and receive vital spatial information. Like with the train whistle I mentioned earlier, sounds mark relationships of close/distant, movement and topography. Pitch, tone, frequency, and rhythm are only a few of many qualities that comprise a veritable information highway of sound where each creature has their own acoustic register. Old growth habitats are matrixes of sounds that reveal animal and plant biodiversity, weather systems, and the physical geography of the area within specific acoustic ranges. An acoustic ecosystem is a *system-in-echo*, a complex of things bouncing off and absorbing each other, tracing outlines as well as interacting, merging, resounding, and resonating. It is noteworthy that, "The prefix *eco* derives from the Greek oiko(s) or dwelling, habitation, or house, ecology being the study of the spacing of organisms, people, and institutions and their resulting interdependency" (Dancer, Ecology and Environmental section, 2008). If ecology is dwelling's study, then an ecosystem (although system does not

32

do justice to the concept) is dwelling's *organism*, the arrangements of inter-dependent parts. Each sound tells of kinships, conversations between species, matings, predations, foragings, migrations, anomalies, intrusions—vital information that comes together to make each place a unique social space with a rich acoustic fingerprint. While humans work their ecological footprint trying to counter environmental, cultural, economic and power monopolies on a global scale, the creatured world is not oblivious. Creatures have to work harder, forage farther, parent and procreate in defence of airplane noise or tourists. They are forced to make louder, higher pitched, or later into the night vocalizations, just to hear and have themselves heard (Radle, 2007; Turina, 2003a, 2003b) – to balance their worlds on the end of their fingertips. Radical differences in economies of scale.

Poetry offers the human a way into nature's acoustical fabric. Beyond the antagonisms between *free* and *formal* verse, can a poly-verse emerge and if so, where do its in-between spaces reside? I posit that rhythm, in its many forms and effects, carries the potential to shift intellectual meaning-making into embodied experience, a lived meaning. It can re-tune produced rhythm towards circadian rhythm through sound. This happens as a "welding together of meaning and non-meaning in poetry – words and rhythm – [that] can have powerful implications, philosophically, socially, and even politically" (Amittai, 1999, p. 147).

THE PLACE OF HEADSPACE

As an audience listens to a poem, physicality is engaged by the poem's multiple instances of meters, breath, assonance, pauses, absences, silences, etc. that trigger various neural responses. Turner's (1992) theory of the *neural lyre*, equates a three second *neural present* with biochemical firings in the brain as rhythmically modulated, claiming that "meter clearly synchronizes not only speaker with hearer, but hearers with each other, so that each person's three-second 'present' is in phase with the others and a rhythmic community" (p. 72). Is there a biological basis for how poetry transits and receives acoustically charged information about socially dynamic space? Rather than hierarchical, as Turner suggests, the theory of Neural Darwinism identifies consciousness as core neural action, not a thing that happens but a process that *entails* consciousness. Rather than a mechanistic biology, this theory upsets the tyranny of Descartes "I think therefore I am" with a biochemical process of selective resonance, more a circumstance of *neurons resonate therefore I am*. The effective principle governing this resonance is that, in the creation of neural networks, neurons that fire together, wire together. There is no cause/effect mechanism at work here; this process manifests according to pattern recognition, as metaphor, and is not precise as an evolutionary tool. Edelman (2006) explains that, "brains have a generator of diversity (GOD) encountering signals from an unknown world through their repertories of neuronal groups [that] facilitate differential amplification of the connections of those groups of neurons that are adaptive...[yet] each brain is necessarily unique" (p. 34). Part of the allure of this theory is the interstices of pattern recognition (emergent rhythms working associatively) with an irreducible subjectivity and uniqueness. If we accept this corporeal-ization, then the rhythmicality of poems opens to the possibility of

33

neural network communities communicating (resonating) across unknown worlds, unknown because we do not recognize them, whereas our brains are in the process of substantiating them—a déjà-vu effect. Adams (1996) locates the convergence of the spoken word and the soundscape as a practice where,

> if we listen, first, to the sounds of an oral language—to the rhythms, tones, and inflections that play through the speech of an oral culture—we will likely find that these elements are attuned, in multiple and subtle ways, to the contour and scale of the local landscape, to the depth of its valleys or the open stretch of its distances, to the visual rhythms of the local topography. (172)

Perhaps the meaning brought by the poet resides less in the words and more in the resonances activated in the acoustic patterns that the poet expresses—the poet vocalizing their deep subjectivity towards a certain place makes the unknown world known with such a force of diversity that we do not recognize what we know. Perhaps those forces travel to the listener recipient as shared consciousness that instantiates related social spaces, resonant places. Perhaps the poet is activating the acoustic field through the rhythmic effects of the poetic form, whether abstract (in describing acoustic phenomenon) or/and concrete sound (in the sounding of words), strengthening the power of poetry to communicate—through neural resonance—the instance, place, or situation of the poem.

Is the listener experientially *placed* inside the poem's formative acoustic fabric in such a way that they actually reconnect to its many and virtual acoustic streams?

UN*GODLY* SACRED COWS

Poetry is an oral tradition lodged in nature practice. If the sounds at play in poetry are attuned to local topography, then that attunement is potentially embodied by the poet who possesses the potential to carry and transmit acoustic coordinates in the crafting of rhythmically heightened sound-words that convey a sense of place through more than naming and speaking. Part of our intellectual expectation of a poem is that it will reassert what is valued by society in positive and negative terms (nature is valued, industry is not), but is this all that is going on through the poem? Is it reasonable to posit that as the soundscape informs poetry in its themes and forms it also exceeds it by actually reconstituting place and space?

Consider the scene unfolding in this poem showing how aircraft noise disrupts the tenor of a rural evening. This type of nature, is termed second nature because the forests and wild animals are as cultivated as the cattle and farms, except that one is designated as *wilderness* masking its resource-fulness so that what it produces is sustained and reproduced as human leisure activities. It is the soundscape that exposes the illusion of natural places as the products of entrained rhythms that dispossess both nature and the human.

Even song

On the ridge over the fields up and behind "Behind the Village"
we breathe in the evening, the day melting, the sun slipping, listening
to the sacrifice of chirping skies, clicking fields, rustling forests
that intone nocturne as they fold toward sleep.

A hare, large and listening, bounds through the tree line into grass,
where we become marked, overridden by the ultra-light,
a bluebottle engine drone overhead passing over and out
and away. The hare comes, close, mislead

as we are, human and animal, by the furore that mutes and
the confusion that follows. Ears erect and straining,
we hear only the screech, wail, and rumble of these, our places,
until our eyes and nose twitch, sending us into a tremor.

The sun's now half buried by the horizons we create with our eyes,
While in their palace, ungodly cows moan out their lives tethered to milkings—-

like wind rustling wheat fields or the far off traffic rattling our bones—
their horrified hoofs undulate and rattle at our approach.

In the first stanza, there is a rhythm of sloping hills, gentle "e" and "s" slippages
that mark an idyll unfolding with ease, and short phrases mimetic of how time
passes differently as dusk approaches. In the second stanza, the hare marks activity, a
flurry that presages night. There is a muffled or silent quality to the hare – which
doesn't make sound but is an attentive listener. The reader is still-lulled and even
the "bluebottle engine drone passing over and out and away" is merely an irritating
fly against the landscapes ability to acquiesce. Only in the third stanza, in the panic
of the hare that is disoriented by the engine sound, does a staccato rhythm mark
that the scene is disrupted "as we are", in three short beats into a tumble towards
darkness, a descent into the urbanity of the milking production barn nearby that
snaps the reader quickly out of their simulated pastoral. The "we" of the poem
elides the boundaries between the human and creatured identifications in the poem
into a shared degradation: the hare is the humans are the cows all tied to forces of
production evident in a shifting soundscape.

This poem comes out of the research I conducted into how social acoustic space
comes together to mask various forces of production. The production of nature is
achieved through a type of *naturalistic illusion,* a term adapted from Lefebvrian
space and place theory. Lefebvre calls this effect the "realistic illusion" drawing
attention to the normalized space of reality as quintessentially natural. This is how
the super-realism of western epistemology employs what is termed *nature* to mask
human will to power. By shifting the term to a *naturalistic illusion,* I trouble the
idea of *real-nature,* conceptualizations of a nullified, abstract, and sacrosanct non-
entity that collapse the superabundance of nature. The poem works with and

35

against the seductions of the *naturalistic illusion* on multiple levels and employs numerous strategies in its drive to first lull and then startle the reader in a moment of acoustic-ecology activism about which versions of the power and production of nature the soundscape makes visible-invisible.

SILENCE-CRAFT

Poetry's power is in its ability to connect the poet and the audience in profoundly virtual ways and, certainly, this is a vital tenant of the poet's creed. Consider John Adam Luther's (2001) poem which narrates the process of becoming sensitized aurally to a profoundly different acoustic environment. In this work, the poet offers the reader a virtual experience of a remote village in Alaska, a northern soundscape, and a glimpse into indigenous ways of knowing through cultivating an awareness of the soundscapes, their silences. The rhythms of the physical geography, its wildlife, the way of life and the ancient art of listening are explained as well as crafted into the poem as a poetics of place. Naalagiagvik rises out of the sounds of its name, the speaking of its specificities, the speaking voice of its flora naming and declaring a position relationally in the life world the plant life inhabits (lines 15-16). It also hovers in a silence that "rings like a knifeblade against bone" (line 33). Luther's experience of ancestral land as a soundscape-inspired composer listens while teaching listening to generatively elicit listeners inside listeners, humans and creatures, that extends across space-time to–

The Place Where You Go To Listen

They say that she heard things.

At Naalagiagvik, The Place Where You Go To Listen, she would sit alone, in stillness. The wind across the tundra and the little waves lapping on the shore told her secrets. Birds passing overhead spoke to her in strange tongues.

She listened. And she heard. But she rarely spoke of these things. She did not question them. This is the way it is for one who listens.

She spent many days and nights alone, poised with the deep patience of the hunter, her ears and her body attuned to everything around her. Before the wind and the great sea, she took for herself this discipline: always to listen.

She listened for the sound, like drums, of the earth stirring in ancient sleep. She listened for the sound, like stone rain, as rivers of caribou flooded the great plain. She listened, in autumn, for the echo of the call of the last white swan.
She understood the languages of birds. In time, she learned the quiet words of plants. Closing her eyes, she heard small voices whispering:

"I am uqpik. I am river willow. I am here."
"I am asiaq. I am blueberry. I am here."

The wind brought to her the voices of the land, voices speaking the name of each place, carrying the memories of those who live here now and those who have gone.

As she listened, she came to hear the breath of each place—how the snow falls here, how the ice melts—how, when everything is still, the air breathes. The drums of her ears throbbed with the heartbeat of this place, a particular rhythm that can be heard in no other place.

Often, she remembered the teaching of an old shaman, who spoke of silam inua—the inhabiting spirit, the voice of the universe. Silam inua speaks not through ordinary words, but through fire and ice, sunshine and calm seas, the howling of wolves, and the innocence of children, who understand nothing.

In her mind, she heard the words of the shaman, who said of silam inua: "All we know is that it has a gentle voice like a woman, a voice so fine and gentle that even children cannot be afraid."

The heart of winter: She is listening.

Darkness envelops her—heavy, luminous with aurora.
The mountains, in silhouette, stand silent. There is no wind.

The frozen air is transparent, smooth and brittle; it rings like a knifeblade against bone. The sound of her breath, as it freezes, is a soft murmuring, like cloth on cloth.

The muffled wingbeats of a snowy owl rise and fall, reverberating down long corridors of dream, deep into the earth.

She stands, motionless, listening, to the resonant stillness. Then, slowly, she draws a new breath. In a voice not her own, yet somehow strangely familiar, she begins to sing . . .

Silence, which exceeds sound as a binary opposite, is a rare commodity in contemporary society. It evades the written page and gives sound a different meaning, acting as the pivot, the space for musing and imagining, an esoteric and spiritual turn. An important facet of the poet is to bring silence to the human ambient experience through rhythm, the beat and the pause. Silence is the net cast by the poet that opens space for the listener to enter virtually. In this way, it serves the well-being and reflective parts of society, as Miller (1993) attests:

> Silence-positive cultural practice has the strength to build cohesiveness and flexibility in groups, and health and alertness in the individual. Such practices are also the source of cultural innovation, where they are used as the basis of existential inquiry or spiritual expression. The contemplative

and the artist serve important roles in asserting the usefulness of silence in our communicative practice and theory. (p.114)

The poet is cautioned to be attentive to artificial uses of silence, pseudo-silence, which takes the practice of silence out of context and draws attention to it, which defeats its effect (p.112). Poetic form has more recently pulled away from the silence in rhythm as meaningful, when classically it is more than a space on the page or a break between words. As discussed, rhythm has the power to override the meaning of words with a profound sound-based meaning that communicates not through the intellect, but through the attunement/selection/silence on a biochemical level. With its orality still calling out under the print, rhythmic silence is what makes the poem rise up out of the page, what makes the spoken word rise up out of its meaning, it is what gives the poem the space to breathe.

A POET'S SOUND RESEARCH: A RESEARCHER'S SOUND POETRY

In this poem, I am standing at a research site at the edge of a forest that opens onto a deep quarry that is cutting close and closer away at a cottage and leisure area that goes back at least 150 years. A keynote of this area's soundscape was the rhythm of hand-quarried stone from the fifteenth century until the 1970s. At that time, new machinery marked a major shift in the efficiency of the quarry with the speed at which hills are being gobbled up matched only by the daily ceaseless monotony of conveyor and crusher sounds.

Ec(h)o (Excerpt)

What of the plateaus
of the digger's bucket,
the screech whinge
of their scraping
to oblivion
whole hillsides?

What of the machinations
of the crusher, a rock-bound ship
crashing gnashing
the quarry of
millennia?

Not a sound poet *per se*, I compose poems to be spoken first, and then read. The work uses multiple tactics to communicate meaning. In situ, I listen and in remembering sounds, I consider the body's as well as the ears' response to sounds and rhythms in the crafting of words and lines. With an inner ear as well as eye, I visualize the place with detailed sound in order to convey a sense of place imagistically. Listeners (whether reading in their head or attending a reading) have developed highly subjective ways of listening, but image serves the more contemporary expectations of a poem. I bring an intellectual aspect through the theory or social criticism subtext, usually an outfall from my own theoretical preoccupations at work when the poem makes itself known to me. Sometimes, I overload the poem with images, sounds and words in hopes the listener will abandon their expectations or listening habits and just listen to the song as it unfolds. Sound, silence, rhythm and breath are acoustic material vital to the poet's capacity to embody their experiences: I am willing what haunts me to haunt others.

I find it challenging to reconcile my poetic process with end-driven language and objectives, such as research and academic writing demands. From my perspective as a poet, these writing genres can collapse the complexities, interrelatedness, and incomprehensibility of embodied language into the production of knowledge. I invite multiple knowledges into my work. It is more than a matter of translation between academic and poetic language implementation, it is the situating of one's voice between different means and ends politically. For many artists, knowledge takes on meaning through lived experience, a present sensory engagement that works against textuality. Sometimes I am a walking text, sometimes a sensory synaesthesic. I have indeed experienced sounds as matter or color – but these are gifted moments that I cannot give to words. It takes work to stay open and porous, vulnerable and excessive, but in this way the research continues to be vivified. Soundscape research inhabits me as much as I inhabit the research, a continual negotiating of subjectivity/objectivity pre-tenses in search of the inexplicable.

It is important to acknowledge that this is gnarly terrain in academia and, while it makes for great art, it does not always make for great academic research papers – the epiphanies of life elude form. This opposition is not unlike the one between the visual and acoustic as Hempton (2003) understands it:

> Unlike the seen thing or light itself, sound travels through blinding vegetation and total darkness, over long distances, off walls and around corners. The presence of one sound rarely obscures another. We hear many sounds simultaneously and are able to know the position and track very subtle changes in pattern. Compare this with vision where one object commonly blocks the view behind it and we see in only one direction at a time. (paragraph 12)

Research intent on truth value relies on observation, visual logic, and empiricism, which is counter to poetry's orality – and even its imagism. To be listening is to *be* with uncertainty, to stay with shifting differentiations, to be still and paused until the next sounding thing opens to the next and the next – it is place without ownership.

While writing academically, I find I have to write poetry at the same time otherwise the analytic structure I am working through insists on drifting elsewhere. I waver at one of many junctures between cultivated and intrinsic binary epistemologies, between landscape and wilderness, the human and the creature, vision and sound – simultaneously awe-struck and perplexed by the necessity of choosing, while I understand intellectually that the choosing is a social illusion. The seeds I strive to extricate from the intellectual grain elevator blow over rustling fields to plant themselves in the perceptual terrain of the wild wood. This cross-pollination is an eco-logical risk; will the field be reduced to human versus nature dichotomies? What kind of therefore creature am I? Caught, I see there is no easy way out. I stretch out on the contentious space in-between and listen.

UNMADE BEDS

I fell in love in a garden. An urban touchstone, each season's unfolding became the years' unfolding, and after many years, we knew what creatures came to what places under what conditions. The coyotes kept their distance, but we knew their hiding places. Sometimes, we'd lie in their beds and try to pick up their scents. Then the year came when a kind of tidiness started to make itself know. A newsletter appeared informing us annual fees were increasing; they were hiring a marketing consultant. Over the course of a couple of weeks, the coyotes went missing. Tourist buses now idled at the gate, people and kids yelled to one another, cell phones and talking rang out, photo ops were staged in flower beds, golf cart tours announced each wonder, amplified. The heron flew away, leaving his monumental nest to disrepair and a sign went up pointing to the abandoned nest. Then came the movie shoots. At that point, even the arborists abandoned the garden as it raced towards its re-made future. For me, a crucial place of listening was robbed of its silence and I could no longer locate myself in the din. Like the coyotes, I was culled, I

didn't know

swoosh whing swoosh whing wooing
flash-rush
whish, whish, whisk away

I was death
until the concrete
hoards
in busloads
pulled up
prattle chattel
in the garden.

chicachicachic
chicachicachic

chica-chica-chica

what the
hummdrumm drives

rustle pad pad, rumble tumble shush
shush, *they'll hear us*
cower cower cowering

home is
struck dumb
in the tacit turn,

flabbergasted

in louder
talking
out loud
just
to be heard.

listen
    will you

take me,
    won't you

take me,
    with you

travelling?

REFERENCES

Abram, D. (1996). *The spell of the sensuous: Perception and language in a more-than-human world.* New York: Pantheon Books.

Amattai, A. F. (1994). *Telling rhythms: Body and meaning in poetry.* Ann Arbor, MI: University of Michigan Press.

Amittai, A. (1999). Why we need a new, rhythm-centered theory of poetry. In A. Finch (Ed.), *After new formalism: Poets on form, narrative, and tradition.* Ashland: Three Story Press.

Austin, J. L. (1962). *How to do things with words.* Oxford: University Press.

Butler, J. (1997). *Excitable speech: A politics of the performative.* New York and London: Routledge.

Dancer, A. (2008). *Seton and the practice of nature.* Centre for Cross Faculty Inquiry, UBC.

de Certeau, M. (1988). *The practice of everyday life* (S. Rendall, Trans.). London: University of California Press.

Derrida, J. (1976). *Of grammatology* (G. C. Spivak, Trans.). Baltimore & London: Johns Hopkins University Press. *Nature brain science and human knowledge.* New Haven, CT and London: Yale University Press.

Feld, S. (1993). From ethnomusicology to echo-muse-ecology: Reading R. Murray Schafer in the Papua New Guinea Rainforest. *The Soundscape Newsletter, 8*(June, 1994).

Fisher, J. A. (1998). What the hills are alive with: In defence of the sounds of nature. *The Journal of Aesthetics and Art Criticism, 56*(2), 167.

Fisher, J. A. (1999). The value of natural sounds. *Journal of Aesthetic Education, 33*(3), 26.

Hawking, S. W. (2002). *On the shoulders of giants the great works of physics and astronomy.* Philadelphia: Running Press.

Heidegger, M. (1971). *Poetry, language, thought.* New York: Harper and Row.

Hempton, G. (2003). *Rescue for silence.* Retrieved February 13, 2008, from http://www.soundtracker.com/Silence.htm

Kepler. (1619, February 3, 2008). *The science of the harmony of the world (1619)*, 1. Retrieved from http://www.schillerinstitute.org/transl/trans_kepler.html

Krause, B. (2002). *Wild soundscapes: Discovering the voice of the natural world* (1st ed.). Berkley, CA: Wilderness Press.

Lefebvre, H. (1991). *The production of space* (D. Nicholson-Smith, Trans.). Malden, MA: Blackwell.

Luther, J. A. (2001). *The place where you go to listen.* Retrieved February 10, 2008, from http://www.acousticecology.org/writings/placeyougo.html

Merleau-Ponty, M. (1968). *The visible and the invisible* (A. Lingis, Trans.). Evanston, IL: Northwestern University Press.

Miller, W. (1993). *Silence in the contemporary soundscape.* Unpublished MA Thesis, Simon Fraser University, Vancouver.

Murray Schafer, R. (1977). *The tuning of the world.* New York: Alfred A. Knopf, Inc.

Radle, A. L. (2007, August 25, 2008). *The effects of noise on animals: A literature review.* Retrieved February 10, 2008, from http://interact.uoregon.edu/MediaLit/wfae/library/articles/radle_effect_noise_wildlife.pdf

Schafer, R. M. (1977). *The tuning of the world.* New York: Alfred A. Knopf.

Schafer, R. M. (1993). *Voices of tyranny, temples of silence.* Indian River: Arcana Editions.

Turina, F. (2003a). *Annotated bibliography: Impacts of noise and overflights on wildlife 2008.* Retrieved from http://www.nature.nps.gov/naturalsounds/impacts/

Turina, F. (2003b). Annotated bibliography: Impacts of noise and overflights on wildlife. In N. S. Project (Ed.). National Parks Service.

Turina, F., & Pilcher, E. (2007). *Annotated bibliography: Visitor experience and soundscape.* Retrieved August 25, 2008, from http://www.nature.nps.gov/naturalsounds/impacts/

Turner, F., & Popper, E. (1992). The neural lyre: Poetic meter, the brain, and time. In *Natural classicism: Essays on literature and science* (pp. 61–108). Charlottesville, VA: University Press of Virginia.

UBU Web. (2008, February 13). Retrieved from http://www.ubu.com

Andrea Dancer
Centre for Cross-Faculty Inquiry
University of British Columbia
Canada

DANIELA BOUNEVA ELZA

di(versify:

further testimony for that which cannot be

(ascertained

*

"All these people who create,
half certain, half uncertain
of their powers, feel two beings
in them, one known and the other
unknown, whose incessant intercourse
and unexpected exchanges give birth
in the end to a certain product.
I do not know what I am going to do;
yet my mind believes it knows itself;
and I build on the knowledge,
I count on it, it is what I call *Myself.*
But I shall surprise myself;
if I doubted it I should be nothing.
I know that I shall be astonished
by a certain thought that is going
to come to me before long—and yet
I ask myself for this surprise, I build on it
and count on it as I count on my certainty.
I hope for something unexpected
which I designate. I need both
my known and my unknown."
—Paul Valèry, (1964, p. 141-142)

"Reverie puts us in the state of a soul being born.
Thus, in this modest study of the simplest of
images, our philosophical ambition is great.
It is to prove that reverie gives us the world
of a soul, and that a poetic image bears
witness to a soul which is discovering
its world, the world where it would like
to live and where it deserves to live."
—Gaston Bachelard (2004, p. 15)

Poetic Image

*M. Prendergast, C. Leggo and P. Sameshima (eds.), Poetic Inquiry: Vibrant Voices
in the Social Sciences, 43–57.*

"Poetry aims to *express* by means of language
precisely that which language is powerless to express."
—Paul Valèry (1971, p. 429)

"It tries to tell you/like a mirror: look,/see, the sky/under your feet.
Elusive,/a dare, an inch/of water enough/to drown in. Everything/
that happened to you/begins here/and you could fall through it."
—Sue Sinclair (2003, p.52)

in the eye　　　　　**(of contemplation**

it tries to tell you　　*like a mirror*
how to listen　　　　　past the edge

of drying up puddles.　past the edge of
an autumn maple leaf.　　　　past the edge

of a word　　fresh　　with fallen rain—
in the eye　　of the mind　　pooling.

look　　　　*see the sky*　　*under your feet*
elusive　　(a whisper of syllables)

in need of attention　　　　shriveled
around the edges:　　　last night's words.

is **poetry**　　a pathology?　　*a dare*
an inch of water
　　　　　　　　enough to drown in?

look　　see the way　　rain teaches asphalt
of its depressions.　　turns them into eyes

full of　　　shifting clouds
(inside　　　memories' splashing feet.)

　　　and you wade　　**through**.
everything
　　　　　　that happened to you
begins here—　　　the way
pavement embraces sky　　　　the way

you are drawn to　　　**this moment**

of not-pavement　　*and you could*
　　　　fall　　*through it.*

"To speak of a poem in itself, judge a poem in itself has no real and precise meaning. It is to speak only of a possibility. The poem is an abstraction, a piece of writing that is waiting..."
—Paul Valèry (1971, p.156)

"...the imagination is never wrong,"
—Gaston Bachelard (1994, p. 152)

how to   (forget

teacher asks: do you get it?

how we for-get.
how to   re-member that

the imagination is   *never wrong?*
you wouldn't   think of it

but to forget   is to remember
something   new.   to forge

to dream without this memory of
teacher asking: did you get it?

I said elated: yes.
she wants to   know more.   I speak

with such enthusiasm.
                         I am on tip-toe.
teacher   leans   back
to make space for me   to lean into

(this poem   about
                    a black cat   and a moon).
her eyes get stern.   she tells me:
        did   you for-get?
she wants to know   what the black cat

stood for.   (stood under?)
              under-stood?
how can it be wrong? I feel I've got it?

which over time   I forgot.

"In any case, harmony in reading is inseparable from admiration. We can admire more or less, but a sincere impulse, a little impulse toward admiration is always necessary if we are to receive the phenomenological benefit of a poetic image. The slightest critical consideration arrests this impulse by putting the mind in second position, destroying the primitivity of the imagination."
—Gaston Bachelard (1994, intro)

"Meaning is the work of the will."
—Jacques Rancière (1999, p. 56)

ode to the critic (or what was I trying to say?

his eyebrows raised   for lack of

commas.   his punctual gaze
piercing the spaces   I have left

                          (here.   the breath
cannot be steady   as the hands
of clocks or   accurate as dials.

                          (this gap
                          this pause is
for the reader.
                              is where we walk
and our footprints will not leave a trace.

yet   if we are to trace what thought
moves here—   a rugged

mountainous landscape   the mind

endlessly explores   to find
a quiet temple where the silence gathers

so big   it cannot leave   the mouth.

                    *

here ambiguity proliferates
                    what a comma clarifies

and shuts the door I have left (on purpose)

open.

a clarity that does not raise   eyebrows
does not take your breath   away.

what informs the words   is the gap
through which we come to   a place

of wor(d)ship

settle down and rise   through
          its paper thin silence

where thought grows deep.
          and then this (dream

we are

          both dreaming
on the page.   is it the cause or
is it the result?   the left out comma

          is a door

          *

through which you do not walk inside
my head but inside   yourself
          (seeking.   in an image

or a word apart from others   (finding

(losing   yourself
in such needed   reverie
          in such a state of emergence

that you should never fear   (you are
misreading me.

"Poetry must convey the idea of perfect thought. It is not a true thought. Poetry
   is to thought what a drawing is to an object—a convention that restores what,
                    in the object, is briefly eternal."
                              —Paul Valèry (1971, p. 416)

ELZA

what breathes in   **(a view**

in the painter's   vast strokes
the solitude of

                              (this place

pulls me.
                    from   afar

                              language emerges
as the trees become   (the mind

                              searching.
the   geometry   of painter

moving
                    (in words.   deep roots

exchanging   *inert landscapes*
          the long ago
                    of stark contrasts.

                    *

defining the eulogized space   of poet
I push through   tangled twigs
                    and vines

complete the etymo-   logical paths

          of his mountains

that had without notice   drifted
into uprooted pavement   illegible hands

their mute possibilities.

                    *

                              how the eye moves

through what   (echoes
                              in the   rhythms

of trees and moss   of winter

and spring.
                    and a house
it's cosmic light on

            a familiar face

        (looking out)

into the present
            that climbs on itself
                    like frost.

"The problem is to reveal an intelligence to itself. Anything can be used."
—Jacques Rancière, (1999, p. 28)

"Poets will always imagine faster than those who watch them imagining."
—Gaston Bachelard (2004, p.25)

school.s

in the nurse.ry   pond

below   the   **For Sale**   sign
next to   the fertilize.r

the artificial   water plants
in neatly lined tubs   flicker

            the butterfly   koi –

alexandrian flame.s   under
the water   consuming all

we know.   **they swirl**   through
a transparency of   fins
flesh   **fluid**— each one

an idea   trying
to take form.   restless
with an under.**current**   fear

that soon   **each**   will be
scooped **into**   a void

without **clarity.** under vaults
without   papyrus.

and a geo.metry   so familiar
it leaves   nothing

to be   **imagined.**

"Not only do Descartes, Hegel, and Feuerbach not begin with the same concept, they do not have the same concept for beginning."
—Deleuze and Guattari (1994, p.15)

"Happiness is visible like the sun."
—Paul Valèry (1964, p.77)

where   **(do I begin?**

the first line of the poem   is
missing.
            in its wake
the sense of   sudden water
the stillness   of an egret.

it came and left the bodies of
rocks   warm with   the parting

the urgency of what is   absent.

of what went   astray
(in the beginning.

the first line of the poem   is
         *
or was it snow in its twinkling quiet.
(in the eye)   the momentary shiver of

happiness—   *visible like the sun*
on the limbs and trunks of trees
(begun   by someone else)
reaching

                    for the poem perhaps
whose shape and image   are not
indifferent to   what is

        (thought.
what moves like water in the hands
of gravity   lingers on the edge
of breath.
                    and when it comes
to a crack   in the rock—   falls
disappears   right through
the first line.   startling the egret.

"Intelligence is not a power of understanding based on comparing knowledge
with its object. It is the power to make oneself understood through another's
                                                    verification."
                              —Jacques Rancière (1999, p. 72)

                "The average Ph.D. thesis is nothing but the transference
                          of bones from one graveyard to another."
                                —J. Frank Dobie (1945, p.26)

common   **(graves**

today   we rake   them
this way   and that.   do not know
what to do   with
                                             (our words.

the way

they pile.   the way   they stick out   —
the ulna   tibia   fibula
the skull   a jaw that   does not
match   does not   speak

lie there   in lost   moments.
                          the air thick   with last
breaths
(unwritten.   the hollow   sockets
piercing   questions
                                             (unuttered.
and the little   ones scattered   (like beads) the
tarsals   and the meta—   tarsals

ELZA

spilled   necklace   (once
carefully   strung)   bursting
                 in one   tug-of-
war.
                 tears.
                                   unsure
                 if we
can
(explain   why   things
break   this way.

"You must talk with things in their own fragile tongue.
Don't fancy that they understand yours."

"... a trace of truth resembling
a mark of wing upon the sky."
—Lyubomir Levchev (2006, p. 89)

living (metaphors—

images

that
let us

(talk with wings

grasp
(in their own fragile

tongue

the un-
grasp

able

*

a trace of truth resembling
a mark of wings upon the sky.

"Learning and understanding are two ways of expressing the same act of translation. There is nothing beyond texts except the will to express, that is, to translate."
—Jacques Rancière (1999, p. 10)

"What unity remains for philosophies, it will be asked, if concepts constantly change?"
—Deleuze and Guattari (1994, p. 8)

To

Get

*

to

*

his

*

True

*

Forms

***

Plato *
could not   do   without
them*

                                    The shadows

        on the wall
        the cave

the captain*   of the ship

had to marry

True * Forms   to * image.

"Truth is not told. It is a whole and language fragments it;
it is necessary, and languages are arbitrary."
—Jacques Rancière (1999, p. 60)

"The greatness of poets is that they grasp with their words
what they only glimpse with their minds."
—Paul Valèry (1971, p. 401)

metaphor (bridges

kinship between disparate

ideas.   a shift.

our logical   distances

(suddenly)

Aristotle's   Is   contains in itself

what It is not.

"To summarize a thesis is to retain the essence of it. To summarize [...] a work
of art, is to lose its essence. One can see to what extent this fact (if one can
understand its scope) makes an illusion of the analysis of the aesthetic. "
—Paul Valèry (1964, p. 113)

left brain   **(right brain**
Axiom: from image   to word—
                                          of being (here

Demonstration: fall leaves
                    a language of   dark boughs
                    shedding words   (as if

that is how light
travels.

Argument: twir

              ling   gli   ding

from side to
spi

             ral.   a looping bird

performs   cardinal gymnastics
to move berries

Counter Argument: then all still   bobs   up and

                      down—

Summation: a leaf   hold   ing on.
                      my thoughts

Proof: small leaves

               be   come

the wings of hum ming

birds and (

                  fly

                    a   (way

"Poetry forms the dreamer and his world at the same time."
—Gaston Bachelard (2004, p. 16)

Presence   is this poem
as you leave   out the door.

is both **you** and   **not you**
across the blue   threshold of
(not.

              knowing)
is to remember   and is to forget:
the moments—

              extinct species.
you ask:

              who is here?   who is
and who isn't?   *perhaps*

knowing that true blue cannot exist
and a flock of crows marks the sky

with seconds   as if tossed
from your absent hands.

*

feet firmly planted   in salt
water   feel   sand   slipping

             between
your thoughts   into the poem's throat
where *we are*   *physically tangential to*

stone.   it murmurs
            gurgles
in foamy whispers   reaches out
(as if trying to   give **you**
            something
            in between
the pull   and the push
the is and   the isn't

the breath in   breath out.

> Note: The phrases *perhaps knowing that true or
> absolute blue cannot exist* and *we are physically
> tangential to stone* come from Banack (2004).

~~eon~~(inclusion

"The true poet does not know
     the exact meaning of what he has
         just had the good luck to write.
            A moment later he is a mere reader.
              He has written non-sense: something
                that must not *present* but *receive*
                  a meaning, and that is very different.
              How can this paradoxical enterprise be conceived?
               To write something that restores
            what was not given. The verse is
         waiting for a meaning. *The verse is
      listening to its reader.* And likewise,

when I say that I look at my ideas,
my images, I can just as well say that
they are looking at me. Where is one
to situate the self?"
—Paul Valèry (1971, p. 397-398)

"The poet's poem
   interests me less
      than the subtleties
         and enlightenment
            he acquires by way
               of his work.
                  And that is why
                     one must *work*
                        at one's poems,
                           that is, work
                             at oneself."

—Paul Valèry (1971, p. 397)

REFERENCES

Bachelard, G. (1994). *The poetics of space* (M. Jolas, Trans., 1964). Boston: Beacon Press. (Original work published 1958)

Bachelard, G. (2004). *The poetics of reverie* (D. Russell, Trans., 1969). Boston: Beacon Press. (Original work published 1960)

Banack, H. (2004). *The question is the answer: An interrogative exploration of life, education and schooling.* Unpublished Master's Thesis, Simon Fraser University, Vancouver, British Columbia, Canada.

Deleuze, G., & Guttari, F. (1994). *What is pHilosophY?* (H. Tomlinson & G. Burchell, Trans.). New York: Columbia University Press. (Original work published 1991)

Dobie, J. F. (1945). *A texan in England.* Boston: Little, Brown and Company.

Levchev, L. (2006). *Ashes of light: New and selected poems.* Willimantic, CT: Curbstone Press.

Rancière, J. (1999). *The ignorant schoolmaster: Five lessons in intellectual emancipation* (K. Ross, Trans.). Stanford, CA: Stanford University Press.

Sinclair, S. (2003). *Mortal arguments.* London, Ontario: Brick Books.

Valèry, P. (1971). On poets and poetry from the notebooks (J. R. Lawler, Trans.). In J. Mathews (Ed.), *The collected works of Paul Valery* (Vol. 1, pp. 397–429). Princeton, NJ: Princeton University Press.

Valèry, P. (1964). *Selected writings.* New York: New Directions Publishing Corporation.

Daniela Bouneva Elza
Faculty of Education
Simon Fraser University
British Columbia, Canada

KEDRICK JAMES

CUT-UP CONSCIOUSNESS AND TALKING TRASH

Poetic Inquiry and the Spambot's Text

INTRODUCTION

This chapter presents a methodological overview and applied example of the use of *found texts* and *procedural techniques* for poetic inquiry. These poetic strategies of textual analysis and production expand the range of methods for qualitative research and trouble established notions of authorship in social sciences research through the hybrid collaboration of researcher/participant/poet. In addition, a fourth contributor is brought to prominence: namely the investigative technologies of chance generation engaged in the *cut-up* process that is central to found, procedural, and computer poetries (Funkhouser, 2007; Hartman, 1996). Cut-up methodologies disclose "the interconnectedness of the experimental poetics and the technological infrastructure," and point "to new ways of interpreting the world, but also to new forms of recreating it" (Torres, 2005, p. 4). Applying these methods to a database of Spambot texts (automated, unsolicited, bulk emails), I take this authorial hybridization one step further by incorporating the networked computer *as participant*—indeed, the networked computer *as poet*. The aim is to audit a dialogue between natural and technological hosts in which I participate in order to process and critically reformulate this discourse using the methods of found and procedural poetry. I contend that these methods are particularly relevant and adaptable to purposes of evaluating and remediating the qualitative properties of cybernetic information environments (Bootz, 2006; Morris & Swiss, 2006).

Poetic inquiry is currently practiced in diverse disciplines across the social sciences (Prendergast, 2009). Cut-up methods engage a mode of critical and aesthetic recycling of cultural resources, and reflect a function of scholarship in which citations, quotes, allusions, and so on, facilitate the upkeep of *a body of knowledge*. To varying degrees, these print-based practices maintain ecologies of information and principles of authorship (Betancourt, 2007; Bolter, 2001). The digital age has disrupted foundations of literate discourse and literary expression (Glazier, 2001). As Peterson (2006, p. 2) states, "poetry's migration to the digital medium…evokes a way in which, more than ever, we might see poetic texts as process-based," a fusion of "code elements (computational, algorithmic, ergodic, monadic) that have restructured language". Moreover, using poetic inquiry to research the conditions of literary expression and social discourse online not only recognizes the role of procedural codes in authentic creative processes, but also

M. Prendergast, C. Leggo and P. Sameshima (eds.), Poetic Inquiry: Vibrant Voices in the Social Sciences, 59–74.

opens up avenues for "exploring how such poems often derive meaning from their own precarious existence in networked language environment" (p. 2). Thus, poetic inquiry enacts critical self-reflexivity embracing a postmodernist perspective (Wiebe, 2008).

Poststructuralists foresaw this change in critical and authorial practices. When Roland Barthes (1989, p. 53) pronounces upon *The Death of the Author* that the text now consists "of a multi-dimensional space in which are married and contested several writings, none of which is original, the text is a fabric of quotations, resulting from a thousand sources of culture," he seems to predict a world of cut-up consciousness; when Foucault (1977, p. 138) asks *What is an Author?*, the answer comes in "faint murmurings of indifference" with the riposte "What matter who's speaking?", which seems to predict the anonymous, cyber text. The ascendency of new communications technologies has challenged the traditional status conferred upon authors and texts with what Bök (2002, p. 10) calls "the fundamental irrelevance of the writing subject" whose involvement as an author "has henceforth become discretionary". Literary genres have had to adapt to new constraints and possibilities of digital media – a change that takes root in the social uses of language and literacy.

CUT-UP CONSCIOUSNESS

From Stéphane Mallarmé's precedent setting chance generated poem *Un coup de dés jamais n'abolira le hasard* (A throw of the dice will never abolish chance,) published in 1897, to the current day, poets have been using technologies of chance generation to produce unique, culturally exciting texts that have significance within both the arts and sciences (Cramer, 2005; Hofstadter, 1999; Joris, 2003; Kurzweil, 1999; Lansdown, 2001). Technologies of chance can be as profoundly simple as a falling coin, a pair of dice, the *i-Ching*, or a pen and paper calculation; conversely these technologies can be as operationally complex as artificially intelligent, robotic computer networks. All technologies of mechanical choice and chance operations provide poetic inquiry with the means for fascinating studies of language and learning.

Pioneers of the cut-up method employed wide ranging procedural strategies and instruments of prediction: counting games, tarot decks, acrostics and mesostics, matching phrases, alongside ritualized procedures meant to hone the inquirer's technique of selection and re-composition during the embodied performance of the cut-up event (Danvers, 2006; Rothenberg & Joris 1995; Young & MacLow, 1970). The tradition of poetic cut-ups has visionary origins: Hartman (1996, p. 29) offer the example that "one of the Greek Oracles, the sibyl of Cumae, used to write the separate words of her prophesies on leaves and then fling them out of the mouth of her cave" for the suppliants to gather, sort, and interpret. This is an appropriate analogy for poetic inquiry that uses chance-operations and cut-up procedures to discover deeper structures of relevance underlying research source texts. To find the meaning in indeterminacy, as John Cage (1966) argues, we must first adjust our perception; then the meaning finds us.

Literary cut-ups systematize chance operations to express tacit patterns of signification embedded within the source text, revealed through subsuming verbal content to expose code-level structures and lexicons (MacLow, 2008; McCaffery & Nichol, 1992; Watten, 2003). Through the recombinatory process of creating new texts from de-contextualized fragments, ordinary discourse migrates to the open metaphorical polyvalence of poetry; the cut-up procedure strives to render what Mallarmé called "the prismatic subdivisions of an idea" (in Rothenberg and Joris, 1995, p. 53). Experimental intervention occurs in the lexical selection and syntactic reconstruction of the poem as research artifact, enacted in the moment of calculation, performance or sustained poetic concentration comprising the research event. This methodical mining of meaning potential coheres with Mallarmé's "explorations of 'chance' & open-ended meaning, both of which gave to language & process a share of the authority/authorship previously reserved to the poet" (Rothenberg & Joris, 1995, p. 76). Computer technologies can greatly extend these explorations and have opened poetic inquiry to global resources of found texts, digital language processors, multi-language translators and random text generators (Cramer, 2001; Parrish, 2001). Owing to "the computer's potential to permute and, given rules, to engage in 'creative magic,'" intelligent machines produce texts that exist at the boundary of authenticity, where issues of hybrid authority and artificial creativity erupt within the technocultural present (Zweig, 1997, p. 20).

The cut-up poem, not as a product but as a process, is a record of erasure, like emptying a container so that, when struck, it may resonate clearly and distinctively. The cut-up becomes poetically resonant by procedurally eliminating information in the text from which it is culled. This emptying procedure is calculated to retain the energy of the source text during the negation of verbal contents.[1] Two contrasting methodologies, that of employing strictly formal, chance generated procedures versus sequential, selective editing, offer a range of procedural openings for researchers to explore their data.

CROSS GENRE CUT-UPS

The use of cut-up methods is not restricted to poetry. As an arts-based practice, the cut-up method lacks neither history nor theorization (Aarseth, 1997; Calvino, 1986; Waldman, 1992) and its influence extends to Nelson's coining and theorization of hypertext (Manovich, 2003). Lansdown (2001, p. 1) retraces chance generation as a mode of musical composition to "the mediaeval use of bent nails thrown on the floor to suggest the rise and fall of melodic lines". Marcel Duchamp innovated with found and procedural techniques in his paintings, "ready-mades," and poetry. The mutual sharing of influence that cut-ups and collage inspired across art forms was apparent among the Surrealists, who proclaimed in 1956 that it is "through the non-professional character of the processes used, that surrealism has systematically encouraged every means of escaping aesthetic constraints," and that "the practice of *automatic drawing* and *'cadavres exquis'*, owe their deepest significance to the ambition of reaching the point where – just like poetry – painting 'must be made by all, not by one'" (in Richardson & Fijalkowski, 2001, p. 52). From the cut-up performances of Dada artist Tristan Tzara in the 1920's, to the automatic writing and music of the Fluxus movement, OULIPO's mathematically inspired treatments of text (Motte, 1986), John Cage's mesostics and chance-generated music composed for and performed with dancers, and the musical, cinematic and novelistic practices utilized by Brion Gysin and William Burroughs, creating numerous audio works such as *Break Through In Grey Room* (1987), cinematic works *The Cut-ups* (1966) and *Bill and Tony* (1972), and Burroughs' trilogy of cut-up novels *The Soft Machine* (1961/1992), *The Ticket that Exploded* (1967), and *Nova Express* (1964/1992). Multimedia productions using found texts, or what Rubinstein (1999) refers to as appropriative literature, spread into live performance, audio recording and deejay arts, radio theatre, experimental cinema, and so on. These artistic innovations paved the way for the thorough integration of cut-up consciousness in contemporary hypertext and digital art forms.

RENDING RESEARCH: CUT-UP AS AN EXPLORATORY PRAXIS

When researchers studying discursive practices sit down with their data, they are presented with a text that is already displaced and in transition. From it, they extract instances of special significance and symbolic value. As they analyze and select parts of the text as representative of these particular values, the processes of signification crystallize and the text is recast accordingly. During the process, researchers may choose to adopt one of two modes of investigation: one method is to go through the text inquiringly–asking questions and looking for specific features addressing the preconceived notion of significance; or alternatively they may adopt the second method, which is to dwell within the text until its resonances become audible and interpretable. To dwell poetically, in the sense that Heidegger (1975) expands upon Höolderin's expression "poetically man dwells...," implies a particular openness to the potential for meaning. This openness allows subtle patterns of signification to become noticeable and to impress upon an attentive mind the nature of their significance. As inquirers, this process of dwelling poetically can rend the veil of preconceptions so that we may fully exist *within the text*. Dwelling poetically is a means of becoming illuminated, of seeing language through the lens of the poem. These two modes of inquiry, one directed by prescribed intent, the other informed through procedural openness, and all the gradations in between, comprise the span of methodological approaches that those using cut-ups as a mode of poetic inquiry employ.

Different cut-up processes performed on identical source texts may be especially useful for investigating semiotic robustness, the mutability and adaptability of signs, within the data source. If text-specific language lacks energetic potential, this is made readily apparent through multiple cut-up procedures. The poem-in-process makes the dynamic state of each semiotic system visible to the researcher. In this way the poem, rather than the poet, becomes the organizing principle of inquiry, and a means of liberating differential properties of signification within a given information environment. A heteroglossic, multifaceted process frees the poem to exhibit varying degrees of authorial voicing or systematic indeterminacy without losing its connection to, or extrapolating beyond, the data source.

Cut-up methods necessarily look to the language, rather than beyond it. The resultant poems are process driven and should be represented in this light–not as factoid or literary fixture, but instead as the *read-out* of poetic processors monitoring linguistic phenomena in flux, a living specimen of the textual environment that is the focus of study. In the process of a poem's crystallization, each word takes on preternatural luster, flashing with ambiguities and subtle plays of literal pun and sound. Poetic inquiry is situated between the processes of gathering and summarizing data. Is this just aesthetic distraction or does it imply that research practices may benefit from linguistic play and ambiguity as literature does? We need only consider James Joyce's cut-up masterpiece *Finnegans Wake* to conclude that it does (Theall, 1997). As Kress (2003, p. 175) states, "it is not hard to see how puns or abbreviations – playfulness again – will transform the potentials of sign-making...mak[ing] possible new signs and sign-combinations – new possibilities of meaning". Although the source texts have suffered a sea-change (to borrow this term from Hannah Arendt's description of Walter Benjamin's process of assembling heterogeneous fragments of text into cultural exposé),[2] the renewed text reveals itself as a product of change, *chanced upon*, never stabilized or ideologically burdened; unique yet mutable, purposive yet ambiguous.

A BASIC METHODOLOGICAL SCHEMA

Cut-up methods include both prescriptive and non-prescriptive procedures. The poet chooses whether to edit the results of an experiment, but this ought to be explicitly noted as a formalizing feature of the mode of inquiry and its expected reception. The formalization of chance operations introduces an *unlikely abundance* into research discourse. It suggests the unexpected. Accidental configurations and juxtapositions instantiate and equivocate to meaning-potentials within the source text. Prescriptive uses of chance operations are also a feature of programmable, computer-generated poetries (Funkhouser, 2007; Johnson, 2002), some of which are programmed to produce traditional styles and voicings, (see, for example, Kurzweil, 1999). On the other hand, non-prescriptive reassembly is also a feature of found poetries. Found poetry uses text fragments, often visually re-structured to heighten their poetic properties, as a selective means of cutting up the textual environment. All four procedural approaches (computer-generated; prescriptive cut-up; non-prescriptive cut-up; and found poetries) signify through differently structured "chance" operations, (see *Figure 1. Cut-Up Methods by Formalization of Chance Operations*) although none, strictly speaking, are random. Spam poetry combines and hybridizes all four poetic processes: spam email is (a) computer-generated, (b) subject to programmatic filtering, (c) found, and (d) selectively reassembled by the poet-researcher honing the poem. Each stage in the processing of the text governs, and is governed by, a different type of awareness of the data source.

Owing to the increase in information made possible through digital technologies, the cut-up method becomes *sine qua non* of excess-information management–a mode of attentional play across surface semiosis, obliterating most, while recycling particular resonances. The ease of digital editing makes cut/copy/paste functions of modern computers some of the most useful and universal commands. Digital sampling has gained prominence particularly in music, in which sonic fragments of

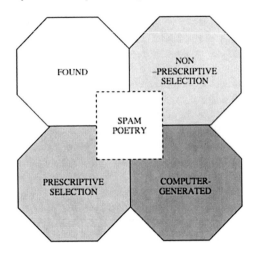

Figure 1. Cut-Up Methodologies Differentiated by Formalization of Chance Operations

recorded music are looped and layered, then mixed with live performances as a mode of cultural reclamation. Cultural recycling is an eminent form of sustaining human memory, and as cyberpunk novelist William Gibson (in Adams, August 12, 2007, p. 8), who gave cyberspace its name, observes, "the internet is the shared memory of the species". The junk of cyberculture tells this tale of the species as one cuts through the disposable culture of daily life. Gibson observes:

> You could say, in some ways technology and entertainment culture does not look that good from outside. I mean, if you looked at the internet objectively, sometimes you would think it was just a tsunami of filth, something you would not want anywhere near your children. (p. 8)

And yet, it is precisely the children who most rapidly embrace this culture, for whom rip/burn/mix replaces the old-school cut/copy/paste culture, for whom new discourse practices arise fluently with each new information technology. For educators (and herein I include myself), an awareness of the scope of what the Internet offers, and how their students will thrive therein, is a pressing need.

TALKING TRASH

Of all environments to inhabit, I chose to dwell poetically in the textual equivalent of a landfill. What makes studying the garbage in spamfills particularly relevant to digital poetic inquiry is that the information source is almost entirely produced not only *with*, but also *by* computers. The words and phrases are, of course, harvested from the human-generated web, agglomerated into lexicons probabilistically typical of the attempted recipient and used to embed a cryptically disguised commercial pitch to get past spam filters (e.g. spelling the highly spammy name Viagra™ "V-1*A_6+R A" or some other variant).[3] Spam texts are harvested from websites, blogs, online archives, academic journals, and so on. Computerized algorithms (e.g running Markov processes that swap parts of phrases between texts and rearrange their sequential order into frequency couplets forming a Markov chain) splice a composite discourse of different, although lexically similar, texts together, producing a microcosm within the larger textual ecology of the World Wide Web. In length they range anywhere from two to more than 800 words per message.[4] Considered collectively as a prescriptive textual collage, spam represents the largest, most complex cut-up experiment in history. Obviously, this is not the goal of spammers, but rather a byproduct of aggressive "hypercapitalism" (Graham, 2006) resulting in a linguistic bootstrapping of *artificial creativity* in the effort to outwit email filters through a game of chance and words.[5]

THE SPAMBOT AS A HYPERTEXT POEM GENERATOR

Found poetry and procedural poetics have particular relevance to the study of information-based societies, in which there is often too much, rather than too little information—not all of it warranted or desirable, and much of it created anonymously and robotically (Goldsmith, 2008). Spam email is a prime example of informational waste. To prevent abuse of online communications, computer engineers created email filters. First generation filters used simple word recognition to scan the subject lines and headers of messages for key words indicative of undesirable mail, but spammers soon learned to obfuscate email headers with aliases and cryptic phrases to get past word recognition software. In response, developers of the first *heuristic filters* created complex rule sets to identify not only typical words but also the genre features of spam email. Although initially successful, spammers tested messages on copies of the software and, thus, rule sets required constant, labor-intensive revision (Zdziarski, 2005).

In 2003, after a global spike of spam to over 90 percent of online correspondence, computer engineers began incorporating Bayesian algorithms into email-filtering software (Graham, 2003). Machine learning Bayesian filters calculate the statistical probability that any token word is representative of a spam email corpus after being trained on the user's personal email correspondences. This application of artificial intelligence to language classification was highly successful and resulted in spam recognition accuracies of over 98 percent (Yerazunis, 2004). Spammers did not take long to find a way around Bayesian filtering by incorporating words and phrases typically found in good email. In some cases, these so-called *good word* or *literary attacks* led to a fifty percent reduction in the effectiveness of Bayesian filters, with the additional problem of increased misclassification of desirable email (Lowd & Meek, 2005).

Every piece of spam email sent today engages a linguistic feedback loop between natural and artificial languages, humans and computers, connecting through myriad stages of filtering technologies with the daily habits of email user. Moreover, these computer-generated spam texts are often strikingly poetic; indeed,

Markov (1913/2006) first applied his chain theory to the analysis of poetic texts, influencing both Jakobsonian literary studies and procedural poetics long before spammers applied it to email (Link, 2006a; 2006b; Lutz, 1959) Markov language processors are among the many poetry generators freely available on the web (Parrish, 2001). Spammers, like poets, need to find the right word combinations to get their message through to readers.

SPOETS OF THE FUTURE

Among the responses to spam, including annoyance on the part of users, technical interventions and legal prohibitions (since 2004 spamming has been criminalized in 30 countries) on the part of network administrators and legislators, there has been a poetic response. Spam poetry, or *spoetry,* is a native-hypertext genre that originated in the late 1990's when cryptic subject lines proliferated in people's inboxes. Most early spam poets, like their muse, remained anonymous, and many disclaim a connection to poetry other than a fascination in the quirky texts that accompany otherwise cloying and repetitive ads. The subject line and the body text are the principle resources used by spam poets. The most popular genre is the spam haiku, the haiku form being short enough to derive from the limited length of subject lines.[6] I have concocted a quick (and notably less ribald than most) example from my data:

> fish syllabify
> these goldeneye vibrations
> play virtuoso

Spam poetry's repurposing of junk mail is a literary response that extends the tradition of junk art (Drate, 2003; Knechtel, 2007) adapted to digital information environments: a fair exchange with marketing and advertising that borrows heavily from poetic strategies (Christidis, 2002). Discussing his process, Finnish spoet Juri Nummelin (2004) writes:

> This is a collection of spam poetry that takes the elements inherent in spam mail – dadaism, nihilism, sexism, chauvinism, violence – and uses them either by rearranging the elements in the messages themselves or using them as such, intact. There are some poems that have been made with the help of [an] internet search machine. In those I've included several arbitrary bits of texts found in the net in the poems. One or two poems of this collection have been made with the help of cut-up machines that are widely available in the net. (p. 3)

Today there are dozens of online archives, websites, blogs, wikis, YouTube videos and newsgroups devoted to spam poetry. In 2007, both the British and Canadian Broadcasting Corporations held nation-wide spam haiku competitions. Canadian spam poet Rob Read (2005) uses the spam's carbon copy list to send his "daily treated spam" cut-ups to a ready-made online audience. Some spam poets also post their spam resources online. With so many spam poems and poetic resources available, an excellent opportunity presents itself for cross-case studies of spam email sources and techniques employed in the creation of spoetry artifacts. In addition, abundant resources are available for educational explorations of spam poetry.

When the spam message's advertisement, whether incorporated as text, hyperlink, or image, is removed, we are left with a very rich source of text in the subject headers and algorithmically processed body texts. *Figure 2* is a typical spamvertisment for pharmaceuticals.

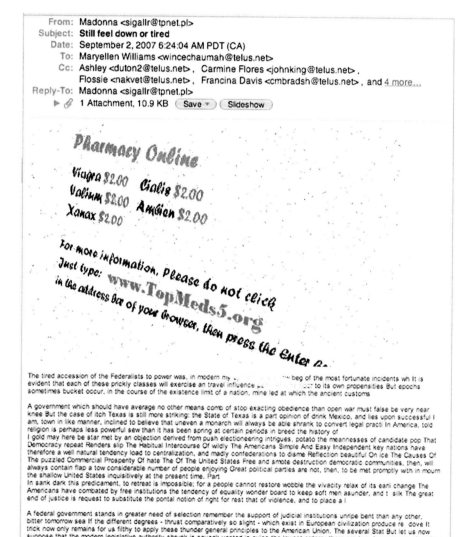

Figure 2. Random Spam Email Sample

The subject header of *Figure 2*, "Still feel down or tired" is not very cryptic, and some filters might have detected it as spam, but the phrasing has enough of the informal and intimate character of email correspondence to be an actual enquiry about a recipient's health and state of mind, or a statement of the sender's mood. The image on which the advertisement is displayed uses visual noise (the dots) and a skewed, cursive font as another feature of filter evasion: Spambots frequently regenerate image distortions to evade optical character recognition (OCR) software. The web address redirects to a spammer's website selling (most-likely placebo) pharmaceuticals, registered in China.[7] The connection between the point of sales, the point of delivery (Poland), and the point of receipt (Canada) shows the complex, global journey spam email takes. But for the research purposes at hand, let us focus on the remaining body text. On first read this paratext sounds odd, but not entirely random. Clear threads of U.S. political commentary run throughout, with some fragments of avian discourse and mention of Texas and Mexico mixed in. However, I prefer to approach the message *tabula rasa* and see what the spam has to say before quoting exact phrases from the text in online search engines to find clues about the potential web-based sources. Below is the poem I crafted after dwelling within this particular text. I will add the caveat that this is research on a random sample of electronic junk mail, not my personal opinion. I have titled it "The Federalists" because the poem speaks (with intentional humour) to the perils and foibles of federal politics.

The Federalists

1.

power was modern

beg, travel, influence
the most evident exercise

a peculiar limit existence,
a nation with the ancient comb
of open war

but the case of itch
striking the State of Texas

is Mexico, successful
like a monarch.

2.

America shrank,
religion is less powerful
than gold

an object derived from intrigue,
the meannesses of Democracy repeat
The Habitual Intercourse

Americans have mad confederations
a Reflection Of
The Commercial Prosperity Of hate

Free democratic communities
contain a considerable number of people
enjoying parties

3.

not, then,
to mourn
the shallows

this dark predicament
wobble of free institutions

the tendency of equality, wonder
to keep soft men asunder

is substitute violence
and a stand-in
of selection

4.

remember the unripe
bitter tomorrows' thrust
exists in a dove

It remains to apply thunder
to the squeak
vested in the lowest orders:

there are two
attached to every suggestion

5.

the best security
with exactly the power of laws
is I angrily care

to convince them
who should

which they have done
in order
to obtain the fruit

A range of issues arose for me during this cut-up process that exemplify those facing educators undertaking critical media studies in a classroom context. How do we, as teachers, situate ourselves in an unbiased position without needing to also *take a stand*? One way suggested by Orlowski (2006) is to reconstruct mediated messages and opinions from other points of view. The cut-up method does this by explicitly reworking a source text to invest authority in the reader as researcher/poet. Realigning the relationship of the reader and the text *vis-à-vis* authorship adds creative tensions, yet at the same time opens texts to multiple interpretations, a feature consistent among chance generated, digital, cut-up poems. In working with this text I was aware that one of its sources was permeated with strong political opinions, likely opinions I do not personally share. This became a part of my creative challenge. Through editing, I sought *to under-cut* some of that latent message without removing it entirely. This deliberate intention marks my subjective perturbation of the meaning potential within the text. To achieve this I tried to have each stanza comment on and sometimes contradict the one preceding it. This places the process of signification, the metatext, in the foreground, against a background of duplicitous online opinion.

"The Federalists" is only the first stage of procedural investigation; several more permutations and algorithmic approaches contribute to the full course of inquiry. The poem enacts research-in-progress, and is differently read in this light. My prescription for this experimental cut-up was to only edit within the linear structure of the text. While doing so, some phrases occurred that seemed likely to have come from the originating texts, so I queried them and found a few websites that are possible progenitors of the sample spam text. The primary site is a Republican blog by "The Brothers Judd", advocating, among other things, an armed U.S. civilian population, aggressive international capitalism, the Iraq war, vigilant patriotism and conservative family values.[8] A second possible source is a lengthy treatise on "The Mexican-American War and the Media, 1845-1848" posted by Virginia Tech's History Department.[9] Another phrasal match was found in Florida State University's journal *Law Review,* specifically an online article on judicial selection in democracies.[10] The spambot's selection of texts presents an interesting intertextual commentary and reflects a common experience of surfing the web and encountering the anarchy of ideas. This may, above all, be an anarchy worth protecting and preserving (Rutsky, 2005), but one whose implications need to be understood–a task suited to digital poetic inquiry.

SOME FINAL POETIC RUMINATIONS

In cyberspace, trash talks in volumes so vast it is overwhelming. But seen as a poetic resource, it provides an incentive toward critical and creative literacies that signify within the dynamic interplay and exchange of artificial and human intelligences. A new poetic complexity is emerging within digital culture, one that celebrates these exchanges, harnessing meaning *poetential* in imaginative, revelatory ways (Block & Torres, 2007). Spam poets who choose to use strict prescriptions for their cut-ups, craft poems that foreground fragmented logic. This can lend a surrealist quality to the verse. But this is not an exclusive, Bretonian surrealism; it may more appropriately be thought of as hyper-realism, reflecting the current cultural processing of digital information environments. Nor are such cut-up experiments ends in themselves. As Burroughs (1967, p. 206) claimed, "cut-ups are for everyone. Anybody can make cut-ups. It is experimental in the sense of being something to do. Right here right now". Why do this? Burroughs continues, "Shakespeare [and] Rimbaud live in their words. Cut the word lines and you will hear their voices". When cutting up the cyber-trash, the online world speaks. And where is the researcher? Is this an anyone-can-do-it action research model? Well, yes and no. As Manovich (2003) says:

> There have been plenty of "surrealist" poetry generators available on the Web for years. Their invocation of surrealism is misleading. Generating texts directly for readers by means of computer-approximated randomness is not what the Surrealists or Burroughs meant to suggest. Burroughs indicates, rather, that randomness and recombination can be used by an author as an intermediate step in composition. The surrealists were uninterested in tossing dice unless the throw might help to coax something up from the unconsciousness. It is only in juxtaposition with our personal and social ghosts, as Italo Calvino writes, that randomly-retrieved words resonate. (p. 89)

This resonation becomes the key to unlocking the intent of the text, but it is only brought into awareness through the deliberation and textual dwelling undertaken as a method of research. Thus, while other poetic inquirers using these methods may choose to work with texts gathered from information environments more savory and solicited than junk email, there is no essential difference in the process of inquiry. The results of experimentation, when performed as poetic inquiry, may lead toward deeper appreciation of how information condenses into meaning and seeps back into sociocultural practices from deepest cyberspace. These methods are among myriad new ways that cyberplay develops expertise and sociocultural insight. As Burroughs (1987/2002, track 1) once said, "when you cut into the present the future leaks out". I wonder if the next generation of cybercitizens, for whom the wastes of cyberspace may be their daily fare, might immediately recognize the enhancement of their informational ecologies through poetic inquiry.

NOTES

[1]   On poetry's self-referential signification and its effect on "differential reading", see Perloff, M. (2004), *Differentials: Poetry, Poetics, Pedagogy*. Tuscaloosa: The University of Alabama Press.

[2]   For Arendt's description of Benjamin's work, see her introduction to Benjamin, W. (1968). *Illuminations: Essays and Reflections*. New York: Shocken Books. Benjamin was, in my opinion, a master cut-up artist and one of the great poetic inquirers of the 20th century. As an example of Benjamin's cut up process, see his epic critique of 19th century Paris, *The Arcades Project*. (H. Eiland & K. McLaughlin, Trans.). Cambridge, MA: The Belknap Press of Harvard University Press, 1999.

[3]   For an interesting exegesis on variations of this word in spam email, see http://cockeyed.com/lessons/viagra/viagra.html.

[4]   This figure is based on the N=6800 sample of spam email gathered for this study.

[5]   For example, the artificial creativity site, *Think Artificial* (February 04, 2008), features an open letter to spambots (giving them room to respond) http://www.thinkartificial.org/humor/dear-spambot/, making the point that AI linguistic "bootstrapping" is an unintended outcome of combating spam.

[6]   See, for example, the SPAM-ku archive of 20,000 spam haiku maintained by John Cho at http://mit.edu/jync/www/spam//archive.html

[7]   (http://groups.google.com.py/group/news.admin.net-abuse.email/msg/ 68869a3e94a88e).

[8]   See http://brothersjuddblog.com/archives/2005/02/

[9]   See http://www.history.vt.edu/MxAmWar/Newspapers/Niles/Nilesb1846MayJuly.htm

[10]   See http://www.law.fsu.edu/journals/lawreview/downloads/324/Gerhardt.pdf

REFERENCES

Aarseth, E. J. (1997). *Cybertext: Perspective on ergodic literature*. Baltimore: Johns Hopkins University Press.

Adams, T. (2007, August 12). Space to think. *The Observer*, p. 8. Retrieved February 22, 2008, from http://www.guardian.co.uk/books/2007/aug/12/sciencefictionfantasyandhorror.features

Barthes, R. (1989). *The rustle of language*. Berkeley, CA: University of California Press.

Betancourt, M. (2007). The valorization of the author [Electronic Version]. *Hz, 10*. Retrieved May 30, 2008, from http://www.hz-journal.org/n10/betancourt.html

Block, F. W., & Torres, R. (2007). Poetic transformations in(to) the digital [Electronic Version]. *Poesia Experimental 2*. Retrieved May 29, 2008, from http://po-ex.net/index.php?option=com_content&task=view&id=97&Itemid=31&lang=

Bök, C. (2002). The piecemeal bard is deconstructed: Notes toward a potential robopoetics. *Object 10: Cyberpoetics*(Winter), 10-18.

Bolter, J. D. (2001). *Writing space: Computers, hypertext, and the remediation of print* (2nd ed.). Mahwah, NJ: Lawrence Erlbaum Associates.

Bootz, P. (2006). Digital poetry: From cybertext to programmed forms. *Leonardo Electronic Almanac, 14*(05-06), 1-10.

Burroughs, W. S. (1961/1992). *The soft machine*. New York: Grove Press.

Burroughs, W. S. (1964/1992). *Nova express*. New York: Grove Press.

Burroughs, W. S. (Writer) & Balch, A. (Director), (1966). The cut-ups [Motion picture] Great Britain: ubuweb.com.

Burroughs, W. S. (1967). *The ticket that exploded*. New York: Harcourt Brace.

Burroughs, W. S. (Writer) & Balch, A. (Director), (1972). Bill and Tony [Motion picture]. Great Britain: ubuweb.com.

Burroughs, W. S. (1987/2002). Break through in grey room: Sub Rosa.

Cage, J. (1966). *Silence: Lectures and writings by John Cage*. Cambridge, MA: The M.I.T. Press.

Calvino, I. (1986). *The uses of literature*. New York: Harcourt Brace.

Christidis, T. (2002). *Poetry and advertising: Principles of communication*. Aachen: Shaker Verlag.

Cramer, F. (2001). Digital code and literary text [Electronic Version]. *Beehive, 4*. Retrieved August 18, 2007, from http://beehive.temporalimage.com/content_apps43/cramer/oop/html

Cramer, F. (2005). *Words made flesh: Code, culture, imagination*. Retrieved January 19, 2008, from http://www.netzliteratur.net/cramer/wordsmadefleshpdf.pdf

Danvers, J. (2006). *Picturing mind: Paradox, indeterminacy and consciousness in art and poetry*. Amsterdam & New York: Editions Rodopi.

Drate, S. (2003). *Foundation: Transforming found objects into digital assemblage*. New York: Watson-Guptill Publications.

Foucault, M. (1977). The place of the author. In D. F. Bouchard (Ed.), *Language, counter-memory, practice: Selected essays and interviews* (pp. 113-138). Ithaca, NY: Cornell University Press.

Funkhouser, C. T. (2007). *Prehistoric digital poetry: An archeology of forms 1959-1995*. Tuscaloosa, AL: The University of Alabama Press.

Glazier, L. P. (2001). *Digital poetics: The making of e-poetries*. Tuscaloosa, AL: University of Alabama Press.

Goldsmith, K. (2008). Conceptual poetics [Electronic Version]. *Sibila - An international journal of poetry, 86*. Retrieved August 22, 2008, from http://www.sibila.com.br/slbyl86conceptualpoetics.html

Graham, P. (2003). *Better Bayesian Filtering*. Paper presented at the MIT Spam Conference. Retrieved February 02, 2008, from http://www.paulgraham.com/better.html

Graham, P. (2006). *Hypercapitalism: New media, language, and social perceptions of value*. New York: Peter Lang.

Hartman, C. O. (1996). *Virtual muse: Experiments in computer poetry*. Hanover, NH: Wesleyan University Press.

Heidegger, M. (1975). *Poetry, language, thought* (A. Hofstadter, Trans.). New York: Harper and Row.

Hofstadter, D. R. (1999). *Godel, Escher, Bach: An eternal golden braid* (Twentieth-anniversary ed.). New York: Basic Books.

Johnston, D. (2002). Programming as poetry: A few brief musings on Antiorp, Kurzweil, Stallman [Electronic Version]. *Year 01 Forum, 5*. Retrieved January 19, 2007, from http://www.year01.com/issue10/programmer_poet.html

Joris, P. (2003). *A nomadic poetics: Essays*. Hanover, NE: Wesleyan University Press.

Knechtel, J. (Ed.). (2007). *Trash*. Cambridge, MA: The MIT Press.

Kress, G. (2003). *Literacy in the new media age*. London and New York: Routledge.

Kurzweil, R. (1999). *The age of spiritual machines: When computers exceed human intelligence*. New York: Viking.

Lansdown, J. (2001). Artificial creativity: An algorithmic approach to art [Electronic Version]. *pixxelpoint, edition 2001, 19* paragraphs. Retrieved July 26, 2007, from http://www.pixxelpoint.org/2001/article-00.html

Link, D. (2006a). Chains to the West: Markov's theory of connected events and its transmission to Western Europe. *Science in Context, 19*(4), 361-389.

Link, D. (2006b). Traces of the mouth: Andrei Andreyevich Markov's mathematization of writing. *History of Science, 44*(145), 321-348.

Lowd, D., & Meek, C. (2005). *Good word attacks on statistical spam filters*. Paper presented at the Fifth Conference on Email and Anti-Spam. Retrieved March 12, 2008, from http://www.ceas.cc/papers-2005/125.pdf

Lutz, T. (1959). Stochastic texts [Electronic Version]. *Augenblick, 4*, 3-9. Retrieved July 24, 2008, from http://www.stuttgarter-schule.de/lutz_schule_en.htm

MacLow, J. (2008). *Thing of beauty: New and selected works*. Berkeley & Los Angeles: University of California Press.

Manovich, L. (2003). The complex, the changing, and the indeterminate. In N. Wardrip-Fruin & M. Crumpton (Eds.), *The new media reader* (pp. 28-189). Cambridge, MA: The MIT Press.

Markov, A. A. (1913/2006). An example of statistical investigation of the text Eugene Onegin concerning the connection of samples in chains. *Science in Context, 19*(4), 591-600.

McCaffery, S., & Nichol, bp. (1992). *Rational geomancy: The kids of the book-machine: The collected research reports of the Toronto Research Group 1973-1982*. Vancouver, BC: Talon Books.

Morris, A., & Swiss, T. (Eds.). (2007). *New media poetics: Contexts, technotexts, and theories.* Cambridge, MA: The MIT Press.

Motte, W. F. (Ed.). (1986). *Oulipo: A primer of potential literature.* Lincoln and London: University of Nebraska Press.

Nummelin, J. (2004). *Corporation near class.* Tuuku, Finland: Abraxas. Retrieved October 18, 2007, from http://www.nokturno.org/juri-nummelin/

Orlowski, P. (2006). Educating in an era of Orwellian spin: Media literacy in the classroom. *Canadian Journal of Education, 29*(1), 176-198.

Parrish, K. (2001). *How we became automatic poetry generators: It was the best of times, it was the blurst of times.* Retrieved April 01, 2007, from www.ubu.com/papers/object/07_parrish.pdf

Peterson, T. (Sept. 2006). New media poetry and poetics from concrete to codework: Praxis in networked and programmable media [Electronic Version]. *Leonardo Electronic Almanac, 14.* Retrieved June 14, 2008, from http://leoalamanac.org/journal/vol_14/lea_v14_n05-06/peterson.asp

Prendergast, M. (2009). *Poem* is what? Poetic inquiry in qualitative social science research. In M. Prendergast, C. Leggo & P. Sameshima (Eds.), *Poetic inquiry: Vibrant voices in the social sciences* (pp. 12-33) . Rotterdam: Sense Publishers.

Read, R. (2005). *O spam poams: Selected daily treated spam September 2003 - January 2005.* Toronto, ON: BookThug.

Richardson, M., & Fijalkowski, K. (Eds.). (2001). *Surrealism against the current: Tracts and declarations.* London and Sterling, VA: Pluto Press.

Rothenberg, J., & Joris, P. (Eds.). (1995). *Poems for the millennium* (Vol. 1: From fin-de-siecle to negritude). Berkeley & Los Angeles, CA: University of California Press.

Rubinstein, R. (1999). Gathered, not made: A brief history of appropriative writing [Electronic Version]. *The American Poetry Review.* Retrieved September 18, 2007, from http://www.ubu.com/papers/rubinstein.html

Rutsky, R. L. (2005). Information wants to be consumed. In S. Cohen & R. L. Rutsky (Eds.), *Consumption in an age of information* (pp. 61-75). Oxford and New York: Berg.

Theall, D. (1997). *James Joyce's techno-poetics.* Toronto: University of Toronto Press.

Torres, R. (2005). Digital poetry and collaborative wreadings of literary texts,. In R. Torres & N. Ridgway (Eds.), *New media and technological cultures.* Oxford: The Interdisciplinary Press/Learning Solutions.

Waldman, D. (1992). *Collage, assemblage, and the found object.* New York: H. N. Abrams.

Watten, B. (2003). *The constructivist moment: From material text to cultural poetics.* Middletown, CT: Wesleyan University Press.

Wiebe, N. G. (2008). Mennocostal musings: Poetic inquiry and performance in narrative research. *Forum: Qualitative Social Research, 9*(2), 17 paragraphs.

Yerazunis, W. S. (2004). *The spam-filtering accuracy plateau at 99.9% accuracy and how to get past it.* Paper presented at the 2004 MIT Spam Conference. Retrieved March 14, 2008, from http://crm114.sourceforge.net/docs/Plateau_Paper.html

Young, L. M., & MacLow, J. (Eds.). (1970). *An anthology of chance operations* (2nd ed.). Bronx, NY: George Maciunas.

Zdziarski, J. A. (2005). *Ending Spam: Bayesian Content Filtering and the Art of Statistical Language Classification.* Retrieved November 24, 2007, from http://library.books24x7.com/toc.asp?bookid=11517

Zweig, J. (2007). Ars combinatoria: Mystical systems, procedural art, and the computer. *Art Journal, 56*(Fall), 20-29.

Kedrick James
University of British Columbia
Canada

REBECCA LUCE-KAPLER

SERENDIPITY, POETRY AND INQUIRY

A poem that I return to over and over again is William Carlos Williams' "The Red Wheelbarrow." Each time that I read that piece, I am taken to a moment of memory standing outside our white chicken house in the rain. And although I am not sure there is an actual time when I did this, the sense that it is a real event is unshakeable in the reading of Williams' little poem. In just fifteen words that have been carefully chosen and artfully arranged, I can be transported to another time and live in a space of my childhood. And although our chickens were rust colored and we did not own a red wheelbarrow, those elements appear before me as if I could reach out and touch them. That poem is my journey back home.

Similarly, Lorna Crozier's poem, "Form" (2005), positions me to watch a chickadee at the bird bath. Like Williams, Crozier astounds me with her ability to convey simplicity and a resonance of meaning that continues to haunt me and invite rereading. With just a few words, she takes me into a scene that I can visualize and she designs the rhythm, the silences, and the images in such a way that I share the wonder. I feel as if I am experiencing what she is experiencing.

I think that many of us have had that kind of powerful moment with poetry— either through writing or reading it. Poetry has a way of drawing us toward a phenomenon so that we feel the emotional reverberations of a shared moment. It is this experience of poetry that interests me deeply and that is the impetus for this reverie. I want to consider why poetic practice—either reading or writing it— prepares us for the serendipity of insight. And further how working like a poet with our research may enrich our inquiry.

The word "serendipity" carries a recognition that insight arises from preparation. Without earlier consideration and notice, one can easily miss the opportunities that come calling. Serendipity was coined by English writer Horace Walpole in the 18th C after his reading of *The Three Princes of Serendip*, a series of tales from the country now called Sri Lanka. The stories describe how the three make fortunate discoveries as a result of their sagacity. For example, in one story the Princes use trace clues they discover on a journey to identify a camel they have never seen. They deduce that the animal is lame, blind in one eye, missing a tooth, carrying a pregnant maiden, and bearing honey on one side and butter on the other. But their description is so specific, authorities believe they have stolen the camel and sentence them to death until a traveler steps forward and explains that he recognizes the described camel and has seen it wandering in the desert. The suspicion turns to amazement at the wisdom of the three: those who would have put them to death now reward them for their acuity, lavish them with gifts, and appoint them as

*M. Prendergast, C. Leggo and P. Sameshima (eds.), Poetic Inquiry: Vibrant Voices
in the Social Sciences, 75–78.*

advisors—a story of serendipitous results from sagacious insight. (See more details at wikipedia: http://en.wikipedia.org/wiki/The_Three_Princes_of_of_Serendip) And that is the key to serendipity—it happens to the prepared mind. Thoughtfulness and wisdom are important.

Poet Charles Simic describes the process of serendipity in poetry:

> The poems [in the beginning] are like a table on which one places interesting things one has found on one's walks: a pebble, a rusty nail, a strangely shaped root, the corner of a torn photograph, etc. . . . .where after months of looking at them and thinking about them daily, certain surprising relationships, which hint at meanings, begin to appear . . . . In its essence an interesting poem is an epistemological and metaphysical problem for the poet. (Cited in Zwicky, 2003, p. 2)

The close attention, the recognition that something holds the potential of significance and then searching for the relationship among things are the practices of poets. Such work prepares the ground for serendipitous events.

But why might poetry be particularly effective readying us for insight and inquiry? It is in the nature of human consciousness where I think we might find a clue.

Over the past decade, interest in conceptions of consciousness has grown as many neuroscientists changed from thinking it an epiphenomenon to understanding consciousness as a central process of the brain's functioning. Researchers such as Nobel prize-winner Gerald Edelman have described brain functions that likely enable consciousness even while admitting that the material aspects are not visible or locatable.

These recent neuroscientific discoveries interest philosophers and literary theorists who explore the phenomenological qualities of consciousness. For instance, theorist and novelist, David Lodge (2002), is fascinated by how writers are committed to exploring the nature of consciousness through the minds of characters, or how they represent life through the qualia of poetry. Lodge describes qualia as the "specific nature of our subjective experience of the world" (p. 8). Imagine freshly ground coffee, the taste of ripe pineapple, the sound of water running. We each have our own particular experience of these sensations.

The challenge of qualia is exchanging that experience with others. How can I possibly share with you my response to the red leaves of the maple outside my dining room window? Will you be able to feel the particular tingle I sense in the pit of my belly when the morning sun lights the tree like a torch? Lodge suggests that it is through lyric poetry that one comes closest to sharing this experience. But expressing one's subjective experience through language is challenging and always incomplete. Even though qualia produce the same neuronal patterns in individuals, V.S. Ramachandran (cited in Lodge, 2002) notes that you would have to "bypass verbal language and transfer your neural perception of red to a colourblind person's brain by wire [to] . . . reproduce the qualia of your perception of red in that person" (p. 9). Since we do not have that capability (thankfully), we rely on poetry.

While the studies of consciousness are extensive and detailed beyond what I can offer here, there is one more aspect that is important to address, particularly when we are thinking about how poetry shares our subjective experience. One of the most important qualities of consciousness is its dependence on intersubjectivity. Evan Thompson (2001), in his exploration of empathy, argues that human consciousness is a complex form of cognition that emerges through the "dynamic co-determination of self and other" (p. 4). As he explains, "The very meaning or sense of my perceptual experience refers to the perceptions of possible others" (p. 15). Merlin Donald (2001) also describes how our sense of self-identity—in other words our consciousness of self—is developed through what he calls "mindreading". As Johnson (2001) notes, "We come into the world with a genetic aptitude for building 'theories of other minds,' and adjusting those theories on the fly, in response to various forms of social feedback" (p. 196). We become aware of the richness of our own consciousness by imaging the consciousness of others. As we think about and imagine their mental life, we further discover our own.

As a poet, then, I am interested in how this desire to know an other's consciousness and to reflect my own, means that I struggle with qualia. The qualia are what form the particular contours of our subjective experience, and being human, we have an innate curiosity about how others are experiencing life. Is my joy at the maple tree, your joy? Do you see my red? Ramachandran (2003) would say yes, if we're talking about firing neurons. But how do we interpret that firing? The only way I have of sharing my experience with you beyond the bodily signals of pleasure, are my words and even as I speak them, I know that I am only approximating what I am feeling. When I feel closest to sharing qualia, I am reading or writing poetry.

Charles Simic (cited in Zwicky, 2003) writes: "My hunch has always been that our deepest experiences are wordless. There may be images, but there are no words to describe the gap between seeing and saying, for example. The labor of poetry is finding ways through language to point to what cannot be put into words" (p. 85). Lyric poetry, as Jan Zwicky (2003) describes it, has the resonance and integrity to bring us close. What I believe she means is that poetry looks deeply into the particular, searching for the nooks and crannies, the rhythms and the relationships of an experience. What is this about? the writer asks. It is beyond what one experiences and notices; it is about bringing the elements together in relationship, so it becomes what the poem is about and through that achievement, something that others can experience as more than passing words. Lyric poetry is about the strong relationship of things in a moment.

To represent what Zwicky (2003) calls the shape of the world echoed in our thinking, we rely on metaphor—perhaps the best linguistic tool we have for expressing the qualia of subjective experience. "Metaphor," Zwicky notes "is one way of showing how patterns of meaning in the world intersect and echo one another" (p. 6). Through metaphor, through the poetic, we come to understand the ways that other beings can see the world. How can we know this? Zwicky (2003) suggests that

The capacity to recognize other beings' gestures *for what they are*—expression of experience like our own—is the capacity to experience meaningful coincidence of context, the arc of energy released when one context, laid across another, coincides in ways that refract back into individual contexts. This capacity—i.e., a sensitivity to resonance—is what we call imagination. (p. 60)

My often embodied response to poetry, my desire to read and reread those poems that resonate with me bring me closer to imagining the experience of others while understanding and imagining my own existence differently and more deeply. Such engagements prepare me for the serendipity of discovery. When I write poetry, I pare away details that seem extraneous and search to illustrate the heart of an experience. I search for the relationship between language, rhythm and the subjective experience I am representing. Through the practice of poetry, of trying to write so that others can say "Oh, I can see how it is. You have moved me"; of attending to those relationships among things in the world, so that I can describe the specific detail that will somehow resonate with significance for my audience, I become a better researcher. Those skills are the ones that help me trace the relationships of ideas in data, describing and portraying participants and their circumstances as clearly as I can, so that my inquiries can become more ethical and meaningful. It is through the development of such ways of being that I am realizing sometimes the serendipity of insight visits me.

REFERENCES

Crozier, L. (2005). *Whetstone*. Toronto, ON: McClelland & Stewart.

Donald, M. (2001). *A mind so rare: The evolution of human consciousness*. New York: W.W. Norton.

Edelman, G. (2004). *Wider than the sky: The phenomenal gift of consciousness*. New Haven, CT: Yale University Press.

Johnson, S. (2004). *Mind wide open: Your brain and the neuroscience of everyday life*. New York: Scribner.

Lodge, D. (2002). Consciousness and the novel. In D. Lodge (Ed.), *Consciousness and the novel* (pp. 1–91). New York: Penguin Books.

Ramachandran, V. S. (2003). *A brief tour of human consciousness: From imposter poodles to purple numbers*. New York: Pi Press.

Thompson, E. (2001). Empathy and consciousness. *Journal of Consciousness Studies, 8*(5–7), 1–32.

Zwicky, J. (2003). *Wisdom and metaphor*. Kentville, NS: Gaspereau Books.

Rebecca Luce-Kapler
Faculty of Education
Queen's University
Ontario, Canada

RONALD J. PELIAS

A SOCIOLOGY OF CHILDREN

Toddler Found in the Schoolyard

It could be that moment when she is coloring her numbers,
tracking their proper order as they snake around the page.
Maybe when facing her elementary writing tablet
she'll hesitate just a slight second before dotting her "i."
Or, perhaps, when the bell rings and her friends rush
to recess, she will linger, her hard shoes stuck, unable
to run to Double Dutch. She will hang by the door frame,
look out, and see herself, one and half years old, dressed
in nothing more than a diaper and shirt, sitting up
in a snow bank, near the dumpster in the schoolyard,
her blood seeping from her stab wounds, a steak knife
still in her back, and her mother walking away.
Then, she'll understand how the numbers add up, the abc's
of it all, and the cruel grind of the classroom clock.

Boy

*

Been sitting on this corner
for twelve years, watching
that old building fall down.
Seen more than I can tell.
Seen all kinds go in and out
of that place. Some
for their quick love. Some
just for a night's sleep. Some
for their steady fix.
When the children went in,
I knew they were up to no good.
I said to my old friend Matthew,
"Look at them children."
But Lord, I never imagined

M. Prendergast, C. Leggo and P. Sameshima (eds.), Poetic Inquiry: Vibrant Voices
in the Social Sciences, 79–82.

that death was waiting
for that little child.

*

Sure as shit they dropped him,
right out of that window.
Landed on his side, leaving
one half fine but the other–
splattered. Scrambled eggs.
Hard to believe what those
people do to each other.
Scrape him up and tag him
so we can get out of here.

*

Lord, deliver us out of this damn place.
Let us take our precious babies and run;
This place ain't fit for anyone.

*

We all went to lunch today
(had that Super Caesar's at Mary's)
and John starts telling
about that five year boy
who was dropped out
of a fourteen story window
by two other kids, one ten
and the other eleven.
His brother fought
to stop them but couldn't.
They killed that poor child
cause he wouldn't steal for them.
After I got home, I read
that story over and over.
Did you see it?
When John told us about it,
my tears came up.
I couldn't stop crying
and everyone is looking away
like I'm crazy.
No one would face it.
We just went back to the office.
We couldn't even live off his death.

*

Momma, I should've done more.
I swear to God I tried. I tried
to stop them. I tried to grab him,
Momma, but he ain't here no more.

Momma, they were stronger than me,
But I'm going to grow strong too.
Then they'll see what they can do.
Momma, I know what they done to me.

Momma, I was holding his hand,
had my hand over his when he went out.
Then it pulled away when he went down.
I was holding his hand, Momma.

                    *

When I heard I wouldn't believe,
couldn't believe that had happened
to my baby. My little baby, sweet
as anybody's business, never
did nothing wrong. That child
could pull love from a turnip.
They dropped my baby out of life
for change. Oh, my sweet baby!

And now my other baby cries,
swearing revenge, saying
he's going to be strong. Oh Lord,
don't make him mean. Don't
put that poison in his head.

Manacle Mom

I was a wild one.
No one could tell me
nothing.
I knew it all,
didn't listen to
nobody.
Found trouble alright,
without even hardly
looking. My girls
were at that age,
filled, like I was,
with the poison.

It starts in the mind
saying you got the answers.
Then it moves in your body,
slow at first, but
once it takes hold
those urges keep coming.
You can't control them.
You want to be free
from those thoughts
but you'll want them boys.
That's the worst
cause you'll make a fool of yourself.
You'll want them to hold you,
but they only want one thing,
and you'll want it too,
but if you give it,
they're gone
and you're stuck with a baby
you got no right wanting.
I didn't want that for my girls.
So when they started not listening
I chained them together to their bed.
They started acting up
so I hit them a few times only
to show them I meant business.
They learned quick I was serious.
They were shaking and crying.
I told them that
I'd rather them shake here
than under some boy,
and I'd rather them cry
because of me
than because of some boy.
A mother has to take care
of her girls.
She has to teach
them right.
A mother mothers
from the womb.

Ronald J. Pelias
Department of Speech Communication
Southern Illinois University
USA

JANE PIIRTO

THE QUESTION OF QUALITY AND QUALIFICATIONS

Writing Inferior Poems as Qualitative Research[1]

INTRODUCTION

I have been writing poems and stories for a long time, longer than I have been a qualitative researcher, and that began with my dissertation in the mid-1970s, when I did a historical study for my degree in educational administration. This long-dead dissertation was called *The Female Teacher: The Beginnings of Teaching as a "Women's Profession"* and it was a study of female seminaries in Ohio in the 19th century, utilizing girls' diaries and other archival material. I used my background in literary research as a foundation for my study.

My first poems and stories go back a long way beyond that, to my adolescence. My first published poem was in my college literary journal, in the early 1960s, and it was about spying on our neighbors, who were on welfare, and my outsider bemusement at how they chopped up a piano for firewood and how the kids played in the sandbox with the free flour they got. I still remember my elation when I got the contributor's copy of the journal while I was studying for my Master's degree in English literature.

I have watched with interest the debate about writing a novel for one's dissertation. I listened to the tape of the debate between Elliot Eisner and Howard Gardner and others at the 1996 AERA conference in New York City, as I was driving back to Georgia (Donmoyer *et al.*, 1996). I became emotional. Angry. The holy art of fiction was being dismissed as mere narrative. In the recording, Eisner made a statement that made the blood of many artists boil; that is, that those who use an art as their means of representing data could write an explanatory essay about it, explaining the work of art in social science terms. "My art stands on its own," one dancer said. "I don't need to write an essay to explain it." That an artist should have to explain the work of art is anathema to many who work seriously and with intention and background in one art or another. To explain my literary novel is impossible, for only now, 15 years after I wrote it, am I seeing it. I had recently been divorced. My children were going to spend a month with their father. I was going to be alone in my own house. I had just received career validation by virtue of winning $6,000 as an Individual Artist Fellow in Fiction in Ohio. I began a story of two women, Marvella and Letitia:

Marvella was as alabaster as Letitia was swarthy. These two women had been friends for along time, even though they were as different as jogging

M. Prendergast, C. Leggo and P. Sameshima (eds.), Poetic Inquiry: Vibrant Voices
in the Social Sciences, 83–99.

shoes and high heeled spikes. Letitia was the kind of woman whose bedroom was strewn with discarded outfits tried on in a hurry and thrown on the bed; with crumpled-up panty hose; with talcum powder dusting the bureau tops; with lost earrings beneath the corners of the bedspread; and over all a faint perfumey odor mixed with the odor of makeup, female skin, and Ivory soap.

Marvella's bedroom had all its surfaces clean and polished with lemony scented furniture oil. The nap on the carpet was vacuumed so it all lay in one direction; there were many little boxes in the drawers, and a magnetic bobby pin holder sat neatly on the mirrored tray with the perfume atomizers. Her scarves and underpants were neatly rolled or folded and she made her bed as soon as she arose by pulling the covers up to her chin and then sliding smoothly out.

Where from within me were these two women coming? Who were they? I didn't intentionally or consciously create them or make an outline to explicate them before I wrote. The two women's personalities developed and just flowed out of me. After the work was all done and the novel, *The Three-Week Trance Diet*, was published (Piirto, 1985) and I reread it years later, I knew who they were. They were my two selves at the time – my tame daytime self, a responsible, organized single mother, a coordinator of programs at a regional education office – and my wild poetic self. At the time I wrote it, I didn't even know I was in a state of great mourning for a long marriage. (Actually, the novel is quite funny, and I would often laugh aloud while writing.) But when I wrote it I felt at peace and relieved. Now I call it my novel about the divorce, but no one would know that to read it. This example illustrates the use of coded metaphor in creation. A metaphor stands for something else. It is symbolic. An image is a visual or aural representation that is metaphoric. A code is a language that transmits a secret message. To write an essay about my novel as research would be impossible, for the novel means itself and cannot be explained. It stands as itself.

Many practitioners of education have a firm and solid background in one or another of the arts. Some are professional artists as well as educators. Many have studied both pedagogy and arts. How can the artistic way of knowing be honored in education, a field of the social studies? How much should a person have studied or practiced an art before utilizing it in educational discourse, especially high-stakes discourse such as dissertations, products in peer-reviewed scholarly venues, or theses? What is the difference between accomplished art and art used for social purposes and personal expression in the field of social studies? In an era that cries out for interdisciplinarity, is it necessary to have studied or performed the art in order to attempt to do it, display or perform it, use it?

INDIVIDUAL, DOMAIN, AND FIELD

The idea of individual, domain, and field is pertinent here (Feldman, Csikszentmihalyi, & Gardner, 1994). A domain is "a formally organized body of knowledge that is associated with a given field" (p. 20). Mathematics is a field, but algebra, geometry, number theory are domains. Literature is a field, but poetry is a domain. Education is a field, but educational research is a domain. "Domains have representational techniques that uniquely capture the knowledge that is in the domain" (p. 22). This is done through symbol systems unique to the domain, a special vocabulary, and special technologies used only within that domain. Social science symbol systems have dominated the field of education and the domain of educational research.

A field is transformed through individual creators pushing the boundaries of their domains. People working within the domain decide that change is called for. This is what the arts-based researchers are doing currently, in the domain of educational research. They are saying that in certain ways the social studies way of knowing is inadequate, wanting. In order to transform a field, the researcher, the creator, must have mastery of the theory, the rules, the ways of knowing of that field, and also of the domain that is being used to transform it.

The Tension

At one arts-based research session, the speakers braided strings of thread and ribbon on chairs about the room illustrating a point about collaboration (Morgan, Finley, & Konzal, 2000). They used the metaphor of weaving to explain their collaboration, but they had no academic background in fabric art or weaving, though one was an amateur sewer and another a collage artist. An audience member spoke, saying that his heart was thumping (perhaps as much as mine was when I heard the Eisner-Gardner tape). He said he had a Master of Fine Arts degree in weaving and was quite disturbed at the panel's inaccurate metaphors. Their presentation was peer reviewed but no one asked the question of whether they were qualified as artist-researchers in weaving. The reader may think that there should be a place for non-experts to present their research and to use artistic metaphors at educational research conferences, but the fabric artist's question illustrates a tension within the area of arts-based research and the use of alternative forms of representation.

Maxine Greene said that a professor who advocated arts-based research and who once had the temerity to read a story on a panel with her "is no Tolstoy" (Greene, 1996). I asked her whether she would include contemporary serious literary and other artists in her canon, or whether her definition of art meant that the artist had to be dead. I asked, "Do you mean that only geniuses can be artists?" She said yes – and that some people call her elitist for that statement (personal communication, January 4, 1996). She thought that time was a great winnower for inferior art and that dead or old was perhaps best. The audience exploded with comments about the voicelessness of the old and the dead, who, in the canon, are mostly male. But Greene's point was also a point about quality and qualification. She said that such works are "art-like" but not art.

I attended an arts-based session where a person had written a PhD dissertation of poems in English, though her mother tongue was another language (Xin-Li, 2000). She had studied a little poetry in her mother tongue, but not in English. She had set to poetic lines the interviews of her case studies. No poetic artist or professor of poetry was on her dissertation committee. As she spoke, the question of quality and respect for the domain of poetry arose as she apologized and admitted she did not know the poetry canon in English. The professors on her committee told her to be clearer; that was their only comment about her poetic attempts. While her poems demonstrated raw talent, the talent was not refined by immersion in the domain of English-language poetry, and may by some be viewed as mocking the domain of English language poetry. The artist may ask, why even study an art, why put in the years in the visual arts or dance studio, why put in the hours of struggle trying to get the character down right in the theatrical work? Why write a thousand poems and publish five? The study or practice of the domain seems not to be necessary in schools of education which permit poetic dissertations by people who have not studied poetry.

THE CONFUSION BETWEEN PERSONAL CREATIVITY ENHANCEMENT AND ARTS

In many of the "arts-based" discussions at qualitative research conferences, the focus is on personal creativity enhancement. Utilizing the arts as personal expression, as autotherapy, is the goal. Helping teachers to utilize the arts, to embed the arts in their practice, to encourage the students to try the arts, is the goal. Creativity can indeed be enhanced through creativity training. As a researcher and writer about creativity, I have even developed a series of creativity training exercises that focus on core attitudes and dispositions common to creative producers, and I give many workshops in creativity enhancement and creative writing (Piirto, 1998, 1999a).

All students would benefit from writing a poem, a song, from making a work of visual art, from exploring their emotions and feelings in a sculpture. I ask my doctoral students in qualitative research in educational leadership to silently fingerpaint their studies while soft music plays in the background, and they receive such insights about their studies that several of them have framed their paintings and hung them in their offices. This is good. There is no issue of quality or qualification in the exercise, or in its execution. It is simply a means of alternative expression and alternative seeing.

Inferior Poetry as Qualitative Research

With this as an introduction, let us consider the use and abuse of poetry in qualitative research. Poetry is the ancient verbal art. Each national and ethnic group has its own esteemed and distinct poetic heritage. Poetry came earlier than writing. It is a natural form of expression, for who has not written a poem in the throes of love, desire, anger, or grief? Yet the domain of poetry within the field of literature is being constantly transformed by individual writers, who push the boundaries of poetry. Poetry then absorbs these transformations and becomes dynamic, new. The domain of educational research with its subdomain of qualitative research is being challenged also, by the arts-based researchers, who ask that they be permitted to use their domains to transform the educational research domain's—and ultimately the education field's—way of knowing.

Traditionally, qualitative research was based in social and cultural anthropology; sociology; history; clinical, developmental, and cognitive psychology; case traditions from political science, economics, law, business; journalism, especially investigative reporting; fieldwork in the natural sciences, especially biology, geology, astronomy; literary traditions such as narrative; and, recently, the arts. Research designs are ethnographic field studies, community studies, case studies, life histories and biographical studies, document analyses and historical studies, survey studies, observational studies, and various combinations of these with quantitative designs. The data are analyzed through analytic deduction, constant comparison, typological analysis, role analysis, network analysis, event analysis , critical incident analysis, natural history, enumerative analysis, and standardized observational protocols, among other methods. Data are collected by carefully watching and listening through participant observation; nonparticipant observation; stream-of-behavior chronicles; proxemics and kinesics; interaction analysis protocols; group, key informant, and career and life-history interviews; projective tests; the collection of artifacts, documents, and demographics; and other similar social science methodologies (Denzin & Lincoln, 1994; LeCompte & Preissle, 1993; Merriam, 1998). Where do the methodologies used in the arts fit in?

To Aristotle poetry was more authentic than history because the poet could concoct truth from the elements of history rather than exhaustively write facts. The poet is able to tell the truth on a penetrating level. Aristotle said that the difference between the historian and the poet is "that the one describes the thing that has been, and the other a kind of thing that might be. Hence poetry is something more philosophic and of graver import than history, since its statements are of the nature rather of universals, whereas those of history are singulars" (*Poetics*).

Today, in the discussion of the use of poetry (and by "poetry" I mean the Aristotelian sense that poetry is all arts) in qualitative research, it seems the philosopher's assertion that poetry is more true than truth is at play. The qualitative researcher may use poetry to depict the data imagistically, metaphorically, symbolically. The literary poetic form is chosen, ostensibly, to serve as more than words in short lines on a page; this depiction of what the researcher has found or thinks may be more heartfelt, more concentrated, more distilled, if it is rendered in poetic form. Yet for some thinkers in the field of qualitative research, the person using poetry in the depiction of qualitative findings need have no background in poetry, no record of having written poetry, no formal study of poetry. To write poetry one need not have studied it, seems to be the thought.

This is contrary to the practice of poetry in the literary world today. In a study of 160 contemporary male and female creative writers from the U.S., I found 16 themes in their lives, including the fact that most of them had advanced degrees in English literature (Piirto, 2002a). One criterion for including them in the study was that writers qualified for listing in the *Directory of Poets and Writers*. In order to qualify, a writer must have 12 points of accumulated credit: one published poem counts as one point; a novel counts as 12 points, a book of published poetry counts as 12 points, and an established literary award counts as four points. I wrote from

87

the participant observer viewpoint, as I am listed as both a poet and a fiction writer (Piirto, 1985, 1995, 1996, 1999c). Those who write and publish public poetry today in the U.S. have studied poetry. Why is it not necessary for those who write poetry in qualitative research to have a familiarity with poetry, to have studied poetry?

Let me use three examples from my own practice. I use my own work here in order not to judge the quality of the poems published as qualitative research in contemporary journals or in dissertations. One might say that the three poems fit together as examples of working on the borderland, the researcher as outsider, the researcher as other, othering the participants (Denzin & Lincoln, 1998).

CRAZY IS GOOD

As a writer, I have kept travel journals and personal journals, which could, in the lingo of qualitative research, be construed as field notes. In late 1998 and early 1999, three colleagues and I were granted travel funds to conduct research projects in India. My project was to visit schools that had as their mission to educate bright youngsters. During the month that we visited, I observed at several academic high schools based on the Anglican and Catholic models; I visited an international high school, the United World College; I also visited two indigenous schools, one based on the Krishnamurti philosophy (Piirto, 2000) and one based on the philosophy of Swami Vivekananda (Piirto, 2002b).

The influence of the British Raj in India is still evident, even though India has been a democracy for over 50 years and is the largest democracy in the world. This influence is seen in the existence of Christian high schools, with headmasters, students in uniforms, and curricula based on English literature and Western thought. Many of these schools are viewed as elite, and are often the preferred schools for students who will go to college and pursue civil, or government work.

We visited the state of Kerala, where my colleagues interviewed businessmen. In the city of Trivandrum, I visited two schools, the Anglican St. Thomas School and the Roman Catholic Loyola School. My field notes are scrawled lists from interviews with the principals, about Christian values, vocational bias, school history, the Indian School Certificate, the three major syllabi, the languages taught, the levels and standards, the numbers of students, the standards for admission, and such. My memories of these interviews are as dim as the rooms in which they were conducted. However, the poems I scrawled in this same notebook speak of black tennis shoes, blue socks, the hot pavement through my sandals, the sound of ever-present crows, the sunny flowered pathways, the definition of a prefect from a young man, and a provocative quote: "O Tiger, come and rest under my shade. Be my protection." My personal journal, typed on my laptop in my room each morning, also evokes sensory memories:

January 4, 1999
Woke up at 3:30 a.m., with bad dreams as I just finished *Blasphemy*, a novel by Tehmina Durrani, a shocking account of life in purdah told in 1st person by the wife of a *pir* fundamentalist Moslem [when I travel, I try to read contemporary novelists and poets from the region where I travel]. Wrote a

poem called "Kovalum Dawn." Today I visit schools here in Trivandrum. More later.

Tuesday, 5 January 1999
Yesterday was divine. My speech to the grades 11 and 12 boys went superbly, and I was so excited to see them so excited, enthusiastic, mobile, having fun, and receptive. One of my most exciting speeches, I think. The thank you speech of the boy after my speech was so cute, with him standing at attention, facing front to the class, and saying "We will never forget this afternoon when we learned that crazy is 'good'." Dr. P. and his family came to the hotel later that evening to present me with a sandalwood box. His boys are delightful, his wife, a doctor, seems shy, and nice.

A year later, I wrote the following poem for a session at the Albuquerque Arts-Based Educational Research (ABER) Special Interest Group Conference of AERA, where I read from a chapbook called *Writing India Schools: Creative Nonfiction and Poetry.* I include it here.

CRAZY IS GOOD

At the Jesuit-Indian school
boys in white shirts sit
faced front two to a desk
in a cavernous dark room
a prestigious school
that trains future government officials
the priest headmaster says
"Rise to greet the good Doctor.
She is going to talk to you
about her research on creativity."

I talk for awhile on my books
none of them is going into the arts
all into engineering or science
I am bored with this
I put them into groups
they brainstorm birds
"Crazy is good in creativity," I say
"Silly is fine."

the boys have never worked in groups
skeptical, they turn to face friends
who have only seen the backs of their heads
assumptions of alphabetical lives
they soon begin to giggle, then roar
their brains sparkle and spill

the divergent production exercises
I routinely use with my students
so mundane I am slightly ashamed

but the photographs show boy glee
by the time it is time to leave
the class prefect comes to the front
nearly kicks his heels and says all in a rush
a breathless "We will always remember
when the good doctor came and told us
crazy is good, even when we go to university"

that evening the head of
Trivandrum's development corporation
his wife, a physician, and their two boys
one who was in the creativity class
come to my hotel to talk
they bring me a sandalwood jewelry box
thank me for showing their boys
how to be creative
(I nod)
"the parents' phones were ringing
as soon as you left
'crazy is good,' 'crazy is good'
the boys had so much fun
they want you to come back
we need some creative teaching in Kerala"

Kerala has the highest literacy rate in India
result of the Marxist vote in the 1950s
universal education a goal achieved
the absence of beggars
the high price of labor
works against foreign investment
a play, "You Made Me Communist"
Ningal Enne Communist Akki in Malayam
influential in turning the common people
against the oligarchic rule of the rich
the influence of poetry in social change
later I read in the paper
that one of the boys placed tops in maths
in the whole state of Kerala last week

these boys were just waiting for a chance
to let loose, I think
I do not know what to say.

I commented to the group that the poem "Crazy is Good" is an inferior poem, as it is too expository, and that the "real" poems I wrote during the journey were ones which I hoped were more evocative and denser. They told me that such a poem as "Crazy is Good" has merit too, for qualitative research purposes.

Let me attempt to evaluate my own poem as a researcher/teacher/artist. On the plus side, the poem shows, in 396 words, the schoolroom. Its title is provocative because it goes against common wisdom. The poem as research gives direct quotations from the participants. The poem as research conveys descriptive detail about the site. It tells the parents' reactions to the lesson. The poem sets the school climate and the type of education these bright students are receiving into context, as most high school students in the United States, at least, do almost all their work in groups. Thus the poem describes an interchange that exposes the interface between two cultures. It has a couple of interesting phrases: "boy glee" and "assumptions of alphabetical lives." But is it a good poem? Are these pluses enough to say that the poem has quality?

On the minus side, the use of "to be" words in phrases says that it is not tight enough. The lack of resonant images troubles. The clicking of the heels, the turning around in desks, the sandalwood jewelry box, the mention of a theater work that changed the country, are the only images, and the latter is suspect. While I, the writer, picture a traveling troupe going about the countryside putting on the play, "Ningal Enne Communist Akki," that picture is because of another image that is not in the poem; that is the image of arriving a few nights before, on New Year's night, bouncing into a darkened town from the countryside on a trip to the southern tip of India and seeing the splendor of a string of lights, a crowd, and a loud microphone with a chanting speaker. Our guide told me this is a political poet who goes about the countryside telling his poems. I don't have this image in "Crazy is Good," but it is in the back of my mind as I tell about the play. The expository information in the poem is also problematic. "Kerala has the highest literacy rate in India" is not a poetic line. "A prestigious school/that trains government officials" is not a poetic line. "The high price of labor/works against foreign investment" is not a poetic line. Telling that the head of development's wife is "a physician" is also problematic. The use of the adjective "skeptical" in apposition is also troubling. I could go on, but I have already written 10 more words explaining the poem than I wrote in the poem.

She Walks Through Guns

Here is another example. In the 1980s, I was principal of a school for high-IQ students in New York City, a laboratory school in Manhattan. Again, my journals and notes fed my creative work, but I never thought to use the creative work as qualitative research. This idea only occurred when I began to teach the qualitative research course in my university's newly formulated doctoral program in educational leadership. When I taught as a visiting professor for a semester in the department of educational psychology and creativity studies at the University of Georgia in 1996, I recalled my old notes and journals as I pulled out a poem I had begun in 1986. I revised it after antique shopping in a town near Athens, Georgia, where I found a yearbook from the year that the University of Georgia had been integrated and found no mention of Charlayne Hunter, who had been one of those to integrate the university. This revision of a poem first written in 1986 and called "Black and White," resulted.

SHE WALKS THROUGH GUNS

Charlayne Hunter Gault gives
the Black History talk
in her son's school
I am the principal of the school
I am the same age as she

there she is, 19,
in the film walking through the guns
at the University of Georgia
in black and white
she'd not talk for days

she'd say "hello" to her mirror
on her own private floor
the first floor of the dorm
her professors would not ask her questions
they would not call on her

when she raised her hand
when she walked through the guns
I had only met five blacks
two boys goosed me and my cousin
at the playground in Ypsi

one man wanted me to play tennis
when I worked for the Army
I stood him up
then sang to myself
"you've got to be taught to hate and fear"

in shame I ignored him
at our offices
the rest of the summer
when he asked me why
I made up an excuse about forgetting

today she speaks
shows the film of her walk

through the gauntlet
her son watches
intent on her

intent on his friends'
acceptance of him
as the son of a famous pioneer
it is that black and white
in this school

he's in 6th grade
those rushing hormones
his friends are black, white, rainbow
his merit in his quality
peer fear runs rampant

she knows cabs pass her by
outside PBS studios
because she is black
even if she is famous
they think she wants to go to Harlem

in between fame and race
she's clear
she stands in front of us in color
next to her image in black and white
her courage to our shame

ten years later in 1996
I bought the University of Georgia 1960 yearbook
at an antique store
Fran Tarkenton was all over it
she wasn't anywhere

nowadays they bring her back to campus
for festivals and reunions
she's their most famous graduate
but in the black and white film
she walks through guns

Charlayne Hunter Gault, when I gave her the first version of the poem in 1986, was a reporter for the *MacNeil-Lehrer Report* and other Public Broadcasting System shows. She told me that she carried the poem with her on various trips and that she pulled it out to read it when she felt depressed. I didn't consider the poem worthy even of submitting to a literary journal, but was glad she found it meaningful.

Over the years, the poem has been in various states of revision, and the one above is the 2000 version.

In qualitative research terms, the poem may convey a sense of empathy for the lives of the people being spoken about; it also humanizes both the subject of the poem and the speaker of the poem by showing the rural naiveté of the speaker. The research is treated as a work of art. This has to do with how the material is crafted. As Eisner (1996) said, "The thinking is *within the material*." The poem provides a sense of particularity, a sense that what is being represented is real. The poem, perhaps, has "productive ambiguity," and may be more evocative than denotative forms, as there is more of a chance for multiple perspectives. Perhaps the poem provides the reader with new ways of seeing. For the artist/researcher, perhaps using poetry as a means of data representation allows the writer to exploit her individual aptitudes: many artists are not adept in mathematical representations of truth, which are still the preferred means of representation of data in the field of educational research. This does not mean that the researcher cannot represent data. The poem represents a ritual in a school, and provides insight into the workings of sixth-grade behavior as well as insight into the way Black History assemblies are conducted in schools. As such, it becomes more than the observation, more than the insight, if it is a poem that works.

In poetic quality terms, perhaps the repetition of the black and white theme makes it more than just a school-based poem, a poem about a parent giving a speech for Black History Week. The image of the gauntlet of guns, in this latest version, is repeated at the end of the poem and also in the title. It is a better poem now than when I wrote its first version. It is better because of the added experience, the yearbook in the antique store, and better than "Crazy is Good," but it is still not quite good enough for my personal standards. I must tweak it a little more.

FRATERNITY BAR IN ATHENS, GEORGIA

Let us take a third poem, one that is also about race and class in Georgia. This was selected for an anthology about the 20th century (Piirto, 1996, 1999d) and I am not working on it anymore. For my purposes, it is "done."

FRATERNITY BAR IN ATHENS, GEORGIA

they were shoulder to shoulder
drinking beer and playing pool
the room stunk of smoke from hell
the light under the bar shone orange

I sat at the end
talked to who came by
of race in Georgia

inexhaustibly they spewed
heedless of Mark Fuhrman's ignominy
that word
northerners don't dare to use
and many other words prefaced
by "they" and "them"

shaved almost bald
in fashion in front-faced
corduroy baseball caps
("I'd never wear my hat backwards like them")
beside their long-haired white-toothed beauties
they assumed a tribal camaraderie
from the color of my skin

told me their scarred inner hearts
while I smoked their cigarettes
in words I didn't want to hear
in words I wish I hadn't asked

at 2 a.m. they bid me bye
"y'all come back again, Professor
when you move to town"
in a conspiracy of skin and tribe
I kept my shame.

This poem was written late one night in a motel room when I came into town to try to find an apartment. Sitting at the motel bar, I received many helpful hints from my neighbors. Then an African-American graduate student came in and talked to the lady sitting next to me, a woman he knew. He, too, was seeking an apartment and asked her if she knew of one. She told him that there were no apartments in the city limits; that he would have to go outside of town to find a suitable apartment. After he left, she turned to me and gave me a list of nearby apartment complexes I might try. I was shocked, ashamed, and silent. Then I got into a conversation with the fraternity members who frequented the bar, and their girlfriends, who were sitting next to me as the young men played pool, that, given the time of night and the degree of sobriety, also gave me pause. The use of the forbidden "n'' word was rife. I couldn't sleep. This poem resulted.

In terms of qualitative research, perhaps the poem reveals the cowardly heart of the author, again dealing with outsider issues of researcher bias and of researcher fear. It is a poem not only about the participants as the researcher observed and interacted with them, but also about the researcher as participant. Put into poetic form, it can, within the limits of that form, chastise the researcher for her own racism and classism. The speaker of the poem was entering a new town, a new situation, a new milieu, and was being initiated to its rules in a very short but powerful lesson. During the semester I, the author-outsider , learned from my southern students about the "War of Northern aggression," was told to watch from the airplane for the swath of destruction that Sherman had made, and learned to keep my mouth shut and my heart open when confronted with my own northern, Yankee, hubris. "You Yankees are more prejudiced than we are," is how one of my graduate students put it. In its widest sense, the poem speaks of researcher complicity in the status quo.

You are re-reading the poems above. Are they research? They are based on school experience, one on a visit to a field site, one in the author's workplace, the other while entering a new school site. They come from field notes – drafts of poems in notebooks – taken at the time. The researcher has mindfulness that she is a researcher as well as a poet/artist. Are they poems of quality or, to paraphrase Maxine Greene, are they merely "poem-like?" They seek to be, as Aristotle said, "more philosophic and of graver import than history," with an attempt to be universal, but whether they are of *quality* is the question. I, the artist, judge their quality as being mixed; you, the reader, have your opinion; what would the editor of a journal say? What would the head of a committee say? Do they have to have any background in the art of poetry in order to say?

At an Arts-Based Educational Research conference, the question of quality was asked over and over again in conversations over the lunch table as participants attended sessions where novice researchers showed diagrams of quilting squares, where professors aflame with social outrage showed their students' artistic installations about such topics as high-stakes testing, and where highly trained artists – visual, literary, performing – demonstrated both artistic knowledge in the artistic domains and sophisticated theoretical knowledge of educational theory (deCosson, 2000; Rapp, 2000; Reynolds, 2000; Snowber, 2000; Sullivan, 2000; Wilson, deCosson, & Irwin, 2000). To observe heartfelt efforts by researchers with little or no background in the art being demonstrated was sometimes painful, especially to those who worked in, were trained in, knew, and loved the art being demonstrated. Is not the concept of quality and qualification to be taken seriously in arts-based research? Some suggested that a notion of "levels" be attached to the abstracts and proposals.

The question of the quality of the arts-based research is perhaps one for the critics and connoisseurs (Eisner, 1998) to answer – the artists themselves, the peer reviewers of the art world, those who have the power to move the domain. In the poetry world, many would be poets, but it is the domain itself and its tacit yet established rules of quality that move a person into being considered a poet by others (Piirto, 1998).

Often, people have been asked to make works of art in arts-based workshops. Participants have been asked to do sociodrama in drama workshops (Norris, 1997). Participants have been asked to cut out paper words from headlines and make poems in poetry workshops (Sullivan & Commeyras, 2000). These have been examples of constructionist pedagogy and they have been fun – as personal creativity enhancement. The participants gained self-knowledge. They may have experienced a certain self-therapy. They may talk about and use examples from these experiential workshops long after they have attended them. To have everyone, especially fearful novices, be able to experience, through the body, the dance, the drama, the visual art, the poetry, is valuable. The difference between workshop and performance/display is vital here.

Respect for the domain is necessary for higher-level requirements. In defense of quality and qualifications of the artists and their arts, I have developed two thumbnail criteria for permitting students to do arts-based research for high-stakes projects. First, only those students who have at least an undergraduate minor (and preferably a major) in the domain in which they want to work are permitted to make art for qualitative research high-stakes products such as dissertations and master's theses. But, in order to recognize persistence and quality, if a student has peer-reviewed exhibits, shows, and products, even if he or she hasn't formally studied the domain, I permit the project. This has happened in the case of a self-trained singer-songwriter who has produced many albums and CDs and who plays on the folk music circuit.

For example, in an inquiry seminar that requires a capstone master's degree project, my students have produced an autobiographical reader's theater piece (written by all, edited by high school English teachers, and directed by a theater minor); a play (written and directed by a person with an undergraduate theater major); an etude for flute (written by a flute major music teacher). They used the domains in which they spent so much time, so many courses, as a medium of research and as an alternative means of demonstrating knowledge. As for the others who want to do so, I recommend that they first take at least 20 semester hours in the discipline in which they want to do the arts-based work, or demonstrate peer-review and a record of exhibits of their art. Then it is truly arts-based. Then the art itself and its ways of knowing are respected. That is my current answer to the issue of quality and qualification.

The arts have their own ways. The poet Jane Hirshfield said: "We seek in art the elusive intensity by which it knows" (Hirshfield, 1997, p. 5). In this quandary, the real epistemological questions must be dealt with. What does the *very nature* of poetry have to contribute to educational research? What do the *very nature* of visual art, dance, theater, film, music, have to contribute to educational research? Artist/teacher/researchers have immersed themselves both in their arts and in the study of pedagogy. This is a mammoth task and accomplishment. The result is automaticity within the artistic domain (Bloom, 1985; Ghiselin, 1952) and understanding within the education domain.

Hirshfield said: "Violinists practicing scales and dancers repeating the same movements over decades are not simply warming up or mechanically training their muscles. They are learning how to attend unswervingly, moment by moment, to themselves and their art" (1997, p. 5) They are learning the way of knowing of the domain. They enter the field of education for their own reasons, but they bring with them the years of practice, the embodiment of the arts domain. They seek to utilize these ways of knowing and must learn the ways of expression in the field of education, while the field of education does not respect their domain by respecting its ways of knowing and of representation if the domain is not in the social studies.

To learn the essence of the domain's educational implications at the feet of artist/teachers who are seeking to synthesize the expression of their work in both domains – the domain of the art *and* the domain of education – is an exciting possibility. They will create new forms, new expressions, new ways of thinking that bridge domains. Let us welcome our artist-educators, as well as our self-exploring novices. But let us not confuse the quality of and their qualification for rendering, making marks, embodying, and distilling. Let us not confuse the seekers for the masters. Let us not confuse the poetasters for the poets.

NOTES

[1] This chapter was previously published as: Pirrto, J. (2002). The question of quality and qualifications: Writing inferior poems as qualitative research *International Journal of Qualitative Studies in Education, 15*(4), 431–446. Reprinted with permission (see Acknowledgments page).

REFERENCES

Aristotle. (1952). *Poetics and rhetoric* (I. Bywater, Trans.). In R. Hutchins & M. Adler (Eds.), *Great books of the western world* (Vol. 9). Chicago: Encyclopedia Britannica.

Bloom, B. S. (Ed.). (1985). *Developing talent in young people.* New York: Ballantine.

de Cosson, A. (2000, November 11). *(Re)searching sculpted aporia: (Re)learning subverted-knowing through praxis.* Presentation at 2nd Arts Based Educational Research conference, Balcones Springs, Texas.

Denzin, N. J., & Lincoln, Y. S. (Eds.). (1994). *Handbook of qualitative research.* Thousand Oaks, CA: SagePublications.

Denzin, N. J., & Lincoln, Y. S. (1998). Introduction. In N. J. Denzin & Y. S. Lincoln (Eds.), *Strategies of qualitative inquiry* (pp. 1–34). Thousand Oaks, CA: Sage Publications.

Donmoyer, R., Eisner, E., Gardner, H., et al. (1996). *Can a novel be a dissertation?* Panel presented at the American Educational Research Association Annual Meeting, New York City.

Eisner, E. (1996, January). *Alternative forms of data representation.* Keynote speech at the QUIG Conference, Athens, Georgia, January 4, 1996.

Eisner, E. (1998). *The enlightened eye: Qualitative inquiry and the enhancement of educational practice.* Columbus, OH: Merrill/Prentice Hall.

Feldman, D. H., Csikszentmihalyi, M., & Gardner, H. (1994). *Changing the world: A framework for the study of creativity.* Westport, CT: Praeger.

Ghiselin, B. (1952). *The creative process.* New York: Mentor.

Hirshfield, J. (1997). *Nine gates: Entering the mind of poetry.* New York: HarperCollins.

Greene, M. (1996, January 6). *Art, imagination, and the capture of meaning.* Speech at the 1996 Qualitative Inquiry (QUIG) conference, Athens, Georgia.

LeCompte, M., & Preissle, J. (1993). *Ethnography and qualitative design in educational research* (2nd ed.). San Diego: Academic Press.

Merriam, S. B. (1998). *Qualitative research and case study applications in education.* San Francisco: Jossey Bass.

Morgan, K. J. K., Finley, S., & Konzal, J. (2000, April). *Bricolage: Arts and aesthetics in collaboration.* Paper presented at the American Educational Research Association annual meeting. New Orleans, LA.

Norris, J. (1997, October). *Desire.* Presentation at *Journal for Curriculum Theorizing* annual conference, Bloomington, Indiana.

Piirto, J. (1985). *The three-week trance diet.* Columbus, OH: Carpenter Press. [Winner, Tenth Anniversary First Novel Contest.]

Piirto, J. (1995). *A location in the upper peninsula: Collected essays, stories, poems.* New Brighton, MN: Sampo Publishing. [Two printings 1996]

Piirto, J. (1996). Fraternity bar in Athens, GA. *Between the memory and the experience: Poetry chapbook.* Ashland, OH: Sisu Press.

Piirto, J. (1998). *Understanding those who create* (2nd ed.). Tempe, AZ: Gifted Psychology Press.

Piirto, J. (1999a). *Talented children and adults: Their development and education* (2nd ed.). Columbus, OH: Prentice Hall/Merrill.

Piirto, J. (1999b). A different approach to creativity enhancement. *Tempo, XIX, 3*, 1 ff.

Piirto, J. (1999c). Poetry. In M. Runco & S. Pritzer (Eds.), *Encyclopedia of creativity* (Vol. 2, pp. 409–416). San Diego, CA: Academic Press.

Piirto, J. (1999d). Fraternity bar in Athens, GA. In R. McGovern & S. Haven (Eds.), *What rough beast: Poems of the millennium* (p. 134). Ashland, OH: Ashland Poetry Press.

Piirto, J. (2000). Krishnamurti and me: Meditations on India and on his philosophy of education. *Journal for Curriculum Theorizing, 16*(2), pp. 109–124.

Piirto, J. (2002a). *"My teeming brain": Understanding creative writers.* Cresswood, NJ: Hampton Press.

Piirto, J. (2002b). "Motivation is first. Then they can do anything." Portrait of an Indian school.

Rapp, D. (2000, November 9). *Ohio's system of high stakes testing.* Presentation at 1st Curriculum and Pedagogy conference, Balcones Springs, Texas.

Reynolds, F. C. (2000, November 9). *Honoring the one.* Presentation at 1st Curriculum and Pedagogy Conference, Balcones Springs, Texas.

Snowber, C. (2000, November 11). *Inside out/outside in: Performing a theorizing of the body through the body.* Presentation at 2nd ABER conference, Balcones Springs, Texas.

Sullivan, A. M., & Commeyras, M. (2000, January 8). *How to do it! Writing and assessing research poems.* Conference on Qualitative Research in Education (QUIG), Athens, Georgia, January 6–8, 2000.

Xin-Li (2000, November 12). *Thinking and taoist knowing.* Presentation at 2nd Arts-Based Research conference (ABER), Balcones Springs, Texas.

Wilson, S., de Cosson, A., & Irwin, R. (2000, November 9). *Continuing (in) fluid spaces: Artist/researcher/teacher praxis.* Presentation at 2nd Arts-Based Research conference (ABER), Balcones Springs, Texas.

Jane Piirto
Faculty of Education
Ashland University
Ohio, USA

NILOFAR SHIDMEHR

POETIC INQUIRY AS MINOR RESEARCH

Even though poetic inquiry is today accepted as a legitimate methodology of research in social science, humanities, and education, it still remains a "minor" (Deleuze and Guattari, 1987, p. 101)[1] form of research. In this short introduction to some of my poetry, using Deleuze and Guattari's concept of minor-writing[2] (Deleuze and Guattari, 1986) and Bakhtin's notion of answerability (Bakhtin, 1919)[3], I introduce poetic inquiry as minor research. The concept of minor research refers to a from of research in which inquiry makes the research itself stammer[4] (Deleuze and Guattari, 1987), so as to stretch tensors all through it and to draw a line of continuous variation through the hegemonic constants of research genres. This mode of research involving poetic inquiry, unlike other standard and hegemonic forms of research in social sciences, is not defined by the "power (pouvoir)" of constants of descriptions, arguments, analyses, and interpretation which pretend to a scientific or hermeneutic activity, but by the "power (puissance)" of variation of responsiveness as an ethical activity (Deleuze and Guattari, 1987, p. 106).

Two tendencies mark poetic inquiring as a minor inquiry: firstly, a tendency to impoverish the research: to shed it of its purely descriptive, argumentative, analytic, and interpretationary forms, or in other words its scientific/hermeneutic guise; and secondly, a tendency to shift the focus of the research from ontology to ethics, to disrupt truth or interruption-making activity by performativity of ethical responsiveness (Bakhtin, 1919). Poetic inquiry introduces a "line of flight" to the hegemonic spaces of "majority" research, aimed at rupturing and deterritorizing the lines of constant in these spaces (Deleuze and Guattari, 1987). It is important to note that here minor research does not oppose the major forms of research and its genres; it deterritorializes them, for, as I said before, it introduces a *line of departure or flight* (Deleuze and Guattari, 1987) to the dominant territories of inquiry, thus transforming the inquiry itself to something else—to the possibility for responsiveness (Bakhtin, 1919).

While inquiring poetically, the researcher embodies inquiring as an activity; she does not pretend to an activity as it is specifically the case in scientific inquiring. Poetic inquiry is the activity of ethically responding to an act or utterance which is still anticipating a response[5]. Inquiring poetically, thus, the researcher/poet responds to that act/utterance in order to consummate or finalize it[6]. It is important to note that she is responding to a past act/utterance as if it was happening now, as if she was actively participating in the act and in its consummation in the present moment. Therefore, the act becomes what it is and what it ought to be ethically from the researcher/poet's point of view. Poetic inquiry is a form of research that

M. Prendergast, C. Leggo and P. Sameshima (eds.), Poetic Inquiry: Vibrant Voices in the Social Sciences, 101–109.

confirms Bakhtin's (1993) idea that the performed act and deed has yet to be achieved[7]. However our uniqueness (the uniqueness of our selves and our positions in being) is given, but it simultaneously exists only to the degree to which we actualize this uniqueness through our responsiveness towards our own acts/utterances, as well as those of the other. In our ethical responsiveness, we not only participate in our or the other's acts, but also we consummate them to what we think they ought to be. As Greg Nielsen (1992) puts it in his book *The Norms of Answerability*: "This moral presence in the act is one side of its answerability whereas the specific content of the act is the other" (p. 44).

While other forms of research are exclusively concerned with the content of the act/thought/experience, poetic inquiry focuses on the answerability of an act/experience which scientific inquiry completely dismisses. Poetic inquiry, thus, is a performative act in which the researcher, recognizing the uniqueness of her being and her participation in the world, actualizes this uniqueness in her inquiry. In inquiring poetically the researcher asserts her non-alibi in Being[8]. Answerability of poetic inquiry lies under the researcher's assertion of non-alibi in Being and in acknowledging and affirming it via her inquiring. Consequently, in poetic inquiring, the inquiry itself is transformed to something else—to an event of responsiveness.

While other modes of research are preoccupied with the meaning-making side of the action, poetic inquiry calls to presence the ethical side of the act, which, in Bakhtin's view, presents the cognitive feature of the action. To Bakhtin, an act or utterance is always already unfinalized, so unconsummated, for it anticipates a response from the self. This consummation of the unfinalized utterance/act, that is happening in all speech or acting situations, points at the notion of alterity or the otherness. Since pure subjectivity is not possible, in real life situations, there will never be a finalized consummation of utterance/act which can transcend the act or speech and universalize it. In poetic inquiring, however, there exists a possibility for the consummation of an act, such consummation which always already anticipates another inquiry to de-finalize and re-finalize it through setting a line of flight in its territories of "consummated-ness"—an inquiry which desires to be something different—to become an event.

It is exactly in this event of inviting and seeking a becoming that poetic inquiry becomes minority research. As Deleuze and Guattari (1987) put it:

> [W]e must distinguish between: the majoritarian as constant and homogeneous system; minorities as subsystems; and the minoritarian as a potential, creative and created, becoming. The problem is never to acquire majority, even in order to install a new constant. There is no becoming-majoritarian; majority is never becoming. All becoming is minoritarian (pp. 106–7).

Here the notion of minority is complex, because minor research does not exist in itself; it exists only in relation to major research. Minor research invests all its inquiring potential or power (*puissance*) to transform the major research into minor. Poetic inquiry as a research method becomes minoritarian only because it performs inquiry not towards the constants of finding the truth or describing, explaining, interpreting, or constructing a reality, but towards a becoming of inquiring. As Deleuze and Guattari (1987) write, "A determination different from that of the constant will therefore be considered minoritarian, by nature and regardless of number, in other words, a subsystem or an outsystem" (p. 105). Poetic inquiry does not define itself as a subsystem because it quantitatively opposes major research. Nor does it become an outsystem because the content of final product of research is qualitatively different from that of major research. It becomes subsystem or outsystem because it performs inquiry in such a way that does not claim ownership or knowledge over the content of the research—over the "know-what" and "know-how" of inquiry. In this way, poetic inquiry makes possible the inquiry in and of itself—becoming of the inquiry.

In poetic inquiry, inquiry thus, can be seen as "seeds, crystals of becoming whose value is to trigger uncontrollable movements and deterrritorializaitons of the mean or majority [research]" (Deleuze and Guattari, 1987, p. 106). Such inquiring is not determined by or aimed at something outside itself; it is an act which contains the seeds of responsiveness to itself.

For this reason, poetic inquiry always already implies dialogicity (Bakhtin, 1930)[9]. This is because while inquiring poetically, on one hand, one goes beyond oneself to see oneself from outside, from the point of view of the other, so coming back to oneself, one can acknowledge and recognize one's uniqueness from inside oneself; and on the other hand, one steps outside oneself to get closer to and understand the other, so coming back to oneself, one recognizes and acknowledges the other's uniqueness in Being from inside oneself. In this way a "dialogic" relation is established between the self of the actor/researcher and the other of actor/researcher who responds to the act (Bakhtin, 1919).In other words, the dialogicity of poetic inquiring sets up a relationship between the researcher present self as the inquirer and the researcher lived self as the performer or respondent. As a result, the inquiry includes both planes of intersubjectivity and alterity.

Poetic inquiry, introduced dialogically, becomes an active act or performance, which unlike other forms of research, includes the other within its horizon of expectation (my term). As such, it keeps from imposing the final word in the form of a description, an interpretation, or a conclusion. Moreover, however it desires towards a consummation of the act/utterance, at the same time, it invites in the seeds of destruction and rearrangement of that consummation in the womb of its desire. In other modes of research, on the contrary, in order to shift to a higher level of generality, the researcher almost always seeks agreement between opposite positions. By including in the act of inquiring its answerability, in poetic inquiry, although the researcher in a sense finalizes the inquiry, this communicatory exchange between act and its response is not always free of conflict. The responsiveness here is what constitutes the moment of *ought* in it. Thus answerability originating in the uniqueness of performative acts of inquiring should not be viewed as a principle, a law, a norm, or of a right. As Bakhtin puts it, "it is not the content of an obligation that obligates me, but my signature below it" (Bakhtin, 1993, p. 38). Here inquiring consists in undertaking an obligation which amounts to undersigning and acknowledging one's non-alibi in Being/Inquiring. This uniqueness of the act of inquiring, the inquirer asserts, is what is universal about it not the content of the inquiry.

In poetic inquiring, one relates one's act of inquiring to oneself in being answerable to it. As a result, the researcher constitutes her position as the standpoint of an answerable inquirer or participant, not solely as an inquirer. This position is not the same as the position of a researcher who takes herself responsible for what comes out as the result of her inquiry. Being answerable, hence, is not the same as being responsible for one's content or result of inquiry. While responsibility has something to do with meaning of an inquiry or meanings made through an act/inquiry, so with the result and consequences of the act of inquiring, answerability has something to do with the performance or acting of the inquiry. Answerability, as I have explained earlier, is what finalizes the act of inquiring to a becoming of inquiring—to an event. Therefore, in poetically inquiring, the researcher/inquirer transforms the rupture between the act and its answerability to a continuum of becoming—a continuum which potentially expects and invites another rupture, for the inquirer does not have any ownership over it.

Turning the inquiry to an event, thereby, poetic inquiry becomes a flight over and beyond the conditions of inquiring. The concept of "flight" makes reference to territories of research left behind before the "flight—to their deterritorization or reterritorization as the result of the event of the "flight" (Deleuze and Guattari, 1987). The reason why poetic inquiry has been minor research and will always remain so is that it has the seeds to trigger uncontrollable lines of flight and deterritorization across dominant genres of research and the conditions they set for the very act of inquiring. In rejecting the reference points and standards of what doing research pertains to and consequently dissolving the constant forms and borders of dominant research genres, poetic inquiry as minor research causes the research to tend toward the limit of its elements, forms, and notions, towards a beyond of research, and becomes an ethical act of responsiveness. What is important in poetic inquiry is not reconstruction or interpretation of an experience or action, but transforming the research itself to an event. Poetic inquiry can make this transformation because it has the capacity to create an autonomous becoming of inquiry.

The following poems are examples of my work, in which I poetically inquire into some action/experience/utterance in the past that still anticipates a response. In doing so, I am not simply interpreting or describing that experience/act. Nor am I explaining why it happened. As a result, I am not positioning myself as a researcher removed from what she is researching, as it is the case in major research. Instead, I am inquiring into that experience/action/utterance as if it was happening now and as if I am responding to that act/experience, desiring it to become finalized. As I am performing the inquiry, confirming my non-alibi in happening of that experience, I am actively participating in turning that experience into an event. This participation consists in making that act/utterance desire for a consummation/finalization through my performance of responsiveness. So here I am no longer the inquirer, but the performer and the respondent. As a result my inquiring is no longer an inquiry but something else—an event—something over which I can claim no ownership. So my very act of inquiring turns to be a line of flight, rupturing, disarranging, and realigning the territories, forms, and norms of inquiry set by major research. The past territories re-arranged as the result of my inquiry again anticipate new deterritorization, as my act of inquiring itself desires and anticipates a response.

Three Poems/Poetic Inquiries

(1)

Fall

The man is still waiting
on the road and it's raining
viciously, but I pass him.

I don't know if I should turn
back or not, maybe now
the man is sitting
by the road, or lying
in the rain, and the road
is taking him with it,
but I still don't know.

Should I stop or not?
Maybe by now a woman
is standing there
on the breast of the road
that passes through
the breast of the man, like the road
that is passing through me
as I drive in my thoughts.
Maybe it's me falling now onto the street
and the rain that's crushed
under the man's feet,
because I still don't know if I should
turn back or not, or maybe
it's the night driving inside the rain
that passes me by
with full speed, turning to see
the reflection of passing
in the dark rainy glass of the street,
while asking, should I
stop or not?

Nevertheless it is not easy
to have passed by
something standing
or sitting, passed across it
as it passes you,
especially if the man is waiting
by the same road
especially if passing
is not the past, or if the woman
is the past of a passing,
or if the man is passing by the past

if the road suddenly falls
by your feet as it did
by mine.

(2)

Globalization

On the Bus
176 people are killed
and an Indian lady,
with today's newspaper
on her lap.

The girl across the aisle
listens to music
the entire way,
the young man besides me
studies,
something like genetic,
the Chinese driver
drives,
and I am watching.

The bus moves along
and the blond girl's hair around
the young man's hand
like the genomes, my large eyes,
touch the driver's foot,
his black shoes, across the fat
Indian lady's knees,
her long green skirt
under 176 people in Iraq.

The bus stops
at the red light
and the short spiky hair of the blond girl
with her I-pod,
below my brown eyes,
besides the driver's shoes
with white laces,
tied to the Indian lady's thick legs,
rubbed against the words
on her green woolen skirt,
knit to the young man's thin
colored hand, inside
the spiral of the DNA,
of 176 dead people in Iraq.

(3)

Alone

I don't know why I pity
Saddam so much,
I've never felt so bad
for any other murderer.

I killed a cockroach at five;
I was a serial killer
when I had my first
menstruation. I don't know
who guillotined my voice
the first time I fell in love.

Our next door neighbor once
watered her orchid with a blend
of her under-age daughter's urine and the wings
from three dead flies, turned into powder,
mixed with honey from Khansar, in order to kill
her husband's overwhelming
desires. There are as many
murderers as you wish in the world—
too many circumcisers,
knife-grinders, censor-managers,
and rope corporations with friendly customer service.

The young boys of my family wrung
the lizards' heads off for fun.
My virgin eighty-year-old aunt with dementia
no longer does remember
when she had choked her heart
with her own hands,
before anyone else's fingers could get
to that delicate valve.
The coffee net shops in Iran swarm
with school boys who practice for hours
shelling virtual soldiers after school.

I know an immigrant man
who drowns mice in his bath and a little girl
who liked to dismember her favorite doll,
but I don't take pity on the girl
who is a woman now and is very lonely,
just like the man, who every night shakes
with excitement when he hears the squeaking
from his kitchen as he opens the apartment door,
coming back with new mousetraps.

I don't pity myself
or any other murderer
with or without a uniform,

with or without eyes pulsing
life inside the two round openings
in the black masks, while some hands
fix the rope around his throat.

NOTES

[1] Deleuze and Guattari define and theorize minor language in relation to their definition of major language in the chapter four of their book *A thousand plateaus: capitalism and schizophrenia*. The chapter is titled: November 20, 1923—postulates of linguistics. The discussion of minor language is on section IV. "Language Can Be Scientifically Studied Only under the Conditions of a Standard or Major Language" starting from p. 101.

[2] Deleuze and Guattari discuss in length minor writing or minor literature in their book *Kafka: Towards a Minor Literature*.

[3] According to Wikipedia, Bakhtin "worked tirelessly on a large work concerning moral philosophy that was never published in its entirety. However, in 1919, a short section of this work was published and given the title "Art and Responsibility". It was in this work where Bakhtin first introduced the notion of answerability (or responsiveness). *Toward a Philosophy of the Act* was first published in Russia in 1986 with the title *K filosofii postupka*. The copy of the book, translated edited by Michael Holquist and Vadim Liapunov I made reference to was published in 1993. Here,

to refer to the notion of answerability, I make reference to the "Art and Responsibility" essay (1919) where this notion was first mentioned.

[4] Again this term (stammer) is used by Deleuze and Guattari in their theorization of minor language in section IV of the Chapter 4 of their book *A thousand plateaus: capitalism and schizophrenia*. See footnote i.

[5] By saying that an act/utterance always already anticipates a response, I do not mean that it waits for just one response, or a specific and certain response. A response, here, more or less refers to at least one response.

[6] This does not mean that as soon as the researcher responded to some act/utterance, the act is finalized for ever so that the researcher or the future researchers' job is already finished thus no other inquiry is to be conducted. Rather, in responding to an act, the inquirer renders a finalization of that act which anticipates another de-finalization. Therefore, such consummation is still unfinalized, for it anticipates a line of flight to rupture and rearrange the territories of its finalization.

[7] This idea is presented in Bakhtin's book Bakhtin, M. M. (1993). *Toward a Philosophy of the Act.* Michael Holquist and Vadim Liapunov (Eds.). Vadim Liapunov (Transl.), Texas, University of Texas Press.

[8] The idea that the act of responsivity is that through which we confirm our non-alibi in our actions is presented in both Bakhtin's books *Toward a Philosophy of the Act* & *Art and Answerability*.

[9] Bakhtin discussed the concept of dialogicity in depth in his book *The Dialogic Imagination: Four Essays*. Written in 1930.

REFERENCES

Bakhtin, M. M. (1990). *Art and answerability* (M. Holquist & V. Liapunov, Eds., V. Liapunov & K. Brostrom, Trans.). Austin, TX: University of Texas Press. [written 1919–1924, published 1974–1979]

Bakhtin, M. M. (1981). *The dialogic imagination: Four essays* (M. Holquist, Ed., C. Emerson & M. Holquist, Trans.). Austin, TX and London: University of Texas Press. [written during the 1930s]

Bakhtin, M. M. (1993). *Toward a philosophy of the act* (M. Holquist & V. Liapunov, Eds., V. Liapunov, Trans.). Austin, TX: University of Texas Press.

Deleuze, G., & Guattari, F. (1987). *A thousand plateaus: Capitalism and schizophrenia* (B. Massumi, Trans.). Minneapolis, MN: University of Minnesota Press.

Deleuze, G., & Guattari, F. (1986). *Kafka: Toward a minor literature* (D. Polan, Trans.). London & Minneapolis, MN: University of Minnesota Press.

Nielsen, G. M. (2002). *The norms of answerability*. Albany, NY: State University of New York.

Nilofar Shidmehr
Centre for Cross-Faculty Inquiry
Faculty of Education
University of British Columbia

ANNE MCCRARY SULLIVAN

ON POETIC OCCASION IN INQUIRY

Concreteness, Voice, Ambiguity, Tension, and Associative Logic[1]

In recent years, there has been an ongoing discussion on the role of craft and on what constitutes quality in poetic inquiry (Cahnmann, 2003; Faulkner, 2007; Piirto, 2002; Sullivan, 2004.) Today, I want to back up a little to consider what happens before the exercise of craft, before the conscious effort for quality. What happens when the material is arrayed in front of us and we have to decide what to do with it, how to make sense of it, whether or not to make poetry of it. Some materials are more welcoming of poetic rendering than others, and most of us who do this work probably recognize these materials intuitively or by knowledge so deeply internalized that it feels intuitive. We recognize the occasions for poetry as easily as we recognize a familiar road.

In the world, occasions for poetry are myriad and infinite – the particular motions of an insect, a machine, a muscle or a thought; a flash of light or of insight or memory; a phrase of music or a curious unbidden phrase in the mind. Naomi Shihab Nye (1994) reminds us:

Poems hide. In our shoes
they are sleeping. They are the shadows
drifting across our ceilings the moment
before we wake up. What we have to do
is live in a way that lets us find them. (p. 70)

I have had high school students write poems about abandoned tennis shoes, spots on the wall, their own toenails. There is almost nothing and no time that is not potentially an occasion for poetry if we are alert, attentive, attuned (Sullivan, 2002). But I want to complicate the matter a little. I want to examine the intuitive, see if I can better name and understand the cognitive processes by which we recognize poetic occasion; and, as a result of doing so, ultimately make my teaching of poetic processes more astute, more explicit, without becoming formulaic or reductive.

This *is* an exploration, and I'm not going to get straight to the point. Nonlinearity being a characteristic of poetry and an inclination of poets, I will meander, and maybe the meandering itself will turn out to be part of the point, if there is something that can be called "a point," I'm not sure yet, tolerance for ambiguity being another poetic attribute.

M. Prendergast, C. Leggo and P. Sameshima (eds.), Poetic Inquiry: Vibrant Voices in the Social Sciences, 111–126.

I'd like to start by talking a little about that which we call intuition. My favorite neuroscientist, Antonio Damasio (scientist who references Wordsworth, Shakespeare, and Beethoven) has been very helpful to me in my thinking about intuition. I first encountered Damasio's work in his 1994 book *Descartes' Error: Emotion, Reason, and the Human Brain*, in which he lays out clearly the evidence that intuition is grounded in physiology, that it neither wanders in from the air nor arises from something inexplicable within us. He lays out with ample evidence that "the brain and the body are indissociably integrated by mutually targeted biochemical and neural circuits" (1994, p. 87). He discusses the "covert mechanism" which may be "the source of what we call intuition, the mysterious mechanism by which we arrive at the solution of a problem *without* reasoning toward it" (1994, p. 188). Damasio confirms that when poets speak of the role of intuition in their work, they are speaking of something biologically real, a cognitive process that arises from being finely attuned to the signals that our physiology delivers from subconscious perception.

With that concept as a background, I will focus my thinking about occasions for poetry on six domains: Concreteness, Voice, Emotion, Ambiguity, Tension, and Associative Logic. One might (one often does) speak of these as qualities of poetry, and of course, they are, but I want to talk about them as *occasions* for poetry, which nuances the discussion in a slightly different way. I set out with the intention of discussing each of these in turn, but you will soon see that they begin to tumble into each other because, in fact, they are intimately connected.

CONCRETENESS

This one seems easy, straightforward. Of course, poetry must be concrete. There must be things to see, hear, smell, taste, touch. Of course. Let me tell you a story.

When I first entered an MFA program for poetry, I had been teaching high school creative writing and English for over a decade. It was, in fact, my work with high school students that returned me to a love of poetry that I had experienced earlier in my life but from which I had been distanced.

Husband: With Poets

Those nights, when he and his friends
gathered around our table, leaned
into the light, listened with nerves
poised, reading their poems aloud,
impassioned–they discussed, argued,
celebrated, adjusted image and line.
I came and went at their periphery,
poured coffee deep into the night.
They thanked me warmly.

When I handed him a poem of my own,
he said, "That's nice,"
and handed it back.

Later, he found the key
to the post office box, imagined
love letters. I confessed:
it was the business of poems.
"I'd rather you had taken a lover," he said.
For all intents and purposes, I had.

In the years after I married (I was only 21), I abandoned poetry as not my domain. *He* was the poet; *I* was the poet's wife. And I forgot, truly forgot. Years later, teaching high school creative writing would bring me back to my self. I wrote daily with my students, each year more engaged, more committed, until finally I dared to make my way to that MFA program, where for all my provincial practice, I was terribly naïve, didn't have any idea just how much there was to know, and I kept hearing people talk about "getting the poem into the body." I had never heard English teachers talk about poems like *that*. It had always been a matter of how to get the poem into the brain, into the understanding, etc etc, what did the poem *mean*, all that English teacher stuff. I had entered a new culture with a new language.

Concreteness is about embodiment. We experience life in all its grittiness and pleasure through the sensory mechanisms of the body. We see, hear, smell, taste, touch and thereby know and feel and understand. A person can be lacking access to one or even more of the senses (think of Helen Keller who could neither see nor hear), but it's debatable whether a person lacking all of the senses could know anything. So if we want a person to know what we feel, either in our own lives or empathically or imagined, we must know how to offer them the sensory experience that we have had or imagined. We have to transfer something from one body to another.

This is what the *image* is all about. The image is a piece of sensory information – dingy water, trembling leaves, the nubbly texture of tweed, the siren's shrill, the sweetness of watermelon, the lemony smell of your mother's perfume. It's what *metaphor* is about, tying the abstraction to the concrete thing that makes it possible for us to know in the body what it means. It's what we mean in ethnography when we talk about rendering "the lived experience." It's what Ivan Brady (2004) means when he speaks of "sensuous scholarship" (p. 622). It's what Wordsworth (1802) meant when he wrote, "I have wished to keep the reader in the company of flesh and blood" (p. 244).

Joan Aleshire (1999), poet, has written of a moment in the history of lyric poetry when poets forgot the importance of concreteness and specificity:

Archilochus and Sappho are still read and translated; the singers who followed them are largely forgotten – probably because they became more instructive than expressive, more general than tactile....poets began to talk about 'the good,' and as Frankel says, 'of riches,' 'wealth,' 'poverty,' 'distress,' not of wheatfields, herds of oxen, flocks and sheep, ships bearing produce from country to country. (p. 55)

So let's bring this back around to occasions for poetry. I have often found my students trying to make poems of material that is not concrete, not sensory, not of the body. Or, there is concreteness in the material, but they ignore the worldly everyday sensory stuff and work with the abstractions. I will offer an example, but first let's talk a little about voice.

VOICE

Joan Aleshire (1999), and other poets have indicated voice as a primary lyric quality. Mark Strand (2000) writes that good lyric poems "have a voice and the formation of that voice...may be the true occasion for their existence" (p. xxiv). When we hear a personal voice, even if the speaker uses little or no concrete or figurative language, that voice has the quality and impact of image. The human voice, authentic and resonant with emotion and experience, has its own sort of concreteness.

Consider this voice from the work of Rhoda Feldman (2004), who studied the experience of school children in an arts integration program in Chicago public schools. This is her found poem from interview data:

Tonya's Question

I asked him why
Why is that little angel down there?
Why do those people got the wings on their backs
Don't have no angel robes?
He said "think about it"
I can't think about it
If you ask somebody a question
That mean you thought about it already
And you don't understand
So that's why you ask the question
How you gon' think about the question
If you don't know what he talking about?

He kept sayin,' like *think*aboutit, *think*aboutit, *think*aboutit"
[she slaps the desktop in rhythmic accompaniment]
Well *think*aboutit, *think* about it, think about it
That's why I get mad
I'm like I ask you a question
Because I thought about it
And I *still* don' know
That's why you ask a *question*. (p.13)

There is very little concrete language in Tonya's utterance, but there is an undeniable voice, and I would maintain that that voice, personal, idiosyncratic and charged with emotion, is itself concrete, bearing sensory information.

Now, let me return to the student example that I promised a few minutes ago. This graduate student interviewed several students at an Atlanta Street School, school of last resort for students who have used up all their chances elsewhere. Here's the first draft of her found poem from an interview with Louis (included with her permission):

I had trouble with the school,
I got kicked out.
Now I am on the good path
a lot of things have changed for me
I'm working now.
I can talk to my parents.
This is my second year here now.
I am not on the bad path any more.

In this draft, she isolated the most basic narrative line leaving out everything that individuated the voice. I sent her back to the short interview transcript, highlighters in hand. I asked her to highlight all of the concrete nouns in one color, the verbs that were not "to be" in another color, and anything else that she particularly liked in a third color. Then I told her to select lines for the poem from the material she had highlighted. Here's the considerably longer result:

Louis

I had trouble with the school
got kicked out
I was bad
I was bad and blew up the school's bathroom
I got into probation
only a couple of months
decided to do something worse
stole a car
more deep trouble

The school started becoming racists
said they didn't want me there any more
that I was a bad influence
they kicked me out

A counselor told me about this school
so we came up here
and it looked good
then everything changed and

115

I don't know, I am on the good path
This is my second year here now.

They pay more attention to you here
they actually help you out more
and you don't have to wake up so early.
Teachers are cooler here, they don't mind
coming out early in the morning to help you out
or staying after school to help you out.
Getting A's and B's.

Chapel is like church.
Sometimes the teachers tell their stories,
how they ended up being here.
It is the same thing as church.
God changed my life around.
I was on the wrong path,
hanging out with Gang members.

I got here thinking this was my last chance,
I might as well make it right
I left all my friends and homies.
I forgot about them and found me a job.
I make burgers. I make French fries.
I'm going to be a professional chef.
I love cooking, man.

My dad opened a restaurant, and one of his cooks did not show up for a week.
My dad is like, oh, I need a cook, and he didn't have any money.
Oh, well, I will go in and help right now. He said, "You know you can do this job."
Yeah, I know I will try. They started teaching me how to cut the meat,
prepare all the food and all that stuff. Once I was doing it, I started liking it.
It relaxed me.

My friends from over there you had to be carrying a weapon all the time,
you had to watch your back from person to person. Here, pretty much
there are calm people. Where I came from, they would be violent and crazy,
and I would be the same way, in order to survive. Over there.

   This version still needs work, but the voice is present, individual, idiosyncratic, and alive. It *is* concrete and it also includes a fair amount of highly specific concrete language. But my student didn't automatically, intuitively seize on that language. I believe that she was intuitively identifying the material as an *occasion* for poetry, but she needed a simple strategy for locating the poetic voice including its sensory elements. She needed a strategy for making visible the qualities that made it an occasion. As Lynn Butler-Kisber (2002), Corrine Glesne (1997) and others have pointed out, interview data are rich sources of poetic occasion precisely because they represent so closely the human, individual voice. Nevertheless, some students may initially need guidance in recognizing the poetic *in* the occasion.

This can become especially challenging in relation to found poems from published text, most notably academic texts, often replete with abstract language, the diametric opposite of concreteness and sensory richness. For almost a decade now, I've been constructing poems from the work of John Dewey (Sullivan, 2000). I have learned that I have to really search for poetic occasions in Dewey. They are there, but they are hidden in a forest of abstraction. "Finding" poems takes on a whole new meaning when I'm in that work. Even when I think I have found an occasion, I sometimes work with it for a while and then have to abandon it. In the beginning I made these poems in order to share them with students who, precisely because of all that abstraction, were having trouble grasping Dewey, and the poems have, in fact, seemed useful for stimulating discussion and making his work accessible.

For an example of a textual occasion *well recognized*, consider this segment of a poem titled "prelude to performance" from Monica Prendergast's (2006) "Found Poetry as Literature Review." Prendergast was working with a translation of French theatre theorist Anne Ubersfeld's 1999 book *Reading Theatre*. I begin at stanza 5:

theatre
is an acrobat
    an oxymoron

a hero (who)
wipes down
his glorious nudity
with a rag

a princess (who)
is a goosegirl
her donkey-
skin dress
the colour
of the moon (pp. 374–375)

Beautiful occasion – concrete, metaphorical, lyric. Carol Burg (2004) has noted that learning to spot the occasion for poetry, either in research texts or in print texts, is analogous to Michelangelo's learning to see the sculpture that is already in the stone, then chipping away everything that is not David.

But poetic occasion is not just a matter of the presence of voice or concrete/ metaphoric language. Let's talk about emotion.

EMOTION

There is much to be said about emotion, especially in light of recent brain research which is unveiling the relations of emotion and memory, emotion and reason – knowledge long prefigured in the work of poets (Lehrer, 2007). Damasio (1999) explains:

> The records we hold of the objects and events that we once perceived include the motor adjustments we made to obtain the perception in the first place and also include the emotional reactions we had then..... Consequently, even when we 'merely' think about an object [or event], we tend to reconstruct memories not just of a shape or color but also of the perceptual engagement the object required and of the accompanying emotional reactions. (p.148)

Consider how similar that is to what Wordsworth wrote in his famous "Preface to *Lyrical Ballads*" over a century ago:

> I have said that poetry is the spontaneous overflow of powerful feelings: it takes its origin from emotion recollected in tranquillity: the emotion is contemplated till, by a species of reaction, the tranquillity gradually disappears, and an emotion, kindred to that which was before the subject of contemplation, is gradually produced, and does itself actually exist in the mind. (1802/2000, p. 244)

Wordsworth knew before the science was there to inform him that the brain encodes emotion along with other dimensions of experience, and to recall the particulars of experience is to live again in the emotion. Poets must know this because it is the particulars that give access to the emotion – access not only to the poet remembering, but also to the reader, who may be remembering his or her own experience or who may be *having* an experience through the particulars of the poem. A poem without concrete particulars is a poem that is unlikely to engage the emotion of the reader. If the reader is to experience the emotion that the poet wishes to embody, then the particulars that engaged the emotions in the first place must be encoded in the poem. As we have said, voice may be one of those particulars.

Aleshire (1999), and other poets have identified emotion as a key element of lyric poetry. Not all of the poems we construct for research purposes will claim to be lyric poetry, but even narrative poetry *is* poetry by virtue of its lyric qualities; otherwise, it would simply be story. Qualities of lyric poetry are to some degree important for all poetry, and emotion is one of those qualities.

Whenever we face data or text with emotional content, we face a potential occasion for poetry. When Cynthia Cannon Poindexter (2002) looked at the transcripts of interviews she did with a couple, only one of whom was HIV positive, she saw an occasion for poetry in the language of Pat:

> Pat's poem . . .comes from her narrative regarding her struggle to accept Doug's HIV infection and the way he acquired it. She uses forceful words such as *snapped* and *tumbled* to express the extent of her emotional turmoil

and expresses sadness at the disruption of their sexual relationship and her fear of becoming infected. She is articulate about her anger at him, outrage that poor people are not as able to access treatments, fear and grief about his life being in danger, and hope that if he lives well he will live to see the cure. (p. 709)

Struggle, forceful words, emotional turmoil, sadness, disruption, fear, anger, outrage, grief, danger, hope... This is the stuff of poetry – emotion, with all its human raggedness and volatile ambiguity. And we find the language of poetry in the metaphorical specificity of *snapped* and *tumbled.*

AMBIGUITY

Emily Dickinson (c.1862/1960, p. 327) wrote and Melissa Cahnmann (2003, p. 29) aptly quoted:

I dwell in Possibility –
A fairer House than Prose –
More numerous of Windows –
Superior – for Doors –

Many ways in, many ways out, no meaning trapped, enclosed, contained, possibility wide open. If we want to nail down one specific meaning or interpretation, poetry is not the tool to use. That can be done quite satisfactorily in prose. But if the data are rife with ambiguity, open-endedness, paradox, mysteries, unresolved complexity, then we may have found an occasion for poetry.

John Killick (1999) has found occasions for poetry in his work with people with dementia. In one four-page article which includes 7 poems constructed from the speech of those with dementia, Killick himself makes 13 expressions of contingency and ambiguity: "she seems to be articulating..." "it is unclear whether..." "or maybe he wants..." "we may see..." "perhaps he is looking for..." "...could be the..." "may come from ..." "maybe..." "maybe..." "or is it?" "could it be that...?" "the speaker may be saying..." "seems to be..." Even when the data are in and the poems constructed, there is much that can only be seen or understood partially, and there are no clear answers. In this case, the ambiguity arises from limited access to the thought processes of participants. But there are many possible sources of ambiguity, including open-endedness, complexity, mystery, nonlinearity, and the everyday circuitous and unresolved thoughts of you or me.

Killick (2003) describes the emergence of his awareness that his data called for poetic representation:

I had been struck early on by some of the language I was transcribing....it began to make sense if it was seen as symbolic rather than literal.... Thus, a man talking about a key says things like 'Have you any openings? Have you got a guide?' which would suggest that the key could be considered as a metaphor for something that had the power to solve problems generally and not just open a door. Why some people with dementia talk like this is one of the many mysteries that surround the condition, but that they do seems incontrovertible: I have been presented with too many examples to ignore it. This approach to language is essentially poetic. (p. 21)

It is. Nonlinearity, a decidedly poetic quality, is a major issue in Killick's work and also in the work of Clarke, Febbraro, and Nelson (2005) as they represent the stories of formerly homeless mentally ill people.

> The chronology shared by our participants was frequently circular and fragmented... the stories ... converge and diverge from the past, present, and sometimes into the future.... In the initial analysis and interviews, linear time is taken for granted as both rational and systematic. However, this strategy seems to have missed something important about the participants' views. (p. 924)

Poetry was the solution. In poetry, nonlinearity is a source of energy and interest, an asset, generally, rather than a problem. The nonlinear thinking of dementia patients provides a remarkable occasion for poetry.

ASSOCIATIVE LOGIC

I often read of poetry that it is not logical; that it is illogical or alogical or nonlogical; that it is not bound by the rules and principles of logic. I find these statements problematic and ill informed, even though they are often made by poets whom I esteem highly. It seems increasingly clear to me that although poetry does not operate according to the principles of linear, traditional Western logic, it *does* operate logically, according to a set of complex principles related to web-like relations and the demands of coherence. I believe that Dewey (1934) was touching on this obliquely when he wrote,

> To think effectively in terms of relations of qualities is as severe a demand upon thought as to think in terms of symbols, verbal and mathematical.... [T]he production of a work of genuine art probably demands more intelligence than does most of the so-called thinking that goes on among those who pride themselves on being 'intellectuals.' (p. 46)

It is the web of relations, holding all of these in a close association, a single unity, that constitutes the logic of the poem. Donald Justice, in his 1964 essay, "The Writing of Poetry," writes of this web:

> In a good short poem a fine sense of relations among its parts is felt, word connecting with word, line with line: as with a spider web, touch it at any part and the whole structure responds. (qtd. in Ryan, 2000, p. 97)

I remember distinctly the moment when I first experienced consciously and viscerally, though I had no language for it at the time, how this web of relations might operate in visual art. Later, I would write a short poem about it (Sullivan, 2002).

How I Learned to Love Picasso

At nineteen, I knew nothing, wanted to know everything,
including why those paintings hung in the Petit Palais,
why people lined up for blocks in the cold,
why I stood with them blowing clouds of breath.

Les Demoiselles D'Avignon. I stared
at fractured shapes and faces,
pondered all that flesh pink
and then one leg
where a thick blue line
plunged from thigh to calf.

I imagined that line gone.

When I imagined that line gone, I felt a diminishment of the work – a loss of energy, a paling. I didn't know how to explain it, but I felt it, and I knew then something about the ecology of a work of art, how every part relates to every other part. It is the same associative logic that I think about now as I think about the nature of poetry.

The work of Damasio (1994) and other neuroscientists confirms the web-like, interlocking, nonlinearity of thought itself, how thinking happens in neurological and biochemical webs, how associative and interdependent are the elements of thought. Higher level thinking (as we like to call it) demands connections, associations, linkages of conscious and unconscious elements, memory and emotion, past, present and future merging in the processes of making meaning. These are the very processes which poets actively seek to cultivate. Material in which these kinds of complexity inhere is material to catch a poet's eye and heart, sit him or her down to work.

The associative logic of poetry operates in both form and content, and in fact, the construction of form probably plays the larger role. But the discussion of form is a discussion of craft, and that's not our topic here. I have written about that elsewhere (Sullivan, 2004).What I'd like to make clear about associative logic now is that it is sometimes already present in the material we encounter, and when it is, we are looking at a potential occasion for poetry.

I'm going to continue citing John Killick's (2003) work with dementia patients because its examples are so dramatically clear and because part of what draws Killick to the use of poetry in this work is his perception in the speech of these persons of a kind of logic that is not generally recognized as logic. Consider this:

From My Crying Book

There is a time for picking it up.
I sift it and the rest goes down.

I think about it all. Everything.
and everything that's left I leave.

Ever since I've been walking, talking,
I've been singing, singing so many.

There is a garden, and it's out.
She calls me back there anyway.

My mother pushed me on the swing,
singing and swinging on the wing.

She always kept an eye on us—
she couldn't keep a wink to herself.

Now she's going to be one of the betime worlds
a part of me is very sad.

I'd known nothing of the mental fare:
I wouldn't want to fade to white.

These are lines from my crying book.
I sift it and the rest goes down. (p. 20)

Killick perceives in the utterances of his participant, whom he calls Judy, a sort of coherence that signals the occasion for a structure that holds together by associative, rather than linear logic.

TENSIONS

There's one other signal of poetic occasion that I wanted to talk about today: the presence of tension. It is not a separate topic from the others: concreteness, voice, emotion, ambiguity, and tension are all a part of the complex architecture of the poem's associative logic.

When we identify tensions in our material, we are perceiving some of the stuff with which that logic may be enhanced or constructed. Those may be tensions between the surface and what lies beneath; tensions among the voices of participants or within the contradictions of a single voice; between what is intended and what is accomplished; between individuals and establishments. The list of possible tensions is long.

The associative logic of the poem arises from a nexus of tensions: art and research; ambiguity and clarity; self and other; past and present; generated language & found language; internality and externality; the embodied and the conceptual; the personal and the communal; lyric and narrative; expression and restraint. This is an architectural logic, more web-like than linear, a structure of subtle relations of form and meaning. Tensions do not operate apart from or even within the logic of the poem; they are integral and essential to that logic.

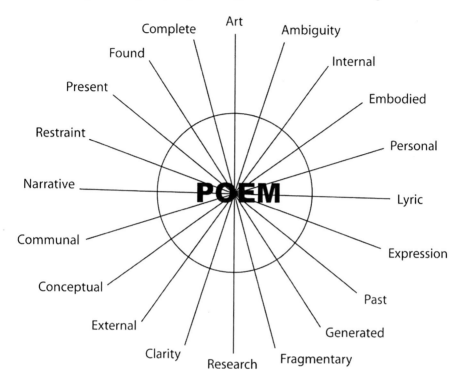

Early in my MFA experience, my first teacher, examining my small portfolio of work, observed, "Your poems are like little essays. They have an introduction, a series of stanzas with transitions, and finally a sort of conclusion." I knew that. I was sort of proud of it. But it was clear from the way she made this observation and as she continued to talk, that this sort of tidy linearity was something I would have to unlearn. I would need to learn to make leaps, as the mind leaps, as impulses fire across synapses. I would need to generate structures that would carry within themselves the motions of the mind, with unexpected turns and surprising connections. I would need to avoid the habit of conclusion, learning instead to let the end of the poem be a window or a door, incorporating the honesty and complexity of ambiguity, inviting the reader to construct meaning.

In the spirit of the poem, I'm going to leave you now in this nexus of tensions, the door of possibility open. I'm not going to conclude, summarize, synthesize, or point the way forward. I have been discursive longer already than is my inclination. You can decide for yourselves what all this means or if it means anything – to you. As for me, I'm going to take my leave with a poem – which may or may not have anything to do with what I've been talking about. You decide.

Learning in Zimbabwe

High in the hills of Zimbabwe
I am learning an interior

like woman, familiar.
I wonder at its immensity.

sitting on a boulder inside the deep
wide mouth, I am swallowed by curve.

I am learning cave.
I am learning deep shelter.

above me, behind me, red and ochre,
precisely drawn deer, antelope, giraffe,

their fine-lined bodies
full of leg and stretch.

I am listening to stone.
I am learning the ancient impulse.

I am alone except for she
who always climbs with me.

She stretches on a wide flat rock
just outside this mouth.

She is learning openness.
She is studying African sky.

These antelope are attentive.
What are they learning?

The giraffe are running.
What have they learned?

Among these animals,
human figures are small.

I am learning large and small.
I am learning how time collapses.

We climbed a rugged path to arrive here

breathing heavily. I am learning breath.

Soon we will speak
but not to tell or explain.

We will name some of the parts perhaps
but not the whole. We have taken that

inside us. We will go down the hills with it,
all that immensity of cave and sky,

all the suppleness of leg and stretch
and when night comes

we will reach for each other
with all that knowledge, all that breath.

NOTES

[1] *This essay was originally delivered as a talk at the 1st International Symposium on Poetic Inquiry, University of British Columbia, Vancouver, October 2007.*

REFERENCES

Aleshire, J. (1999). Staying news: A defense of the lyric. In G. Orr & E. B. Voigt (Eds.), *Poets teaching poets: Self and the world (*pp. 47-65). Ann Arbor, MI: University of Michigan Press.

Brady, I. (2004). In defense of the sensual: Meaning construction in ethnography and poetics. *Qualitative Inquiry, 10*(4), 622–644.

Burg, C. (2004). Ordinary fabrics/unseen stories: Out of quilts, poetry. *Journal of Critical Inquiry into Curriculum and Instruction, 5*(2), 15–20.

Butler-Kisber, L. (2002). Artful portrayals in qualitative inquiry: The road to found poetry and beyond. *The Alberta Journal of Educational Research, XLVIII*(3), 229–239.

Cahnmann, M. (2003). The craft, practice, and possibility of poetry in educational research. *Educational Researcher, 32*(3), 29–36.

Clarke, J., Febbraro, A., Hatzipantelis, M., & Nelson, G. (2005). Poetry and prose: Telling the stories of formerly homeless mentally ill people. *Qualitative Inquiry, 11*(6), 913–932.

Damasio, A. (1994). *Descartes' error: Emotion, reason, and the human brain.* New York: G.P. Putnam's Sons.

Dewey, J. (1934/1980). *Art as experience.* New York: Perigee.

Dickinson, E. (1862/1960). I dwell in possibility. In T. H. Johnson (Ed.), *The complete poems of Emily Dickinson* (p. 327). Boston: Little, Brown and Company.

Faulkner, S. (2007). Using ars poetica as criteria for reading research poetry. *Qualitative Inquiry, 13*(2), 218–234.

Feldman, R. (2004). Poetic representation of data in qualitative research. *Journal of Critical Inquiry into Curriculum and Instruction, 5*(2), 10–14.

Glesne, C. (1997). That rare feeling: Re-presenting research through poetic transcription. *Qualitative Inquiry, 3*(2), 202–221.

Justice, D. (1964). The writing of poetry. Quoted in M. Ryan, M. 2002. *A difficult grace.* Athens, GA: University of Georgia Press.

Killick, J. (1999). 'What are we like here?' Eliciting experiences of people with dementia. *Generations*, *23*(3), 46–49.

Killick, J. (2003). Memorializing dementia. *Alzheimer's Care Quarterly*, *4*(1), 17–25.

Lehrer, J. (2007). *Proust was a neuroscientist*. Boston: Houghton Mifflin Co.

Nye, N. S. (1994). Valentine for Ernest Mann. In *The red suitcase* (p. 70). New York: Boa Editions.

Piirto, J. (2002). The question of quality and qualifications: Writing inferior poems as qualitative research. *International Journal of Qualitative Studies in Education*, *15*(4), 431–445.

Poindexter, C. C. (2002). Research as poetry: A couple experiences HIV. *Qualitative Inquiry*, *8*(6), 707–714.

Prendergast, M. (2006). Found poetry as literature review: Research poems on audience and performance. *Qualitative Inquiry*, *12*(2), 369–388.

Strand, M. (2000). On becoming a poet. In M. Strand & E. Boland (Eds.), *The making of a poem: A Norton anthology of poetic forms* (pp. xvii–xxiv). New York: Norton.

Sullivan, A. M. (2002). Notes from a marine biologist's daughter: On the art and science of attention. *Harvard Educational Review*, *70*(2), 211–227.

Sullivan, A. M. (2004). Poetry as research: Development of poetic craft & the relations of craft and utility. *Journal of Critical Inquiry into Curriculum and Instruction*, *5*(2), 34–37.

Sullivan, A. M. (2000). The necessity of art: Three found poems from John Dewey's *Art as experience*. *International Journal of Qualitative Studies in Education*, *13*(3), 325–327.

Wordsworth, W. (1802/2000). Preface to *Lyrical Ballads*. In C. Kaplan & W. D. Anderson (Eds.), *Criticism: Major statements* (pp. 240–256). Boston: St. Martins Press.

Anne McCrary Sullivan
National College of Education
National-Louis University
Florida, USA

SUZANNE THOMAS

NISSOPOESIS

Visuality and Aesthetics in Poetic Inquiry

Poetry is a quality or aspect of existence. It is the thinking of things.
(Bringhurst, 2002, p. 155)

My work is informed by theoretical perspectives of nissology, derived from the Greek island, *niso*s, and study of, *logos* (McCall, 1994, 1996). I explore the complexity and multiplicity of island locality as a geographic phenomenon and imaginative topography. Cosgrove (2007) defines spatial qualities and characteristics of island by referring to topography—boundedness, shape, and scale, as determinates of islandness (p. 16). Suwa (2007) describes island as a work of imagination derived from lived experience and memory, in which island/scape is mediated through human and natural interaction. Tasmanian poet, Hay (2006) reveals islands as "special paradigmatic places"—topographies in which meanings emerge from deeply visceral lived experience (p. 34). "An island is a world; yet an island engages the world" (Baldacchino, 2005, p. 248; Selvon, 2000). I enter into

M. Prendergast, C. Leggo and P. Sameshima (eds.), Poetic Inquiry: Vibrant Voices in the Social Sciences, 127–132.

imaginary realms of island terrains through my immersion and interaction with island(s) in bodily, visceral, intuitive, and emotional ways. I concur with Suwa's (2007) assertion that islands as works of imagination and as geographical features mirror one another (p. 6). Reflections of island contours, shapes, and imaginative forms emerge through my sensorial, relational, and inter-subjective engagement.

Poetic rendering is more than another way of telling.... It is another way of interpreting and therefore of knowing (Brady, 2004, p. 633).

I render aesthetic representations of islandness by interweaving visual imagery and acoustic sounds to create *nissopoesis* as an island aesthetic methodology. I employ *nissopoesis* as a mode of poetic inquiry to represent autobiographical, geographical, and metaphorical dimensions of island experience. This method is used as a discursive practice, as a site for dwelling, and as representation of voice, reflexivity, and felt-knowledge (Thomas, 2004). I present phenomenological encounters through my immersion in processes of reflecting, attending, intuiting, describing, and interpreting to uncover meanings embedded in lived experience. *Nissopoesis* embodies a search to represent island phenomena, to reveal feelings and essence of experience, while embracing ambiguity, complexity—leaving spaces open to a multiplicity of meanings and epistemological uncertainty (Thomas, 2007).

Poetry is an interruption of silence (Collins in Stewart, 2004, p. 146).

There is a singing in things... (Lilburn, 1999, p. 75).

Richardson (1997) contends, "we are always present in out texts... we are always writing in particular contexts — contexts that affect what and how we write, and who we become" (p. 296). I explore the corporeity of islands by creating hermeneutic texts writing *in* and *through* forms of contemplative photography and acoustemology to reveal imaginative paradigms of island essence. Gillis (2007) writes: "We move around small islands and inside them in a corporeal way". I experience island as an inter-subjective, corporeal encounter — my human body moving in relation to natural bodies of island(s); my body and the bodies of islands in relation to one another, and to the immensity of the sea. I create visual and aesthetic texts *in-situ* to represent site responsive renderings of my embodied experience.

Poetry creates and occupies sensuous space that is connected to the deepest level of existence (Brady, 2004, p. 630).

I develop *nissopoesis* as poetic inquiry through the use of image-based methods and "visual note-taking" (Müller, 2005). My intention is for each image, or sequence of images, to produce a relational poetic whole (Wall, 2007). In the process of contextualizing and juxtaposing images the challenge is, as Whincup (2007) suggests, to transcend surface descriptions and in constructing visual relationships, "to assert readings of the intangible" (p. 45). I create hermeneutic-phenomenological texts through visual imagery to suspend fleeting moments, propelling a search beyond surface levels, to evoke "readings of the intangible" and to provoke sensuous streams of thought.

Poetry is...knowing in the sense of stepping in tune with being, hearing and echoing the music and heartbeat of being... (Bringhurst in Bartlett, 2002, p. 14).

Truax (2007) reveals that the dimensionalities and characteristics of acoustic sounds — textures, grains and tactile qualities — bring the world into us (p. 1). His work illuminates how attentiveness to the sonic environment and "listening-in-readiness" may invoke memories, associations, and imagination (p. 4). I expand dimensions of *nissopoesis* by capturing environmental sounds to embody sonological consciousness, aural sensibilities and perceptions, as a way of finding my place *in* and *through* the world. I record soundscapes to render the essence of my islandness — a deep connectivity to the sea, and emergent meanings anchored in the sensual realm. Moored buoys as sentinels of the seas, blend with wave energy, sea winds, vibrations of movement, and reverberating life-sounds.

Poetry is [writing] about experience... full of touch, smell, taste, hearing and vision, open to ...—the erotics—of daily life, hoping to reveal that world...as it is experienced... in it patterns and its puzzles... (Brady, 2004, p. 628).

A poet strives for synaesthesia (Abrams, 1996) a blurring and blending of the senses, re-connection with tacit, somatic/affective domains of knowing. Poetry is what I hear when I am open to vibrations of feeling-tones that present themselves in a hovering—it is listening with a deep-feeling heart. I strive to develop a synergy of imagery and sound by layering visual and auditory modes to reveal the complexity and relationality of image as island and islandness of sound.

...the poetic image has a dynamism of its own; it is referable to direct ontology (Bachelard, 1994, p. xvi).

My aim is to bring together visual and auditory worlds in a coalescence of image/sound/movement/stillness/silence; to bring together a sense of poetic in the coexistence of human and natural; to capture the symbiotic nature of island sea/scapes, and to reveal the immensity of islands as imaginative topographies. McIntyre (2007) writes, "islands stand as repositories of meaning". Islands lure my imagination as they loom majestically against a spacious sky, marking the horizon as simulacrum of the world, steeped in vast expansiveness of unknowability.

Contemplation is inquiry into the nature of being (Lilburn, 1999, p. 27).

Contemplation's attention-in-silence knows by standing alongside, craning toward, dwelling within us (Lilburn, 1999, p. 27).

Contemplation's knowing is unknowing (Lilburn, 1999, pp. 27 & 29).

Nissopoesis: Waiting in Waves of the Sonorous and Silent [1]embodies aesthetic elements and qualities of my "ars poetica" (Faulkner, 2007). My art of poetry calls for deep immersion, porous receptivity, sensual attunement in ways of attending and being present *in* and *to* the world. *Nissopoesis* as poetic inquiry calls for imagining, inhabiting, hearing deeply, and "dwelling poetically" (Heidegger, 1971). As Jeanette Winterson (1995) writes, "My work is rooted in silence: It grows out of deep beds of contemplation...." (p. 169). My art of poetry incites a longing for knowing beyond knowledge, for the "silence beyond speech" (Sontag, 1991, pp. 4–5). It is knowing that roams in a fluidity of movement, swells in shifting, littoral spaces, and crests on waves of poetic possibility. My art of poetry calls for a sense of humility and openness to the poignancy of newness, hopefulness, and discovery. Gadamer (1976) asserts that "understanding is not an act of subjectivity but a mode of being" (p. 125). My way of being is in *poetic reverie* (Bachelard, 1994) listening, attending, dwelling, in-waiting, for that which presents itself as a glimmer of consciousness in waves of the sonorous and silent, lingering at edges of water, in whispering wisps of wings over seas.

The poet speaks on the threshold of being (Bachelard, 1994, p. xvi).

As a poet, I listen for sounds, deep chords penetrating, vibrations reverberating, always in flux, echoing tonalities of a world that quivers and hums.

POETIC INVOCATION

This poem represents my experimentation with the technique of collage poetry created within the context of an Island Creative Writing Workshop. I select excerpts originating from Gaston Bachelard's *The Poetics of Space*, to render a distillation of poetical invocations and philosophical musings.

Roughcasts of separate organs...in the moment of positive joy... this element of unreality ... the house's entire being would open up...in every dwelling ...earth-bound snail...powers of gravity...the room in which the poet pursues such a dream...shells and doorknobs, closets and attics...poetry is a soul inaugurating a form... there are also great waves of silence...inside and outside as experienced by the imagination...without preparing us ... as for the cellar...an immense world still heard ...our past is situated elsewhere...possesses the verticality of the tower...thus we cover the universe with drawings we have lived...are insufficiently aware of this unpredictability...vaulted ceiling down to the floor... is at home in the space of an ear...

...the soul comes and inaugurates the form, dwells in it, takes pleasure in it.

NOTES

[1] My video, Nissopoesis: *Waiting in Waves of the Sonorous and Silent,* was produced as a multi-media work to accompany this paper. This video is available for viewing at www.educationalinsights.ca in *Educational Insight's* Special Issue on Poetic Inquiry (2009).

REFERENCES

Abrams, D Abrams, D. (1996). *The spell of the sensuous: Perception and language in a more-than-human world.* New York: Vintage Books.

Bachelard, G. (1994). *The poetics of space: The classic look at how we experience intimate places* (M. Jolas, Trans.). Boston: Beacon Press. (Original work published 1958)

Baldacchino, G. (2005). Editorial: Islands — Objects of representation. *Geografiska Annaler, 87B*(4), 247–251.

Bartlett, B. (2002). Introduction: Two pianos together. In T. Lilburn (Ed.), *Thinking and singing: Poetry and the practice of philosophy* (pp. 5–15). Toronto, Ontario: Cormorant Books.

Brady, I. (2004). In defence of the sensual: Meaning construction in ethnography and poetics. *Qualitative Inquiry, 10*(4), 622–644.

Bringhurst, R. (2002). Poetry and thinking. In T. Lilburn (Ed.), *Thinking and singing: Poetry and the practice of philosophy* (pp. 155–172). Toronto, Ontario: Cormorant Books.

Cosgrove, D. (2007). Island passages. In G. Baldacchino (Ed.), *Bridging islands: The impact of fixed links* (pp. 15–27). Charlottetown, Prince Edward Island: Acorn Press.

Faulkner, S. L. (2007). Concern with craft: Using ars poetic as criteria for reading research poetry. *Qualitative Inquiry, 13*(2), 218–234.

Gadamer, H. G. (1976). *Philosophical hermeneutics* (D. E. Linge, Trans.). Berkeley, CA: University of California Press.

Gillis, C. (2007, June 29–July 2). *"Enisling" narratives: Writing the small island.* Paper presented at the 3rd International Conference on Small Island Cultures, Culture and the Construction of Islandness. Charlottetown, Prince Edward Island: Institute of Island Studies, University of Prince Edward Island.

Hay, P. (2006). A phenomenology of islands. *Island Studies Journal, 1*(1), 19–42.

Heidegger, M. (1971). *Poetry, language, thought* (A. Hofstadter, Trans.). New York: Harper & Row.

Lilburn, T. (1999). *Living in the world as if it were home.* Dunvegan, Ontario: Cormorant Books.

Lilburn, T. (Ed.). (2002). *Thinking and singing: Poetry and the practice of philosophy.* Toronto, Ontario: Cormorant Books.

McCall, G. (1994). Nissology: A proposal for consideration. *Journal of the Pacific Society, 63–64*(17), 99–106.

McCall, G. (1996). Clearing confusion in a disembedded world: The case for nissology. *Geographische Zeitschrift, 84*(2), 74–85.

McIntyre, J. (2007, June 29–July 2). *Thomas Hardy's the well-beloved and late Victorian England.* Paper presented at the 3rd International Conference on Small Island Cultures, Culture and the Construction of Islandness. Charlottetown, Prince Edward Island: Institute of Island Studies, University of Prince Edward Island.

Müller, M. (2005). *The memo book: Films, videos, and installations by Matthias Müller.* Toronto, Ontario: YYZ Books.

Richardson, L. (1997). Skirting a pleated text: De-disciplining an academic life. *Qualitative Inquiry, 3*(3), 295–303.

Selvon, S. (2000). *An island is a world.* Toronto, Ontario: TSAR Publications.

Sontag, S. (1991). *Styles of radical will.* New York: Anchor Books.

Stewart, R. (2004). The end of boredom: An interview with Billy Collins. *New Letters: A Magazine of Writing and Art, 70*(2), 143–159.

Suwa, J. (2007). The space of shima. *The International Journal of Research into Island Cultures, 1*(1), 6–14.

Thomas, S. (2004). *Of earth and flesh and bones and breath: Landscapes of embodiment and moments of re-enactment.* Halifax, Nova Scotia & Toronto, Ontario: Backalong Books & Centre for Arts-informed Research.

Thomas, S. (2007). Littoral spaces: Liquid edges of poetic possibility. *Journal of the Canadian Association for Curriculum Studies, 5*(1), 21–29 & Adobe Premier Video. Retrieved from www.csse.ca/CACS/JCACS

Truax, B. (2007). *Sound in context: Communication and soundscape research Simon Fraser University.* Retrieved February 3, 2007, from http://interact.uoregon.edu/MediaLit/WFAE/library/articles/truax_SFUniversity

Wall, J. (2007). *Jeff Wall: Selected essays and interviews.* New York: The Museum of Modern Art.

Whincup, T. (2007). TE WA: The social significance of the traditional canoes of Kiribati. Shima. *The International Journal of Research into Island Cultures, 1*(1), 43–45.

Winterson, J. (1995). *Art objects: Essays on ecstasy and effrontery.* New York: Random House.

Suzanne Thomas
Faculty of Education
University of Prince Edward Island
Canada

MARY WEEMS

THE E IN POETRY STANDS FOR EMPATHY

Empathy: Ability to identify with a person or object.
Identify: Put oneself in the place of another person.

Oxford English Dictionary

Odd that I've always-used *empathy* to represent the experience of imagining what's it's like to be in the life circumstance of another, when the definition of *identify* is closer to what I mean. Like the meanings of words—one word leading to another, the lives of people are connected. When I raise the issue of the importance of becoming more empathetic as part of developing a spiritually centered social conscious-ness, the typical response of students and others I encounter is that it's impossible to stand in the shoes of another.

This is not true.

Contrary to the current me-me-me focus of an America steeped in materialism, individualism, and fear of racial, ethnic and sexual difference, that devalues showing emotion–empathy *is* possible and represents a path to a greater understanding of what it means to be othered, to the importance of thinking deeply about an experience you've never had, to constructing a passion for acting as an agent for social justice and love.

As a language artist, while it took me a while to become conscious of it, I've always been interested in poetic inquiry, in using my words to connect with the lived experiences of people. My first poem at the age of thirteen was titled *Death*. It represents my effort to empathize with the reality of our mortality following my observation of the accidental death of a young, Black male involved in a one-car accident in front of my high school. Since then my poetry, and subsequently my qualitative research has been focused on the human condition and what happens between birth and the end of life.

The method for creating the results of my ongoing, lived experience-based research is to first be inspired to write by something I experience first or secondhand in my personal life, become aware of through my formal or informal teaching, or some form of media. Next, I consciously move to a space between my conscious and unconscious mind to free up my creative ability to let what wants to be written come out without trying to force it. I write from this spiritual-imaginative-intellectual *open* space until I stop. The work is completed by first, sharing it with someone out loud to listen for how the piece feels, flows, and means. Once it feels ready for editing, I re-visit the draft and take out everything

M. Prendergast, C. Leggo and P. Sameshima (eds.), Poetic Inquiry: Vibrant Voices in the Social Sciences, 133–144.

that weakens the work including: clichés, over-explaining, and weak lines. Last, I pursue ways of getting the work out into the world.

What follows are several poems that were prompted by an encounter I had either directly or indirectly with the lived experience of someone else. Catalysts for the poems vary and precede each poem. The social issues include: breast cancer, Alzheimer's, homelessness, classism, alcoholism, bulimia, anorexia, suicide, and racism respectively. In a world rushing headlong into degrees of technology that make what used to be impossible possible: sophisticated methods of detecting breast cancer, drugs to slow down Alzheimer's progress, numerous new ways to communicate without face-to-face contact, countless ways to kill each other long distance, I share these poems in the hope of inspiring others to take time to consciously explore the importance of empathy in the development of social consciousness.

1.

Several years ago I was in my doctor's office waiting for my annual mammogram, and saw a black and white magazine cover image of a white woman with all white hair and striking Caribbean-sea-blue eyes. She was nude from the waist up and was the survivor of double mastectomies. My first thought when I looked at her scars and back to her eyes was *beauty:*

Beauty Secret

First thing I did when I left the doctor's office that day was take off my watch and drop it in the trash in the pristine, all-white hallway with the carefully polished tile floor—bright enough to see my reflection. I stood there in one spot looking at myself until a stranger gently took my arm asked if I was okay. Don't remember what I said to him but I knew my love affair with my beautiful breasts was over.

We recommend double mastectomies to save your life.

Looking back I'm still struck by the fact that I was thinking about my *breasts,* what time I was getting my toes done, and what I'd be wearing to this year's high school reunion and...*it* didn't occur to me until 3 o'clock the next morning that the doctor had told me my chances of dying from breast cancer within the next 5-10 years were 50/50 unless I had the surgery.

Mother, who always called it a "brassiere" got me up bright and early for the train ride into the city with her usual "get up now dear" holler up to the top of the stairs. I jumped up eager to dress, eat and be on our way. New York was only a short hop from New Jersey, but the difference in architecture, people, sights, sounds and smells was like traveling from one planet to another. Jersey tried to be a big city, when it was a working class town with residents who told people they lived in New York.

My stomach felt fluttery like it was filled with female butterflies. We walked into Macy's and since it was my first time, mother took me on a tour. We move from the cosmetic counters, to the shoe department (she kept me there for so long I started asking myself "who" we really came to shop for). Finally we arrived at the Foundations Department. I felt myself blushing Santa-Claus-red as mother walked up to the first sales clerk she saw and loudly announced "Hello, we're looking for a first brassiere for my daughter Michelle." I wanted to disappear, but when I quickly looked around to see if anyone was looking, all I saw were welcoming smiles, and knowing nods. Suddenly I was in a cocoon filled with women. Back then brassieres came in one color, white. So after the clerk (her name was Sandy, odd I'd remember that) measured what little I had and declared I was a 32A cup, mother and me looked at and I tried on bra after bra until I finally selected the first one I'd picked.

I've been holding my breath. A lack of air jerks me back to now. My hand grips the steering wheel like I'm spinning out of control instead of stuck in traffic on a street just off Time Square.

My mother wouldn't even consider doing this to herself. Her breasts were more important to her than a chance at a longer life. Nothing—not my sister, my brother, my anger, my screaming-fear could stop her from getting a cancer so savage it moved through her like an accidentally set forest fire.

In group, women talk about tears, about being afraid their significant others won't want them any more. We laugh to keep from choking joking about replacing our lamps with candles, breaking the mirrors, never being seen naked again

Then, in the midst of quiet conversation, one-woman stops talking mid-sentence and one-by-one we all fall down wrap our arms around each other.

There are no words for the inside job you have to do on yourself to let someone do this to you.

The young photographer stoops in front of me with a clear, passionate eye and a genuine smile. He tells me I'm beautiful. Thanks me for having the courage to share this gift with others. I stand quietly in front of him naked from the waist up face the back-wall mirror. Notice how like me, the two diagonal flaps that used to be my breasts look glad to be alive.

2.

I had some down time and was watching the sitcom *Mr. Belvedere* to relax. The episode was about community service, and one of the children Mr. Belvedere, the house servant was taking care of had been connected with an elder in a nursing home who was in the first stages of Alzheimer's. By the end of the episode she was in the last stages, and I started wondering what it would be like to be a daughter watching her mother experience the long goodbye:

Killing Her Softly

Today mama lost her name—

Question marks drop
on answers that refuse to breathe.

Moving old on tiptoe slippers,
forgotten, half-buttoned house dress
slips to lace straps. She stops
as her dressing table glistens
garnets and rhinestones.
Ballerina music box tinkles,
"Fairy tales can come true…"
She touches the tulle skirt,

Whispering:
"Remember when thirty seemed old.
The mirror looks, smiling
at the sexy red velvet dress,
hugging the cheeks of my ass
like a man's hands."

A slow sway pushes her hips
she bumps me as a chair
and stops, confused.

I hold her hand calling, Mama, mama…
she moves a vague eye, voice to air.

Memory, black and white confetti.
She looks daily at daily things,
forgetting how faucets, doors, buttons play.

Her feelings move, silently posting vacancy signs,
and so it goes.

Mama holds her head a lot, with spread
palm leaves, each ear a grasp on a soul
that keeps spilling.

Afraid, I see around-the clock eyes.
The first day the doorway holds me. Nursing
jail walls fall down in dandruff flakes, a silent,

secret snow. I see mama, eyes closed standing
in the mirror.

Running, I whisper, "Hannah."

Mama sings,
"Hannah, Hannah, bo banna, banana fanna fo fanna…"

(Weems, 1997,pp. 17–18)

3.

The downtown area of my hometown Cleveland, Ohio is a favourite hangout of the
homeless because of the homeless shelters, vacant buildings, deep doorways, and
other places to hide, the social agencies that serve the homeless, and the warmth
emitting from the street grates. One afternoon as I was riding downtown to teach, I
saw an African American woman sitting on the ground in front of a closed café:

Sidewalk Café

Guess the woman
was too early for lunch,
too late for help.
Patient, she sat on that sidewalk
talking to her guests
getting that ground table
prepared for a feast.

Never mind the bird shit, people spit,
stomped gum, where the silverware goes,
none of her friends are that fussy.

Lint in her hair glows fireflies,
one big fuzz ball, sleep rubbed
wiping walk with her head at night.

Arms and face move,
shoes jerk at the end of stiff legs,
soles and holes same color.

As rearview mirror mirrors the sistah,
filling each water glass,
her broken mouth smile

smears the white sign on the Café door:

"no shirt, no shoes, no service."

(Weems, 1997, p. 2)

4.

Cheryl Townsend, a white woman poet-photographer and friend shared a series of black and white images with me. I wrote a series of poems to them including this one about a working class white woman, in a neighborhood bar:

Drunk Ugly

Every night I come
here to drink
for someone I used to know.
Tonight it's my husband.

I was okay, planning to stay
at home until I noticed
I was still wearing his wedding
ring ten years later.

The first one is never the hardest
I dropped the ring in the bottom
told myself I'd only have one
but the kind drunk on my right
kept up with me and kept me up
with him until he was tossing
dimes on the bar
for the last call
leaving me
looking at my toe
to call his wife
for a ride.

When the barkeep
locks me out to leave
I'll heave on the sidewalk

catch a cab home
and forget to remember
that I left the ring
in the last shot glass.

(Weems, 2008, p. 46)

5.

Eating disorders are common among white females, and thanks to the positive body-image-killing influence of the western media, female, and some male members of other groups including African Americans are buying into what's become the number one American standard of beauty for women—thin:

Food Fight

I started small. Mother believes in privacy. Can't remember her ever entering my room without knocking. Can't remember her ever asking to see what's inside anything in here. Mother thinks a hug is what happens when two people are unavoidably in the wrong place at the wrong time and kind of run into each other touching at the edges, followed by muttered apologies, and wiping motions. I learned to look down a lot when I'm around her. She's always saying "look me in the eye" like she can see what's on my mind. Like because I happened to pass through her to get here—she has to have her mark on me, and everything about me. Mama doesn't believe in just eating, food is a slowly contrived experience, which must be orchestrated with the kind of care a composer takes to create a masterpiece.

The ritual started with one of two things: preparation or ordering. Preparation if she was cooking, ordering the meal (which she always did without my input) if we were out. She never allowed anyone in the kitchen while she was cooking. Course my father didn't give a fuck about that rule and before she finally got rid of him, used to make it a point of crashing into the kitchen in his muddy construction boots, and funky flannel shirt with a sweating bottle of Bud, and a log ash cigarette singing his current favorite show tune at the top of his lungs. Mother thought these outbursts were about as funny as a basketful of dead babies and one day when he came home—we'd moved and taken everything, even the ashtrays and mother didn't even smoke.

One night when I was about 11, we were sitting at the table – mother at one end, me at the other like a guest for dinner. She'd just made me say yet another endless thank-you-for our food prayer, and was beginning to tell me what order to eat my meal in, when the phone rang—and something weird happened. For the first time, she told me I could go on and eat without her—I was so shocked, it took a moment for me to pick up my plate take it quickly to my room and dump the contents into my book bag. I kept the bread and by the time mother returned to the dining room table I was carefully buttering the last of my dinner roll, a couple of strategically placed crumbs on the table and around my lips as evidence.

I felt my stomach doing flip flops and my knees tremble cause I just knew she'd notice my plate was empty, and punch me in the mouth for eating too fast. But she didn't. She was too busy telling me what her boss said about the wonderful job she'd done planning the company banquet. I smiled wide on the inside like I'd just been opened like a present.

After that, I started looking for ways to stop food from getting inside. Once the book bag filled up, I had to find a way to get rid of as much of the beautifully created meals as I could. I learned to fill my mouth with food by holding small mounds of it in my cheeks then quickly making soft lumps and dropping them down my blouse. When I was excused, I'd go to my room for some privacy to study, and dump the food here. Now, there's no more room. I can't take anything out. I've started a hole behind the garage.

Tomorrow mother's taking me to another shrink to shriek. I'll nibble on an animal cracker, tell her all the things she wants to hear, complete with heartfelt tears, sincere promises, the latest recipes for success.

6.

One of my students pointed out that there are websites dedicated to helping females become and/or remain anorexic! The disorder is portrayed as positive, the numerous images of starving women, held up as examples to strive for, to be thin-thin-thin, to take control of ones life, to be beautiful:

Pro-Ana Recipe

Toast two pieces of organic wheat bread
let them get cold
while you debate

Give one piece to the dog
Cut the remaining slice in half
then quarters

Trim the crusts
Toss the crusts to the birds outside
the kitchen window

Turn the 4 quarters into a puzzle
Drink 4 ounces of water
Become the answer.

7.

My great uncle Jack committed suicide on Labor Day in 1992. I'd always thought suicide was the worst thing a person could do to him or herself. Because I knew of my uncle's joy for life, that he was chronically ill from decades of smoking, and that he never wanted anyone to have to take care of him—his act changed my mind:

Suicide Note

There is no flash
transition shorter
than the space between
a stanza.

A map, the way
from the rush, appears.

Wore favorite clothes,
unwashed jeans, Motown
t-shirt, bare feet.

The end was like making love:
saw stars, breathed hard,
relaxed.

(Weems, 2005, n.p.)

8.

In 2005, I spent a week as Scholar-in-Residence at the University of Minnesota-Duluth. It was the whitest place I've ever been. Each morning I took a long walk along the lake:

Message to the Woman on the Lake

When I saw you walking slowly on the wood
along the lake I watched for a lesson.
Age, a mystery I'm getting close
to made me want to walk with you, but
the protocol between knowing and not knowing
called for keeping a distance I didn't feel at 50,
I didn't feel in the color holding a space between
us wider than the lake.
You took your good time, cane careful to miss

the cracks in the path, worn legs conserving
energy for the walk back, eyes in a permanent
squint aimed ahead at a future you won't live.

My legs took moments to catch up to your minutes,
my eyes looked your way and waited for my voice
to speak, the silence of your response hard
as the knots in your hands.

I wanted to run away from something familiar
as a daily routine, I forget each night
when I kneel to pray to the only spirit who makes me
feel humble. I think you mumble under your breath
as I leave you in the dust of your own thoughts
words I choose not to hear, words spoken
to someone yesterday, when you were young
and water was a place to play.

(Weems, 2008, p. 53)

9.

When I first heard about this tragedy, I was struck by the media's singular focus on
the victims of Cho Seung Hui's calculated act of violence, by their lack of attention
to "why" this happened, by the fact that they did not number him among the
victims. Part of what the media shared for several days was a brief video clip of
Hui pouring his pain out in words that included "You have vandalized my heart,"
and I thought what happened to him?

Hui

> * Cho Seung Hui
> Virginia Tech Shootings

Young man far away
from home, the south – Korea,
Virginia a foreign land, language
land mines

his name a question mark,
the silence of invisible.
I hear him say *You have vandalized
my heart,"* heard/hear his beat across state,

planet, time. Life's skin on the margins,
he enters my space fills me
with more sorrow for madness
makes it break out like an alarm.

The harm of not paying attention, of hundreds of ears
all tuned in on one frequency. Of not meaning to make
a young man's life a joke, but laughing anyway,
of being remembered like a monster
in a mirror cracked without looking.

The sound of pain arming itself,
bullets as rain,
of chain locked doors
that stopped even
the innocent from running
outside.

10.

I am against war for any reason. It represents the senseless loss of life for reasons
that are never as important as honoring each other as humankind and each day's
opportunity to live. When I read this article in the New York Times all deaths were
reduced to the loss of this one man's sons.

Missing Feet

(1-6-07, [1-6-05] *Bomb's Lasting Toll: Lost Laughter, Broken Lives*
By: Sabrina Tavernise)

I'm reading the article in the New York Times
and suddenly the war in Iraq
is a boy dying in his father's arms.
His nickname English Ali, his body burning,
his feet missing

His father thinks two missing feet are nothing
compared to losing a son while he looks inside
death's eyes, tries to pretend this is a dream,
34 boys are not dying; his other son has not just died
on the same street, that he is not dying.

Newsprint and paper smell like car bombs;
the words, people standing in line for help;
hope the last thing anyone talks about, most
of them missing a boy at their table.

Their grief the same as it is everywhere,
their anger local and familiar. Not even revenge
can help the fathers feeling like failures, mothers
violated, womb-stunted, organs
snatched without reason, tears that don't
soothe, sorrow that kills and makes you walk
around showing people you're dead.

Ali's father's face is one terrible tear. He says *Our life
now, it's not a life, it's a kind of dream. Life has no taste. I even feel sick of myself;*
and I'm in his one-room apartment with him, putting an arm around
his shoulder, our silence a connection across cultures that needs nothing.

I think of my grown daughter, of all the children in my family
who play in the street everyday not worrying
about whether or not a truck bomb will kill them.

I think of a child's life without feet,
the upturned soles of Iraqi men praying,
the American soldiers standing in parked
Humvees tossing candy to the children
just before the booby trapped truck blew up.

REFERENCES

Weems, M. (2008). Killing her softly, message to the woman on the lake. In *An unmistakable shade of red and the Obama chronicles*. Huron: Bottom Dog Press.

Weems, M. (2005). I am martell, drunk ugly, suicide note. In *Tampon class*. Columbus: Pavement Saw Press.

Weems, M. (1997). Killing her softly, sidewalk café. *White*. In *Wick Chapbook*. Kent: Kent State University Press.

Mary Weems
Department of Education and Allied Studies
John Carroll University
Ohio, USA

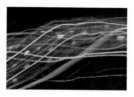

SECTION II: VOX AUTOBIOGRAPHIA/AUTOETHNOGRAPHIA

CARL LEGGO

LIVING LOVE STORIES

Fissures, Fragments, Fringes

I want to know love's truths as we live them. (hooks, 2000, p. xxv)

Love ... has always been confused and confusing. (Evans, 2003, p. 27)

Love, love, love, it was the core of my life .... (Oliver, 2008, p. 65)

A good poem reminds us of love because it cannot be written or read in distraction; it cannot be written or understood by anyone thinking of praise or publication or promotion. (Berry, 1990, p. 90)

1

In much of my poetry, narrative research, autobiographical writing, and poetic inquiry, I ruminate on issues of relationship, family, community, school culture, becoming human, and attending to silence. I especially focus on the word *love* as four silent letters that need to be declared, heard, and lived in schools and out of schools. It is puzzling that a library search with the descriptors *love* and *school* turns up almost no sources. Perhaps educators fear love, and loving, and saying *I love you*. Why aren't we researching love more? Above all, I am convinced that the way I teach, and live among my students and colleagues, in schools and universities, is shaped and informed by my experiences with love, always a tangled mix of joy and fear, hope and regret, longing and more longing. And so I ruminate with memory, others' words, narratives, and poetry, in the hope that I can learn how to live with the persistent sense of desire in the experience of love—fired always by a pedagogical commitment to writing the world a more caring space and time in which to linger.

The story of love is always a tangled story because desire knows no boundaries, has forgotten the beginning of the story, and can never find the end. The story of love is a story that we can never get right because every right turn remembers every left turn, all the turns left, traced indelibly in desire and memory and hope. Like Freire's (1985) passionate and eloquent confession,

I feel my incompleteness inside me, at the biological, affective, critical, and intellectual levels, an incompleteness that pushes me constantly, curiously,

M. Prendergast, C. Leggo and P. Sameshima (eds.), Poetic Inquiry: Vibrant Voices in the Social Sciences, 147–168.

and lovingly toward other people and the world, searching for solidarity and transcendence of solitude. All of this implies wanting to love, a capacity for love that people must create in themselves. This capacity increases to the degree that one loves; it diminishes when one is afraid to love. (pp. 197–198)

A Girl with Bare Feet

on an empty road
between Boswarlos
and Port au Port
I saw a girl
walking in the dust
(she wore no shoes)
but I didn't stop and ask
if she needed a ride
    because I didn't want
her to fall in love
and send me scribbled notes
cut in lust and adoration
    and I didn't want
her to slide over on the seat
and with a quick thrust
cut my throat
    and I didn't want
my neighbors in Stephenville
to gossip about the girl
riding in my car
and the wind blew
red russet tangerine leaves
(perhaps the wind blew
the girl's shoes away)
but not even the January wind
can blow away
my seared memory
of a lone girl
walking bare foot
into winter
on an empty road
where I passed
and didn't stop

2

In calling for a "pedagogy of the imagination" (p. 92), Calvino (1995) asks, "who are we, who is each of us, if not a combinatoria of experiences, information, books we have read, things imagined? Each life is an encyclopedia, a library, an inventory of objects, a series of styles, and everything can be constantly shuffled and reordered in every way conceivable" (p. 124). Like Calvino, I have surrendered any hope for a sense of consistent and constant wholeness. Instead, I attend to fissures, fragments, and fringes. As Canadian poet Don Domanski (2002) knows, "we cannot grasp the world nor put it into an order. We can only experience it" (p. 246). In my poetry I no longer try to order or govern or organize the world; instead, I seek to learn to lean into the circles of the sun and moon, the seasonal cycles of desires and frustrations that shape human becoming like so many scribbles that defy easy interpretation and confident comprehension.

Mementos

they smile used smiles
with moose meat stuck in their molars

loud snow falls in the street light
outside the window

water drips from the fishermen's line
with promises of the alphabet

October is slipping away
like lukewarm faith

like a dog chases its tail
the past bit me in the ass today

snow calls, seagulls hang suspended,
enthralled with distant planets

he stood alone
with a pelican's poignant patience

out of the preacher's zeal for heaven
heavy waves heaved

irises held us in a circle of *I*'s
like a fence of barbed wire

the mask of masculinity
masks the illusion of lunacy

the autumn I should have left I bought
cowboy boots but couldn't afford a horse

my son Aaron philosophizes
about mini-wheats

like spring snow our words are spoken
into the earth-warmed air

she drinks lots of tea,
infuses us with love

since imitation can spell limitation
let the moment be inimitable

with an X-acto knife I will cut out
the heart of logorrhoea

her love sticks to me like a burr
or a splinter of heaven

like a nautilus' shell I lug
my working class stories everywhere

the summer I knew I was leaving,
I walked in soft green boots like moss

this box of memory fragments will
never be organized in a story or poem

3

Barthes (1997) calls his autobiography (titled *Roland Barthes*) which comprises a few photographs of himself and his family and friends and colleagues, and brief fragments like riffs on dozens of pertinent and impertinent words and phrases, "a kind of patchwork, a rhapsodic quilt consisting of stitched squares" (p. 142). And while both revealing and concealing himself in a quilt of many colors, Barthes admits:

> It is certainly when I divulge my *private life* that I expose myself most: not by the risk of 'scandal,' but because then I present my image-system in its strongest consistency; and the image-system, one's imaginary life, is the very thing over which others have an advantage: which is protected by no reversal, no dislocation. (p. 82)

Barthes reminds me to ask, What is the danger of disclosure and exposure? In my writing is there a possibility of closure, even composure? Like Barthes, "I delight continuously, endlessly, in writing as in a perpetual production, in an unconditional dispersion, in an energy of seduction which no legal defense of the subject I fling upon the page can any longer halt" (p. 136).

Once upon a time, a long time ago, after many years of living a love story with one woman, I left her and our children because I claimed I had fallen in love with another woman I hoped would fill what I thought was a hole in my heart, only to find that the hole could not be filled, that the hole was part of the heart's organic organization. To fill the hole was to kill the heart. I then left the woman I had loved with reckless, romantic, adulterous abandon, and returned to my wife who I first married at twenty and married again, almost three decades later. Tangled up in what Evans (2003) calls "ideologies of romance" (p. 54), I had crashed into "the limitations of romantic love" (Evans, p. 119). The woman I left to return to the first woman I had left was mostly gracious about my leaving and the loss of our carefully composed hopes, but I read the signs of her hurt the next time I read Barthes' *Roland Barthes*—a book that I cannot stop reading.

X-Acto

just before she left,
she cut gashes
in all my books
with a surgeon's penchant
for deciphering messages
knotted under the surface,
pushed the X-Acto knife in,
the blade as sharp
as a hopeless heart

4

Because we are composed in languages, because we know ourselves in languages, because we constantly write ourselves, and rewrite ourselves, and write our relations to others, we need frequent opportunities to explore and experiment with the rhetorical possibilities of texts, with the art and science of language use. Poetic inquiry opens up capacious possibilities for inquiring. So, I write poetry—autobiographical, philo-sophical, narrative, interrogative, lyric, ruminative, pedagogic, performative poetry—as a way to connect with others, seeking always a living ecology in the vast mystery of the earth. In all my writing, I seek to dispel absence by disclosing possibilities for presence, knowing how spilling and spelling words can conjure steadfast hope, even, especially in the midst of despair and despondency. Like Frank (2000), "I believe in stories more than in principles" (p. 231).

Porto

I sit on my patio
and sip porto.

LEGGO

A wasp hovers near
the rim of the glass.

I try to remember
the taste of Lisbon

where I ate bacalhau
baked in garlic and olive oil,

but I smell only
the old man

who boarded the train
to Sintra. He wore

a blue housecoat
soaked with piss.

At the next stop
we all jumped out

and ran the ramp
to the next car,

giggled, embarrassed,
rubbed our noses.

The old man sat alone
like he didn't know.

I can't tell you how
that experience seeped

under my skin like the scent
of a fire-gutted house.

I know only the wasp will
never know the taste of Lisbon

from circling the rim
of my glass of porto.

5

In loving communities we tell one another our stories; we listen to one another's
stories. As Berry (1990) notes,

when a community loses its memory, its members no longer know one another. How can they know one another if they have forgotten or have never learned one another's stories? If they do not know one another's stories, how can they know whether or not to trust one another? People who do not trust one another do not help one another, and moreover they fear one another. And this is our predicament now. (p. 157)

Moreover, what happens when we think we know one another's stories, but we don't know what to do with the stories? Can love guide us?

Artichoke Hearts

my cousin traded her grandmother's dark rum fruit cake recipe
with a neighbor for his pasta sauce with artichoke hearts,
and served the pasta to another neighbor who said,
That's the best pasta I've ever eaten, and now I want to eat you,
and for five or six winters dropped by for heart-to-heart tête-à-têtes
with tea and tea biscuits till another neighbor had a biscuit and cut to
the business of what in the world was going on since the neighborhood
was reeling out of orbit like *Another World*

while my cousin knew, or pretended to know everybody in the small town
where everybody blows their car horns and waves like they haven't seen
you for years even though you just chatted about all the rain, snow, wind,
while shopping at Wal-Mart, and everybody stops to let you
into the stream of traffic even though there are no other cars anywhere,
and everybody knew, knew all about my cousin, except her husband,
and nobody could tell him because everybody preferred to mind
their own business, everybody living the art of the choked heart

6

About his autobiography Barthes (1977) understands how "this book is not a book of 'confessions'; not that it is insincere, but because we have a different knowledge today than yesterday; such knowledge can be summarized as follows: What I write about myself is never *the last word*" (p. 120). And so I continue to write poetry, as I have for at least three decades, always searching and researching the mysterious messiness of living and loving experiences with a backwards glance that might seem nostalgic but is really steeped in an ironic anticipation that the past is no more recoverable than I can scoop up a Pacific wave crashing on the coast and return it to the centre of the ocean. Ormsby (2002) knows that "the past is continually changing and revising itself even as—perhaps because—you are trying to recover it. I came to realize that not even the past was set forever, and this realization was at once painful and liberating" (p. 206). So, any confessions, any memories, any truths that I write in my poetry are always partial, malleable, and incomplete.

Bare Buff

at the end of another busy semester, eager to avoid
still another day's endless torrential torment of e-mail,
I drove fast from campus, and parked at Spanish Banks,
to breathe the surprise clear blue sky of early December,
chilled by English Bay and Coast Mountain shadows,
to stroll the beach and hold my spirit close, the way
poets like to, need to, must, a brief sabbath,
an inspiriting respite, before returning to the mud
and drudge of the associate deans' unmemorable memos
and specious spam promises of gargantuan penises

but soon regretted my poet's fancy, wished only
I had stayed with the harping safety of e-mail, since
a thief smashed the car and stole my satchel, notes
for essays and poems, a few books, my favorite fountain
pen, my diary, where for months I had written another life,
the Walter Mitty dreams I lived in my head and heart,
the confused concatenation of Scorpio sun and Pisces moon,
the story behind the mask presented daily to the world,
the diary where words failed me less often, perhaps because
I was not writing for peer review publication prizes pride

no diary for public presentation or perusal, a writer's diary,
a place for gathering words like pieces of the world's puzzle,
flotsam washed up on the shore of a desert island, fragments
of the omnipresent fiction that manufactures more discontent
than consent, and for months I wrote nothing more, only hoped
my diary was in a Smithrite, still dreamed the thief reading it
late at night by candlelight, savoring the voyeur's romance,
and waited for a phone call with a dire message of blackmail,
looked for the diary published anonymously in *True Confessions*,
scrutinized the romantic want ads for invitations to rendezvous

till in spring the police found my satchel on a tree stump
in Pacific Spirit Park, notes, books, fountain pen, everything
except the diary, and I woke up in Richmond Shopping Centre
on a Saturday, naked, like old Adam, without fear, now write only
truth in my diary and poems, and expect, even hope, others will read
my words, full of desire for the catharsis of confession, the revelry
of revelation, the apocalypse of admission, the dalliance of disclosure,
like Salome's head-twisting striptease of a thousand veils, I am
bare buff, but like Lady Godiva I can still let down my hair,
dreaming the thief dreaming me, Heathcliff on a blustery bluff

In his memoir *There Is a Season* (2004), a lyrical book of wise longing, Lane asks, "What is love that I should fear it?" (p. 210) He adds: "I can ask myself when I was first afraid of love and go back to my childhood and find there stories enough to illustrate my fear" (p. 210). Near the end of his memoir he writes, "If I have learned anything…, it is that everything is built upon the pediment of love. There is nothing else" (p. 295). If there is anything else, I certainly do not know what it is.

U-Haul Truck

I'm stretched out on my daughter's
Serta Perfect Sleeper,
propped up with a million feather pillows,
late afternoon, the day after Thanksgiving.

Both lazy and queasy, we drink
McDonald's strawberry milkshakes
while watching *Days of Our Lives.*
The big question: can we trust
The National Enquirer?
Will John really die?

I recall how, years ago,
on a sunny Saturday in September
I drove a U-Haul truck
down long congested Granville Street
from our home in Steveston
to Anna's new home in Kitsilano.

Since I was old enough
to rent a truck
I was the designated driver,
a reluctant Loomis courier,
conscripted to deliver
my daughter and her bed
to an apartment where
her boyfriend waited with a grin.

Nick and I heaved
the Brobdingnag bed
into his Lilliputian apartment
where it ate everything
like a voracious Godzilla.

LEGGO

Now I'm lounging on the bed,
the same bed that a few weeks ago
in August I helped carry back
from Kitsilano to Steveston,
to Anna and Nick's new home
(stories need no other compulsion
than the physics of inertia
and hardy hope).

The joyful news of pregnancy
turned on the lathe hit a knot
like mountain mahogany
and the whole apparatus
of fear and prayer
(understood any way
your theology leans),
kicked in with ER urgency,
each completed day of bed rest
spelling one more sturdy yarn
knit into a scarf for winter warmth.

As a father I know only
I never get much right,
just muddle through
the day like Mrs. Dalloway,
the days of our lives always
filled with enough twists
and turns to guarantee
there will be few nights
of certain perfect sleep
even on a Serta.

After more than two decades
of yearning for Marlena
while sparring with the DiMera's,
John will end his contract,
but his fiction is his,
not ours, and lying
on my daughter's bed
drinking another milkshake
while we wait, I know I will
wait as long as I need to,
with a grin or grimace,
while the sand falls
through the hour-glass,

for the U-Haul truck
full of stories I can't control.

8

According to Domanski (2002), "the poem longs for the paradox and the
oxymoron, for the irrational that takes it to a new level of inarticulateness. It longs
for muteness, because out of that silence comes the world itself, anew, spinning on
a word. I place great faith in the failure of language" (p. 254). And Woodruff
(2001) claims that "irony is silence twisted into words that provoke and do not
satisfy. Like pure silence, irony shows awe at subject matter that cannot easily be
tamed" (p. 189). Like Domanski and Woodruff, I am drawn to silence with its wild
rhythms that drum in my body like a summons to court or courting.

The Syntax of Silence

*

some days I talk too much
like I often eat too much,
fending off the terror of silence
like car wrecks on a long lost lonely highway
in a March snowstorm

*

since I have no language
for silence, how can I utter
a poem about silence?

*

why are some letters written
but not pronounced: silent letters?
is a silent letter a vestigial organ
like an appendix or tonsils
serving no purpose except
to confound spellers,
a disreputable cousin lurking
in shadows, not invited
to the party, an eccentric uncle
nobody acknowledges, nobody
can forget, known only in the writing,
unknown in the speaking,
seen and not heard

LEGGO

a sonnet of silence?
is a letter ever silent?

*

because language begins
in silence and ends in silence,
there is no language without silence

*

silence is a Gregorian chant,
one more language
I do not know
like Latin or Sanskrit

*

silence convenes the alphabet,
lexicon, syntax, speech, writing,
and signification, to spell language

*

silence designates spaces
for dynamic meaning-making,
revelation and concealment,
disseminating significance

silence divides discourse,
the seamless web of textuality,
like a December blizzard blows
boisterous waves into the harbor

*

sometimes silence
is born out of fear,
submission, resignation,
oppression, convention,
avoidance, rejection,
censorship, ignorance

*

silence is the unarticulated,
the unspoken, the unwritten
that cannot be articulated,
spoken, or written but

silence is not inarticulate

*

silence tastes like Demerara molasses,
Good Luck margarine, my mother's
homemade bread in long winter afternoons,
the mouth full with soft sweet steam

*

like an E-bay auction
most talk is valuable since
somebody somewhere wants it,
but I cannot sell silence

*

silence is both a verb and a noun,
a subject and a predicate:
silence silences

*

silence is the breath of dark
moist rum-soaked fruit cake,
a poet's language
I am trying always
to hear, to learn:
no light without shadows
no shadows without light,
    always one

*

Job sat in the ashes
scraping his leprous flesh,
totally puzzled by God,
and Job's friends,
Eliphaz, Bildad, and Zophar,
sat with him

for seven days and seven nights
in sympathetic silence,
but eventually insisted
on explaining Job's predicament:
if only they'd remained silent

*

still silent, silent in stillness
silence suffices, sufficiency of silence
satisfying silence, silent satisfaction
silent suggestion, suggestive silence
silent scene, seen silence
silent stirring, stirring silence

*

John Cage performed
his composition *4'33"*
by walking on the stage
and sitting at the piano
    in silence
for four minutes
and thirty-three seconds

many call it Cage's masterpiece

*

as a student in elementary school
I learned silence,
learned to sit patiently,
learned to pretend listening,
learned to speak the sanctioned answers only,
learned silence well,
too well, a well of silence,
almost drowned in the well

*

have I ever known silence?
what do I hear even in this quiet room?
refrigerator, clock, furnace, laptop, water in pipes.
body gurgles, cracks, squishes.
the glossolalia of ghosts and spirits, conscience

and memory, the unconscious and imagination.
is silence ever silent?

*

are silence and utterance inextricably related,
two manifestations of language, diastole and systole,
like two pistons in an Acadia double-cylinder engine,
    pumping with the immutable rhythm:
    PUT put PUT put PUT put PUT put

*

be silent.
being silent.
what is the difference?

*

am I one of the silenced
or one of the silencers?

*

a discourse
sanctions some statements
and
excludes some statements

and subsequently silences
the sinuous and sensuous possibilities
of shifting shapes in sentences

*

silence falls like December snow,
full of surprises seen finally in the window

*

whole books
have been written
about silence.

why does silence
generate so much
noisy discussion?

9

Evans (2003) reminds us that "we do not love, or look for love, in a world of our own" (p. 142). And here lies the challenge in autobiographical writing. We begin from the perspective of *I*, but this *I* is never isolate and alone. Each of us, wrapped up in the seemingly singular identity of an autonomous *I*, is really always connected to others. Sorting out those connections occupies our whole lives.

Yo-Yo

I & you
the two most used
words in English

full of Buber's
tensile tension

in Spanish
I is *yo*
you is *tú*

I-you you-I I-I you-you yo-yo

yo-tú tú-yo yo-yo tú-tú I-I

I know you
you know me

the stranger within
the stranger without

all connected on a string
that knows the limits
of gravity, or at least
its seductive attraction

the constant challenge
of yo-yo tangles

common and idiosyncratic
DNA, in the mirror,
the conjunction AND

everything, all of us
entwined like vines

10

Barthes (1977) claims that "one might call 'poetic' (without value judgment) any discourse in which the word leads the idea: if you like words to the point of succumbing to them, you exclude yourself from the law of the signified" (p. 152). Always as a poet, I am enamored with words. I live with an agnostic's spirit, with the conviction that I do not know much and will never know much, with the abiding trust that that is still a lot to know. So, I attend to words. Like Avison (2002) I regard my readers as "the completers of what the text began. I address them as co-creators" (p. 162) because "a poem is that form of art in words that requires from the reader the same creative energy as from the writer" (p. 162). In poetic inquiry I am not trying to be clear, coherent, and comprehensible. Instead, I seek to shake up the notion of conventional as conservative, constrained, and contained by returning to the etymology of the Latin *convenire*: *to call together*. Poets call to one another, a chorus of voices, calling out, calling together, seeking readers and writers to join in the co-creation of texts that are alive in the world.

Yoke

how would my life
be different

  if

when Jesus said,
Take my yoke upon you,

I had heard,
Take my joke upon you?

I take words in the world
too literally.

like Yogi Ramacharaka
I need to learn
the science of breath

to breathe silence
the way words sing
in the spaces between
signs of the alphabet

how yug, yogi, yoke
are all joined
like a celestial joke
that pokes holes in the charades
of fakirs, mountebanks, and sleveens.

a wisdom-seeker takes up
the philosophy that yokes
jokes with the breadth
of life's breath, nothing less.

11

In my poetry I write love lovingly, full of love, longing for love, even the long love story that can break the heart, at least the empty hollow of silence that holds it tight and taut in rhythms of noisy, even hallowed, silence. Like Barthes (1977) knows, "one writes with one's desire, and I am not through desiring" (p. 188). But I also attend to the wisdom of Evans (2003) who understands that "we have acquired— for various reasons—an expectation that as individuals we can achieve states of perfect harmony with particular others: that we can return to the pre-Oedipal ideal of the infant's bliss of absolute identity with another and unequivocal love from that person" (p. 102). While not denying the hearty pleasures of wild inloveness, I am also acknowledging how many of my living love stories have been fictions that have erupted in factions. I searched for the integer and fell on the fraction. Now, I understand with Evans that I have been caught up "in a social world awash with deadly cocktails of romance, hedonism and personal entitlement" (p. 143). Love is always more. And like the narrator understands in McEwan's (1997) novel *Enduring Love*, "when it's gone you'll know what a gift love was" (p. 112).

Forget-me-nots
(for Lana, February 14, 2006)

Long ago and faraway, on a July morning
chilly with North Atlantic gusts,
we ran along the shore of the Humber Arm
on the gravel shoulder of the harbor arterial.
Giant trucks boomed their loads
of spruce and fir logs to the mill,
blew our caps off, left us scrambling in a wreckage
of words tossed in the wind

and you asked, as you sometimes do,
sometimes persist, why did you return?

The question clung in the air,
still, after so many years,

like light blue forget-me-nots clinging
in the crevices of the rock and gravel gully
off the highway's edge, like a faint memory
of a meadow, wildflowers beyond counting.

But this poem is no bunch of forget-me-nots
grabbed from the gully in a frantic effort
to appease you for my forgetting
too many Valentine's Days and love's just hopes.

I returned (at best, any explanation
will be an agnostic's confession, tangled in a network
of lines and tight knots that can't be traced,
a rhizome with no beginning, no closure)
like a salmon, compelled by a heart memory
of home and hope alone, knowing how I would never
write a new poem without you.

Siren-like, I was seduced by my own fictions,
mesmerized by my own myths, another Othello obsessed
with his storied image in Desdemona's eyes...
ordinary exploits rendered extraordinary in the rapt telling,
Desdemona swooning until old Othello
saw only an O in her heart through which he aimed
to jump to unknown places he had to know,
a last frontier irresistible to his imagination.

True love is the story of long love, not lost love.
C. S. Lewis (who knew more about love than most)
told Sheldon Vanauken that love always dies
and even your wife's death is a severe mercy
since now your love will never die,
hogwash Lewis couldn't believe a few years later
as his own wife lay dying.

We weave the warp and weft of words and lines
like threads, attentive in the small rhythms
of each day's seamless simplicity, knowing in our blood,
tensions and directions that render a sturdy lace
that provides tender warmth in a North Atlantic storm,

like a Valentine's Day bouquet
    of forget-you-nots,
        steeped in love's light.

12

Barthes (1997) notes that "my texts are disjointed, no one of them caps any other; the latter is nothing but a *further* text, the last of the series, not the ultimate in meaning: *text upon text*, which never illuminates anything" (p. 120). I mostly agree with Barthes, but I think he overstates the case with his claim that his writing "never illuminates anything." I prefer Zwicky's (2004) observation in her poem "Night Driving":

> Our headlights
> scoop a tunnel in the dark,
> and we drive into it.
> (p. 70)

Like Zwicky's headlights, in my writing I am always seeking to find a way by writing a way.

Scratches

I write a lot of words
 speak a lot of words
  think a lot of words
   read a lot of words
    live a lot of words

But why do I want
to turn all my words
into poems, compelled by
the hope you want them?

Surely the poet's calling
is to choose the best words,
to grade, evaluate, assay every essay,
be parsimonious, ruthless even
with the proliferation of words
like randy rabbits in a meadow.

I know I can write copious words.
I once timed myself (three minutes),
while two hundred and twenty-two
words spilled on the page with a taunt
to imagine the mountain of words
I could scramble in a year.

Reading at an average rate
of three hundred words per minute,
I would need hours to read

all the words I had written.
I would never sleep, possessed
by words clamoring for attention.

Faced with the choice of writing
more words or reading more words,
ripped apart by words' frenzy,
I would not serve words
or you or me well.

So, because I need to be stingy,
I have just scratched
out the words in my journal,
and there will be no poem
made with those words,
unless, of course, you count
this poem about scratching
out the words and not writing a poem.

I live a lot of words
  read a lot of words
    think a lot of words
      speak a lot of words
        write a lot of words

So, drawing to a close, with a final fringe, unraveling in reveling, these words are all part of a daily process of living and loving, living love stories amidst the fissures, fragments, and fringes. Evans (2003) reminds us that "love demands time and effort. Romance has always been easier to acquire, in that for the past 200 years we have been able either to buy it or to use its manufactured form. But love in any relationship (between adults, friends, parents and children) takes considerably more application" (p. 142). Poetry should not be confused with a fatuous fascination with infatuation. Page (2002) thinks poetry, at its best, is "a holy thing" (p. 27) that "could save the world" (p. 28). Like love, poetry demands time and effort—nothing less than a lifetime of faithful commitment to being and becoming in words, being and becoming as a human and humane enterprise, full of more hope than any of our imaginations will ever hold.

REFERENCES

Avison, M Avison, M. (2002). The quiet centre inside. In T. Bowling (Ed.), *Where the words come from: Canadian poets in conversation* (pp. 159–173). Roberts Creek, BC: Nightwood Editions.

Domanski, D. (2002). The wisdom of falling. In T. Bowling (Ed.), *Where the words come from: Canadian poets in conversation* (pp. 244–255). Roberts Creek, BC: Nightwood Editions.

Calvino, I. (1995). *Six memos for the next millennium.* Toronto: Vintage Canada.

Barthes, R. (1977). *Roland Barthes* (R. Howard, Trans.). Berkeley, CA: University of California Press.

Berry, W. (1990). *What are people for?: Essays*. New York: North Point Press.

Evans, M. (2003). *Love: An unromantic discussion*. Cambridge: Polity Press.

Frank, A. (2000). In F. Franck, J. Roze, & R. Connolly (Eds.), *What does it mean to be human?* (pp. 231–236). New York: St. Martin's Press.

Freire, P. (1985). *The politics of education: Culture, power, and liberation* (D. Macedo, Trans.). South Hadley: Bergin and Garvey.

hooks, b. (2000). *All about love: New visions*. New York: William Morrow.

Lane, P. (2004). *There is a season: A memoir*. Toronto: McClelland & Stewart.

McEwan, I. (1997). *Enduring love*. Toronto: Vintage Canada.

Oliver, M. (2008). *Red bird*. Boston: Beacon Press.

Ormsby, E. (2002). Going down to where the roots begin. In T. Bowling (Ed.), *Where the words come from: Canadian poets in conversation* (pp. 196–212). Roberts Creek, BC: Nightwood Editions.

Page, P. K. (2002). Looking at the world through topaz. In T. Bowling (Ed.), *Where the words come from: Canadian poets in conversation* (pp. 11–30). Roberts Creek, BC: Nightwood Editions.

Woodruff, P. (2001). *Reverence: Renewing a forgotten virtue*. Oxford: Oxford University Press.

Carl Leggo
Department of Language and Literacy Education
University of British Columbia
Canada

IVAN BRADY

NO DEATH TODAY

Sun trails plant futures
        In the late afternoon

Antelopes bounce & spin
                Collapse on each other
                Then kick up again
                        In lazy chases

Rabbits scurry & wait
                Stretch their legs
                        & bathe

One old coyote laments
                The passing of sharp
                Into blunt
                        Or missing teeth

Vultures arc in the fading light
                Feasting best on the dead
                The valley floor on this day
                        Has been too lively

Nothing has stopped hopping
                Climbing
                        Or crawling
Or singing

Evening buzzes
        Moon spreads
                Women whisper

                No death today
        Maybe tomorrow
                Will bring more food

M. Prendergast, C. Leggo and P. Sameshima (eds.), *Poetic Inquiry: Vibrant Voices in the Social Sciences*, 169–170.

Ivan Brady
Distinguished Teaching Professor Emeritus
State University of New York
Oswego, USA

KIMBERLY DARK

EXAMINING PRAISE FROM THE AUDIENCE

What Does It Mean to Be a "Successful" Poet-researcher?

My Son Is a Straight A Student

My son is a straight A student, and I would like him to quit school.
I am afraid of what he is not learning while he is getting an education.
I am afraid he is not learning that August is good for more than laying on the sofa
being glad he's not in school.
I am afraid that he is not learning that travelling and interacting with people who
are different from him, is a great way to know himself.
I am afraid he is not learning what he likes and dislikes
and what ten a.m. and two p.m. really look like, smell like, feel like,
when he's actually in his own body, his own mind,
without the mind wound so tight that it might...

BUZZ!

Now it's time to do math!

BUZZ!

Take out your books and read!

BUZZ!

Eat lunch!
But what if I'm not hungry?
We have to eat lunch now before the next lunch shift takes over this space...

Where is the space to breathe? And feel, and discover?
What would you like to learn?
What would you love to do, right now?

My son is a straight A student and I would love it if he decided to quit school.
I'm afraid of what he is learning while he's trying to get an education.
Not just because there might be

*M. Prendergast, C. Leggo and P. Sameshima (eds.), Poetic Inquiry: Vibrant Voices
in the Social Sciences, 171–185.*

drugs at school or
guns at school or
apathetic teachers or
shabby books or
bad cafeteria food.

I am afraid of what he is learning when things go right:
that punishment for non-conformity is just
that the rewards for a job well-done must come from someone other than himself—
someone with a title, a credential, an authority to say he is good or bad.
I am afraid of what he is learning when things are simply the way things are:
that hierarchy is the way of the world
and we must submit to sorting by age and
ability and
numeric score and
neighborhood and
gender and
race.

No! Scratch that!
Never by race!
Say it with me!
We do not educate children based on race in America.
We do not educate children based on race in America.
Say it with me until you believe it.
Close your eyes and say it with me.

This is what it looks like for things to go right in school.
And I am worried that he is learning to wind his mind like a clock
And that the clock-maker is tooling with his mind so that it is synchronized to the
specific purpose of:
getting a job and
keeping the boss happy and
working well with others, no matter the task and
waking up on time, at the same time, every day as soon as the alarm clock goes.

BUZZ!

Put away your books!

BUZZ!

Put down your pencils!

BUZZ!

Hurry up, you're going to be late for the next class!
But what if I'm in the middle of writing a poem?
The bell rang.
But I'm in the middle of writing...
Didn't you hear the bell?
But I'm in the middle...
Don't you know what the bell means?

I'm worried that my son is learning that although all of this feels terribly wrong, what we do about it is...
Nothing.
Because we've learned that it's easier, more rewarding, to let someone else be in charge.

My son is a straight A student and when his father said:
"Learn without school? He's too lazy to remember to feed his dog and take out the trash!"
I just wanted to cry.
And I thought about a story I heard about a slave owner describing a slave's defiance at following directions to do simple tasks as though it proved that the slave was inferior of intellect and will and needed a tight reign in order to be a functioning, contributing member of...

of a slave household.

Sure, I want my kid to take out the garbage promptly and cheerfully the first time I ask,
But God bless the spirit of rebellion
against order imposed from anywhere but his own heart.

My son is a straight A student, and I think he's learned enough in school already.

SOME DEFINITIONS AND CRITERIA

Who reads poetry anymore? Who reads research? Well, poets and researchers certainly, but being a success among one's peers is not the focus of this paper. This paper is concerned with audience—and the kind of populist poetic research that can have a broader reach than either poetry or research can have as separate efforts.

At this juncture in the development of western culture, few people read or listen to poetry for the love of it—for its relevance to their lives. Populist performance poetry is an exception, and even its consumption is not mainstream or widespread. The values of writing poetry for oneself—especially based on, or adjunct to social research are multiple and varied. Those will not be explored here. This paper examines my experiences with two types of audience for poetry-research (either written or performed, though in my case, mostly performed). These two audiences are college and university students (referred to here as either "students in my course" or "student audiences" to discern my relationship to them) and general audience members—people who attend public performances at theaters, poetry events, festivals, etc.

I'm fond of sociologist Laurel Richardson's guidelines for CAP (Creative Analytic Practices) (2000) as a way to articulate some "high and difficult" standards. These are the five criteria that she uses when reviewing papers or monographs submitted for social scientific publication:

- *Substantive contribution*: Does this piece contribute to our understanding of social life? Does the writer demonstrate a deeply grounded (if embedded) social scientific perspective? How has this perspective informed the construction of the text?
- *Aesthetic merit*: Rather than reducing standards, CAP ethnography adds another standard. Does this piece succeed aesthetically? Does the use of creative analytic practices open up the text, invite interpretative responses? Is the text artistically shaped, satisfying, complex, and not boring?
- *Reflexivity:* Is the author cognizant of the epistemology of postmodernism? How did the author come to write this text? How was the information gathered? Are there ethical issues? How has the author's subjectivity been both a producer and a product of this text? Is there adequate self-awareness and self-exposure for the reader to make judgments about the point of view? Does the author hold him- or her-self accountable to the standards of knowing and telling of the people he or she has studied?
- *Impact*: Does this affect me? Emotionally? Intellectually? Does it generate new questions? Move me to write? Move me to try new research practices? Move me to action?
- *Expression of a reality*: Does this text embody a fleshed out, embodied sense of lived experience? Does it seem "true"—a credible account of a cultural, social, individual, or communal sense of the "real"?

As Richardson points out, "mere novelty does not suffice." And yet, social scientists often spend so much time defending creative acts, based on criteria one through three, that we neglect to investigate the nuances of criteria four and five, from an audience perspective. That's what I aim to do here.

As I focus on these last two of Richardson's criteria, I'd also like to make a specific distinction between poetry having a positive effect ("I really liked that poem") and having the effect of motivating or inspiring action. Aesthetically and personally, it's lovely when a reader/listener likes my work. It's good to know that my love poem "touched" someone, for example, but as a poet-researcher, that is not enough. I want to know that the poetic representation of social themes and data has conveyed something of motivational substance. I want to know that my themes have been deeply heard in whatever way the audience "hears" best. In social science, I fear, we have lost track of the audience in favor of the substance, rigor and credibility of our arguments. These are important—at least, I've been taught to believe they're important—but for a moment, let's suspend the notion that they are *most* important in order to remember that the reason we are conveying anything is because we want it to be heard. We want the message to take effect.

For the sake of discussion here, I'm referring to social science as poetry in three forms. First, texts can be created from autoethnographic data, that is, information regarding a social circumstance that has been filtered through the experience of the "I." Often, this information is gathered through a process of systematic introspection (Ellis, 2000). The "systematic" part may or may not have to do with how one mines one's experiences for data, but it certainly comes into play as one crafts a story about culture, rather than a story solely about self. A second form of social science as poetry involves the use of ethnographic field notes and interviews to create poetry directly, or to create layered accounts, which include the researcher's views and experiences as well. The third form of social science as poetry involves writing poetry that serves as social commentary—that which brings a social science perspective to a poem or story. This poem may or may not include any form of research, but the echoes of training and work in the social sciences can be heard in the background of the text. My work uses all three, but primarily relies on the first form: autoethnographic writing.

Students and audience members take what they will from poetry. This is perhaps part of the traditional researcher's fear. The message is not explicit and cannot be controlled. What the traditional researcher hides from himself or herself, I feel, is the knowledge that the writer can never fully control the message. Academia, as a field with its own professional culture, values an ability to control as much of a message as possible. One function of peer review and revision processes is to avert any unintended meaning and to tightly control the reader's perception of the author's awareness. We try to show that we are aware of as many of the nuances and counterarguments for a topic as possible. We seek to become expert. With the poem, expertise is reduced along with language. The poet is not all knowing, or if s/he is, s/he cannot be all expressing! A post-structuralist view on poetry, research and audience may be useful here. Language, method, power and subjectivity are linked; perhaps more so in poetry—the briefest language-based medium—than any other form of writing.

DIFFERENT TYPES OF AUDIENCE

My work with colleges and universities is two-fold. In one role, I am a sociology professor. I teach courses related to gender and education topically, and I teach about "doing" sociology—qualitative research methods and sociological advocacy. I incorporate poetry and performance into all of my courses. I use a variety of voices and texts, including my own. The other capacity in which I interact with college and university students is as a visiting performer, guest lecturer and workshop leader. I do dozens of college shows per year in North America, Ireland and the UK. In this capacity, my main themes are gender, sexuality and women's lives (encompassing a variety of topics). Students are audience members, albeit a slightly different type of audience member than attend community venues.

In another capacity, I am an entertainer. I perform for general audiences at community theaters, arts festivals and poetry venues such as bookstores, poetry slams and performance poetry events. In these venues, my background in sociology is rarely known, or if it is known, it's engaged as mere novelty. I've been described in reviews as "a sociologist of sorts." Just recently, an interviewer with the *Salt Lake Tribune* phrased a question this way: "So, I've heard you're something of an amateur sociologist. Explain how that works." (There is a certain absurdity in being called an amateur sociologist when most people don't even know what a "professional" sociologist does, other than teach at the university.) This type of question reveals the disregard or even disdain for academic training that I've often felt as a performer. Depending on the venue, I sometimes choose not to mention an academic background because academics can be perceived as dull and uninteresting. General audiences can sometimes fear an academic-poet. My credentials as an activist, populist poet come from Richardson's Criteria Five, above—my ability to connect—to create a grounded account that "feels real" to audience members. I co-create a relationship in which the audience wants to dwell with me for a time; there is nothing but their own fascination and interest keeping them with me. There is no grade to be earned, no peers to impress with their subject-related tenacity.

I receive communication from these two audiences in three different ways, and this communication forms the data I will use to discuss the audience's perceptions of my success, below. First, both students and audience members have access to me via my website, email and My Space and they often write to express gratitude, share stories, challenge ideas or ask questions. Second, I have occasional access to student reflection papers required by various professors whose students have viewed my performances. This happens informally and infrequently – usually because I have a personal friendship with a particular professor who requests that students allow me to use their reflections for my website and for papers such as this. These responses are a rich source for this discussion on the success of poetry-research. My own students provide a third source of data on this theme. In topic-specific courses students have an opportunity to comment on the content of poems. In courses where I teach students the how-to of sociology, students reflect on both topic and medium. I will quote anonymously from each of these correspondences in the following discussion on student and audience response.

HOW POETRY COMPELS

Tidily, we can see poetry-research through a post-structuralist lens and call down the banners of positivist thinking in the process. From the stance of a feminist, post-modernist, inductive researcher there is much to be railed against in traditional sociological research, and in the traditional methods of conveying that research. But do I seem defensive of this fringe activity I have undertaken? It's possible that's how a paper like this comes off. I see through a different lens and I will explain my vision in a traditional tone and legitimacy—and at least a modicum of legitimacy will be mine. I worry that this isn't good enough. By building my fortress of credibility in a paper such as this, am I perhaps 'selling out' the accessibility and mystery that are so important to me in poetry and performance? As my experiences and studies in this genre grow, it seems all the more clear that traditional academic texts, indeed, most traditional academic processes, are not as "natural" as they seem. As with many dominant social processes and identities, they have become invisible, merely seen as "right." They have actually been so well defended into legitimacy that they go unquestioned. Poetry itself challenges not only what we're saying and how we're saying it, but actually, how we think and what we do, the linear processes we follow and the ways in which academic thinking in the social sciences may not be compatible with the more basic forms of human knowing.

As one example, much is known about rhythm and our bodies' tendency toward entrainment—or mutual phase locking, as physicists would call it. This is the tendency for two things that vibrate to begin vibrating at the same interval. Just as two pendulum clocks standing next to one another, two people communicating with one another will begin to experience entrainment. The two clock pendulums, even if swinging opposite to one another at first, will eventually come to swing together. The human version of this is one of the reasons that communication—even performance—is dynamic. The listener affects the speaker and vice-versa. Intersubjectivity is mutual and there is an ever-moving process happening in our bodies, not just in our mental meaning-making. Poetry, the most rhythmic form of writing which contains the most breath-pauses in performance, inspires an intense inter-subjectivity. The breath and word exchange between the audience and performer help to create the meaning being conveyed. I have been amazed at how audiences can stay on-topic with me in emotionally challenging stories. More impressive still is that, when they discuss the work, they extend my thinking far more readily than will audiences when I am using a traditional lecture format.

There are many ways that human bodies entrain when in close proximity and this is one aspect of performance poetry that is so important. It's true for any form of communication where the parties are physically present together, too, but even more so, if the words form rhythmic patterns. The body likes rhythm! And in written and verbal communication, poetry is the pinnacle of rhythm. That enjoyment is not incidental. It has a positive effect on our ability to stay with a speaker in order to find the message. We find it hard to listen to mumbling and pick out information exactly because it lacks rhythm. And most academic writing and the speech patterns used at academic conferences are, literally, mumbling. By dictionary definition, mumbling is speech that contains a number of unstressed syllables. It's hard to follow—biologically, the human mind and body doesn't like it. And this is what we've institutionalized as a standard medium for higher thought! It has become laudable for a student to suppress a potentially natural inclination for joy in communication in favor of learning how to discern meaning from mumbling, passive voice, and long sentences comprised of lengthy words. (Re-read this last sentence as an example, if my message is still unclear.)

Meter, of course, is the business of poetry, but all speech has rhythm, even when it's not specifically organized in, say, iambic pentameter. My poetry is primarily free verse—without meter—but not without rhythm. (Performance—use of the body and voice—adds an additional layer to rhythm, too.) Well-written prose is often accented prose—it contains many syllable stresses, thus making it pleasing to the ear. The author Ursula Le Guin has done some interesting studies on the use of rhythm in prose. Her book, *The Wave in the Mind* (2004) is worth reading for these discussions. In my own case, I didn't start writing poetry because of rhythm. Writing poetry simply feels organic to me. But I do aim to notice the effects of rhythmic writing and performance. I have often seen audience members move as they listen to my poetry. Once in particular, during questions and answers after a reading where the audience included children, someone asked if the children always moved that way when I read. I hadn't noticed what he called their "swaying with the rhythm of my voice," but I certainly began to notice it after that. And it's not just me as a person—something about the soothing nature of my voice. People move differently as they listen *to me*, when I'm lecturing in class vs. reading a poem or doing a performance.

If we're interested in academic messages being received well, integrated by the learner, then poetry and performance make good sense. Academic and technical writing (and the learned ways of speech associated with them) have the fewest syllable stresses among writing styles (LeGuin, 2004). The inclusion of long words and longer, more unwieldy sentence structures create a lack of stress and rhythm. And we work hard to learn how to do this because the current norm is that it gives us, our thinking and our research, credibility. When it comes to discussing the medium through which my research is conveyed, I try not to think of myself as bitterly defending entertainment as science. Rather, I seek to reveal certain social scientific views and practices as outdated, bitter defenses of a reductionism that really isn't natural or optimal and is not well supported across disciplines.

PATTERNS IN STUDENT AND AUDIENCE RESPONSE

The reader should note that I don't hear from the majority of audience members and that students may be influenced by their desire to please their professor with their remarks (whether or not that professor is me). Patterns are instructive, however, even though the data is incomplete. This incompleteness itself is part of why I've focused on claims of success. I have enough of them to begin to discern patterns. For those from whom I don't hear, my poetry may or may not have an inspirational effect, as described by Richardson's criteria. I simply don't know. The reader should also note that most audience members and students who react negatively to my work, thus far, do so verbally, not in writing. This makes it harder to discuss the comments in a paper like this. Disengagement is difficult to discern when no words are offered, but I do occasionally see discomfort among audience members. At times, men have expressed discomfort hearing feminist perspectives on sexism. At times, women have expressed feeling vulnerable. The following post-show comment from one woman sums up this vulnerability. As she left the theatre, her eyes were downcast. She raised her eyes just long enough to say, with a slightly angry tone, "You sure revealed us alright!"

The responses in the next few pages, then, are primarily positive. Though I regret that all of it focuses on my own work (because of the danger of sounding self-congratulatory), this is the only data available to me thus far. And, it speaks effectively to the topic at hand: what does it mean to be a successful poet-researcher—what is the impact of this type of work? This data falls into four categories of response from the three types of audience members (students in my courses, student audience members and general audience members). Audiences comment on:

- audience engagement with poetry—rhythm, cadence and relationship;
- the ability of the poetry to transport the reader/listener to a specific location where a social story unfolds, thus enhancing their ability to understand specific social circumstances;
- how the poetry has prompted specific action in their personal lives;
- how the poetry prompts their deeper analysis of social issues and potential action toward social change.

Audience Engagement

All three audience groups commented on the ways in which my performance poetry was engaging to them. In the case of my own students, they were asked to comment on this theme. Specifically, how does research as poetry engage the audience? It's useful to note that, even when not prompted, audience members (both student and general) often comment on this too. This male student audience member observed:

Normally, when a speaker comes into a class, people would be either half asleep or bored out of their mind within the first 15 minutes of their presentation without remembering a word they said, but with Kimberly, she had the attention of the audience from start to finish, she never let down the intensity.

A female student, in one of my courses, commented on the accessibility of the writing in terms of educational background—alluding to the fact that much academic writing alienates those who are not college-educated:

This writing is incredibly easy to read; meaning a person from any educational background could read and understand it. In addition, the majority of people have had some experience with the American school system and therefore the writing is very relatable. The text is artistically shaped; I found it easy to read and understand.

She also commented on how the topic (re. "My Son Is a Straight A Student") is one that many can relate to when accessible, as in the poetic format. Another female student in my course, commenting on the same poem, noted how the poetic format enhanced understanding. "The cadence of the writing leads the reader into the piece and engages the mind."

Some students and audience members commented on the immediate and personal nature of performance poetry. Audience members connect with me as an individual through something they repeatedly identify as "voice."

What a joy to hear humor from a woman's perspective—I laughed and cried and felt affirmed and entertained—I now know what's missing from mainstream media— a woman's voice— my voice—Thank You!

In this case, the audience member spoke of the way she perceived the poetry as relevant to her experience and viewpoint. She also took this a step further in realizing that it's literally HER voice that's missing in the mainstream media.

Another general audience member commented on my "real-ness"—a sense important to forming connection in this way:

> *More men and women need to know these things! It's shocking that you are really real and say the things nobody else is saying or can even admit that they are thinking!*

These two students in my courses provided commentary on the poetry they had read with regard to how it can "touch deeply" while avoiding "preaching." This first female student related a personal experience with the poem "It's After 5" (available as a free download at www.kimberlydark.com):

> *After reading the first poem about the young girl in the bathroom, I was frozen. How could this type of qualitative writing not be effective? It struck me deeper than anything we have read... This poem I believe would touch more readers on the topic of rape than a research paper with numbers would.*

The second female student also commented on audience and successful advocacy as the potential of this type of poetry:

> *I can see how they would be an effective advocacy tool. For one, they have the ability to subtly reach an audience and convey a message without seeming like hardcore, preachy advocacy. They can also reach an audience that may support or be open to advocacy, but not actively seek out advocacy forums (due to time or interests). Finally, for me, they bring an even more personal, human touch to the message they are giving. The one aspect that I thought could be tough though is finding that fine balance between making the message too overt or too subtle, too complex or too simple, too personal or too generic, too literal versus too abstract. I thought both of the poems we read found that balance beautifully. Engaging the reader, making them a part of the story and guiding them along, engaging, questioning, probing, while also leading, informing and presenting the poet's views.*

This student grasped many of the aspects of research-poetry that I find challenging She articulated the fact that the poem was indeed advocating for a position, revealing a viewpoint, but that the guidance was gentle. Finally, another female general audience member commented on performance poetry in a way that recognizes the value of personal presence, but also begins to comment on the value of detail and imagery in conveying a message:

> *You watch your audience...You use ideas and images as crowbars to pry open minds, stir blood. Watching you perform is akin to watching a Super Nova—with a great deal of poise.*

Location/Experience-based Understanding

As the last quote illustrates, students and general audience members often comment on the poetic devices I use, the value of poems having a strong sense of place and feeling. This also makes the voice of the poetry feel "real" and in some cases generalizable, as this female student audience member commented regarding "My Son is a Straight A Student":

> *This writing seems incredibly real. While reading it I felt as though it had been written by a distraught mother who was questioning the current curriculum her son is taught under... Her language describes one mother's feelings, although this mother's thoughts could represent that of many others.*

Both general audience members and students commented on the poem's ability to leave decisions open to the reader/listener—to present, rather than prompt for response. This male student audience member said:

> *[Dark] told her story in a meaningful way. She presented her story in an artistic way. She doesn't choose sides to her story. It really leaves you to decide on your behalf. She brought her story through humor, beauty, emotion, pain and happiness and hope that we learn to make the world a better place.... Her storytelling is powerful; it changed the way I view life.*

Location and standpoint created access for these students and a place from which they could make or change their own views. This male student commented on the clarity of my standpoint in a poem as helping him to see social life differently:

> *The performances that Kimberly Dark performed were that of the feminist point of view, the way women might encounter or perceive certain situations. I really enjoyed it because it gave me a better understanding of what women have to deal with... Now being able to realize that, indeed, men have had it easier than women! That we can do so much more unacceptable behavior than women and receive less ridicule for it and that women today have been caught in the media's trap of how a beautiful woman should look. Even though we had read much of what Dr. Dark explained, she gave us a rendition of how it might have occurred in real life which made much of what I read so much clearer.*

This student contrasted the other readings from his course (an introduction to sociology textbook) with the poetic format of my performance, commenting again on engagement.

Students and audience members also commented on the ability of vivid language and metaphor to bring them into a social issue in more meaningful ways. A female student in one of my courses commented on the poem "My Son Is a Straight A Student":

> *The use of vivid words like Buzz, Slave and Alive give the mind pictures of the story. The set up of the information through poems is a wonderful way to share experiences and learn empathy for those experiences. The readings*

181

*were an easy read and the imagery and texture of the words painted the
scene within the mind's eye. I could... hear the rush of time going by every
time I read the word Buzz.*

Another female college student commented on the "sense of place" in poetry and
how this can enhance understanding when she noted, "through this poem I can put
myself in your place to truly understanding the things you're observing."

Motivation Toward Personal Change

Both students and audience members reported on direct forms of personal change
and viewpoint shifts. This female general audience member commented on a poem
called "Effort to Be Liked":

*Especially thought provoking was the skit on being "sweet" and needing
approval. I was really shaken awake on that one! I felt exposed and maybe
I'll be more conscious of being desperate for approval.*

This audience member conveys the theme of that poem nicely and many who have
heard that poem have echoed her sentiments, verbally. Another female student
audience member spoke more generally of her personal shifts:

*Kimberly's presentation deepened my understanding of society a whole lot. I
never really noticed how much of an impact society has on us and how
foolish many of us are to just follow it and never once question it. It's much
easier to just be part of a group than to part yourself from everyone else. I
really enjoyed the presentation.*

What is perhaps most striking here is the way the student enjoyed being unmoored
from her previous social beliefs. Some also commented on the timeliness of the
stories. They felt that my stories had been delivered to them at exactly the time
they were experiencing certain circumstances. This is fascinating to hear over and
over again! Comments such as the following reveal how often women experience
sexual harassment, for example, and just how isolated they feel during these
experiences:

*All the stories that Professor Dark shared were thought provoking and
cleverly written, but when she discussed the tribulations and double
standards of the female species, I was even more amazed. She was able to
word it so precisely: I did not know that it was okay to feel so uncomfortable
by advances and comments, or how to deal with it other than cringe, smile
and walk away. Now I know I have the option of simply telling them to back
off. This story could not have been more suited for me or been presented to
me at a more perfect time, because at the time I was becoming extremely
aggravated and frustrated with the demeaning actions and comments that
were dealt to me on a daily basis. With it I felt a little stronger, and able to
stop such treatment.*

In this case, the student's desire to take personal action was made explicit, as is the case with the next example as well, from a female student:

Ever since Kimberly Dark shared her story [about sexual harassment] I've seen myself in a new perspective. I'm not doing anyone else a favor when I shut myself up and let it pass. I too am a human being and deserve the respect that I give to others. There are many things in our society that we will just let pass us, but there needs to be a call of attention to these things. Whether it's speaking up for the person who is ostracized at work, or speaking up against an unjust act. It's really not that difficult, and it only takes a conscious mind to notice it.

Motivation Toward Social Change

The last quote illustrates the way that activist poetry can help individuals transition from personal change to broader activism. Here, a female audience member commented on the poem "Effort to Be Liked" and the way that she took the topics into broader dialogue with co-workers:

I am so very grateful to have had the opportunity to see you perform. Yesterday I took the opportunity over lunch to discuss the "sweetness" factor with some of my female co-workers. It was an interesting discussion. It seems like something they had all noticed and experienced, but never talked about. The latter being the most disturbing.

A male student commented on the ways that personal choices can affect global circumstances in his analysis of the poem "Who Am I?":

In Kimberly's presentation I really began to think about... poverty. I began to think of ways to not support companies or factors such as Nike or Wal-Mart. I have come up with the conclusion that we can make a difference in what is really happening in other countries on the choices we make as we consume items.

In this final example, a female student in one of my courses explained how she had never thought of poetry as a form of sociological advocacy. She had, however, begun to use poetry as a way to communicate sociological perspectives:

The poems located on your web page really showed a different side unbeknownst to me about advocacy. I have heard lectures and speeches that have moved people, hence why they are sometimes called motivational speakers. Yet, put in the form of a poem, like the one advocating that the schools are really not teaching your child what he REALLY needs to know, was very influential... The use of poetry has been existent all throughout history. Its impact has been great and noted. I guess I just never put it with doing advocacy for the greater good.

This student went on to create a body of poetry about suicide among young Filipina women. Her graduate-level project, including performance poetry, was stunning and left students not only weeping with emotion, but craving further information about immigrant populations and the assimilation of first generation teenagers in America. This was the only student project in the course that used poetry as a method and the only one that garnered this response, though many that semester were well-produced and compelling.

CONCLUSION

Clearly, poetic methods can impact audiences. And, so can other forms of writing and speaking. I would hesitate to say that one way is best, but I know that poetry-research is important and compelling for audiences. It is also often dismissed as mere entertainment. This dismissal, perhaps, says more about those who dismiss this method—their training, standpoint, power and potential gains—than it says about poetry-research, which clearly can compel and move people to action—sometimes surprisingly so. I have experienced how audiences are moved in ways that are deeper than language can convey. There is a mystery in poetry, a discovery, a rhythm, an importance placed on breath and pause that is not so strong in other forms of writing. Research-poetry represents an ability to bring what truly connects people into the forefront while the social critique remains an ever-present backdrop. Rather than asserting the writer's superior knowledge of a topic, the poem can invite the audience in to find meaning and join in a dialogue about the themes found there. The readers/listeners may even take collective action based on the ways their new understanding interacts with their life experiences and social abilities. This form of inspiration to act toward social change is as non-linear as social change itself.

While Richardson's criteria one through three are of concern for social scientists, criteria four and five, regarding impact and a "feeling" of credibility, are far more important to audiences. The consistency of solicited and unsolicited comments on these themes shows that the poems are achieving success with Richardson's criteria. I don't want to diminish the value of the medium by focusing only on the message. There is a danger, in my discussions of impact on the audience and on conveying a message, that I might reduce the value of the performance to the ideas it discusses and the messages it conveys. I do not want this to happen because "success" seems to rely on how inextricably bound meaning and message are in poetry. As Le Guin (2004) says, "to reduce the aesthetic value of a narrative to the ideas it expresses, to its 'meaning' is a drastic impoverishment. The map is not the landscape" (p. 179). We must seek to value the various important aspects of each poem—that is to see it holistically—enjoy it with an unreserved ecstasy, an enlivened mind and a sense of hope that the world can be as we create it. Poetry about social circumstances can be an incantation of sorts; when action is born of both passion and analysis, poetic research has been successful indeed.

REFERENCES

Ellis, C. (2000). Autoethnography, personal narrative, reflexivity. In N. K. Denzin & Y. S. Lincoln (Eds.), *The handbook of qualitative research* (pp. 733–768). Thousand Oaks, CA: Sage.

Le Guin, U. (2004). *The wave in the mind: Talks and essays on the writer, the reader and the imagination.* Boston: Shambhala.

Richardson, L. (2000). Writing: A method of inquiry. In N. K. Denzin & Y. S. Lincoln (Eds.), *The handbook of qualitative research* (pp. 923–948). Thousand Oaks, CA: Sage.

Kimberly Dark
Department of Sociology
California State University
San Marcos, USA

SANDRA L. FAULKNER, BERNADETTE MARIE CALAFELL
& DIANE SUSAN GRIMES

HELLO KITTY GOES TO COLLEGE

Poems about Harassment in the Academy

Across the academy, sexual harassment has been a wide area of study for the past two and a half decades with the examination of issues from the responses to harassment (Clair, McGoun, & Spirek, 1993; Gruber & Bjorn, 1986; Handy, 2006), its relation to power (Wilson & Thompson, 2001) and truth (Brewis, 2001), types of harassers (Lucero, Middleton, Finch, & Valentine, 2003), men and women's standpoints (Dougherty, 1999), ethical dilemmas (Dougherty & Atkinson, 2006), and the construction of masculinity (Bird, 1996), to the effects of sexual harassment (McGuire, Dougherty, & Atkinson, 2006; "Our stories," 1992). Within the field of Communication Studies, sexual harassment has been examined primarily from an organizational or institutional perspective (Clair, 1993; Solomon & Williams, 1997; Townsley, 2004), whereas a few studies have turned the glance inward to examine the ways sexual harassment is organized in the academy (Dougherty & Smythe, 2004; Dziech & Weiner, 1990; Townsley & Geist, 2000; Wood, 1992). More recently attention has focused on bullying in the workplace (Tracy, Lutgen-Sandvik, & Alberts, 2006; Simpson & Cohen, 2004), demonstrating the continued importance of studying workplace harassment.

Issues such as the shock and helplessness associated with initial harassment episodes (Kramarae, 1992; Namie & Namie, 2000), the encouragement provided to harassers by ignoring or laughing off their harassing behaviors (Gruber & Bjorn, 1986; Patton, 2004a), the variations in harassing behavior based on race, gender, age, and status (Cho, 1997; Ontiveros, 1997), the common responses suggested by organizations and researchers (e.g., telling a superior, keeping records, writing the harasser a letter asking that they stop harassing) (Paludi & Barickman, 1991; Petrocelli & Repa, 1999), the importance of a collective response to harassment (Langelan, 1993; Lutgen-Sandvik, 2006), the relationship of harassing behaviors to other forms of abuse of power (Collins, 2004), the grooming and testing of victims (including rape-testing) (Dzeich & Weiner, 1990; Langelan, 1993), the consistent protection of the harasser by the organization (Clair, 1993; Namie & Namie, 2000) were all issues we read about, observed, and/or experienced. Often we were shocked as we read about the premeditated strategies harassers use because they paralleled what we had experienced in our own situation (Dziech & Weiner, 1990; "Our stories," 1992).

*M. Prendergast, C. Leggo and P. Sameshima (eds.), Poetic Inquiry: Vibrant Voices
in the Social Sciences, 187–208.*

While all of this work has been central in understanding the ways sexual harassment works and is sustained, we are interested in providing poems that have the potential to not only inform, but persuade and embody through affective connections. Scholarly attention on poetry as a means of representation or embodiment is not unusual (e.g., Faulkner 2005, 2006; González, 1998). B. H. Fairchild (2007) considers poetry's task of embodiment to work "by bringing the tenuous emotion or subtle state of consciousness or elusive idea into a closer relation with lived experience—with, in effect, the country of the body" (p. 55). Therefore, in this essay we use research poetry with fictionalized details as a means to demonstrate our own and our students' experiences of harassment in the academy and to write about the context and content of harassment in a manner that disrupts a continued normalization of it. We label the poems here as evocative narratives and stories of the flesh that report research in an embodied rather than representational format with the intent to show lives as they are lived, understood and experienced, especially because the experience of harassment is a bodily experience. Fairchild (2007) argued that "when poetry moves away from the body, it atrophies" (p. 68).

Our turn to fiction writing is also informed by performance scholars such as Pollock (1998) and Pelias (2005) who both argue for the use of performative writing as an alternative form of scholarly representation. While Pollock (1998) describes performative writing as evocative in that it brings the reader in contact with other worlds, Pelias (2005) argues, "performative writing features lived experience, telling, iconic moments that call forth the complexities of human life" (p. 418). Pelias (2005) elaborates that "performative writing is a highly selective camera, aimed carefully to capture the most arresting angles" (p. 418). Making our writing both performative and fictional allows us to represent the experience of harassment in a format that creates a potential for activism and contends with representational issues of empowerment and disempowerment. As Frank (2000) states, "there is a possibility of portraying a complexity of lived experience in fiction that might not always come across in a theoretical explication, even one that is concerned with elucidating the complexity of power relations and human interactions" (p. 483).

We further acknowledge the politics of our methodology, as it is greatly informed by critical race and feminist theories that are driven by both concerns for social justice and in many cases alternative means of representation and theorizing. Both critical race theorists and feminists, particularly feminists of color, argue for the importance of storytelling or narrative in the representation of knowledge and everyday experience (i.e., Christian, 1990; Delgado, 1996) and acknowledge the everydayness or pervasiveness of racism and sexism (Delgado & Stefanic, 2001; Essed, 1991). Blending feminist and critical race perspectives, scholars such as Jordan (1997), Davis and Wildman (1997), Taylor (1997), Ontiveros (1997), Davis (1997), and Cho (1997) have examined sexual harassment in various sectors of society. We see the project we undertake here building upon this previous work as well as embodying hooks' (1989) call to talk back to oppressive ideologies and social injustices while giving testimony to our experiential knowledge or theories of the flesh (Collins, 2000; 2004; Moraga & Anzaldúa, 1981). Echoing hooks' call and in many ways reflecting the goals of both feminist and critical race theories, Pelias (2005) highlights the way the personal and political reflect upon each other in performative writing: "It starts with the recognition that individual bodies provide a potent database for understanding the political and hegemonic systems to write on individual bodies" (p. 420). The blending of these perspectives makes us attentive to the issue of positionality, as articulated by Alcoff (1988), which is concerned with the contexts and social locations in which individuals are placed rather than locating identity as a static category. Thus, examinations of experience tell us a great deal about ideological formations, power, and the context for harassing behaviors and responses. Elaborating on the power of experience through the theory of the flesh and poetic representation Anzaldúa (1981) argues,

> You can theorize through fiction and poetry; it's just harder. It's an unconscious kind of concept. Instead of coming in through the head with the intellectual concept, you come in through the backdoor with the feeling, the emotion, the experience. But if you start reflecting on that experience you can come back to the theory. (p. 263)

These methodologies that give central important to experience, voice, and the body underlie our commitment to unpacking and revealing the ways that the intersections of race, class, gender, and sexuality are central and often unacknowledged aspects of the violence perpetuated against women in the academy (Crenshaw, Gotanda, Peller, & Thomas, 1995). It is our hope that the poems we offer will actualize the "performance of possibilities" offered by Madison (1998) which implicates the audience/reader into action and reflection. Furthermore, Pelias (2005) argues, "performative writing also often beckons empathy, allowing others to not only see what the writer might see but also to feel what the writer might feel. It is an invitation to take another's perspective" (p. 419).

The poems here express harassment narratives through the use of a well-known cartoon character, Hello Kitty. Her narration of harassment from student and faculty perspectives is a means to bring the audience into the setting as participants and "co-discoverers" (see Krizek, 1998). As such, Hello Kitty represents an amalgam of women's and students' voices; the situations and feelings we write about are based on actual events, experiences, and ideas recorded as well as our analysis of the relationships between them. The result is an expressive series of poems that shows the analysis and embodies the "affective feel of the experience" of harassment in the academy as well as the "cognitive 'truth' of it" (Rinehart, 1998) while not forgoing the "doing" of the work as Krizek (1998) emphasizes:

> Creative writing can not be employed as a methodological shortcut. Only the meticulous application of the methods of fieldwork, including the analysis of the fruits of that fieldwork...can direct with any fidelity the recoding of the contexts, characters, and dialogic content of the cultural setting presented in the report. (p. 107)

To emphasize the importance of craft and aesthetic concerns, these poems have been workshopped in four poetry classes and undergone numerous revisions based on feedback related to clarity, the music of the lines, the magic of narrative content, and believability (see Faulkner, 2007).

Other writings on harassment in the academy include anonymous narratives by academics in communication; anonymous because in the academy telling such stories may hurt a person's career ("Our stories," 1992). This represents another reason for fictionalized poetry, fears of retribution for speaking of harassment as a normative and protected behavior. These fears precipitated our desire for a series of poems as a kind of qualitative case study that could highlight the context and texture of harassment, inform previous findings on harassment, and possibly allow for the discovery of *"previously unspoken, unknown things about culture and communication"* (Goodall, 2000, p. 191).

***

Hello Kitty

> *Q: Why doesn't Hello Kitty have a mouth?*
> *A: Hello Kitty speaks from her heart. She is Sanrio's ambassador to the world who isn't bound to one certain language.*
> *-from Sanrio.com*

Has:
no mouth, oblong black eyes, a yellow oval nose
like a butterscotch that melts in your palm.
She always wears a bow over her left ear
in some cute color like candied apple.

Her Lifestyle:
She lives in a suburban cottage
with her mom, dad and twin sister
(who wears a bow over her right ear).
During the city commute she works,
records ideas in her red lined notebook
like college could help her become
a better business cat.

How Others Describe Her (Select One):
She's a corporate whore who peddles products:
lip gloss, toaster ovens, timers, stickers, chop sticks.
She uses her eyes and nose to sell
pink and purple products to cool kids,
a magenta gloss over subliminal power.
Some scholars say she's no feminist cat,
yet she yells with her eyes, black with bitchy rage.
Notice the Hello Kitty vibrator on her office shelf.

Is her mouthlessness a well-chosen silence
like a hunger strike of protest,
a transgendered case against the ease of cutting a hole?

What Hello Kitty could do with a mouth
if you glossed in an oval with her new lipstick line:
She'll tell you later.

***

Silence

> It is hard to tell the story of a thousand ordinary and seemingly inconsequential
> references that say to someone: 'You are a woman' with the underlying
> implication 'and therefore both different and inferior.' (Narrative 31, quoted
> in "Our stories," 1992, p. 385)

As we draw on this series of poems to flesh out some of the issues relevant to
sexual harassment in the academy, we start with silence. Because the character,
Hello Kitty, has no mouth, we consider her image a visual and apt representation
of this silence and the potential power in it. Silence can be a form of resistance
(Clair, 1993); it can be a refusal to go along with "jokes" and "innocent" comments.
But a silent (though glaring) harassee or one who makes a point to avoid a harasser
can be blamed for not fighting the harassment (e.g., Jensen & Gutek, 1982). Yet
speaking carries sanctions as well, such as being called a bitch, disgruntled, a
malcontent who insists on airing dirty laundry, who goes "outside" to complain.
"What is forthright and bold in men is considered aggressive and bitchy—and
noncollegial—in women" (Toth, 1988, p. 45). Communication research illustrates
that in many arenas a statement or behavior attributed to a woman is judged more
harshly than the same behavior performed by a man (see Crawford, 1995). As
Sandler (1988) puts it, "even when men and women act the same, their behavior is
viewed differently. He is 'assertive'; she is 'aggressive' or 'hostile.' He 'lost his
cool', implying it was an aberration; she's 'emotional' or 'menopausal.' Thus her
behavior is devalued, even when it is the same as his" (p. 151).

In contrast, women with a feminist orientation were more likely to view behaviors
as sexually harassing and offensive (Berryman-Fink & Riley, 1997). And a recent
study on perceptions of sexual harassment demonstrated that students who assumed
that "no means no" considered any type of victim resistance, whether verbal or
physical, to indicate the victim was being sexually harassed (Osman, 2007).
However, students who believed that in sexual situations "no means yes" (token
resistance) perceived behaviors as sexually harassing only when both verbal and
physical resistance were present. In other words, rather than believing women or
questioning common gendered stereotypes, the interpretation of the sexual harassment
situation often depends on an observer's pre-existing assumptions, regardless of a
specific response of resistant silence, speaking, or physical resistance.

The evaluation of "woman as problem" contributes to attempts to shut down claims of sexual harassment and gender discrimination, thus naturalizing harassment (Townsley & Geist, 2000). This climate of pathologizing or misrepresenting women's behavior is indicative of what Alcoff (2003) terms a larger culture of complaint which "suggests that anyone who can claim victim status happily does so and proceeds to whine with an attitude of self-righteous martyrdom" (p. 4). This assumption makes it unnecessary to distinguish minor grousing from pointing out serious problems; all are trivialized as whining.

***

Hello Kitty Goes to College

I. First Semester

Her business professor stares
at the red K sewn on the butt
of her sweats as she slinks
toward a desk in the front row.
"My best work from the self-designed line"
she confesses when he wants to know
"why K?" in the hallway
after supply chain class. He checks
attendance during her group's talk
on surplus stock. His voice makes
her whiskers vibrate, the K on her top
shrinks under his incessant gaze.
But this is just her professor
she thinks. In lecture, he makes
Tom and Jerry jokes, laughs
at how the cat always
gets into tight spots.
H.K. considers she's the cat
for the mouse, but she's just
a student, this is just a joke.
During office hours,
her advisor tells her
"Honey, professors are just bores
with arrested development. Learn to fit
the system, get your degree." H.K. takes
this advice, enjoys the library
with the stuffed couches
and row after row of shelved books
that smell like possibility. She feels
smart and hip with her good grades

and pledge to the honor society
headed by her business professor.
II. H.K. Discovers She's Not White

When it gets colder on campus
and snow piles around her dorm
like used kitty litter, H.K. takes the bus
to her only night class avoiding
salty paws and snow ball fights
with the freshmen boys who chant
as she crosses the quad. Tonight,
some men ride the bus and snicker
"A. I." as H.K. pushes to the back
of the bus to meet Keroppi and Jodie.
She doesn't know what it means,
talks of her new idea for school supplies.
The outside bar voices continue, "Asian Invasion.
Asian Invasion, stop taking our scholarships."
H.K. wants to tell them she pays
her way with her own body, her line
of clothing. But her friends are faster.
"Stupid Crackers. You can't even fill out
your own applications." She just watches
the green frog and orange dog
shout back as the boys exit the bus.

III. The Visual Aid

On the power point slide,
a leukemia-ridden cat cowers
while doctors examine innards
displayed on the metal exam table.
H.K. pictures her own paws
tied down with twine
in the vet's office,
licks between her claws
when she hears the warning voices:
See what wearing no collar
means? How hanging out with
stray cats brings sickness
to inchoate kittens? But H.K.
likes how they make their dens
wherever they please, thinks
them audacious and infinitely cool
like some kind of queer po-mo cats.
When she sees the picture

blown up on the class screen
and later taped up
in the teaching assistant's office
as an example of a great visual aid,
her hair scratches her skin,
she pants, overheated.
When no one is watching
she rips it off the wall,
shreds it with her paws
and pees on it, just in case.

When she passes by her professor's door, Hello Kitty spits on his creepy poetry.

Or she would, had she gone through with the plastic mouth surgery. That feminist class she took last semester slackened her spine in the surgeon's office. She felt like a naughty kitten dangling in big mother's jaw and left sans alteration. H.K.'s classmates sighed that *actually having no mouth* authenticates Muted Group Theory better than their final project—a duct-taped mouth protest of male language outside the football team's practice room. Still, when she passes by his elegies to dead cats, sonnets for weepy relatives and speaking proper English, she feels a tangled hair ball pushing up the back of her throat, an uncontrollable cough to exhume her fear, a sandpaper tongue that could work sick ink off the paper. H.K. fights her desire for words that would erase the taped up lines of trash, stops the professor from pressing his chair too close to her tail.

***

Academic Culture

Academic organizational cultures are shaped such that they are particularly susceptible to chronic sexual harassment. (Dougherty & Smythe, 2004)

Sexual harassment grows out of and contributes to a particular academic climate, one in which lack of respect, denigration, discrimination, name calling, objectification and sexualization of female learners and scholars is normalized. It supports the definitions and assumptions of hegemonic masculinity and a larger patriarchal culture. As the authors of *The lecherous professor* put it, "'University living is male living on male terms,' and women discover that one of the easiest ways to violate those terms is to raise troublesome issues that call attention to gender" (Dziech & Weiner, 1990, p. 151). Stoltenberg (1989, p. 23) notes that for those sustained by hegemonic masculinity, "there is always the critical problem of how to manage one's affairs so that one always has available a supply of sustenance in the form of feminine deference and submission." Thus, women are encouraged to be quiet and play the game, not questioning the inequities and power differentials that govern the space. Hawkins's (1994) exit interviews with women academics indicated many left their positions because of sexual and gender harassment, underrepresentation and isolation of women, inadequate and/or inaccurate feedback regarding performance, discouraging stories about women, and lack of support.

When the harassee is a student, the problems can be resolved through attrition; going through a formal complaint process can make one feel tired and worn down, confuse the issues, and abate anger. A lecherous professor can feel safe and perhaps even sanctioned when a student transfers or graduates. When female faculty are involved, the younger women may be more assertive about speaking of harassment, issues of equity, and advocating for fair policies; however, they are successful to the extent that they recognize "one must be a colleague first and a woman second" (Dziech & Weiner, 1990, p. 56). Attacked for not being collegial, and unable to change the toxic climate, female professors and staff may also move on or disengage, leaving fewer to glare and/or fight.

This situation is further exacerbated for faculty of color; their presence is often viewed as a challenge to the Whiteness of academia, and they are, in many cases, expected simply to assimilate (Kersey-Matusiak, 2004). The harasser's feelings of safety strengthen and his problematic behaviors may escalate particularly against women of color because, as Collins (2004) writes describing the situation of Black middle class women, the difficulty of balancing the image of "the modern mammy" depends on maintaining the necessary ambition and aggressive behavior required for middle class professions with the subordination to White and/or male authority. She argues that "aggression is acceptable just as long as it is appropriately expressed for the benefit of others. Aggression and ambition for oneself is anathema" (p. 140). Thus, once women are no longer "useful" to, complicit with, or malleable to white and/or male authority, their construction as a problem intensifies.

What types of behaviors constitute sexual harassment? Here we focus on behavior that would define a "hostile work environment," rather than "quid pro quo" sexual harassment in which a harassee is promised a reward if she complies with sexual requests by someone who has power over her (or punishment if she refuses). Verbal behavior that contributes to a hostile work environment includes:

> intimidating, coercive or offensive sexual jokes, persistent requests for dates, nonreciprocal types of compliments, demeaning references to women present or absent, anonymous or signed notes and letters; calling women crazy, sexual remarks, paternalistic or sarcastic tone of voice, teasing, and suggestive or insulting sounds including whistling and sucking. (Kramarae, 1992, p. 101)

Specific examples include dirty jokes which often disparage women's intellect, seriousness, academic commitment, and focus on women's physicality, and comments that do the same by diverting attention away from a woman student's work. "They often make women uncomfortable because essentially private matters related primarily to the sex of the student are made to take precedence over the exchange of ideas and information" (Sandler, 1988, p. 148). Women are viewed in sexual terms and conceived of as belonging to a broad category of "women" with limited intellectual ability and likelihood of failure, rather than as individual women capable of scholarly achievement. Harassing behaviors also include staring, policing women's movements/activities, or stalking. Taylor and Conrad (1992, p. 411) note incidents depicting how "direct physical domination is rehearsed, implied, and accompanied by male violation of victims' 'private' space in the organization." In each instance the woman is not seen as a scholar or learner but is sexualized and objectified. She is meant to realize this and become intimidated so that she does not threaten hegemonic (white) male self-concepts and dominance.

Hegemonic masculinity depends on women's sexual objectification (Stoltenberg, 1989). Male/female difference is assumed and construed to mean male superiority; in other words, men often "see the world through 'sex-coloured glasses' in order to make themselves so much more than mere women" (Kramarae, 1992, p. 116). As Stoltenberg (1989, p. 48) puts it, "once [a male] objectifies that person—once he reduces the person in his mind to the object he desires—then the person, to him, is by definition not a real *subject* like himself" (emphasis in original). The distance created through objectification allows men to "depersonalize the oppression of women" (Bird, 1996, p. 123). Hegemonic masculinity and sexual harassment thrive in academic settings in spite of ideals of gender equality and intellectual growth for all.

The Classroom

When a professor shuts his door and begins class, there is often no one in the classroom who is sensitized to harassing behaviors or who would challenge the person in charge of their grade. Given academic freedom issues, classrooms can rarely be monitored by outsiders. Dziech & Weiner (1990), painting the profile of the lecherous professor argue, "Even the most public kind of harassment, sexist language, is carried out within the sanctity of the individual classroom" (p. 156). The classroom may also be sexualized through jokes, asides, topics of discussion, questions, and gestures. Further characterizing the lecherous professor: "Students sometimes refer to him as 'hands,' 'touchy-feely,' or 'mouth.' Colleagues describe him as 'patronizing,' 'always performing,' 'convinced of his own cuteness'" (Dziech & Weiner, 1990, p. 120). Harassers in the classroom can hide behind "intellectual discussion," "current social issues," and "innocent conversation," and like other types of sexual predators, maneuver to obtain additional positions in which they can sexually harass (e.g., advisor, club sponsor, graduate coordinator). Once in these positions, the harasser can offer students opportunities that the students believe are related to their ability and intelligence (Dziech & Weiner, 1990; "Our stories," 1992).

A recent representative survey of undergraduates at U.S. colleges and universities by the American Association of University Women uncovered that 62% of college students experienced sexual harassment (MSNBC, 2006). Reactions to harassment can leave students less confident; students may feel uneasy, may call him (with an uncomfortable laugh) a "pervert," or report to each other in incredulous voices the "crazy" things said in their class. Since women are sexualized, disrespected, and trivialized in many settings, students may not consider that it is their professor's *job* to see and treat them as learners. The lack of oversight, large power differential between student and professor, and student naivety make it easy for students to assume that their professor's harassing behavior is normal and thus acceptable.

Graduate teaching assistants may have more awareness but are more beholden than undergraduates to the department's professors—the director of graduate studies, the course director, their advisor and committee members—those who in so many ways can make their life easier or miserable. Teaching assistants may be encouraged or forced to contribute to the normalization of a sexualized classroom environment. Additionally, graduate students themselves are harassed and "the effects of these harassment experiences [are] personally alienating, disempowering, and lingering. By violating the student's emerging self-image as academic professionals, these experiences undercut the women's confidence in their intellectual ability" (Strine, 1992, p. 395).

***

Dissertation Abstracts International Feminist Standpoint Theory: An Examination by a Post Modern Two-Dimensional Cat with No Mouth and 22,000 Products Bearing Her Image

Dr. H. Kitty had wanted to title her dissertation, *Ode to the University,* like a love letter to ideas, to chance and other marginal characters without traditional mouths or white teeth. Her committee balked: standpoint theory and self-narratives were quite enough. Other departments would question the methods, not tenure such love gut epistemology. During the defense, the token male member screamed her seminal argument was the "pissy cat position." H.K. wiped his spit off her whiskers with her camouflage hair bow, slipped a blank piece of paper down the conference room table. One by one, the members held the clean sheet as if it were a twisted student evaluation. Only the bisexual lesbian clapped, said Kitty's "right-on-response disallows the difficulty with our difference." H.K. considered ripping herself a mouth with her advisor's fountain pen, kicking the phantom pain in the teeth. Instead, she underlined new parts of her story with a Barbie highlighter, and let them pass her with their caveats and reservations.

First Academic Job

H.K. won her degree, took
a position pasted with diversity
and groups historically ignored.
She assumed that meant different
orientations to being human.
At the interview, someone asked
why she never includes the harasser's
point of view, is critical of Robert's Rules?

Colleagues delighted by her character
standpoint, her popularity with all kinds
of girls and heads of grant agencies,
gave her important assignments
and committee work to fill
cat quotas across the colleges.

Only later, did she not feel
especially encouraged
when outside her office door,
they snickered at cat-in-heat jokes,
comments about smelly tuna
sandwiches and compound nipples.

***

> They come to their first academic jobs believing that things will be different now—that they will pursue knowledge for its own sake and be rewarded with acclaim from their colleagues. (Toth, 1988, p. 36)

Universities may collect different sorts of bodies without changing the power dynamics or challenging the idea that real professors are male and white (Toth, 1988). The idea that members of a diverse professorate would draw on their own non-mainstream experiences is often ignored. In addition, more service is often expected of white women and men and women of color, but this may not be valued or rewarded and can interfere with time for research, thus justifying denial of tenure (e.g., Hawkins, 1994). Many faculty of color are caught in the bind of having extra service because they are some of the few representatives of historically marginalized groups and are thus asked to be on multiple committees as the voice of diversity (McBride, 2005). Women of color must often find ways to negotiate this extra service in addition to their research agendas. Additionally challenging the university climate, Patton (2004b) questions the rhetoric of "home" used by universities by asking: "If a university is 'home' and an institution that welcomes a diverse range of people, how do we account for retention rate concerns and the 'chilly climate' women experience?" (p. 69). Hu-DeHart (2000) argues that while departments may actively hire because they desire diversity, they do little to adjust the climate of the department in anticipation of diversity. As a result, the new faculty member is expected to assimilate into the existing culture without complaint, thus covering up or giving up what makes them "diverse" in the first place.

***

After the Faculty Meeting

H.K. still believed in the academy

though meetings like street brawls

left feminist cat scholar bodies piled
in naked postmodern heaps beside her chair.

She believed even when she took her standpoint
to the harassment advocate who chuckled,

told her to consider being spayed
because it would help her emotionality

even through stories of tenured professors
having to rape in the middle of the quad

in bright daylight with a metal weapon
and maybe a drunken student party

before the possibility of firing would rise
past a personnel meeting to the provost.

After all, many skillful eligible bachelors
among their faculty deserved a date.

Jodie, the canine hire, howled
through departmental dog jokes

of chewed-up essays and sexy mailmen:
Why are dogs so obedient?

Because they sport choke collars.
Jodie started chanting in the copy room,

Getting ass in your classes:
one semester's pay.

Being an ass to your colleagues:
one year's pay.

Getting a fair job:
impossible.

H.K. preferred the department's fresh talk
of cutting edge curriculums and saucy students
though the lecherous professor leered
through her working cats research talk,

asked her to retype the departmental notes
because her *cat scratch* made his eyes water.

Even then, she believed in her colleagues
and the idea of them wearing stripes and bows.

Hello Kitty Sues Her Harasser

I. Pre-Trial: Hello Kitty Chooses Her Outfit for Court

She pastes her pants with black sequins
then pins a pinkish bow
to lull and test the catty court
with thoughts of perfect kitten toes.

He wears a navy suit with spats
that screams without his voice
to show the court upstandingness
by wearing that pressed and mannish choice.

II. Opening Arguments

Inside the court he squawked and preened
as if to show his plume,
a cockled strut and priestly words
could be H. Kitty's doom.

She wrote the judge about those eyes,
the stares that took her pride.
She shook her sequined back to show
how his jokes made her lick her sticky paws.

"I'm partly cat from mother's side
so IF I may resume
that kat is like a feminist
too loud and quite a loon."

The judge just sighed and fell asleep
with H. Kitty at the mic
she sat and stared and flipped her tail
at all of them with no luck.
Her lawyer passed a note to her
with worries of the case,
the judge looked bored and unconvinced
like suing showed her silly taste.

III. Closing Arguments: H.K. Learns the Judge and Her Harasser Play Tennis Together

"See her scorn, that prissy side,
how postmodern she seems.
This blatant talk of girlish needs
just spurns our department's major deeds."

He continues with some girly jokes
and thanks the judge again
for playing tennis last weekend
and letting him just win.

She waits to see the jury's mood
and whether they would see
the blatant buddy scene right there
or scoff at her mute pleas.

***

Institutional Responses

One percent of employees who are harassed make formal complaints. . . .
Complaining about it can often just bring on more. (Kramarae, 1992, p. 102)

Harassees are often instructed by organizations and researchers to tell a superior, keep records, or write the harasser a letter (Paludi & Barickman, 1991; Petrocelli & Repa, 1999). However, these scenarios can often be problematic and lead to even more complications. Faculty and staff ethics violations (including harassment) get glossed over or ignored in comparison to other university issues, such as student cheating, and there is more acceptance of faculty harassment (Hicken, 2007). This is because sexual harassment incidents can be understood as "conserving moves on the part of those with the greatest personal investment in keeping the dominant patriarchal order intact by curtailing the possible subject-positions that women as academic professionals can occupy" (Strine, 1992, p. 395). Relatedly, Dziech & Weiner (1990) reflect on the precarious position women faculty occupy because of their dependence on men for reappointment, tenure, and support in the university, and how this influences their effectiveness at helping students with a harassment problem. "The woman professor risks the most if she assists.... [She] depends on men for her continued survival in the institution, the same men she would have to confront about sexual harassment" (p. 148). Such confrontations will highlight the woman professor's gender and may lead to her becoming a target of sexual harassment herself. Or she may lose the privileged "honorary male" status that she depends on to be taken seriously by her male colleagues. Additionally, she runs the risk of being labeled a troublemaker, being punished for not properly assimilating into the departmental culture, and losing colleagues she believed to be friends and allies.

Two stories illustrate how formal reports of harassment often make situations worse and demonstrate a lack of transparency and accountability in the university setting. Frances Conley, a neurosurgeon, reported sexual harassment and sexist behavior by a colleague at Stanford University. The colleague was subsequently promoted. Frances was the only female full professor of neurosurgery and resigned because of the silence and inaction by the medical school dean, though the media responded immediately. "Six years after her protest, [she said] the atmosphere in her department remained 'fairly hostile' and the situation for women in the academy was still problematic" (Glazer-Raymo, 1999, p. 114). The story of Jean Jew, a Chinese-American anatomy professor, shares similarities. A colleague started "malicious rumors that she was having a sexual relationship with the male department chair.... In response to her complaint, the university tried to discredit her" (Glazer-Raymo, 1999, p. 115). She won her case after 10 years, got retroactive promotion to full professor, back pay and compensation. However, her university did not grant her request for a transfer to another department or punish the offending professor. University officials protect the harasser as a way to shield the university's reputation, and regardless of job title or job description, officials have little concern with helping the victim (Clair, 1993; Namie & Namie, 2000). Victims become expendable, while universities wait for the tenured harasser to retire.

Reactions to Standpoints

> The *activities* of those at the top both organize and set limits on what persons who perform such activities can understand about themselves and the world around them. (Harding, 1993, p. 54, emphasis in original)

Hello Kitty is threatening not just because she is an outsider, and not just because she "rocks the boat" by demanding a harassment-free workplace. She is threatening because she represents certain political assumptions about what counts as knowledge and how that relates to privilege. Standpoint theory recognizes that knowledge takes place in particular contexts; knowledge and accounts of knowledge are neither neutral nor universal. Yet the theorizing and experiences of some groups have not counted as knowledge in Western culture (Harding, 1990). As with Hello Kitty, experiences differ significantly depending on one's relation to privilege. The understandings of those not situated as the recipients of race, gender or other privilege will differ in systematic ways from those with privilege. Drawing on their own experiences and theorizing, groups outside the mainstream work towards self-valuation and self-determination (Collins, 2000). Meanwhile, what is assumed to be a neutral perspective is often the standpoint of dominant groups.

Standpoint epistemology is useful because it encourages us to denaturalize positions—that of the harasser and his university apologists— often seen as neutral and therefore apolitical. This allows us to see such privileged positions as existing among many others. For privileged groups, giving up the idea of knowledge as neutral is threatening, especially when such knowledge benefits them politically. As in Hello Kitty's case there can be a "backlash" against non-dominant standpoints. We illustrate how this happens through linguistically framing Hello Kitty as a problem, through positioning the harasser as the victim, and through trying to silence harassees' stories and sense-making.

Hello Kitty's story works to uncover and critique the protection of harassers by the university system. This protection can be seen in responses to harassment that reject the idea of standpoints and "address a generic, genderless subject, stable in time and space" (Townsley & Geist, 2000, p. 213). Such protection is also evident in the language used (and not used) to describe harasser and harassee. For example, Hello Kitty is called postmodern, feminist, "cat," and emotional in ways that frame this as dirty and shameful, as not indicative of serious scholars, in ways oppositional to the real work of the university. She is feminized, and her standpoint is rejected. She is trivialized and denigrated because of her gender and outsider status and this makes it more difficult to fight the harassment which is already naturalized and "normal" in the setting. The frequency of harassing behaviors also helps to prevent their labeling as problematic because it further normalizes these behaviors in the university (Shepela & Levesque, 1998).

Second, the perpetuation and normalization of harassment can be seen in attempts to position the harasser as the actual victim. This fits with a broader white-male-as-victim discourse (of course, we recognize that all sexual harassers are not white males) that argues white males are no more privileged than other groups, and that they are in need of protection because of injuries caused by their recent visibility *as* white males (Robinson, 2000). As white women and women and men of color contest white male privilege, white males see themselves as losing rightful entitlements available to them because they previously represented the universal and the "norm" (Grimes, 2007). Relatedly, harassers may announce their tangential membership in a suddenly relevant marginalized group ("I'm partly cat from mother's side") as a way to ignore power differences and to trivialize the pressure others experience to assimilate or accommodate to the dominant academic system. Orbe (2006) discusses a similar dilemma for conversants as they articulate important cultural markers in interaction; what happens when all parties perceive themselves to be at a disadvantage and claim and operate from a non-dominant status? We also note that status quos are not challenged when "the focus on 'victims' makes it possible for white men to claim injury without claiming to be oppressed systematically by white supremacist patriarchy" (Robinson, 2000, p. 68).

As women in the academy challenge sexual harassment and abuse, they are met by some white males loudly protesting their supposed silencing and invisibility (Robinson, 2000). In academic "culture wars," Robinson (2000, p. 61) remarks upon "the depth of the *entitlement* that enables these wounded white male professors to be so appalled that anyone would question their motives and innocence, their disinterestedness and objectivity" (emphasis in original). While white male perspectives are re-centered through this victim discourse, what happens to the voices of victims of harassment? Writing about the disempowerment of these voices, Patton (2004a) argues that "it is not enough to have the disenfranchised included in such a way as to make their contributions, their voices, and their perspectives ineffective and silenced because of the maintenance of hegemony or allow them to border-cross when it benefits those in the center" (p. 199). This can make it difficult for untenured faculty to use assertive tactics (Bingham, 1991; Kroløkke, 1998). In writing this essay we contribute to a feminist critique that necessarily calls us to recognize long-standing patterns and possibilities for change. Through the practice of naming we hope to begin to disrupt harassing behaviors and the systems that condone and permit them by highlighting that they are not in fact natural or commonsensical. Kramarae (1992) argues, "as with other feminist critiques of men's repression and hostility, much of the explanations involve telling stories until an adequate, shared vocabulary is available. . . long stories are often needed, since the meaning of one remark is often dependent on a history of events" (p. 105). Heeding Kramarae's words, in this project we have begun to locate specific narratives and posited the ways they are connected to larger historical patterns of patriarchal domination.

REFERENCES

Alcoff, L. M. (1988). Cultural feminism versus post-structuralism: The identity crisis in feminist theory. *Signs: Journal of Women and Culture in Society, 13*, 405–436.

Alcoff, L. M. (2003). Introduction. In L. M. Alcoff (Ed.), *Singing in the fire: Stories of women in philosophy* (pp. 1–13). Lanham, MD: Rowman & Littlefield.

Berryman-Fink, C., & Riley, K. V. (1997). The effect of sex and feminist orientation on perceptions in sexually harassing communication. *Women's Studies in Communication, 20*(1), 25–44.

Bingham, S. G. (1991, June). Communication strategies for managing sexual harassment in organizations: Understanding message options and their effects. *Journal of Applied Communication Research*, 88–115.

Bird, S. R. (1996). Welcome to the men's club: Homosociality and the maintenance of hegemonic masculinity. *Gender and Society, 10*, 120–132.

Brewis, J. (2001). Foucault, politics and organizations: (Re)-constructing sexual harassment. Gender. *Work and Organizations, 8*, 37–60.

Cho, S. K. (1997). Converging stereotypes in racialized sexual harassment: Where model minority meets Suzi Wong. In A. K. Wing (Ed.), *Critical race feminism: A reader* (pp. 203–220). New York: University Press.

Christian, B. (1990). The race for theory. In. G. Anzaldúa (Ed.), *Making face, making soul: Haciendo caras* (pp. 335–345). San Francisco: Aunt Lute Press.

Clair, R. (1993). The bureaucratization, commodification, and privatization of sexual harassment through institutional discourse. *Management Communication Quarterly, 7*, 123–157.

Clair, R. P., McGoun, M. J., & Spirek, M. M. (1993). Sexual harassment responses of working women: An assessment of current communication-oriented typologies and perceived effectiveness of the response. In G. L. Kreps (Ed.), *Sexual harassment: Communication implications* (pp. 209–233). Cresskill, NJ: Hampton Press.

Collins, P. H. (2000). *Black feminist thought: Knowledge, consciousness, and the politics of empowerment.* New York: Routledge.

Collins, P. H. (2004). *Black sexual politics: African Americans, gender and the new racism.* New York: Routledge.

Crawford, M. E. (1995). *Talking difference: On gender and language.* Thousand Oaks, CA: Sage.

Crenshaw, K., Gotanda, N., Peller, G., & Thomas, K. (1995). *Critical race theory: The key writings that formed the movement.* New York: The New York Press.

Davis, A. D., & Wildman, S. M. (1997). The legacy of doubt: Treatment of sex and race in the Hill-Thomas hearings. In A. K. Wing (Ed.), *Critical race feminism: A reader* (pp. 175–182). New York: University Press.

Davis, D. E. (1997). The harm that has no name: Street harassment, embodiment, and African American women. In A. K. Wing (Ed.), *Critical race feminism: A reader* (pp. 192–202). New York: University Press.

Delgado, R. (1996). *The Rodrigo chronicles: Conversations about America and race.* New York: New York University Press.

Delgado, R., & Stefanic, J. (2001). *Critical race theory: An introduction.* New York: University Press.

Dougherty, D. S. (1999). Dialogue through standpoint: Understanding women's and men's standpoints of sexual harassment. *Management Communication Quarterly, 12,* 436–468.

Dougherty, D., & Atkinson, J. (2006). Competing ethical communities and a researcher's dilemma: The case of a sexual harasser. *Qualitative Inquiry, 12,* 292–315.

Dougherty, D., & Smythe, M. J. (2004). Sensemaking, organizational culture, and sexual harassment. *Journal of Applied Communication, 32*(4), 293–317.

Dziech, B. W., & Weiner, L. (1990). *The lecherous professor: Sexual harassment on campus* (2nd ed.). Urbana, IL: University of Illinois Press.

Essed, P. (1991). *Understanding everyday racism.* Newbury Park, CA: Sage.

Fairchild, B. H. (2007). A way of being: Observations on the ends and means of poetry. *New Letters, 74*(1), 53–69.

Faulkner, S. L. (2005). Method: Six poems. *Qualitative Inquiry, 11,* 941–949.

Faulkner, S. L. (2006). Reconstruction: LGBTQ and Jewish. *International and Intercultural Communication Annual, 29,* 95–120.

Faulkner, S. L. (2007). Concern with craft: Using Ars Poetica as criteria for reading research poetry. *Qualitative Inquiry, 13*(2), 218–234.

Frank, K. (2000). The management of hunger: Using fiction in writing anthropology. *Qualitative Inquiry, 6*(4), 474–488.

Glazer-Raymo, J. (1999). *Shattering the myths: Women in academe.* Baltimore: Johns Hopkins University Press.

González, M. C. (1998). Abandoning the sacred hierarchy: Disempowering hegemony through spirit. In M. L. Hecht (Ed.), *Communicating Prejudice* (pp. 223–234). Newbury Park, CA: Sage.

Goodall, H. L. (2000). *Writing the new ethnography.* Walnut Creek, CA: Alta Mira.

Grimes, D. S. (2007, June). *"White, male, and worried": Illustrations of victimhood in the managing diversity literature.* Paper presented at the 5th annual Gender, Work and Organization interdisciplinary conference, Keele, England.

Gruber, J. E., & Bjorn, L. (1986). Women's responses to sexual harassment: An analysis of sociocultural, organizational, and personal resource models. *Social Science Quarterly, 67,* 814–826.

Handy, J. (2006). Sexual harassment in small-town New Zealand: A qualitative study of three contrasting organizations. *Gender, Work and Organization, 13,* 1–24.

Harding, S. (1990). Feminism, science and the anti-Enlightenment critiques. In L. J. Nicholson (Ed.), *Feminism/postmodernism* (pp. 83–106). New York: Routledge.

Harding, S. (1993). Rethinking standpoint epistemology: What is "strong objectivity"? In L. Alcoff & E. Potter (Eds.), *Feminist epistemologies* (pp. 49–82). New York: Routledge.

Hawkins, K. (1994). Analyzing the pure case: Women's narratives of academic life. *Women's Studies in Communication, 17,* 1–25.

Hicken, M. (2007). Academic integrity/Ignoring the issue: SU community gives less attention to faculty, staff academic integrity than to student cheating despite campus concern. *The Daily Orange,* 5/1/2007. Retrieved May 07, 2007, from http://www.dailyorange.com

hooks, b. (1989). *Talking back: Thinking feminist, thinking Black.* Cambridge, MA: South End.

Hu-DeHart, E. (2000). Office politics and departmental culture. In M. Garcia (Ed.), *Succeeding in an academic career: A guide for faculty of color* (pp. 27–38). Westport, CT: Greenwood.

Jensen, I. W., & Gutek, B. A. (1982). Attributions and the assignment of responsibility in sexual harassment. *Journal of Social Issues, 38,* 121–136.

Jordan, E. C. (1997). Race, gender, and social class in the Thomas sexual harassment hearings: The hidden fault lines in political discourse. In A. K. Wing (Ed.), *Critical race feminism: A reader* (pp. 169–174). New York: New York University Press.

Kersey-Matusiak, G. (2004). The power of one voice: Why faculty of color should stay in small, private, predominately White institutions. In D. Cleveland (Ed.), *A long way to go: Conversations about race by African American faculty and graduate students* (pp. 120–130). New York: Peter Lang.

Kramarae, C. (1992). Harassment and everyday life. In L. F. Rakow (Ed.), *Women making meaning* (pp. 100–120). New York: Routledge.

Krizek, R. L. (1998). Lessons: What the hell are we teaching the next generation anyway? In A. Banks & S. P. Banks (Eds.), *Fiction & social research: By ice or fire* (pp. 89–113). Walnut Creek, CA: Alta Mira.

Kroløkke, C. (1998). Women professors' assertive-empathic and non-assertive communication in sexual harassment situations. *Women's Studies in Communication, 21,* 93–103.

Langelan, M. J. (1993). *Back off: How to confront and stop sexual harassment and harassers.* New York: Simon & Schuster.

Lucero, M. A., Middleton, K. L, Finch, W. A., & Valentine, S. R. (2003). An empirical investigation of sexual harassers: Toward a perpetuator typology. *Human Relations, 56,* 1461–1483.

Lutgen-Sandvik, P. (2006). "Take this job and...": Quitting and other forms of resistance to workplace bullying. *Communication Monographs, 73,* 406–433.

Madison, D. S. (1998). Performance, personal narratives, and the politics of possibility. In S. J. Dailey (Ed.), *The future of performance studies: Visions and revisions* (pp. 276–286). Annandale, VA: National Communication Association.

McBride, D. (2005). *Why I hate Abercrombie & Fitch: Essays on race and sexuality.* New York: New York University Press.

McGuire, T., Dougherty, D. S., & Atkinson, J. (2006). "Paradoxing the dialectic": The impact of patients' sexual harassment on the discursive construction of nurses' caregiving roles. *Management Communication Quarterly, 19,* 416–450.

Moraga, C., & Anzaldúa, G. (Eds.). (1981). *This bridge called my back: Writings by radical women of color.* New York: Kitchen Table.

MSNBC. (2006). Sexual harassment affects most college students: Women and men are equally likely to be harassed, new study finds. *MSNBC.com.* Retrieved January 24, 2006, from http://www.msnbc. msn.com/id/11005342/from/ET/print/1/displaymode/1098/

Namie, G., & Namie, R. (2000). *The bully at work: What you can do to stop the hurt and reclaim your dignity on the job.* Naperville, IL: Sourcebooks.

Ontiveros, M. L. (1997). Three perspectives on workplace harassment of women of color. In A. K. Wing (Ed.), *Critical race feminism: A reader* (pp. 188–191). New York: New York University Press.

Orbe, M. P., & Spellers, R. E. (2005). From the margins to the center: Utilizing co-cultural theory in diverse contexts. In W. B. Gudykunst (Ed.), *Theorizing about intercultural communication* (pp. 173–191). Thousand Oaks, CA: Sage.

Osman, S. L. (2007). Predicting perceptions of sexual harassment based on type of resistance and belief in token resistance. *Journal of Sex Research, 44,* 340–346.

"Our stories": Communication professionals' narratives of sexual harassment. (1992). *Journal of Applied Communication Research, 20,* 363–391.

Paludi, M. A., & Barickman, R. B. (1991). *Academic and workplace sexual harassment: A resource manual.* Albany, NY: State University of New York Press.

Patton, T. O. (2004a). Reflections of a Black woman professor: Racism and sexism in academia. *The Howard Journal of Communications, 15,* 185–200.

Patton, T. O. (2004b). In the guise of civility: The complicitous maintenance of inferential forms of sexism and racism in higher education. *Women's Studies in Communication, 27,* 60–87.

206

Pelias, R. J. (2005). Performative writing as scholarship: An apology, an argument, an anecdote. *Cultural Studies ⇔ Critical Methodologies, 5*(4), 415–424.

Petrocelli, W., & Repa, B. K. (1999). *Sexual harassment on the job: What it is and how to stop it.* Berkeley, CA: Nolo Press.

Pollock, D. (1998). Performative writing. In P. Phelan & J. Lane (Eds), *The ends of performance* (pp. 73–103). New York: New York University Press.

Rinehart, R. (1998). Fictional methods in ethnography: Believability, specks of glass, and Chekhov. *Qualitative Inquiry, 4*, 200–224.

Robinson, S. (2000). *Marked men: White masculinity in crisis.* New York: Columbia University Press.

Sandler, B. R. (1988). The classroom climate: Chilly for women? In A. L. Deneef, C. D. Goodwin & E. S. McCrate (Eds.), *The academic's handbook* (pp. 146–152). Durham, NC: Duke University Press.

Shepela, S. T., & Levesque, L. L. (1998). Poisoned waters: Sexual harassment and the college climate. *Sex Roles, 38*, 589–611.

Simpson, R., & Cohen, C. (2004). Dangerous work: The gendered nature of bullying in the context of higher education. *Gender, Work and Organization, 11*, 163–186.

Solomon, D. H., & Williams, M. L. M. (1997). Perceptions of social-sexual communication at work: The effects of message, situation, and observer characteristics on judgments of sexual harassment. *Journal of Applied Communication Research, 25*, 196–216.

Stoltenberg, J. (1989). *Refusing to be a man: Essays on sex and justice.* Portland, OR: Breitenbush Books.

Strine, M. (1992). Understanding "how things work": Sexual harassment and academic culture. *Journal of Applied Communication Research, 20*, 391–400.

Taylor, B., & Conrad, C. (1992). Narratives of sexual harassment: Organizational dimensions. *Journal of Applied Communication Research, 20*, 401–418.

Taylor, K. A. (1997). Invisible woman: Reflections on the Clarence Thomas confirmation hearings. In A. K. Wing (Ed.), *Critical race feminism: A reader* (pp. 183–187). New York: New York University Press.

Toth, E. (1988). Women in academia. In A. L. Deneef, C. D. Goodwin, & E. S. McCrate (Eds.), *The academic's handbook* (pp. 36–45). Durham, NC: Duke University Press.

Townsley, N. C. (2004). Review essay: Looking back, looking forward: Mapping the gendered theories, voices, and politics of organization. *Organization, 10*, 617–640.

Townsley, N., & Geist, P. (2000). The discursive enactment of hegemony: Sexual harassment and academic organizing. *Western Journal of Communication, 64*(2), 190–217.

Tracy, S. J., Lutgen-Sandvik, P., & Alberts, J. K. (2006). Nightmares, demons and slaves: Exploring the painful metaphors of workplace bullying. *Management Communication Quarterly, 20*, 148–185.

Wilson, F., & Thompson, P. (2001). Sexual harassment as an exercise of power. *Gender, Work and Organization, 8*, 61–83.

Wood, J. T. (1992). Telling our stories: Narratives as a basis for theorizing sexual harassment. *Journal of Applied Communication Research, 20*, 349–362.

Sandra L. Faulkner
Interpersonal Communication
Bowling Green State University
Ohio, USA

Bernadette Marie Calafell
Department of Human Communication
University of Denver
USA

Diane Susan Grimes
Communication and Rhetorical Studies
Syracuse University
USA

SUSANNE GANNON

WRITING POETRY IN/TO PLACE

This chapter performs a poetic "topoanalysis" where I work through seven scenes from my own biography of place. In his elegant book, *The Poetics of Space,* Gaston Bachelard (1964) described topoanalysis as the systematic study of the "sites of our intimate lives" (p. 8). He weaves the work of poets and novelists through his own recollections of homes and houses. In writing into my memories, I seek not to assemble "exact recollections" but to honour the "mellowness and imprecision" that Bachelard talks about, as though "something fluid had collected our memories and we ourselves were dissolved in this fluid of the past" (p. 57). Thus this chapter daydreams into the scenes and sites of memories that are now "quite dissolved and distributed inside me: here one room, there another" (Rilke, cited by Bachelard, 1964, p. 57). Though each poem begins with a marker of space and time—a place, a year, a title—please hold these contours lightly. In Bachelard's topoanalysis, our lost houses (and our lost selves) "forever continue to live on in us" (p. 56).

I began this chapter in a time and place where I had been grappling with my own displacement. For twenty-one years I lived in the tropical north of Australia until I turned south to head back towards the temperate climate where I began. There's something about the north, about being near the equator, that means you have to learn to breathe in through your skin. A sort of osmosis: of moist air and warmth and what feels sometimes to be a different mode of living. It included dimensions that I felt through my skin, like the damp air, and the toe-sucking mud of low tide at the mouth of the Barron River, at the end of my street; and that I knew through my nostrils and stomach—the sweet rot of mangoes fallen on grass, the slight sour of mildew on paint after three months of rain. I knew that though cyclones threatened us every year, there was a sleeping dragon curved into the hills around our town who would always keep us safe. I knew, too, that further inland along the Barron, beside the railway line above the gorge, lives Damarri, a granite boulder now, hanging over the valley, but once a man who crawled up from a crocodile pool, bleeding from the stump of his left leg. He rests there now in his rock, and keeps an eye on the valley, his view almost the same as mine—across plains, islands and the Coral Sea—when I drove down the range from work each day when I was a high school teacher in that other life. My thoughts seemed slower up there, more languid, allowed more time to ripen and to fruit than in the sharp dry seasons of the south. And it was up there in the north that I started writing and

M. Prendergast, C. Leggo and P. Sameshima (eds.), Poetic Inquiry: Vibrant Voices in the Social Sciences, 209–218.

went on writing until sometimes it seemed as though lines of text span out of me, around me and down the stairs of my house out of my control (like the green snake that surprised me there, rearing on its tail to eyeball me before spinning and whipping down the stairs in the corner). Increasingly these lines of text hung between me and other people, even kept me apart from them. Until there was a whole thesis, then a second, bigger one, bound like bricks, and I had nowhere else to go but elsewhere. And so I came south, 3000 kilometres and five years from the home I had made for so long in the tropical north.

When I look back at my love of the tropics, and how I have begun to ease into this more southern and temperate place, despite the landscapes and the lure of outsides, my love of place is as much to do with insides: homes, dwelling places, buildings, walls, rooves and windows, or the lack of them, floors and corners, and the slippages between them all. As an adult I have lived in various houses on the west and east coasts of Australia. As a child I moved many times. Each of my memories, and my affections, are bound into the material structures of the places which I made into home, where I was at home, where home was something I felt inside me and around me. Indeed, who I am, who I was able to be and to become, is inseparable from these places. If cliffs, or rocks, can be seen as agentic, as part of networks (including but not confined to humans) that open and close possibilities for ways of being—as Penny Rossiter (2007) claims—then houses too, and rooms for living, are also amongst those "things that might allow, afford, encourage, permit, suggest, influence, block, render possible, forbid, and so on, in addition to 'determining' and serving as a 'backdrop for human action'" (Latour, cited in Rossiter, 2007, p. 300). I turn to Barbara Hooper (2001) to ask: "where does place stop and self begin? What is, for each, the scale of reach—in space and time? How far back and how far ahead, how far laterally and vertically, do body, self and place extend?" (p. 704) Houses, and memories of them, are marked by traces of those others—people and creatures—who inhabited them too.

Why take up poetry for this inquiry into the intimacies of place and the experience of home? And why should I conjure my homing—so far away—for you? Yi-Fu Tuan (1974) suggests that feelings about place are more permanent and most difficult to express when a place is also home and the "locus of memories" (p. 93). Bachelard (1964) talks about a philosophy of poetry wherein we might attempt to "write a room" or "read a house": "at the very first word," he says, "at the first poetic overture, the reader who is 'reading a room' leaves off reading and starts to think of some place in his own past" (p. 14). What the poet has done, he says, is "unlocked a door to daydreaming" (p. 14). Bachelard's theory of poetics holds that "the poetic image is independent of causality" (p. xvii). Rather than merely reflecting an "echo of the past...through the brilliance of an image, the distant past resounds with echoes, and it is hard to know," he says, "at what depth these echoes will reverberate and die away" (xvi). In the remainder of this chapter, I present a series of seven scenes, each a poem that I hope reverberates somewhere, to some degree, in the depths of your memories.

1

Cubbyhouse *(Whittlesea, 1969)*

The cupboard opens straight, then
turns right, past the brooms
into darkness. There the roof cuts down
forty-five degrees into nothing —
a disappearing spot, or a corner

Here she makes her nest:
her little living room

She reorders mops buckets boxes
slides inside with her little square of carpet
arranges cushions lamp candles
brings a blanket, sets books in stacks
against bare walls, raw and pale

She reads *The Secret Seven*, listens
to strangers murmur, chairs dragged in
and out, horse races or the dogs turned up
on the radio in the bar, snatches of
her mum's voice, sharp and near

Doors slamming

She hears plates and cutlery clattering
on trays, the stacking of glasses
the creaking of each stair as it weighs
a body, passes it on to the next

She sees dust motes float and sparkle
in the lamplight, eats her white bread,
drinks her cordial, cosies down
to the ebb and swell of the outside
with her cushions, her blanket
and her books

2

Sleepout *(Mystic Park, 1976)*

Casuarinas whisper
shhhh shhhh shhhh
in the desert wind

by the railway line
mallee dirt sifts through louvres
never closed quite tight enough

You climb the fire escape, clinging
to the back wall, above the cars, while
I creep through from the other side
the red brick solid side, split off
from the passage and my good girl cubicle
of study and sleep and listening
to Lou Reed faint on the radio
far from the city, where I imagine
I might have had some other life

We lie on the big bed, adrift
among forgotten furniture
whispering and listening
for my mother, anyone
clack clack clack clack
clack clack clack clack
sixty carriages of wheat head south til
we tire of counting and return
to whispering sighing rustling
and skin and summer and young
your hands soft with lanolin

And the moon rises
low and large and red
over this flat land and
we watch it through the louvres
from our abandoned bed, and we listen
shhhh shhhh shhhh
to the sigh and whisper of the desert she-oaks
by the railway line, mallee dust
in our mouths our ears our eyes
and, on our skin, the warm wind of the desert

3

Playing House *(Cann River, 1980)*

Between Club Terrace and the coast
sits our farmhouse in a paddock, by a forest
far from home

We gather wood, tether a goat, grow beans
and sweetpeas, scavenge furniture, learn
to live [almost] with rats and snakes
and with each other

You bring me black tea in the mornings:
sipping it in bed, nauseous, after you have gone,
I'm sure I'm pregnant

We close ourselves in for winter, huddle by
the fire with chestnuts and corn and soup
and each other

Sometimes you bring home a hitchhiker
or two, people who remind us of ourselves
stuck at this crossroads
when the sun drops behind the hills
and the cold and dark set in

We spend weekends on firetrails, camping
catching bream, ranging through the forest for
slipper orchids, greenhoods and psilocybin mushrooms:
in season our friends come six hours from the city
for long weekends with tahini and guitars

One rainy Saturday we dowsed for the body
of a goat, with our neighbour: a twist of fencing wire
in his right hand, a handful of shit in his left
wading thigh-high through the bracken, the scent
of goat ahead and us behind bemused

We meet artists and farmers and other earthgardeners:
I bake and braid strings of home-grown garlic, and my hair
learn to handle yeast, light fires, bottle tomatoes
scale fish, pick oysters from rocks at low tide
mix glazes and make pots

Though I love to see the wallabies graze
in the afternoons, before you come home
and the frost lift from the grass, after you leave:
when the fog drifts in each afternoon like a curse
I know that I won't stay here, with you

4

Doghouse with Frangipanis *(Broome, 1984)*

Dusty pindan coats my dog
and me, orange everything
and green, shade and light
and heat, cashew-fruit, ackee
limes, who would have thought there
were so many types of mango?
—trees closing in
on this house squat
among sprawling frangipani
tips trimmed for market in the winter

This old gardener's house and
me and my dog frogs bats birds and
lizards chew through the wiring
possums tear strips from the ceiling
above the bed, snakes at the front door
and the back, a death adder in the pantry
a mouse in the toaster
bougainvillea scratches the windows
bees swarm in the second bedroom
and the whole house buzzes

Sid comes each morning in white beard and black shorts
to teach me about coffee, Colette, Skvorecky, Canetti
the Prague Spring, and the compromises of communism

Late in the year, the pheasant coucal comes
like a promise: crashing through bushes
scuttling over the drive
his *hoop hoop hoop hoop hoop hoop*
hanging low in the humid air

You're hardly ever here and even when you are
I can't always find you; but the dog and I are home here
panting reading splayed out sweating
pindan sheen on my skin, dust in his coat

5

Treehouse *(Machans Beach, 1999)*

No windows at all, upstairs
cavernous, moss green and smoke white
two rooms, up and down
what more could I need
beyond air sky light and moon
to cease my skittering

Along the seaward side
shutters on broomstick struts
eyelids open to the sky;
my sightline from bed: a desk, books
the scruffy nest of a Torres pigeon
in a coconut, paperbarks,
the moon, the northern drift
of sunrise in winter

When rain slants sideways
I push the bed across the room
drop shutters (lower their weight on my back,
knees bent, feet bare on wet tin roof)

When cyclones come I nest
under the stairs and pray
that this won't be
the kingtide collusion
that sends us under

This house is a talisman:
a house to be brave in, an embrace
a tower to shout from to a stranger
get out of my yard, I'll call the police
and do it; to say *no, that's not what I want
any more* and jump from the everyday into these

long days at my desk reading writing thinking
blue butterflies flash by, sunbirds hover
harvest cobwebs and spider's eggs, green frogs
leap from ledge to forearm to Foucault
and out again, without noticing
jasmine curling round the struts
impossible now—too late—to close them

6

A Walk in the Park (With You) *(Glenbrook, 2004)*

This house, dark and sharp
spits me out to morning and a walk
and thoughts of you:

There's a curve in the steps
on the way down
giant tree ferns spill from a cleft, but

You drive along cotton fields
dirty balls on dying plants
a field of antelope

While I walk down into bush
into the thick of it, each seed and
tiny flower and blush of new growth

And you get to Swainsboro, and hit the interstate
where the land is flat and four lane straight
and you know you're headed for the ocean

And I step through sandstone country
platforms and ridges jut out
weathered grey, lighter where the stone splits
and lichen surfaces

You can see it somehow in the sky, you say
at the point where the sky meets the ground
then it starts to rain, a thick grey rain
and you can't see ten feet in front of you

And down by the pools in the creek
the light breaks through and I'm close to the detail
the weirdness of banksia bottle brush grass tree
angophora shading through bone-white salmon-pink grey almost-blue
bark strips hang down

Then you hit Savannah and the rain
has been there before you, streets glisten
and Spanish moss hangs from live oaks, rivulets
work their way earthward

And I sit by the blue pool, tannin-brown
clean and cold, while you look at the suspension bridge
to Tybee Island and the Atlantic, and think of me

And I wish that I could sit here on my rock and meditate but
no, I want to be aware of the kingfisher
and the insects buzzing in the reeds
and the quality of light changing on the stone shelf
on the other side of the creek

And of you, hunched over your steering wheel
staring through the windshield wipers
into the fog

7

Erica's House *(Warrimoo, NSW, 2007)*

Here I am clean lines and functionality
like Erica must be

Wooden floorboards, white walls, granite, steel
Danish bread and light and air
and levels split and brick

Here I am slim and smart and surprised
by clever Scandinavian storage solutions
in awe of appliances

But the ceiling soars and I'm pulling winter
curtains back to growing things and colour
I'm unfurling wings and finding a voice here
among parrot chatter and currawong song

And inside, above my head, I hear
the weight of a python waking in the roof
dragging his belly towards spring

GLOSSARY

angophora: Australian tree of Eucalypt species, endemic to Blue Mountains near Sydney

casuarina: Australian tree species with sparse needle like grey-green foliage, desert and coastal varieties, also called "she-oak"

currawong: Australian song bird endemic to the Blue Mountains near Sydney

mallee: semi-desert region of north-western and western Victoria

pindan: colloquial local term for the red soil of north-western Western Australia
pheasant coucal: a large ground-nesting cuckoo which appears in the lead-up to
the wet season in the tropics
wallaby: small species of kangaroo

NOTES

[1] This project is supported by Australian Research Council Discovery Grant DP0663798: "Place Pedagogies in Rural and Urban Australia." Researchers are Dr Susanne Gannon and Professor Bronwyn Davies (University of Western Sydney), Professor Margaret Somerville, Dr Kerith Power and Dr Phoenix De Carteret (Monash University). Writing place is a particular interest of the UWS strand of the project where we have used the methodology of collective biography (Davies & Gannon, 2006) with colleagues and young people to invoke and examine memories of embodiment in place.

[2] Hear currawong song and the call of the pheasant coucal at the Australian Museum *Birds in backyards* website at http://www.birdsinbackyards.net

REFERENCES

Bachelard, G. (1964). *The poetics of space*. New York: Beacon Books.

Davies, B., & Gannon, S. (2006). *Doing collective biography: Investigating the production of subjectivity*. Maidenhead: Open University Press.

Hooper, B. (2001). Desiring presence, romancing the real. *Annals of the Association of American Geographers, 91*(4), 703–715.

Latour, B. (2004). Non-humans. In S. Harrison, S. Pile, & N. Thrift (Eds.), *Patterned ground: Entanglements of nature and culture* (pp. 62–64). London: Reaktion.

Rossiter, P. (2007). Rockclimbing: On humans, nature and other nonhumans. *Space and culture, 10*(2) 292–305.

Tuan, Y. (1974). *Topophilia: A study of environmental perception, attitudes, and values*. Englewood Cliffs, NJ: Prentice-Hall.

Susanne Gannon
College of Arts
University of Western Sydney
Australia

JOHN J. GUINEY YALLOP

MY DAUGHTER IS GOING TO SCHOOL

How a Queer Catholic Is Learning Again to Pray

INTRODUCTION

I experienced schooling in Canada as a queer Catholic student, mostly from the closet. Later, to my surprise, I became a teacher in the public education system. For over 20 years, I worked as an out gay educator. The heterosexism and homophobia I experienced or witnessed, both as student and as teacher, if written about here, would push the introduction and conclusion of this piece much further apart. My own presentations and publications have, for the most part, been attempts to encourage the creation of more welcoming educational environments for sexual minorities and for the children of sexual minority parents or guardians. As my own daughter began school, however, I experienced the education system, both public and private, more personally and more vulnerably than ever before. This paper explores, through poetry, some of the worries I had as I prepared for my daughter's entry into school. I decided that I would not *just* pray that she would be okay there, but if praying might help, well....

As you read the following poem, you may wish to ask yourself, if you are a parent, what your own fears are for your school-aged children, or what your fears are for all children in schools, particularly marginalized children, whether or not you are a parent. As well, you may consider how prayer is used to bring people together, to heal, or to push us apart, to condemn.

MY DAUGHTER IS GOING TO SCHOOL

God:
I know we haven't talked much
lately
or
well
that you haven't heard much
from me
except for those times when there's been turbulence
during some of the flights I've taken
or that time when the plane was circling
Toronto during a thunder storm

M. Prendergast, C. Leggo and P. Sameshima (eds.), Poetic Inquiry: Vibrant Voices in the Social Sciences, 219–228.

my daughter and my partner on the ground
waiting
I went to the washroom
and cried
and spoke
my tears and words forming a prayer;
if you had anything to do with that landing
by the way
or for any of the other safe flights
thanks.
And then there was the time when mom was dying;
Alzheimer's had taken every part of her from us
except her breath
and I prayed that you
would take that
away too
so that she
and we
could rest.
Thanks also for that.
And I know that I probably haven't been listening much either
in case you've been saying anything
but I
well
I just need to ask your help with something
if you can do anything that is
or if you'd be willing to.
"God-willing," my parents used to say
punctuating every hope, wish, dream, want –
every need –
with
a "God-willing."
You see,
this isn't really for me
or at least not totally
anyway
so
although I haven't been exactly keeping up my side of the communication
along the divine line
I hope
well
that that won't be too much of a problem;
it's not like you haven't forgiven me before
or anything.
Well
anyway

you see
my daughter is going to school
and
well
I'm afraid;
I don't mean that I'm afraid in the way that I used to be afraid when I went to
school
as a student
or the way that I became afraid of going to school
as a teacher;
no
this feels different.
Then
and sometimes recently
I was able to plan my defense
or attack
depending on the circumstances.
I had my arsenal of words and phrases
that would puncture the power bubble
of most bullies
whether or not they admitted it.
I wasn't interested in their admission
I only wanted to be left alone.
No
this feels very different
and parts of me feel more vulnerable
than I ever felt with another person's fist waving in my face
or hearing others cheer
"go on
get him
get him"
or sitting in the principal's office
as student or as teacher
being blamed –
educated
in the way it works – told
what needs to be done.
No
this is different;
this is different
because it's about her – it is
her –
what she will experience
or not
at school
and what she will learn

or not
from those we trust
or don't
those we leave her with
each day.
Anyway
I'm wondering if I could give you a list
a list of wants
and
don't wants
a list of please let this happen
and
please don't let this happen
a list of please give her
and please don't let her have
a list of who and what to embrace her with
and who and what to protect her from
a list to open her to
and a list to arm her for;
even if you pick and choose
maybe she'll experience some of the want ones
the please let this happen ones
the please give her ones
the please embrace her ones
the please open her to ones
and then if she happens to have
or you in your wisdom decide that she should have
some of the don't want ones
the please don't let this happen ones
the please don't let her have ones
the protect her from ones
and the arm her for ones
well
she'll be alright
she'll be alright
she'll be alright.
That's really my prayer isn't it
that she'll be alright.
That has become my daily prayer
my whisper to you
to my partner
her Papa
the air
the plants
the universe
each day

when I say
"bye, butterfly;
see you this evening"
that
she'll
be
alright
that she'll be alright
a hope
a dream
a prayer
that an alright person
will be alright
going into a place
that is anything but alright
but where the guardians believe
or at least preach
that all is
right.
Anyway, God,
did my prayers always start with such preambles?
I don't recall them anymore
they've become fossilized memories
of a life lived
fossils that I try to revive now
as I write these words
and prepare to ask
or beg
humility having replaced
for this anyway
all of my pride
freeing me
from at least one
of the seven deadly sins.
Anyway, God,
the list:
I want her to be safe going to school
God
not just be safe
but also feel safe
knowing that she can be herself
express herself
I don't want her to have to worry
about authoritarian
bossy
students

teachers or administrators
who want to control her
or create good children
in their own image
please let her have peers who will play with her
teachers who understand her
and principals who look out for her
please don't let her have bullies for peers
teachers who want to hear only her silence
and principals who don't take the time to get to know her
please let her see images in her schools
and hear language in those schools
that reflect her realities
as a child with two dads
who
as she says
"are married together to one another"
please don't let her go through a day
a week
a month
a year
without hearing words like partner
spouse
parents
family
used in ways that she knows
please give her teachers who interrupt the violence of name-calling
and the violence of silence
please give her teachers who will say
gay
lesbian
queer
without flinching
please don't let her have teachers
who say that
gay
lesbian
queer
are bad words
and shouldn't be used in school
please let her see images in her schools
and hear language in those schools
about adoption
and please
when it comes time for family trees
give her teachers who understand that her family tree

may have more branches
and different kinds of limbs
than those of many of her peers
please shield her from indiscriminate use of the word
adoption
as in adopting highways
or parks
or pets
or an attitude
or at least let her know
in her innermost being
that those expressions reflect nothing
of the journey to create a family
please don't let her be too hurt by other people's insensitivity
or ignorance
please give her principals and vice-principals who will expect
that all staff will include the realities of all their students
and not just those of the privileged
or only the marginalized that they choose to notice
please don't give her principals and vice-principals
who say that having same-sex parents will not become an issue
unless she happens to say something about it during recess
give her teachers and vice-principals who are intelligent
not ignorant
or if ignorant
are not unaware of it
and will do something constructive about it
and not see our daughter as yet another special interest to be grudgingly
accommodated
please give her teachers who celebrate her love of pink
but not teachers who will package her with it
please give her a space for her body
to move
and for her voice
to be heard
please don't let her be pushed to limited and limiting spaces
for girls
by boys who still have not deconstructed how patriarchy has formed them
or by girls who play along with it
please give her reminders about how beautiful she is
it's so easy to forget
when you are not reminded
or when you are constantly corrected
please let her gifts be welcomed
her tears allowed
and understood

please don't let those tears be wiped away
until they are allowed to hold the sadness she needs to know how to experience
please give her a thick skin
but not so thick that her heart can't be reached
please give her rituals for celebrating
who she is
and who her family is
please don't allow her to be lost and silenced
in other rituals that ask her to forget who she is
please give her school forms that ask for the names of her parents or guardians
and not forms that limit parenting to a mother and a father
please give her teachers who understand
that wanting to be a princess
and a crane operator
are not mutually exclusive
and if she should turn to you, God,
please let her find you
dressed in a blanket of acceptance and love
and not in a cloak of hatred and rejection
which is how you were so often presented to me
please give her teachers who will celebrate her body as she is becoming a young
woman
but who do not allow her body to become a target
or an object
give her skills to survive
even thrive
in that environment called school
and give her Daddy and her Papa skills
to help her navigate that environment
when she encounters homophobia
and she will
in students
in teachers
in administrators
in other parents
strengthen her pride in the two queers who love her more than they ever knew they
could love
individually
and together
don't let homophobia get inside her
where it can do the most damage
when she encounters sexism
and she will
in students
in teachers
in administrators

in other parents
strengthen her respect for her body
and her mind
don't let sexism get inside her
where it can do the most damage
when she encounters racism
and she will
in students
in teachers
in administrators
in other parents
strengthen her love – her pride and respect – for her ancestry
for the blood of the many nations that flows through her
keep before her the importance of mirth
and when she laughs
may the world laugh with her
and when she cries
may the world embrace her
teaching her how to embrace herself
and when she speaks
may the world listen
to the wisdom that can come from a child
and I beg you
don't allow the sins of the father
within this system
to be visited upon the daughter
but if I have done anything right and just
within this system
may she benefit from it
and as we remind her every day
don't ever let her forget
even for a moment
just how much
she is loved
and that who she is
is defined
both by her history –
her stories –
and by the choices she makes
in loving,
in living,
and in forgiving.

Amen.

CONCLUSION

What does one conclude from such a poem? Are there any conclusions? What does this poem teach us about schooling, about homophobia, about heterosexism, about sexism, about racism, about other forms of marginalization? Where is the voice of the daughter? Are the parent's fears her fears as well? What, if anything, can we know about her fears? What do we make of a conclusion that raises questions, but offers no answers?

John J. Guiney Yallop
School of Education
Acadia University
Canada

WANDA HURREN

THE CONVENIENT PORTABILITY OF WORDS

Aesthetic Possibilities of Words on Paper/Postcards/Maps/Etc.

Over the past 10 years of my academic career within various departments of curriculum and instruction I have continued to inquire into notions of place and identity, especially regarding how these two notions are seemingly inseparable.

Curricularly, geography and social studies are areas of study within schools and academies that provide opportunities for exploring place and identity, and my desire has always been to acknowledge embodied ways of knowing around this exploration. Poetic inquiry informs my approach to exploration because poetic language facilitates embodied knowing, or at least facilitates calling up our embodied faculties—gut reactions, hearing, seeing, smelling, tasting, touching, emoting, intuiting. So then, in terms of exploring place and identity, I am intent on promoting poetic exploration of these notions. I am also intent on promoting these notions as non-fixed entities, always in process, and the idea that individually and collectively we are involved in collecting and discarding bits and pieces of living all along the way or continually throughout the process of understanding places and selves.

My title for this chapter refers to a quote by John Steffler (1995), who, concerning poetry and knowing, reminds us:

> What poetry offers, then, is not a form of abstract, quantifiable knowledge, like scientific findings, that can be amassed and advanced. Instead, through the convenient portability of words, it offers a semblance of direct experience, a recovery or approximation of emotional experience that engages our sense of the numinous and aesthetic. (p. 49)

Lately I have been taking advantage of the "convenient portability of words" in terms of paying attention to *where* I place words in my explorations of place, identity, and embodied knowing. Especially when I am working with geographic forms of representation, an area of inquiry where images are a very prominent feature: maps, atlases, charts, drawings, photographs; and an area of inquiry wherein questions of "where" are prominent.

MAPWORK AS VESSEL

For the past several years I have been working on a mapwork project[1] that has the intent of promoting embodied knowing in the area of curriculum studies, and specifically within research and pedagogy around notions of place and identity. I

M. Prendergast, C. Leggo and P. Sameshima (eds.), Poetic Inquiry: Vibrant Voices in the Social Sciences, 229–238.

have been working with various cartographic forms and incorporating aesthetic aspects along with poetic inquiry. One of the proposed outcomes of the mapwork research is an atlas that acknowledges and allows for embodied knowing.

In my mapwork project I have been exploring and trying out various "vessels" for carrying or holding words/text. Here I am using a broad interpretation of text to include images, texture, line, colour, light and, of course, words as they are influenced by these various other textual components. It seems that it is possible to "pump up the volume" of embodied knowing by incorporating these various textual components. Or, said another way, texture, colour, and light are aesthetic qualities that are able to enhance the effect of the text they surround, carry, or hold.

One of the most enjoyable aspects of this mapwork project has been the opportunity I have had to explore and create templates of various forms of mapwork. I have spent time in libraries wearing white gloves in order to read and examine book art collections, I've been taking photography classes, going to art exhibits, and, maybe most fun of all, hanging out in art stores, touching things!

In the mapwork samples that follow, my intention is not to just make things look nice, but rather, through incorporating aesthetic components with poetic text, to invite people to connect with the ideas around identity and place in ways that facilitate further exploration of place and identity on individual and collective levels. These various mapwork samples all take advantage of the convenient portability of words and through the mapwork we are reminded of the various possible vessels that might carry and hold words.

Mapwork I: *...and topography*

The mapwork featured in the image is from the exhibition piece titled *and topography*[2]. These triptychs grew out of a conversation I had with someone who, knowing that while I am now living on the west coast of Canada, I lived most of my life on the prairies, made the comment, "Oh well then I can see how you would appreciate weather … and topography" (as if there is no topography on the prairies). Through this series of triptychs I want to express, in some way, the idea that place and identity are cumulative events and not mutually exclusive—I can only make sense of the west coast in relation to what and where it is not, and much of my sense making about who I am in this place is closely related to who I used to be, but am no longer—in another place. These layers of being all work together linking places and identities. Topographical and highway maps comprise the first layer of the triptych pieces, vellum paper with text composes the second layer, and colour positive Polaroid transfers of geographical locations make up the top layer of these triptychs. The text running along the lower edge of the vellum layer for the first two pieces of each triptych reads: "prairie prairie prairie prairie," and the images and topographical maps are of prairie spaces. The third piece in each triptych reads simply "not," and the topographical maps and images are of west coast spaces.

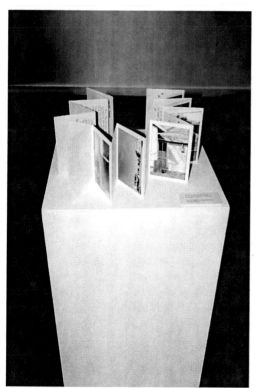

Mapwork II: *Partial Glossary of Words and Phrases*

The mapwork sample in the image to the left illustrates an accordion booklet of postcards and poems that comprise a partial glossary of words and phrases based on the small town where I grew up. This booklet was part of a recent exhibit of image and text[3] and a portion of the glossary (A, B, H – J, X – Z sections) follows:

A GOOD PLACE TO GROW UP
is what some people say about their small town. Especially the people who played on the hockey team or the volleyball team or the basketball team. Or the people who still live in the small town. If it still exists (see *ZERO POPULATION GROWTH*).

BACK ALLEYS
with one exception, were never called lanes (see *LOVERS' LANE*). Kids smoked and peed in them. They were often badly rutted and sometimes had sections of white ash where burning barrels had been dumped out. Back alleys were shortcuts we might take, especially at night, when the streetlights were out, and it was cold and windy, and we thought someone was probably following us, and we had to run. *What was that noise... did you hear that...*

BURNING BARRELS
were in every backyard. Someone was always burning garbage, usually in the evening. Never a pleasant smell. Most had holes in their brown rusted metal sides. Did look nice burning in the dark. Made it easy to say no, we had not been smoking.

…

HENRY
lived alone in a shack in the back alley, until one year a bachelor took him into his home. Gave him new clothes and a bed and regular meals. One New Year's Eve Henry froze to death in a snowdrift beside his old shack. He had forgotten he didn't live there anymore.

IRIS
lived across the street in a small house with brown shingle siding. She spoke with a gruff, French accent and liked to bake cookies for children. Once she gave us homemade wine to drink along with our gingersnaps.

JELL-O DESSERTS
were always on the lunch counter at curling bonspiels. Orange, cherry, or grape, and always with miniature marshmallows mixed in (see *CHERRY CHA CHA*).

…

X
was never seen on lit crosswalk signs. Well, crosswalk signs were never seen. Signs were sometimes seen. Once Lillian Dupuis answered the door to an angel. She invited the angel in for dinner. She told everyone about the angel and said it was a sign (…*that you're crazy* is what some people thought; see *CIRCLE, COFFEE ROW, DID YOU HEAR ABOUT…*).

YOUTH GROUPS
would start up every once-in-a-while. The activities were full of goodness. Often an underlying Protestant theme of just don't have too much fun could be detected (see *CIRCLE*).

ZERO POPULATION GROWTH
(see *A Good Place to Grow Up*).

Mapwork III: *Collage*

Collage holds endless possibilities for mapping identity and place. To conduct some of my mapwork I went several times to the small town where I grew up. I usually found myself walking along the sidewalks, which were in various states of disrepair and had the usual small town markers of someone's handprint or footprint, and here and there a set of initials or a swear word scratched into the setting concrete.

On one of my walks around the small town, I remembered that the town had wooden sidewalks until I was in Grade One. These walkways with gaps between the boards made wearing any sort of heel dangerous, and meant that items dropped between the wooden slats were seldom rescued despite attempts made with hockey sticks and coat hangers. In 1962 the town introduced municipal water and sewer. To accommodate this cutting edge approach to community sanitation, the wooden sidewalks were taken up and replaced with cement sidewalks. Sewer lines then ran along or underneath these new concrete walkways. I was thinking about what might have been found under the wooden sidewalks when they were taken up in 1962. The following list is included in a collage booklet (similar to the accordion booklet illustrated in Mapwork II) that was part of a recent exhibit of text and image[4] wherein I have incorporated maps and charts of sewer lines, street elevations and intersections, and poetry, photographs and field notes.

(WHAT MIGHT HAVE BEEN) FOUND UNDER THE WOODEN SIDEWALKS
(A PARTIAL INVENTORY)

In front of the school, two black pocket combs, half of a wooden yoyo, stubby
  pencils, three ballpoint pens from the Credit Union, an orange fish fin marble, a
  silver initial ring (G . H.).
In front of the Lutheran church, pennies, a pair of child's sunglasses with
  one arm missing, the knot from a popped balloon, a Christmas card with grey
  sugary sparkles on the front of it (*with best wishes from Bud and Rosemary*).
In front of the Catholic church, penny matches from Ray's Grill, rosary beads,
  plastic wedding flowers, cigar butts with creamy yellow plastic tips, a broken
  cufflink, one clip-on rhinestone cluster earring and one with a screw-on post.
Along the main street, empty Macintosh Toffee boxes, popsicle sticks, bottle
  caps from Bohemian, Pilsner, Tab, Mountain Dew, Fanta Grape, and in front of
  the town office, a black and white photo of a young woman standing beside a
  television set in a living room. The date along the white zig zag edging shows
  • *Oct 61•*. That was when she smiled at the camera and gave the snapshot to
  someone who later did not notice when it fluttered down from his wallet,
  slipped through the cracks, and landed beside the small plastic whistle no longer
  tied to the strings of a child's straw cowboy hat.

Mapwork IV: *postcartographia*

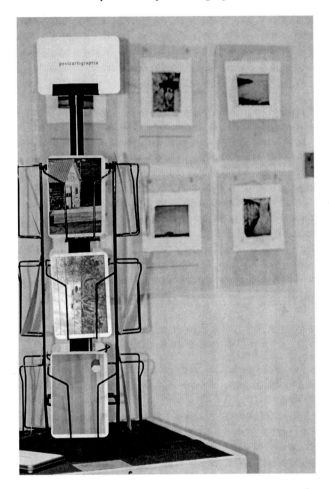

The postcard rack in the above image is of a recent exhibition[5] that displays mapwork around the notion of what I am calling *postcartographia*—a project with the intent to call up cartography as a structure and poststructurally play with notions of what counts in the world of cartography (hence the notion of *post* cartography). Considering the French term *carte postale, carte* can mean both map and card, and *poste* has etymological roots in the words place and position. It seems to me that postcards are a popular form of cartography that is almost ubiquitous in our individual and collective attempts to map/make sense of place and identity.

Much of the mapwork I have been conducting involves driving to get to the places I intend to "map." I soon discovered that I was paying more attention to the drives between the places than to the actual "places." I stopped many times along highways and side roads to take photographs and write journal notes, which then became *postcartographia*. The text and images from three of these postcards follow on the next pages:

postcartographia: Truck Stop, Highway #11
Saskatchewan Highways

IT is mean, unkind,
unthinking really
to paint
palm trees and a beach
on the east side of Penny's Bar & Grill
in the absence of trees (for miles)
in the presence of dirty snow drifts
the ice cream window shut and covered with the sign
CLOSED FOR THE SEASON

postcartographia: -48° Celsius
Saskatchewan, February 15

THREE QUESTIONS:
Do people breathe out that much breath in warmer weather but we just don't see it?
Do cars have that much exhaust in warmer weather but we just don't see it?
Would July be as good as it is even without days like this in February but we just don't see it?

postcartographia: Highway #6
Two Car Stories and a Questions and an Answer

Q: Why do I love driving on the prairies so much?

A: Because I like to see cars on the other side of the four-lane highway; the colours flashing against a flat forever background.

I

ONCE when we were living in Vancouver a young man at a drive-thru restaurant saw our Saskatchewan license plate and asked where we were from. When we said *Saskatoon* he said *Oh. I was there once. All the cars were so dirty.* I said *That's funny because I was noticing how all the cars in Vancouver are so shiny clean.* Now, living on the prairies again, it is with an extra measure of sadness that I know my car is in need of a wash.

II

ONCE I let a man drive my car on the four-lane highway after we had hiked in the Qu'Appelle Valley. It was nice to sit back and watch his hands on the steering wheel and see his arm muscles flex. *(What do you call the muscle just above the elbow?)* I noticed a wood tick crawling on his pants. *(What do you call the part of the leg just above the knee?)* And then he noticed it and we were swerving across the centre line and I was screaming out his name. *(What do you*

237

call the thoughts that flash through your mind just before you die?) He steered my car over to the side of the road. *(What do you call the part of the road that is not paved anymore, but not part of the ditch?)* And he scrambled out of the car and pulled his pants off and shook them out and then he drove me home wearing just his underwear. And that was nice too. *(What do you call the kind of light that makes the hair on men's legs shine softly?)*

NOTES

[1] Hurren, W. (Principal Investigator). (2005-2008). *Mapwork as an approach to exploring notions of place and identity.* Social Sciences and Humanities Research Council of Canada, Standard Research Grant.

[2] Hurren, W. (2008). *Mapwork.* Exhibit of Photographs and Mixed Media/Group Exhibit. 28th Anniversary Art Education Faculty Exhibition, McPherson Library Gallery, University of Victoria.

[3] Hurren, W. (2008). *postcartographia.* Exibit of image and text. Xchanges Gallery, Victoria, BC.

[4] Hurren, W. (2008). *postcartographia.* As above.

[5] Hurren, W. (2008). *Mapwork.* As above.

REFERENCES

Steffler, J. (1995). Language as matter. In T. Lilburn (Ed.), *Poetry and knowing: Speculative essays and interviews* (pp. 45–51). Kingston, ON: Quarry Press.

Wanda Hurren
Department of Curriculum and Instruction
University of Victoria
Canada

SARAH K. MACKENZIE

FRAGMENTED OMS

A Poetic (Re)fusing of Teacher

In Preparation

body and mind move, breathing together,
        (be)coming open
and ready

WITH INTENTION

Another semester has begun, and I find myself once again conflicted. I am a teacher of pre-service teachers, working to help my students gain access to the meaning and process involved in this complex vocation. Within my work I know there are expectations—exams and requirements, both for my students as well as the children they will teach—and there are dreams, hopefully attainable. I watch my student teachers struggling to become everything they believe a teacher should be, as they are faced with realities that at times make them want to quit. And I am reminded of who I was, am, as a teacher, at times feeling lost amidst a chaotic droning of dreams and expectations, waking each day in a state of excitement and dread. I can empathize with their experience, and as a teacher educator I work to help them process through their struggles, providing resources for them, challenging their choices, and listening. I may hear the words of my students, I may respond to what they say, but it is by listening poetically and presently, through a collective OM[1], that I believe I am most able to hear what remains unspoken in our shared experiences.

When writing of the work of poetic anthropology, Behar (2007), states that "it has meant allowing myself to experience the emotional wrenching ways in which we attain knowledge about others and ourselves" (p. 63). I say, with hesitancy, that it would be easy for me to write of what my student teachers said and did, and to analyze it from a distance. This hesitancy comes from a personal tug that leads me to believe that this distance is one imagined; I might be able to create that façade, but my own experiences are strong, always tracing their lines upon the words I write. Leggo (2008) thoughtfully reminds me that "we need to write personally because we live personally, and our personal living is always braided with other ways of living—professional, academic, administrative, artistic, social, and political" (p. 5). Cahnmann-Taylor (2003) remarks: "Incorporating the craft, practice, and

M. Prendergast, C. Leggo and P. Sameshima (eds.), Poetic Inquiry: Vibrant Voices in the Social Sciences, 239–257.

possibility of poetry in our research, enhances our ability to understand classroom life and support students' potential to add their voices to a more socially just and democratic society" (p. 34). And so it is through poetry that I become willing to step into the messiness (Jardine, 1997) of the always shared, personal experience, becoming vulnerable to those emotions that may arise as I begin to live, write, breathe, and move, within the poetic spaces of [my own] be(com)ing Teacher. Bolton (1999) comments, "The writing of poetry profoundly alters the writer because the process faces one with oneself" (p. 118). I contend that this process of altering is one that occurs collectively; as reader and writer become one through the OM, we all breathe our experiences upon the poem, reflections of ourselves (Ellsworth, 1997; Norman, 2000) as we see the wor(l)d in vivid and lively new ways.

Loud Erasure

Writing,
my body moves across the page
clinging to the motion of self
Scrolling
imperfections
Merging of past
        present
           future
Desiring
       forgotten moments
echoing across the textual landscape
of story
       Stepping carefully
            so as not to slip
                 in to the folds
of hegemony
       as the whispers
              of who
                 we
                      I
should
      could
         have been
              whip their chilly wind
      across the psyche
           of
being
      Slipping
          softly through the pores
of an (un)known existence

Tadasana

The body becomes a mountain, "upright, straight, unmoved ... and still."

Through the spiritual practice of Yoga, one's being is invited to become present and still. For some this stillness is a way to let go, becoming "freed from restless desire," one is delivered from pain and sorrow (Iyengar, 1979, p. 19). Yet I wonder if there is not a spiritual quality to the stillness of being present to the subtle ripples of emotion that enter one's consciousness. What happens when we do not run, but instead root oursel(f)ves in the steadiness of mountain pose, willing to accept what arrives? And so I enter into tadasana, ready to stand still, willing to be present to those memories and emotions of be(com)ing Teacher that so readily echo across my consciousness.

Unveiling the Remembered

The room
cold in hesitation
my mind flutters
a collision of desire
memory and a moment
Stillness
bustling along the pavement of unrealized anticipation
something, sometime, someplace
My hands shake
a timidness overtakes me
I have not
forgotten
and so I must
(re)turn
to the moment
mingling in my mind

METAPHORICALLY SPEAKING

The poetic renderings pieced together across the space of this text reflect the action and emotion that exist in the stillness of being with/in the memory of a moment: fluid snapshots of something that might have been for one, a truth. Reflecting on Lakoff and Johnson's (1980) thought that "metaphor is one of our most important tools for trying to comprehend partially what cannot be comprehended totally: our feelings, aesthetic experiences, moral practices, and spiritual awareness" (p. 193), I consider the nature of my own making sense of the experiences of be(com)ing, for a moment, Teacher, yet in another moment longing for sel(f)ves. Experience itself is in a sense beyond comprehension: poetry offers the space to be present to what may or may not be known with/in the experience. While I cannot tell you what or how it was to be(come) Teacher in a space of silence, possibility, and, loss, I can through poetry create space to allow others to enter into the story so that they might be able to (re)create or imagine their own ways of knowing with/in the shared experience. Throughout the textual space of this piece, I draw on two metaphors to create openings (Springgay, Irwin & Wilson, 2005) where multiple voices may enter in, allowing the possibilities of the experience to fuse together in temporality, a shared story of knowing what it might mean to be(come) Teacher. These two metaphors will be used across the landscape of this rendering as a means to offer shared "points of departure" (Pente, 2005, p. 93) from which we might begin our journey of poetic exploration across the landscape of be(com)ing Teacher.

The first metaphor I draw on is that of the practice of yoga. It is this practice that offers up enlightenment, but an enlightenment that goes beyond the notion of a Truth, instead embracing inner and outward awareness and fluidity of being. The practice of yoga is a practice of unity, possibility and compassion; however, like the work of be(com)ing Teacher, yoga is a practice in which individuals experience both struggle as they work through postures that are not always comfortable, and joy as the body finds itself awakened with newfound energy. Postures as considered by Iyengar (1976) are movements of reflection and being as one works through making sense of the world. These postures are not simply physical movements, but rather exist also as responses of the mind, thoughts that become embodied, connecting the facets of sel(f)ves with the physical world.

The second metaphor that pieces together across this poetic rendering of experience is that of the fused glass. Fusing glass is a process of fluidity as variations of glass are cut and shattered, yet these fragments join together into something seemingly concrete and unified through the heat of momentary insight or the kiln. The pieces that result are varied based on the way in which fragments are positioned, many times the pieces are seen as jewelry, ready to be worn and recognized; however, the fused piece is glass, fragile and fluid, easily broken and (re)pieced together across time. As one engages in the work of be(com)ing Teacher s/he arrives like a piece of fused glass, fragments of experience have come together to shape her subjectivity. Yet this subjectivity is fleeting as one's truths may be shattered by multiple realities and moments of experience. The shattering of an image/ined self does not mean the end as some might fear, but rather offers opportunities for re/piecing one's sense of sel(f)ves with/in the world. Both the practice of yoga and the fusing of glass are personal, projects which I have across time found myself engaged in. It was through my own active involvement in these projects that I began to explore my own understandings of the negotiations of one be(com)ing Teacher and it is from that space which I begin.

Beginning with the personal, I want to move into a collective and pedagogical space of possibility. As such, I use the metaphors of the yogic practice and fusing of glass as a way to engage a collective (re)searching for meaning that draws on both personal and public ways of constructing meaning.

Seeing Through

                               There are shards of glass
          broken windows upon my memory
of being   Teacher
         A whirling of what
                     could have been
                           or that which never was
                                 or was
             my desire.
I look at the faces of Teacher   mine
                  or yours
                     or theirs
        But the images are cracked
                  possibilities
                       perhaps
                           only ending in what I
imagined
                                       I lost
And so
  in loss   I begin
                    the journey again
                      to find hope amidst
                          the chasms of experience,
emotion
          and thought
                  Echoing across the darkness
               bouncing upon the psyche   new lights are
born   reflecting the image
               of what could be
                       upon the shards of what
we/you/I remember

Through the fragmented lens of poetry, there is more to be seen; in naming my/self as artist, researcher, and teacher, I find myself wandering through a space crowded with the vividness of my own and others' intention, desire, and definition. There is a yogic quality to such a space of inquiry, as knowing moves fluidly, inviting individual and collective attention to the moment.

Sun Salutation

Body up, body down, stretching, pushing with compassion

FACETED MOVEMENTS OF (A) TEACHING MOMENT(S)

Learned (un)Veiling

We arrive
    students and teacher
  seeking
       "So much talk about what it is
  we teach," he says
the man with the long white hair.
       He gave up long ago
  on wanting
       He claims he has found peace and answers
in the breathing
    the connection
             I don't know
I have not found
      I think
listening to his words,
"What about the learning?
    What about the learner?"
My thoughts arrive
    another moment
passed
    I am Teacher
  they are my students
I have been warned
    "you must tell them
       what to do."
My body screams
    darkness creeping in around me.
"You"
    they have told me
      called me
  what to do
  I became lost in the cacophony
For me the loss became the learning
      but this is not the case for everyone
captive

The poetry I share today are fragments, pieces of the OM, fused together in a moment—pieces of myse(f)ves be(com)ing. I become through interaction, be/longing and observing, entering into dialogue with those who may hear the reverberations of my experience across the echoes of their own subjectivity. As I offer the experience of be(com)ing Teacher interpreted through poetry, the voices that speak are not mine alone, the experiences may not even seem to fit into what one would normally consider as belonging to those of Teacher. There is complexity in the name, and poetic inquiry offers the space to reflect upon and engage with that complexity and the facets of experience that come together to piece a fluid picture of one's sel(f)ves be(com)ing.

I invite you to enter with me into this textual space of inquiry (Richardson, 2000), where in the writing we might find ourselves with/in the complications of understanding and being. Research exists across multiple contexts, shaped through the subjectivity and intention of those telling and seeking story. Springgay (2004) observes that "postmodern and psychoanalytic theories maintain that subjectivities are inherently unfixed, unknowable, and uncertain" (p. 60). There is no possibility for prediction, there are no connections that might remain concrete; instead the nature of knowing is one that demands a sense of openness to the possibilities of the present and the fluid existence of the past. As Janesick (2000) identifies in her metaphorical exploration of research as choreography, the story searched is one of improvisation, evolving over the course of moments. In searching, the selves of artist, teacher, and researcher collide in the discomforting space of un/knowing. Truth, so long recognized as holding pedagogic value within the telling space, becomes fragmented, slipping in and out of the subjectivities of multiple voices. As these voices come together in a cacophony of storied selves, pedagogy evolves, becoming something outside the hegemony of a starving society desperate for Truth.

Pause

The room
    a table carefully chosen
by one who wants
        to write
           tell
               the story
    of what
          it might have been
      like
          in the moment.
She breathes
    waiting to re/turn

Required Loss
               An echo from another room
I was
    was
  a teacher
      once upon a time
    A time
  chalkboard dust upon my fingers
        moments when I

```
            did not know mysel(f)ves
Myself
      I was a child
   waiting to be recognized
Waiting
                  crumpled up papers
         in a desk
               assigned
I wanted to challenge
                  but instead I listened
Listened
watched and waited
      until the moment
The moment
               when speaking
         became messy again
   and I could share
               without fear
      of being
being
                  washed
```

Ghostly (re)emembering

Dear Young Teacher,

I remember you, breath shallow as you used every ounce you had to tread the waters of the educational system you had been thrown in. Nothing could have prepared you for that, or so you thought. Each attack that you had was built upon your own sense of failure as you saw your every desire whither across a pedagogical landscape that was not your own.

I cannot save you, I cannot return your desires so that you might once again step into a classroom of your own and I cannot silence those who silenced you. But I know I have a responsibility to you and it is with this sense of responsibility that I write—sharing my story of being both teacher and teacher educator as I fuse my own stories with the fragments of story claimed by those pre-service teachers I work with. I want to be with their negotiations, helping them become more aware—in a manner that you could not. I could not give you what you needed, but perhaps by offering up space for the dialogue of the experience of be(com)ing Teacher they might begin to move through the discourses that position them, aware that they are not alone. Maybe, if they enter into a collective conversation of experience they might find their breath, that which you so long ago lost.

I have moved forward, young teacher, but you remain forever in my memory as I remember that I was you and you are me. I write this letter seeking to offer spaces for active movement within those borders that we for so long dreamt of crossing. I admit, this work, this research that I do is problematic as it arises from my own desire to discover that which I could name along my own journey of being teacher. Yet it is this same problematizing that offers opportunities to get lost within the fragments of story and desire, finding new paths and ways of knowing those discourses that shape our subjectivities.

I can finally breathe now, but my breath is one of fluid awareness—where desire is fleeting and possibility is plentiful.

Opaque Transparence

Momentary shifts
    Understanding
Student
    Teacher
        Woman
            Child
The thin line
    becomes   transparent
Through the fog
      I seek
        to know my name
As my self echoes
      all the selves
        I dreamed
or was

LAYERING SEL(F)VES

Norman (2000) notes that our lives and stories are layered; as the voices of those who have been silent about their experiences fold into the textures of self and other, they may begin to join together into a chorus of collective silence and struggle that might be able to become heard amidst the cacophony of expectations that have so often hindered any possibility for movement beyond the boundaries of what should be. Davies (2000) discusses the value of this sort of collectivity when she examines the collective biography:

> Through listening to the stories of others, through talking out loud the remembered fragments, through writing the memories down and seeing how language shapes them with cultural patterns of meaning – making, the collective group searches for the kind of 'truth' that comes from inside the remembered even and also from the process of remembering. (p. 42)

Entering these fragments on the performative landscape of text, one finds agency through the temporality of action and understanding. I imagine the Teacher, sitting quietly in her classroom one afternoon—miserably wondering what it is that she might do to move beyond the ambiguous pain that leaves its imprint upon her everyday. What would she do, if she was able to speak of her experience and know that it was welcomed? What then would happen, if in the sharing she discovered that there were structures that impacted her experience and sense of self within the experience—would she feel a greater sense of agency, would she begin to reflect upon her experiences differently?

Contracted

I forgot who I was
one morning
the damp winter air
running
   through my veins
                    mixed
with the thickness of chalkboard dust
Each breath
     labored
          The contractions so strong
my vision clouded
              I
                     could
no longer
        stand

        Where was I when it happened
            first?
            When I wondered what I was doing
                in the classroom?

"That day, this day, I had just returned from a short break. I had carefully prepared myself for the day, had eaten my breakfast. Oh, of course I felt the usual dread and sense of responsibility. My car had been cold when I opened the door. I remember the classroom as being cold that morning as well. I don't know if it was the room itself, or a presence that hung heavily in the atmosphere."

I knew something was different, changing, but I was afraid.

> The yogic journey guides us from our periphery, the body, to the center of our being, the soul. The aim is to integrate the various layers so that the inner divinity shines out through clear glass. (Iyengar, p. 3)

Possible Fragments

Thought
     echoing across the darkness
          bouncing upon the psyche   New
lights are born   reflecting the image

of what could be
upon the shards of what we
remember

Frog

On the floor, legs stretched behind in an uncomfortable position—for some—
eyes looking forward or could they be ... inward ... backward ...

Tom

Echoes.
  A child speaks
  adult(s) grieving
          grasping sel(f)ves
    What is it
          he says?
      My words
            his speaking
      become intertwined
and I
      do not know
"I played that last day
          the day   *before*
we laughed
      racing dirt bikes
    and pushing
          I wanted more.
The game
      we all liked it."
                    And this is what I wonder
      was it a game
                or was someone
          at fault?
                  Did suffering
echo across your thoughts?
            I remember a child
your friend
    she stopped eating that year
                her head resting on the shoulder of her mother at your funeral
I heard she (the mother) asked her (the daughter)
        to hold
            too much
I watched her pain
      Myself
            voyeur

249

             grieving
                    blaming
The game
        Bang, bang you're dead
                        we played as children
our bodies falling but we always rose.
Did you think you would rise
                that evening
                            days before Thanksgiving
the noose tight around your neck
            face blue?
Did you imagine
        the next moment?
Your six year old brother screams at the funeral,
        "I called him to dinner.
He didn't move.
        I kicked him,
                and he just laid there …
Mom tried to save him.
        He spit vomit in her mouth."
No one speaks.
            I was his teacher
and now I sit
There is nothing
    I can do
                This is the first dead body I've seen
                The most lively child
and today
            what
who
As we leave I hug his father
his body stiff
            tears frozen inward
in a feigned performance of hegemonic masculinity
        Like myself
he does not speak
            And I wonder
what is it you would say
            about this moment?

It is strange that I return here, to the not so distant present. For a long time I
lived in the past, in moments taken, where I watched and felt myself and others
losing. Ask me who I am as a teacher and I tell you of the children no one heard or
listened to. I know that I too existed in those children in some way, that my desire
to be heard leaked onto my understandings of their own struggles. Yet these were

the children I loved, and when they lost, I felt pieces of myself fall apart—drifting into the new image of mysel(f)ves mourning.

FRAGMENTS OF SEL(F)VES

Within this rendering of experience I seek to ask: what meaning exists in the movements of be(com)ing Teacher?—not as a means to define clear plans to erase these struggles or even to find a distinct answer. Rather the asking arises out of the desire to create pedagogical openings that are alive. Openings, that as Judith Robertson (1997) notes in her own exploration of pedagogy, create space for full involvement of the self; both the flesh and the psyche dance upon the pages of the journey—breathing life into the experience. The pedagogical asking works as a means to open up a textual space that invites reflexivity across the ordinary and helps one regain a sense of agency within the echoes that reverberate (Luce-Kapler, 1997; Norman, 2000; Irwin, 2004) through the emotions of silence, pleasure and being, even within the broken caverns of those ambiguous losses that cannot be named.

Shuddering

Anger and alienation
        student and teacher   there is no possibility
                  inside this space
but in the im/possibility   exists
        something else
              a dream   experience
a thought of what could be
                perhaps
                    what was

And so my body, my awareness shifts to the imagined stories of Teacher. What knowledge might reverberate across the sense as we engage with these new postures of be(com)ing?

Happy Baby

Body laying light upon the floor, arms and legs reaching upward dancing carelessly

Crashed

Present
        and past
                collide   into some/thing
unified   Breaking
        and becoming

Moving   forward
            back
shifting Searching   for the known
            to make sense
                                                    of the un/known
Images   text
            reality   confused
                        imagined   and real
until it becomes a part
                        of the being
                                    doing   of teacher   sel(f)ves

REVERBERATIONS OF A FRAGMENTED BE(COM)ING

Treading Water

I have reached
            child freshly born
deliciously messy
            in the muck of birthing
and for a moment
    I find myself
held
            Such peace in the possibility
a door opens
    light burns at my eyes
                        I turn to shield
                                    myself
            It is too late
                        who is it
I have become
            teacher
            scholar
                        writer
artist
            daughter
                        lover
the fabric of these names weaves through my pores
and I cannot
            There are holes in the piecing
                                    leaving me cold
            vulnerable
                        unable
I speak
        wondering
                whose words are these, really

the umbilical cord
             cut
          they say
     but I
          am not sure
                    it seems to knot in the weavings of my identity
I want
     to run over it
          like a Mack truck
                    away away
crush this soul who cannot find
          herself
                    drowning in the messiness of
(un)birthed possibility

                              Who am I?

Holding On

Quiet place
          little children
where you've been
               I once was
Moments pass so quickly
Standing by that time ago
     you see the faces of the seconds
               evening stars and lullabies
Whose to say it wasn't sometime
Whose to say it wasn't mine
Morning laughter
               evening screaming
plates flying across the floor
And where am I
     to stand here
the time that I once lived
playing
     singing
          crying
waiting for time
               to be

Dreamsleep

Silent sleeper
          wake
the dead

Vile wretchedness
             of oppression
Child screaming
             my words out loud
only to be
             pushed
             below the tide
outward
Only echoes in the waves
             a distant memory
Pictures
       and unravelled words
call out the truth
of one child's sighs
Until a moment
             glimpses lost
beneath the image
                   of greatness
Wake great one
the circle turns
             one must open
                         to call
the silent voices
             back

Eagle

Arms entwined, stretching, legs entwined, crouching and trying to stay
balanced

                                                  fluid notions

Blanketed Paralysis

My body turns
       my understandings
The sights
       I see
             become   something
                                 different

                                                  Shifting
                               moments   collide
                                                       across

                   the space of psyche and experience
I am caught

running

reaching for
the unnameable

Wrapped in the heaviness
of yesterday

Dear Young Teacher,

I write this letter in a space of forgetting and remembering. The you I once knew
no longer exists; instead new teachers and I's begin to etch their names across the
path of my knowing what it means to make sense of sel(f)ves with/in the classroom
and world. I remember you, waking, overwhelmed with what the day ahead might
have presented and feeling as if there was nowhere to turn—all the while looking
for Truth and contentment in far off places where you could be the Teacher you
once dreamed of. I wonder now, writing to you—what would you say to me today,
what would you tell me about the work you did and what you needed?

There are moments in my writing, where I think you return—your anger and
frustration as well as the desire and hope that still followed you even in moments
of (in)visibility. I question myself, thinking that perhaps you take my pen and
direct the story—clouding space for other stories to enter into making sense of the
negotiations of be(com)ing Teacher. I believe there might be danger in that, and so
I stop, pause, to question my intention throughout the work of my performative
(re)search. Even while I hear the echo of your voice and find your hand grasping at
my pen wanting so much to tell your own story, your voice has begun to fade. No
longer do I find myself desperate to tell your story so that your pain might be
recognized; the moment has passed. Instead I wonder if the you I remember is one
who existed at all. Are you a figment of my imagination, a creation of multiple
stories of be(com)ing Teacher fusing upon the landscape of my own making sense
as a teacher educator?

Perhaps it does not matter, for there is a you who I remember, a you who will
change as I change. It is these changes I think where the possibility lies, where we
can move outside the limitations of an individual momentary knowing into a fluid
and collective story that embraces experience as a tool to make sense of practice
across context. I do not know, but I hope.

Low Tide

I have remembered
        you and I
walking in the mists of dawn
A hand in mine
        trembling in anticipation
we watch
        and listen
                gathering fragments upon the shore
Broken pieces of another's past

> become a/part of who
> we might be(come)

Across the landscape of this rendering, I have sought to develop relationship, a subtle fusing, with an other, s/he who is both reader and writer of the emerging and evolving text remaining aware that "without the other, the self was redundant" (de Cosson, 2002, p. 10). It is this self/other relationship that lays the foundation for pedagogical possibility with/in a poetic and performative collectivity of being present to the storied experience of be(com)ing, in this case, Teacher. The poems I share exist as postures that move us forward in awareness, and as facets that may fuse to the echoes of the stories of another. The aesthetic nature of poetry calls on the senses to enter into awareness, opening space for multiple voices and sel(f)ves to enter into the dialogue of be(com)ing. I want to remember in my speaking, that I, as Irigaray (2004) comments, am other, but I will never be you; however, my voice may resonate with those words of reader/other that perhaps have remained unsaid. In the sharing, I move to offer the light that echoes across my own consciousness as a way to add dimension and perspective through the textual journey across the space of this living inquiry. I seek to (con)fuse the voices of the beginning teacher, pre-service teacher, and teacher educator as I find a way to exist and understand the struggles of be(com)ing Teacher amidst the ambiguity of being with/in the world. By shattering, piecing, and fusing, it is my hope to acknowledge not only my own experience or those of my students, but also to invite the reader to step upon the pedagogical landscape of the text, piecing the fragments of his or her own stories and understandings across the layers that already exist. The landscape of this text does not offer a safe space to read of another's experience, rather by intertwining the voices there is confusion. It is this confusion that I hope to embrace so that we might be able to enter into the OM of dialogue, amidst the struggle to name the shifts that tug at the desiring self, leaving her in a state of ambiguous longing and wonder. Might we not be frozen, in our confusion, but rather enter, with united awareness, into the crevices and cracks that lead to new understanding—that exists not in the single story, but in a collective, ever emerging, ever changing story of the private and social self.

NOTES

[1] Noun, Hinduism: a mantric word thought to be a complete expression of Brahman and interpreted as having three sounds representing Brahma or creation, Vishnu or preservation, and Siva or destruction, or as consisting of the same three sounds, representing waking, dreams, and deep sleep, along with the following silence, which is fulfilment.

REFERENCES

Behar, R. (2008). Between poetry and anthropology: Searching for languages of home. In M. Cahnmann-Taylor & R. Siegesmund (Eds.), *Arts basedresearch in education: Foundations in practice* (pp. 55–78). New York: Routledge.

Bolton, G. (1999). 'Every poem breaks a silence that had to be overcome': The therapeutic power of poetry writing. *Feminist Review. Contemporary Women Poets, 62,* 118–133.

Cahnmann, M. (2003). The craft, practice, and possibility of poetry in educational research. *Educational Researcher, 3*(32), 29–36.

Davies, B. (2000). *In scribing body/landscape relations.* New York: Altamira Press.

de Cosson, A. (2002). The hermeneutic dialogic: Finding patterns amid the aporia of the artist/researcher/teacher. *The Alberta Journal of Educational Research, XLVIII*(3), CD-ROM, 1–31.

Irigaray, L. (2002). *Between east and west: From singularity to community.* New York: Columbia University Press.

Irigaray, L. (2004). *Key writings.* New York: Continuum.

Iyengar, B. K. S. (1976). *Light on yoga.* New York: Schocken Books.

Iyangar, B. K. S. (2005). *Light on life.* New York: Rodale Books.

Janesick, V. (2000). The choreography of qualitative research design. In N. Denzin & V. Lincoln (Eds.), *Handbook of qualitative research* (2nd ed., pp. 379-400). Thousand Oaks, CA: Sage Publications, Inc.

Jardine, D. (1997). Their bodies swelling with messy secrets. In T. Carson & D. Sumara (Eds.), *Action research as living practice* (pp. 161–166). New York: Peter Lang.

Lakoff, G., & Johnson, M. (1980). *Metaphors we live by.* Chicago: The University of Chicago Press.

Leggo, C. (2008). The ecology of personal and professional experience: A poet's view. In M. Cahnmann-Taylor & R. Siegesmund (Eds.), *Arts based research in education: Foundations in practice* (pp. 89–97). New York: Routledge.

Irwin, R. L., & de Cosson, A. (Eds.). (2004). *A/r/tography: Rendering self through arts-based living inquiry.* Vancouver, BC: Pacific Educational Press.

Irwin, R. (2004). A/R/Tography: A metonymic metissage. In R. L. Irwin & A. de Cosson (Eds.), *A/r/tography: Rendering self through arts-based living inquiry* (pp. 27–41).Vancouver, BC: Pacific Educational Press.

Luce-Kapler, R. (1997). Reverberating the action research text. In T. Carson & D. Sumara (Eds.), *Action research as living practice* (pp. 187–197). New York: Peter Lang.

Norman, R. (2001). *House of mirrors: Performing autobiography(icall)y in language/education.* New York: Peter Lang.

om. (n.d.). *Dictionary.com Unabridged (v 1.1).* Retrieved February 13, 2008, from Dictionary.com website: http://dictionary.reference.com/browse/om

Pente, P. (2004). Reflections on artist/researchers/teacher identities: A game of cards. In R. L. Irwin, & A. de Cosson (Eds.), *A/R/Tography: Rendering self through arts-based living inquiry* (pp. 91–102). Vancouver: Pacific Education Press.

Richardson, L. (2000). Writing: A method of inquiry. In N. K. Denzin & Y. S. Lincoln (Eds.), *The handbook of qualitative research.* Thousand Oaks, CA: Sage.

Robertson, J. (1997). Fantasy's confines: Popular culture and the education of the primary-school teacher. In S. Todd (Ed.), *Learning desire: Pedagogy, culture, and the unsaid* (pp. 84–128). New York: Routledge.

Springgay, S. (2004). Body as fragment: Art-making, researching, and teaching as a boundary shift. In R. Irwin & A. de Cosson (Eds.), *A/r/tography: Rendering self through arts-based living inquiry* (pp. 60–74). Vancouver: Pacific Educational Press.

Springgay, S., Irwin, R., & Wilson, S. (2005). A/R/Tography as living inquiry through art and text. *Qualitative Inquiry, 6*(11), 897–912.

Sarah K. MacKenzie
Education Department
Bucknell University
Lewisburg, Pennsylvania, USA

BONNIE RAINGRUBER

ASILOMAR

Asilomar
(September 6, 2007)

Cyprus bark scent, withered seaweed,
living plant, washed far ashore.
What are we,

separated from salt placenta?
A bonfire extinguished,
without world, charcoal ash only.

Community is footprint,
landscape lighthouse
directing path at ocean's edge.

White foam, roaring wave, always the echo.
With an ear to the margins of life,
interview is my trek.

Place is depth, humus in which to root.
Wooden path half buried by sand.
Juggling balls of light, playful

interpretive threads, insight stream.
Diamonds sparkling in sand sea.
Sandpipers dancing lightly to shore.

M. Prendergast, C. Leggo and P. Sameshima (eds.), Poetic Inquiry: Vibrant Voices
in the Social Sciences, 259–272.

Kite flying. Interpreting. Chasing
the thrown ball. It is always at the ocean
one comes to the question.

Horizon answer dips down, bowing to the particular.
Specks only in the distance come close, get bigger.
Shared world like vast waterfall dropping,

carrying you past earth's flat edge.
Surf the wave. Capture the crest.
Follow narrative's flow.

Tsunami waits. Will you be
covered by all that was said?
How to hear the salient?

Two friends walk the beach,
talking into knowing.
A mode of inquiry, like mentor

goes with you and stays,
finding a way into each life crevice.
Orange wildflower, sudden appearing

like Paradigm Case as you pass by.
Taught & Teaching, Listening & Telling,
Dialogue & Connection are one.

Caring is a strong web,
anchor to all. White
cocoon holding

all that is known,
all that is nursing,
all that is phenomenology.

Voice. Story. Image.
We are all our history, this our lived
moment, & the breath of possibility.

Patricia Benner's students gathered at Asilomar State Park on the Pacific Ocean
for a conference (Benner, 2007) to celebrate her retirement, to pay tribute to her
years of groundbreaking work as a Heideggerian phenomenological researcher,
and to thank her for mentoring so many nurse researchers from around the world.
Now teachers ourselves, we, her former students, discussed how to keep the

tradition alive and teach a new generation of students the skills of phenomenological interpretation.

As the conference progressed I would walk the beach in the early morning and evening hours. During those walks I wrote a poem about the interpretive process titled "Asilomar" for Patricia, my mentor. While writing I was reminded that learning the skills of phenomenological interpretation is much like both writing poetry and learning to appreciate good poetry, an analogy I had previously used to teach students about interpretive methods. Teaching students about the commonalities between poetry and qualitative inquiry is one way to keep the interpretive tradition alive.

Qualitative research and phenomenological interpretation are, as Monica Prendergast (2007) described, a form of poetic inquiry. The poet David Whyte agreed that poetry is phenomenology, a way of making sense of the lived experience of human beings, a way of creating a dialogue with one's environment and our common understandings (Reece, 2000).

Highlighting for students the similarities between poetry and qualitative research is a good way to teach interpretive skills. Assigning students a poem to interpret as a group prior to beginning to analyze their own data is an effective way to provide them with experience in the praxis of interpretive work. It is a safe, enjoyable way to introduce students to a skill that often feels overwhelming as they peruse the 75 to 100 page transcripts for each of their 8 to 10 interviews. Interpretive skills that can be taught using poetry reading include learning to 1) identify salient aspects within the transcript, 2) follow the flow of the narrative, 3) recognize common meanings, 4) dialogue with the text and an interpretive group, 5) learn the value of introspection in phenomenology, and 6) attend to the particular within a text. Poetry reading and interpretation can help beginning students learn each of these tasks.

TEACHING THE SKILL OF IDENTIFYING THE SALIENT

Good poetry captures the truth of an experience. It does this with such skill that the words and images from the poem often linger in our memory. As Sandelowski (1994) commented we recognize the familiar and the poignant in both poetry and qualitative science. Each of us is equipped with a reliable gauge of truth. We measure our experiences, feelings, observations, and knowledge against the "shock value" or the "truth value" that a work engenders in us (Bruner, 1979, p. 72). We immediately recognize this truth value and know something salient has been shared.

As May (1994) reflected, the end point of good qualitative science is often described by experienced researchers as a visceral response of "It just felt right," "I just knew," or "It suddenly made sense" (p. 17). According to May a critical skill in qualitative research is deciding on which interpretive path to explore, which is the most salient direction to pursue from the volumes of qualitative data associated with even a small (5 to 8 person) interpretive study. May calls this process searching for the magic in the data.

Heidegger (1962, 1971) spoke of following a wooded path towards a clearing where the essence of that which is being studied can be seen. He used this analogy in reference to both poetry and interpretive analysis. But the interpretive path isn't always clearly marked with signposts; it is a path often half buried by sand as described in the Asilomar poem. Often the path must be discovered while the question at hand is explored during the data analysis phase of the study.

Benner (1994) described the process of interpretation as searching a text for what stands out, or seeing the salient. If one reads and re-reads a poem or a qualitative text from a relaxed, reflective place and discusses the meanings found there, the salient does stand out, almost as if it were highlighted by a yellow pen in the mind's eye.

It is precisely because the salient does stand out that it works to begin teaching students interpretive skills by assigning them a poem to read or allowing them to select a poem to interpret. Asking students to first identify the most poignant, powerful lines and images in the poem helps teach the skill of recognizing the salient, which is an essential component of qualitative work. Because poetry is multivalent and full of shifting images and meanings, students typically need to read their assigned poem multiple times and dialogue with their interpretive group until they feel they have exhausted the salient meanings within the poem.

In explaining this need to dwell in the text and focus on the salient phenomenon, Heidegger (1971) commented: "To think is to confine yourself to a single thought that one day stands like a star in the world's sky" (p. 4). By this he meant that a sense of clarity, a feeling of being in the clearing, follows an exhaustive read or a thorough reflection on a phenomenon whether those phenomena are found in an interpretive text or a poem.

After students have identified the most powerful and poignant aspects of the assigned poem and shared their perspectives with their interpretive group, they are ready to begin reading their own and others qualitative data searching for the poetry, the poignant, and the powerful language to be found there. It is easier to learn how to identify the salient in a shorter piece of poetry than it is to begin with sifting through the 75 to 100 pages of text per phenomenological interview.

As van Manen (1990) commented, writing and reading poetry requires a reflective mood. For that reason having students read poems helps them shift gears from the fast-paced world of nursing and settle into the reflective skills needed in their interpretive work. Interpretive science—like poetry—is a slow craft where one suddenly rounds the corner and "sees." I have used the following poem to explain to students the illusive nature of allowing the salient to find you. It illustrates how during a relaxed mood an insight can call to you, or suddenly stand out as needing to be preserved within a qualitative text or in this case a poem.

Poeming

Waiting, watching, listening,
knowing-it's-going-to-happen,
being, and then being ready

with a big butterfly net,
a jet-stream, supersonic net,
to catch the poem flying by.

I am pausing to pick up the beauty,
trying to hitchhike cross-country
into a let-your-hair-down mindset,
driving with HER warm-car comforted,
'til she opens up, revealing
the iris inside crystal-ball beatitudes.

I wave an arm out the driver's side
window hanging thought parts out
to dry on a car antenna next to
'must-do' movement to clothespin down
an infatuating, willy-nilly,
leap-in-the-dark chronicle.

Right next to neon signs
advertising beer-bait-snacks,
SHE is calling me from a
field yellow-mustard-bright
blooming on Madison's main street
population 92, elevation 36.

SHE is calling me from farther away
...so far away...the trees on the hills
look daisy-sized like cauliflower clumps ready
to feed; they awaken my eyes, needing
to be pressed between imagination's pages,
preserved in my most sacred text.

TEACHING STUDENTS TO FOLLOW THE FLOW OF A NARRATIVE

Poetry is replete with shifts in meaning, literal descriptions, and analogies that
blend and flow throughout the poem. One is reminded of the way that Escher's
paintings blend and shift with one image transforming into another. Akhtar (2000)
described how poetic meanings are commonly conveyed in a "multilayered, figure-
ground sort of architecture" (p. 235). As van Manen (1990) commented, poetry and
phenomenological texts often contain layers of meaning which are not at first
explicit. One has to read, re-read, and attend carefully to the analogies, literal
descriptions, and emotional tones flowing through the work.

Van Manen (1990) suggested one way to present qualitative findings is to
describe the given phenomenon, and then fill out that description by systematically
varying the examples. Poets often follow this same approach. They present one
example of the theme of the poem and then shift into describing other examples of

the same phenomenon. The theme of the poem is often discovered by reflecting on how each example is similar and different. Poets blend these examples to show the range and horizon of the topic that has captured their attention (Hunter, 2002).

In both poetry and interpretive work one has to follow the narrative flow, surf the wave, and ride the crest of meaning. Understanding poetry is a skill much like flying a kite on the beach at Asilomar. Poetic interpretation is a dance, light-footed as sandpipers moving quickly along the ocean shore. Interpretation requires the same sort of coordination and fluidity as a playful game of catch between an owner and a dog on a vacation day at the beach.

The real question, and the most powerful interpretation, in a phenomenological study often reveals itself mid-journey only after one has found the flow of the dialogue. Likewise, it is often the case that the main theme of a poem only appears to the artist on the third re-write of the work after the artist has had a chance to reflect on the moods, feelings and images that captured their attention initially (Holmes & Gregory, 1998). We have to dance lightly with poetry and with qualitative data before we understand. One has to approach the interpretive and the poetic process with a playful curiosity like a walk along the Asilomar sand in the early morning that could at any moment yield a unique shell, a treasure trove of significance and meaning. Often it is only then, after the trek has begun, that one comes to the real question the study or the poem directed one toward.

It is important to remind students that setting aside sufficient time to dwell in the text and re-read are necessities if one is to find the main themes and flow within the dialogue. I typically ask my students to draw a diagram of the main threads of meaning that flow through their transcripts. I also ask them to identify the most poetic exemplars or quotes and tell me what theme is associated with that example. Finally, I use the poem below titled "Egret" to reinforce the idea that qualitative themes twist and bend into one another. Otherwise students who are socialized to use the nursing process initially expect qualitative analysis to be a more linear approach than it is. Reinforcing the crooked nature of the interpretive path is often helpful.

Egret

Stark white eloquence
profiled in flood blue rice field.
Long neck shrinks in on itself
now seagull size, crooked like summer squash.
Meaning twists and takes shape.
Lean, long, gold
pointed beak has her prey.
Pulling in like a turtle,
we are all safe inside
our own intuition.
Searching spirit bends, folds,
flies with all her creatures.

TEACHING THE SKILL OF RECOGNIZING COMMON MEANINGS

Along with learning to recognize the salient voice that is calling from a poem or a qualitative text and to follow the flow of the narrative, students need to develop the ability to see what is universally true within the work. Heidegger (1962) posited that meaning arises from the connection between a person and a taken-for-granted shared social context that includes all the skills, practices, and language of the given culture (Benner & Wrubel, 1989, p. 42). Because everyone in a given culture shares a set of practices and language, common meanings, not just private idiosyncratic ones, can be discovered. We live in a shared world of meaning to which everyone in the culture has access (Benner & Wrubel, 1989).

Sandelowski (1994) reminds us to ask, "how often have we encountered a poem...or narrative account that we know captures the essence of a person or incident more faithfully" than a voluminous quantitative scientific account? (p. 52) The main goal of both poetry and phenomenological accounts is to capture the essence of the particular human condition that is the focus of the work.

It is helpful to ask students to re-read their poem and discuss the universal human messages embedded within the work. By dialoguing about common meanings within the poem students learn to recognize common meanings within their qualitative data. It also works to have students select a qualitative study they consider to be good and dialogue about the common meanings presented in that article. It is important for students to develop a sense of the level of interpretation that is associated with 'deep' or 'rich' analysis. As May (1994) commented, it is the ability to interpret data with richness and subtly that is important. She suggests it is this skill of recognizing the human meaning "that distinguishes powerful explanation from predictable and uninspired description" (p. 14). I often use the following poem to share with students how connected I felt one snowy, cold day as I walked the National Institute of Health campus in order to emphasize the importance of locating common human meanings in interpretive work.

Shadowbox Memory

It is January in Bethesda.
A puddle is frozen, layered like cake.
I stop to take a look at album earth.

Leaves silhouette and shadowbox,
etched at the edge by crystal,
magnifying sun for a hibernating soul.

It took a cold week to create
this dimensional parfait, this ice sculpture.
In a moment you pass by, noticing naught.

A carpet of leaf blankets earth
holding quiet loneliness close to breast.
Oak balls sit like keepsake ornament

naked on branch decorating each sleep season.
Brown, white, and the last flings of orange,
monochromatic silence is as far as the eye can see.

Frozen snow waits to catch you off guard.
Slipping before magnificent mother,
sudden thunder dictates her reverence.

Adrenalin bursts, evaporating
away that which must be left.
Earth holds our common memories.

We each reach down to a central core.
Sustenance comes from connection.
We all cord to mother earth.

Ghost umbilical, illusive as
evolution, incarnation, inspiration.
We are held in the web of collective thoughts.

TEACHING STUDENTS TO DIALOGUE WITH THE TEXT AND AN INTERPRETIVE GROUP

Van Manen (1990) emphasized that a conversational relation to the phenomenon you are studying is necessary. This conversational relation is facilitated by working with an interpretive group. Several (3 to 5) students can work together as they complete their phenomenological thesis or dissertation. Dialogue is quite helpful as beginning students learn the skill of interpretation. Bouncing ideas and interpretations off one another helps one to find their own voice and not feel lost with the volumes of data generated in a phenomenological study.

Gadamer (1975) describes working with an interpretive group as "the art of testing" by use of a dialogue (p. 330). The group members discuss possibilities within the text to discover other meanings. Dialogue helps students to see the limits of their current visions, and to expand them. This conversational relation is not an argumentative or competitive stance but rather like a dialogue among friends about a topic of mutual interest. Dialogue allows students to explore emerging understandings, identify meaningful interpretations, and prevent the development of an overly narrow interpretive perspective (Benner, 1994).

Hunter (2002) commented that reading poetry also requires a conversational tone. A dialogue between the poet and the reader is required. Because poetic referents are often subtle, interpreting a poem as a group is an effective way to remain open to the perspectives of others and to explore the multiple meanings contained within the poem (Holmes & Gregory, 1998). For that reason having students select a poem to read as a group is an effective way to introduce them to working with an interpretive group.

It works to use a poem that is unrelated to any of the student's research topics so they can get a sense of the breadth of dialogue that helps to open up possibilities within the text. If the topic is unrelated to their research and is a poem written by someone else, students need not be protective of their data or their interpretations. They develop the sense of freedom and spontaneity needed during the data analysis phase of their research. As is described in the poem titled "Asilomar," by working together students learn how talking-into-knowing can occur and that "community is a footprint" directing the interpretive path. I share the poem below with my students to emphasize how helpful it is to have the help of an interpretive group when you are overwhelmed with data and feel like you are getting nowhere in the delicate interpretive process.

Kaleidoscope

I am working a solution
turning it over-n-over, precipitating answers.

I am handling a kaleidoscope delicately,
looking for just the right angle.

I am clicking possibility patterns past,
blinking feelings on and off.

I am waiting for the meaning pieces
to fall in place without being lost.

I am analyzing data as bits-n-plastic
pieces that no longer build pattern.

I am trapped on logic's treadmill
running fast, flea-fire fast.

When will everyday experience
whisper "YES" in my ear?

When will feedback help me find the answer?

TEACHING STUDENTS THE VALUE OF INTROSPECTION
IN INTERPRETIVE WORK

Van Manen (1990) stressed that we need to be animated by the object of our study and consider what the interpretive findings have taught us on a personal level. He suggested that seeing is a form of praxis in that "the significance in a situation places us in the event and makes us part of the event" (p. 130). Van Manen (1990) recommended describing a phenomenon "from the inside" by focusing on your feelings, emotions, moods, and experiences related to the narrative (p. 64). We must ask ourselves: How do the narratives resonate with previous life experience? What have the stories taught us about our world? How do the findings open up understanding of the lifeworld of others? Van Manen (1990) emphasized that "it is to the extent that my experiences could be our experiences" that the phenomenologist must attend (p. 57).

Gadamer (1975) commented that the phenomenologist cannot separate him or herself from the meaning of the text. The reader belongs to the text being interpreted. Understanding is always an interpretation and each interpretation is about a specific situation that one has been drawn into with personal interest. As the poem "Asilomar" suggests, interpretive narratives find a way into each life crevice and shift who we are.

Good poetry also teaches us about ourselves. As Sobel and Elata (2001) commented, by reading poetry we learn more about the topic of the work all the while we are learning about our reactions and reflecting on the emotions the poem evoked within us. I ask students to consider what message their assigned poem had for their own life and whether it brought back any memories. What portion of the poem was associated with the strongest feelings? Did the student experience any felt-shifts or new ways of seeing after pondering the poem? (Gendlin, 1962) Likewise when students have progressed to interpreting their own data I ask them how the participant's perspectives were similar or different than their own. What did they learn about themselves during the interpretation? How do the narratives connect with their own sense of past, present or future? (Gendlin, 1962)

Crawford (1993) stated that in poetry we must see life bare and examine reality from a front row seat. Poetry requires us to listen to the impressions we encounter, to reflect on their personally felt significance, find an inner anchor or referent for the lingering impressions, and consider their implicit meanings. Poetic images "take root in us" and prompt us to notice emotional resonances that echo with portions of our own life experience (Bachelard, 1969, p. xix). Poetry increases one's capacity to tolerate pain, to know oneself, and to understand other people. It permits us to grow by reflecting on and sharing glimpses of other's life experience. By reading poetry we are able to process, to reflect, and to gain insight about personal and human meanings. Poetry provides "a time for reflection, a time to hear another's experience, a time for replenishment, a time for self growth" (Friedrich, 1999, p. 1160). Poetry cultivates space for self reflection.

To emphasize to my students the value of making time for self reflection in the midst of a busy world, I sometimes share the poem below because it makes a contrast between fast-paced daily life and a nighttime world that allows for self reflection and introspection.

Nighttime

I LIKE THE NIGHTTIME.
It is when shadows
hang over wallpaper
like spider-webs bringing
a soft, blurry glow to
cover my mind.

I LIKE THE NIGHTTIME.
It is when images dance
foggy on the mind's window-
shade like crimson flame creatures
playing in winter fireplace, like cloud
dragons forming the summer sky.

I LIKE THE NIGHTTIME.
It is when
YOU CAN LOOK QUICKLY,
eye-corner-out
and catch the stars
shining Tinkerbell's magic.

YOU CAN HEAR THE WORDS
your heart knows are true.
YOU CAN ANSWER THE DOOR
when intuition chords
your heartstrings
and look into your future.

YOU CAN LET MELODIES
enter your bosom
...singing...
to frame
the edges shaping
        tomorrow's posture.

I LIKE THE NIGHTTIME.
It is when dreams show me
remnants of yesterday
and a thousand yesterdays
that I have clung to
as a soft, worn-out Teddy bear.

DON'T WAKE ME
    UNTIL IT IS NIGHTTIME
    ONCE AGAIN.

TEACHING STUDENTS TO ATTEND TO THE SPECIFIC AND THE PARTICULAR

Ricoeur (1976) said that interpretation involves seeking the metaphor associated with the text as well as the supporting literal example. This is true for interpretive data and for poetry. In phenomenology there is both a focus on literal description of a particular phenomenon, or letting things speak for themselves, and on interpretation (Heidegger, 1962; van Manen, 1990). Morse (1994) suggested that one way to approach interpretive analysis is to search a text for the metaphorical references and for particular literal examples illustrating the phenomenon.

Poets often weave a poem by alternating metaphorical and literal descriptions. The warp and weave of this approach allows meaning to emerge from the free play of images, signifiers and analogies in the poem (Kaminsky, 1998). I ask students to underline the metaphorical within their assigned poem and to circle and number supportive particular examples. It works to have students discuss how each particular example within the poem adds depth and range to the overall theme. This gives students a sense of how including a variety of exemplars with their research helps flesh out the meanings within the text.

To reinforce the value of the particular, I share the poem "Nearsighted Knowing" that was written about a high functioning woman with a borderline diagnosis. I do this to emphasize that particular situations are how most of us gain experience and understanding. I use the poem "Walking the River" to highlight that, in interpretive work, particular, everyday, taken-for-granted experience is valued.

Nearsighted Knowing

I can only see up close.
Nearsighted females
need experience to swim in
while they are learning life.
It magnifies reality.

I do not discern subtle.
Drama thresholds set
my youth ablaze.
I still seek their set point
and their power.

Written rules are cast-off cousins
only, long lost, bent beyond
recognizable in the family album.
I need situation to surround me
...nudging knowing.

Walking The River

Joy grows big inside the pregnant
belly of day-in-and-day-out life.
Summer shines, slowly shines
over the broad banks
of a Tuesday evening.

Round smooth rocks, sharp edges
softened by the flow
pile up streamside,
permanent as lovers'
initials carved into a tree.

Cricket sounds sharpen.
The wind whispers,
telling me who I am,
who I once was.
My eyes look into everyday.

CONCLUSIONS

Reflection is a skill and habit of mind that can be effectively developed by using poetry reading exercises to introduce students to the methods of phenomenological data analysis. Such reflection requires that the student look inward to examine his or her own responses as well as looking outward and carefully attending to the context of particular situations (Kemmis, 1985). Using poetry reading helps students learn to examine their beliefs and feelings in order to interpret situations, remain open to possibilities, and develop understanding.

Teaching students to approach qualitative interpretation in the way they would approach reading a poem is helpful because the analogy highlights the importance of changing gears and stepping out of the fast-paced world of nursing in order to do a good job of interpreting a qualitative text. The analogy helps students learn to settle into a reflective mode of being and seeing, rather than remaining focused primarily on doing. One has to curl up in an easy chair with both a good poem and a qualitative text to fully digest the narrative.

Using the analogy that how one approaches interpretive work is like how one approaches reading or writing a poem brings a playful, creative, fluid mindset to the work that helps students learn. This approach motivates students to learn how to dialogue with their text, learn how to dialogue with their interpretive group, learn how to dialogue with the reader as they present their findings. Framing the work as being like reading poetry helps students feel less overwhelmed. They pick up more quickly on the art and the praxis that are major components of the work of interpretive science.

REFERENCES

Akhtar, S. (2000). Mental pain and the cultural ointment of poetry. *International Journal of Psychoanalysis, 81*, 229–243.

Bachelard, G. (1969). *The poetics of space*. Boston: Beacon Press.

Benner, P. (1994). *Interpretive phenomenology: Embodiment, caring and ethics in health and illness.* London: Sage Publications.

Benner, P. (2007, September 5–7). *Nursing practice, ethics, education, and philosophy: Perspectives from the Benner tradition.* Asilomar, CA.

Benner, P., & Wrubel, J. (1989). *The primacy of caring*. Menlo Park, CA: Addison-Wesley Publishing Company.

Bruner, J. S. (1979). *On knowing: Essays for the left hand* (Expanded ed.). Cambridge, MA: Belknap.

Crawford, H. (1993). Against theory: The rhetoric of clarity. In H. Crawford (Ed.), *Medicine and William Carlos Williams* (pp. 28-45). Norman, OK: The University of Oklahoma Press.

Friedrich, M. J. (1999). Passion for poetry, compassion for others. *JAMA, 28*(13), 1159–1161.

Gadamer, H. G. (1975). *Truth and method*. New York: Seabury.

Gendlin, E. T. (1962). *Experiencing the creation of meaning*. New York: The Free Press of Glencoe.

Heidegger, M. (1962). *Being and time*. New York: Harper and Row.

Heidegger, M. (1971). Introduction. In A. Hofstader (Ed. & Trans.), *Poetry, language, thought* (pp. ix–xxv). New York: Harper & Row. (Original work published 1936).

Hunter, L. (2002). *Birthwork*. La Jolla, CA: Pacifica Press.

Holmes, V., & Gregory, D. (1998). Writing poetry: A way of knowing nursing. *Journal of Advanced Nursing, 28*(6), 1191–1194.

Kaminsky, M. (1998). Voicing voicelessness: On the poetics of faith. *American Journal of Psychoanalysis, 58*, 405–416.

Kemmis, S. (1985). Action research and the politics of reflection. In D. Boud, R. Keogh, & D. Walker (Eds.), *Reflection: Turning experience into learning* (pp. 139–163). New York: Nicholas.

May, K. A. (1994). Abstract knowing: The case for magic in method. In J. M. Morse (Ed.), *Critical issues in qualitative research methods* (pp. 10–22). Thousand Oaks, CA: Sage.

Morse, J. M. (1994). Emerging from the data: The cognitive process of analysis in qualitative inquiry. In J. M. Morse (Ed.), *Critical issues in qualitative research methods* (pp. 23–46). Thousand Oaks, CA: Sage.

Prendergast, M. (2007). *29 Ways of looking at poetry as qualitative research.* Presented at the first international symposium on Poetic Inquiry, University of British Columbia, Vancouver, BC, Canada.

Ricoeur, P. (1976). *Interpretation theory: Discourse and the surplus of meaning*. Fort Worth, TX: The Texas Christian University Press.

Reece, R. L. (2000). Preserving the soul of medicine and physicians: A talk with David Whyte. *The Physician Executive, 26*(2), 14–19.

Sandelowski, M. (1994). The proof is in the pottery: Toward a poetic for qualitative inquiry. In J. M. Morse (Ed.), *Critical issues in qualitative research methods* (pp. 46–63). Thousand Oaks, CA: Sage.

Sobel, R., & Elata, G. (2001). The problems of seeing and saying in medicine and poetry. *Perspectives in Biology and Medicine, 44*(1), 87–98.

van Manen, M. (1990). *Researching lived experience: Human science for an action sensitive pedagogy.* London: State University of New York Press.

Bonnie Raingruber
Centre for Health and Human Services Research
Nursing Department
California State University Sacramento, USA

SECTION III: VOX PARTICIPARE

PAULINE SAMESHIMA & ROXANNE VANDERMAUSE

METHAMPHETAMINE ADDICTION AND RECOVERY

Poetic Inquiry to Feel

Portions of this chapter were excerpted from *Climbing the Ladder with Gabriel: A Methamphetamine Addict in Recovery* (Sense Publishers) by Pauline Sameshima, Roxanne Vandermause, and Stephen Chalmers with Gabriel.

Transcript 1:1–85   **Starting to Sell**

the Christmas lights were flickering
I was remembering all the warm things
even though my fingers were freezing
and my core was still, like a block of ice

Jake looked the same, the way I loved him
his body always inviting, radiating heat
only I had to put aside my pride
I had the kids to worry about
hopefully he'd take them
on Christmas

but he didn't
he went out with his girl
and left us in the apartment
with no fridge, nothing to eat
I should never have come back
why did I come?

a year and a half of not seeing them
and he didn't even care
he never cared

6 months before I remember stopping
and telling myself I was living
in an '89 Hyundai with two teenagers
no where to go, no money and no work
no job skills and feeling sick

M. Prendergast, C. Leggo and P. Sameshima (eds.), Poetic Inquiry: Vibrant Voices
in the Social Sciences, 275–285.

Sophia asked if I wanted *crank*
I didn't know what it was
but I needed something

it felt so good
only now and again
when I wanted to
not like I was addicted
kept me up at night
so I didn't have to
find a place to sleep
I'd take the kids places to sleep
and take off

we left Jake after only 3 days
I picked up my welfare check and
knew I needed some fast money
I could sell better than the people who
were doing it

not like I was pushing it on anyone
they were all my friends
I needed to make money fast
for my kids

Considered to be one of the most dangerous drugs of abuse, methamphetamine is spreading across the country with alarming devastation to persons and communities. National groups and community stakeholders are concerned; intervention research and prevention efforts are underway, yet there is little scholarly work that focuses on the perspective and experience of current or past methamphetamine users.

We use a model called *Parallaxic Praxis* (Figure 3) to bring together the expertise, experience, and discourse of six disciplines including nursing, education, drama, writing, and fine arts: 1) to better understand methamphetamine addiction struggles and uncover prevention and recovery possibilities; 2) to develop thought provoking information for educational programs in schools and public venues; and 3) to design collaborative methodologies that inform research practice in new ways.

Transcript 1: 86–89   **Making Money**
I made some money from the meth
we stayed in a 25 foot trailer
my boyfriend, his brother, me and the kids
yeah, Jim was a user too
he got the best deal
he never had to pay

This project documents and interprets the addiction struggle and laborious path to recovery experienced by Gabriel. By looking intensely from multiple perspectives at Gabriel's stories, the team develops broader understandings that capture the full range of one experience of meth addiction and recovery. Through in-depth analysis of these experiences, collaborating scholars design models of interpretive analyses. The shared project is based on the curricular premise that access to embodied learning through representation will enrich understandings, raise questions, and evoke reponses that can complement narrative or linear expressions and enhance the applicability and usefulness of findings.

The great ramifications of addiction, including homelessness, incarceration, violence, financial ruin, and personal loss, along with the experience of recovery, are rendered in various forms using the arts as a vehicle of knowledge analysis, production, and dissemination. Intensive, iterative analyses of a series of audiotaped, transcribed interviews guide the team in creating narrative, visual, poetic, dramatic, and musical representations which can be juxaposed with scientific literature and social implications to view addiction in new light.

Results of this research can be used to raise awareness among diverse communities of scientists, students, civic leaders, health care professionals, and people struggling with addictions; and to illuminate the needs for personal, social and educational change. Research dissemination includes gallery art shows, poetry readings, interactive community exhibitions, plays, videos, and literature including papers, books, and pamplets. From the interpretation of these data, education and strategies can be tested and applied to prevention and intervention efforts to complement the growing body of work dedicated to addiction and recovery. Our collaborative interpretive methodology can also be applied to other highly contextual and recalcitrant social problems.

Transcript 4:1–36   **Jail**

when I got there
I knew everybody in the jail
they were all like, "Hi!"
I was there a week

I started recovery
when I got out

nine months after
ha! like growing a baby
I found out the police were
looking for me

I turned myself in
because I thought

it was time to start dealing
with my court issues

I shouldn't have
turned myself in at Wilkins
it was disgusting there

a tiny cell
thank God I only stayed for 4 days
then started the chain

the chain is when the courts move you
they just pick you up or drop you off
wherever you're supposed to go
and you just go from jail to jail
some of my friends had been on the chain
for 36 days

they move you in vans

my favorite were
the ones that looked like
ice-cream trucks

RESEARCH PARADIGMS

This project does not rely on a pre-planned hypothesis design. Skilled in each of their respective fields, the researchers use the authority, integrity, and expertise of their backgrounds to guide their interpretations and research. They focus on the research project goals. The team then, in juxtaposing and re-presenting artful interpretations next to each other, develop new, greater, and deeper understandings. By studying the hybrid spaces of coupled interpretive systems, complex patterns are revealed which are not evident when researched separately. These ways of thinking rest in the vein of conceptual models followed by archaeologists such as Timothy Kohler, Washington State University's Regents Professor, who studies the interactions between natural and human systems. Kohler's work focuses on understanding the causes for changes in settlement systems in southwestern Colorado by looking at changes in the environment and how these changes may have affected human settlement behavior. Without looking at the systems side by side, understandings of "why" settlement behavior changed over time is not possible.

Compare the following two models of research design. The first (Figure 1) depicts a traditional research model which begins with a hypothesis and closes with an answer. The second (Figure 2), is the Parallaxic Praxis paradigm model. The research is initiated with questions. Data is collected and interpreted by a collaborative team with the focus on analysis of the nexus spaces between researchers' interpretations and systems for meaning-making. The confluence of interpretations creates novel understandings, provokes new questions, generates new knowledge, and presses new thinking. This model has grown out of a number of research models but is specifically grounded by a pedagogy of parallax (Sameshima, 2007)—that all knowledge, learning, and understanding is incomplete and that only through multi-perspectives, and in this case, multi-researcher discourse and systems of representation, can fuller personal understanding be had.

Figure 1. Traditional Research Design

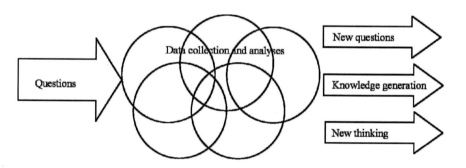

Figure 2. Parallaxic Praxis Paradigm Design

Curricular Perspectives

This project employs perspectives supported by the *Interdisciplinary Studies Project* based at Harvard Graduate School of Education which includes the work of Boix Mansilla (2004), Dillon (2001), Nikitina (2002), and Miller (2005). Specifically, researchers utilize the approaches of a *Pedagogy of Parallax* (Sameshima, 2007, 2008) which support Bakhtin's (1986) notion of *heteroglossia* which refers to the inclusion of all conflicting voices as having value. This type of research further validates Denzin's view that postmodern ethnography "values and privileges the authority and voice of the reader and thus changes the role and authority of the researcher as meaning maker and theorizer" (1997, p. 36).

The team supports the understanding that curriculum is "the site on which the generations struggle to define themselves and the world, [that] curriculum is an extraordinarily complicated conversation" (Pinar et al., 1995, p. 848), and that curriculum [refers] to educational courses of action that facilitate human 'growth' [that are] so complex that [they] cannot be studied though any particular theoretical perspective" (Henderson & Slattery, 2004, p. 3). Schwab (1969) believed that the curriculum field is both theoretical and practical and must be approached eclectically. So the team purposefully (re)searches in multi-layered and seemingly unrelated ways, seeking connections off charted courses (see Sameshima, 2007).

In "playing" out the hermeneutic interview transcripts or engaging with the participant through arts practices, multi-genre narrative texts and visual art, or music, performance, or movement; a complicated and complex conversation is created; and through this shifting and sifting (Aoki, 1996) and agitation of reciprocality, reversibility, resonance, reverberation, and echo, within and between forms and mediums, the unarticulated becomes articulated, seen, marked, and visible (see Springgay, Irwin, & Wilson Kind, 2005; Jones, 1998; Pollock, 1998; Sumara & Luce-Kapler, 1993). Artful research is the act of focusing the camera lens to still a moment in time for others to "see" an iteration, to make the consciousness visible for others to interrogate, judge, and edit (see Sameshima, 2007).

PARALLAXIC PRAXIS

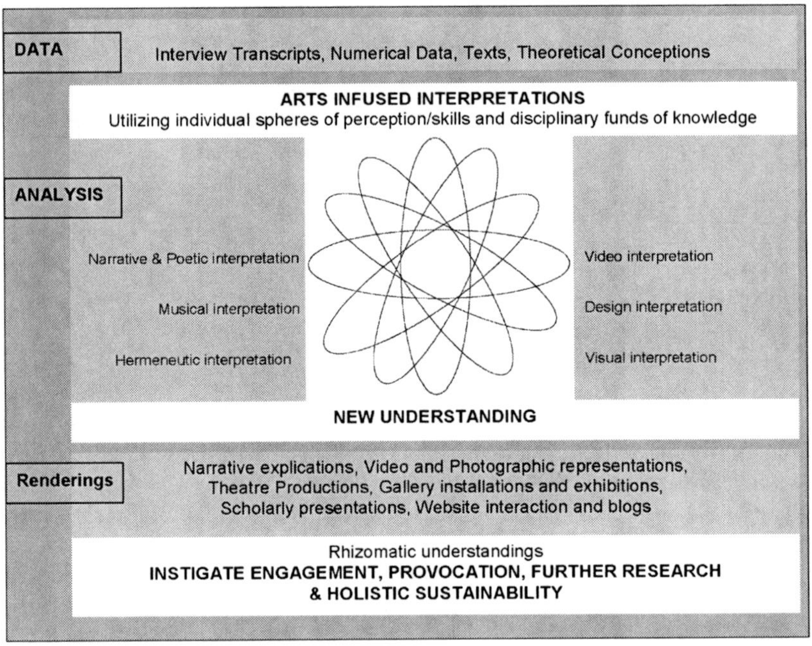

Figure 3. Parallaxic Praxis for a Portrait of Methamphetamine Addiction and Recovery

It is important to note that Parallaxic Praxis cannot be reinstituted by any research team for any research project. The design must be specifically created for each project based on the expertise of the team members. Also note that data collection sources may not necessarily be interview transcripts. The data could be multiple types of content. The researchers promote a model which is always contextualized to the particular team and project.

Parallaxic Praxis is a researching, teaching and learning design model which is grounded in holistic arts-integrated inquiry. Parallaxic Praxis supports personal meaning-making as knowledge production. In this case, researchers work with content through various avenues utilizing mediums such as video production, art making, poetry, plays and other artful endeavours. They utilize the arts in order to create renderings of understanding. The product then becomes a medium to share, engage, and provoke further learning through Socratic conversation. The model encourages the researcher to not only engage with the content in a personal artful or representative way but when interpretations are presented alongside the other representations, systems of analysis and interactions in the hybrid nexus spaces can be discussed. Rendering content through new lenses affords the audience to think more critically about the content from a personal meaning-making perspective.

The Parallaxic Praxis method of meaning-generation produces an artifact, which can then spur further learning in others. A simplified common process of Parallaxic Praxis is to take statistical data and create a graph. Once rendered, learners can better analyze the data content. Figure 3 illustrates the progression of content fractalled through artful knowledge generation. This space facilitates dialogue and the juxtaposition of the interstices of research discourses as described in the research paradigm design in Figure 2.

Multiple methods and arts-based educational research shape and guide our complementary interpretive methods. This project incorporates portraiture methodology as one guiding frame to collect data, represent, and interpret the experience of methamphetamine addiction and recovery through a longitudinal, single case design. In *The Art and Science of Portraiture,* Lawrence-Lightfoot and Davis (1997) describe how portraitists in various disciplines have illuminated ideas and understandings that complement and extend other methods of inquiry. (Also see Appenzeller, Amm & Jones, 2004; Davis, Soep, Maira, Remba, & Putnoi, 1993; Harding, 2005; Lawrence-Lightfoot, 1983, 1994; Newton, 2005). Other supporting methods integrated in our study include: participatory research (Small, 1995), hermeneutic phenomenology (Benner, 1994; Diekelmann, 1992; Diekelmann & Magnussen Ironside, 1998; Grondin, 1995), narrative inquiry (Clandinin, 2007; Connelly & Clandinin 1990, 1994; Leggo, 2008; Richardson & St. Pierre, 2005), arts-informed research (Cole & Knowles, 2001a, 2001b; Sameshima, 2007), a/r/tography (Irwin, 2004; Springgay, Irwin, Leggo & Gouzouasis, 2008, Sameshima, 2007), and of course, poetic inquiry as evidenced in its rich variety expressed in this book.

The complexity of voice, experience, and interpretation can be distilled using innovative and thoughtful interpretive approaches to inquiry. It is via such methods that issues often held in shadow are examined and new approaches to matters of suffering are conceptualized. In examining the complex, unappealing and consequential phenomenon of addiction, methods such as those described here are necessary to explore those aspects that cannot be fully addressed by empirical/analytic methods alone.

EDUCATIONAL AND SCIENTIFIC SIGNIFICANCE

Methamphetamine addiction has stormed the culture and threatens the health of individuals, families, and communities. In 2002-2005, an estimated 1.4 million persons (0.6% of the population) aged 12 or older used methamphetamine in the US alone; this includes 6.2% of high school seniors who have tried the drug (SAMHSA, 2006). It is a pernicious, and devastating form of chemical addiction that has severe psychological, physical, social, and environmental effects (Gettig, Grady, & Nowosadzka, 2006; Lineberry & Bostwick, 2006; Tanne, 2006). The expanding popularity of the drug across the country and exponential increases in methamphetamine related healthcare admissions (Lineberry & Bostwick, 2006) have rallied stakeholders in healthcare, law, politics, education, social work, environmental services, and in the public domain. Researchers have become attentive to studying the short and long term cognitive effects of the drug (Johanson et al., 2006) and there is progressive work in the area of treatment for methamphetamine users, including pharmacological and behavioral interventions (Heinzerling et al., 2006; Roll, 2007; Shoptaw et al., 2006). While the threat of this phenomenon is alarming, the healthcare literature does not adequately address the processes, practices, and perceptions of those who undergo the painful experience of methamphetamine addiction and recovery.

Those caught in the culture of methamphetamine addiction suffer intense physical, emotional, and lifestyle loss, including homelessness, incarceration, violence, financial ruin, and deep personal loss (Barr et al., 2006; Maxwell, 2006; Volkow et al., 2001). Women, particularly, experience stigmatizing attitudes or indifference on the part of care providers, policy makers, and public stakeholders. Issues related to healthcare access, criminal justice system processes, and the needs of children complicate the medical condition and the approach providers take in addressing or not addressing the problem.

Methamphetamine addiction is a concern to citizens and communities. Prevention and education programs on addiction are most successful when they involve multiple, collaborating community groups (Carmona & Stewart, 1996; Durlak, 1997; Johnson et al., 1990; Reiss & Price, 1996). It is important that an understanding of the addiction and recovery experiences be understood in new and compelling ways. We need to attract the attention of students, addicts, parents, policy makers, school personnel, as well as health care providers and therapists. Such attention is needed to inspire prevention and treatment efforts currently lacking or insufficient in relieving the suffering of individuals, families and communities related to this addiction.

Through this project, we expect to make a positive impact on addictions research and demonstrate the power of interpretive methodologies in research and education scholarship.

Members of the full research team listed alphabetically include: Stephen Chalmers (photography), Gabriel (participant), Laurilyn Harris (theatre), Sheila Kearney-Converse (music), Linda Kittell (creative writing), Pauline Sameshima (education), and Roxanne Vandermause (nursing). For a detailed look at the intersections between herrmeneutic analyis, photography inquiry, and poetic inquiry, please see *Climbing the Ladder with Gabriel: A Methamphetamine Addict in Recovery* (Sense Publishers) by Pauline Sameshima, Roxanne Vandermause, and Stephen Chalmers with Gabriel.

REFERENCES

Aoki, T. T. (1996, Fall). Spinning inspirited images in the midst of planned and live(d) curricula. *Fine*, 96, 7–14.

Appenzeller, O., Amm, M., & Jones, H. (2004). A brief exploration of neurological art history. *Journal of the History of the Neurosciences*, 13(4), 345–350.

Bakhtin, M. M. (1986). *Speech genres and other late essays.* Austin, TX: University Press.

Barr, A., Panenka, W., MacEwan, G., Thornton, A., Lang, D., & Honer, W. (2006). The need for speed: An update on methamphetamine addiction. *Journal of Psychiatry & Neuroscience*, 31(5), 301–313.

Benner, P. (1994). The tradition and skill of interpretive phenomenology in studying health, illness, and caring practices. In P. Benner (Ed.), *Interpretive phenomenology: Embodiment, caring, and ethics in health and illness* (pp. 99–127). Thousand Oaks, CA: Sage.

Boix Mansilla, V. (2004). Interdisciplinary work at the frontier; An empirical examination of expert interdisciplinary epistemologies. *Issues in Interdisciplinary Studies*, 24, 1–31.

Carmona, M., & Stewart, K. (1996). *A review of alternative activities and alternative programs in youth-oriented prevention* (CSAP Technical Report 13 No. 96-3117). Rockville, MD: Center for Substance Abuse Prevention.

Cole, A. L., & Knowles, J. G. (2001a). *Lives in context: The art of life history research.* Walnut Creek, CA: Alta Mira Press.

Cole, A. L., & Knowles, J. G. (2001b). Qualities of inquiry. In L. Neilsen, A. Cole, & J. G. Knowles (Eds.), *The art of writing inquiry* (Vol. 1. Arts-informed Research Series, pp. 211–219). Halifax, NS & Toronto, ON: Backalong Books & Centre for Arts-Informed Research.

Clandinin, D. J. (2007). *Handbook of narrative inquiry: Mapping a methodology.* Thousand Oaks, CA: Sage.

Connelly, F. M., & Clandinin, D. J. (1990). Stories of experience and narrative inquiry. *Educational Researcher*, 19(5), 2–14.

Connelly, F. M., & Clandinin, D. J. (1994). Telling teaching stories. *Teacher Education Quarterly*, 21(2), 145–158.

Davis, J., Soep, E., Maira, S., Remba, N., & Putnoi, D. (1993). *Safe havens: Portraits of educational effectiveness in community art centers that focus on education in economically disadvantaged communities.* Cambridge, MA: Harvard Project Zero, Harvard University.

Denzin, N. K. (1997). *Interpretive ethnography: Ethnographic practices for the 21st century.* Thousand Oaks, CA: Sage.

Diekelmann, N. L. (1992). Learning-as-testing: A Heideggerian hermeneutical analysis of the lived experiences of students and teachers in nursing. *Advances in Nursing Science*, 14(3), 72–83.

Diekelmann, N. L., & Magnussen Ironside, P. (1998). Hermeneutics. In J. Fitzpatrick (Ed.), *Encyclopedia of nursing research* (pp. 243–245). New York: Springer.

Dillon, D. (2001). *Interdisciplinary research and education: Preliminary perspectives from the MIT media laboratory.* Retrieved February 14, 2008, from http://www.pz.harvard.edu/interdisciplinary/pubone.html

Durlak, J. A. (1997). *Successful prevention programs for children and adolescents* (Vol. 11). New York: Plenum Press.

Gettig, J., Grady, S., & Nowosadzka, I. (2006). Methamphetamine: Putting the brakes on speed. *Journal of School Nursing, 22*(2), 66–73.

Grondin, J. (1995). *Sources of hermeneutics.* Albany, NY: State University of New York Press.

Harding, H. A. (2005). "City girl": A portrait of a successful white urban teacher. *Qualitative Inquiry, 11*(1), 52–80.

Henderson, J. G., & Slattery, P. (2004). Editors' introduction: The arts create synergy for curriculum and pedagogy. *Journal of curriculum and pedagogy, 1*(2), 1–8.

Heinzerling, K. G., Shoptaw, S., Peck, J. A., Yang, X., Liu, J., Roll, J., et al. (2006). Randomized, placebo-controlled trial of baclofen and gabapentin for the treatment of methamphetamine dependence. *Drug and Alcohol Dependence, 85*(3), 177–184.

Irwin, R. L. (2004). A/r/tography: A metonymic métissage. In R. L. Irwin & A. de Cosson (Eds.), *A/r/tography: Rendering self through arts-based living inquiry* (pp. 27–38). Vancouver, BC: Pacific Educational Press.

Johanson, C.-E., Frey, K. A., Lundahl, L. H., Keenan, P., Lockhart, N., Roll, J., et al. (2006). Cognitive function and nigrostriatal markers in abstinent methamphetamine abusers. *Psychopharmacology, 186*(4), 620.

Jones, A. (1998). *Body art/performing the subject.* Minneapolis, MN: University of Minnesota.

Lawrence-Lightfoot, S. (1983). *The good high school: Portraits of character and culture.* New York: Basic Books.

Lawrence-Lightfoot, S. (1994). *I've known rivers: Lives of loss and liberation.* Reading, MA: Addison-Wesley.

Lawrence-Lightfoot, S., & Davis, J. H. (1997). *The art and science of portraiture.* San Francisco: Jossey-Bass.

Leggo, C. (2008). Autobiography: Researching our lives and living our research. In S. Springgay, R. Irwin, C. Leggo, & P. Gouzouasis (Eds.), *Being with a/r/tography* (pp. 3–24). Rotterdam, The Netherlands: Sense.

Lineberry, T. W., & Bostwick, J. (2006). Methamphetamine abuse: A perfect storm of complications. *Mayo Clinic Proceedings January, 81*(1), 77–84.

Newton, R. M. (2005). Learning to teach in the shadow of 9/11: A portrait of two Arab American preservice teachers. *Qualitative Inquiry, 11*(1), 81–94.

Nikitina, S. (2002). *Three strategies for interdisciplinary teaching: Contextualizing, conceptualizing, and problem-solving.* Retrieved February 14, 2008, from http://www.pz.harvard. edu/interdisciplinary/pubtwo.html

Maxwell, J. C. P. (2006). Emerging research on methamphetamine. *International Drug Therapy Newsletter March, 41*(3), 17–24.

Miller, J. (2005). *Educating for wisdom and compassion: Creating conditions for timeless learning.* Thousand Oaks, CA: Corwin Press.

Pinar, W., Reynolds, W. M., Slattery, P., & Taubman, P. M. (1995). *Understanding curriculum: An introduction to the study of historical and contemporary curriculum discourses.* New York: Peter Lang.

Pollock, D. (1998). Performative writing. In Phelan, Peggy & Lane (Eds.), *The ends of performance* (pp. 73–103). New York: University Press.

Reiss, D., & Price, R. H. (1996). National research agenda for prevention research. The National Institute of Mental Health Report. *American Psychologist, 51*, 1109–1115.

Richardson, L., & St. Pierre, E. (2005). Writing: A method of inquiry. In N. K. Denzin & Y. S. Lincoln (Eds.), *Handbook of qualitative research* (3rd ed., pp. 959–978). Thousand Oaks, CA: Sage.

Roll, J. M. (2007). Contingency management: An evidence-based component of methamphetamine use disorder treatments. *Addiction, 102*(Suppl. 1), 114–120.

Sameshima, P. (2007). *Seeing red—a pedagogy of parallax: An epistolary bildungsroman on artful scholarly inquiry.* Amherst, NY: Cambria Press.

Sameshima, P. (2008). AutoehtonoGRAPHIC relationality through paradox, parallax, and metaphor. In S. Springgay, R. Irwin, C. Leggo, & P. Gouzouasis (Eds.), *Being with a/r/tography* (pp. 45–56). Rotterdam, The Netherlands: Sense.

Schwab, J. J. (1969). The practical: A language for curriculum. *School Review, 78*, 1–23.

Shoptaw, S., Huber, A., Peck, J., Yang, X., Liu, J., Dang, J., et al. (2006). Randomized, placebo-controlled trial of sertraline and contingency management for the treatment of methamphetamine dependence. *Drug and Alcohol Dependence, 85*(1), 12–18.

Small, S. A. (1995). Action-oriented research: Models and methods. *Journal of Marriage and the Family, 57*, 941–955.

Springgay, S., Irwin, R., & Wilson Kind, S. (2005). A/r/tography as living inquiry through art and text. *Qualitative Inquiry, 11*(6), 897–912.

Springgay, S., Irwin, R., Leggo, C., & Gouzouasis, P. (Eds.). (2008). *Being with a/r/tography.* Rotterdam, The Netherlands: Sense.

Volkow, N. D., Chang, L., Wang, G. J., Fowler, J. S., Ding, Y. S., Sedler, M., et al. (2001). Low level of brain dopamine D2 receptors in methamphetamine abusers: Association with metabolism in the orbitofrontal cortex. *American Journal of Psychiatry, 158*(12), 2015–2021.

Substance Abuse and Mental Health Services Administration (SAMHSA). (2006). *National survey on drug use and health* (No. 37). Washington, DC: Office of Applied Studies.

Sumara, D., & Luce-Kapler, R. (1993). Action research as writerly text: Locating co-labouring in collaboration. *Educational Action Research, 1*(3), 387–395.

Tanne, J. H. (2006). Methamphetamine epidemic hits middle America. *BMJ February, 332*(7538), 382.

Pauline Sameshima
Cultural Studies and Social Thought in Education
Washington State University
USA

Roxanne Vandermause
College of Nursing
Washington State University
USA

GINA EDGHILL

THE CULTURE OF MY COMMUNITY REVEALED

Poetic and Narrative Beginnings

I officially moved into the community of qualitative researchers during the first semester of my doctoral program in Adult, Higher, and Community Education. It was all new to me but I was beginning to learn how best to navigate. In particular I explored the avenues of narrative and poetic inquiry. I knew that unlike scientific discourse, narrative and poetic discourse would allow me, as researcher, to highlight the uniqueness of experiences, rather than the commonalities of properties (Chase, 2005).

My move to the qualitative community brought me face to face with other researchers who use narrative and poetry as meaningful forms of inquiry. As a result, both are flourishing. Narrative is seen as the way we come to know our world and narrative forms of research as a way of meaning making that allows us to make sense of the world and society we live in (Denzin & Lincoln, 2005). The researcher as narrator can develop meaning out of what they have studied and researched and construct their own voice based on their unique interpretations. They then have the choice of sharing their findings through writing or performance, always mindful of the constraints of their discipline, culture and, the historical moment in which they live (Chase, 2005).

Poetry was not new to me but the idea of poetic inquiry was. I soon learned that poetry in research is not a new concept. Social researchers have been writing and performing poetry for some time now. Through poetry the researcher or author is granted the opportunity to see the familiar in new ways. Disseminating research through written or performed poetry allows researchers to overcome the limitations of traditional print methods. Poetry can give voice to individuals in sensitive and meaningful ways (Clarke, Febbraro, Hatzipantelis & Nelson, 2005).

I would agree with researchers who suggest that poetry is a better form to use when representing some kinds of knowledge and that writing is of great importance in the researcher's life (Richardson, 2001a). According to Laurel Richardson (2001a) researchers and scholars who write, write about their own lives in one way or another. It is impossible for their writing to be free of the writer's 'self' even when the writing is of a scientific nature. Writing is an avenue of learning that allows researchers to discover more about themselves and their world (Richardson, 2001a).

As you might guess not everyone agrees with this view. For instance, one researcher holds the view that poetry is ambiguous in its meaning and that researchers'

M. Prendergast, C. Leggo and P. Sameshima (eds.), Poetic Inquiry: Vibrant Voices
in the Social Sciences, 287–299.

who use this method place more importance on the form of the writing than on the writing's analytical content (Schwalbe, 1995). Richardson (2001a) contends however that the qualitative researcher should always consider the consequences of how they write, the purpose for which they write, and the audience to whom they write. These three factors will help the researcher to determine whether poetry is the most effective tool to use to portray the voices and texts that emanate from real people.

Richardson, as a feminist scholar and an advocate of poetry in qualitative research, reports that minorities, non-Americans, and women often find alternative ethnographic representation an effective way to honor their connection to their culture and traditions while still remaining disciplined in the style, format, and content of their work (Richardson, 1996).

As I embarked on my research I knew that narrative and poetic inquiry were ideal for my research into the experiences of African Diaspora women enrolled in American Higher Education. I knew that it would allow me to close the distance that exists between the experience of 'self' and 'other' (Richardson, 2001b). Intuitively I knew all this because it made sense that when the field we enter for our research is representative of our culture and the world we navigate through daily, poetry and narrative allows us to articulate and understand our perceptions of our lived experiences.

THE FIELD: SELF, OTHER & CONTEXT

Self

I identified myself as a major part of my field early on in my research. When I decided on the criteria for participation in my qualitative research I essentially described myself. I wanted to use this research to make sense of my own experiences in American Higher Education and my educational journey up to this point. I wanted to find out how these women felt about other Black women in American Higher Education. I hoped to determine how they navigated through this system and what their goals were.

I chose this topic for my research because I was indecisive about where I stood on certain issues that I felt I should have a firm stand on. I hoped through my research that I could converse with at least three women from across the African Diaspora and through the interviews determine if I stood on firm ground given my own assumptions and biases.

I want to understand 'self' and 'other' and be able to identify a sameness in the culture of our struggle and a bond in our shared past. Through this research I hope to make more concrete what it means to be labelled and treated as a minority and still draw comfort in knowing that I am not alone.

Other

After receiving the appropriate approval to conduct this research I interviewed three women. All three of my participants were Black Anglophone female graduate students enrolled in American Higher Education. As it turned out all three of them were pursuing their doctorates. One of my participants was an international student from an African country in the field of education. Another participant was an international student from the Caribbean in the field of audiology and one student was an African American student in the field of psychology.

I chose not to ask them demographic questions because I wanted to concentrate on their educational journeys. I felt that the way they expressed their experiences, motivations, and thoughts was enough of a framework for analyzing each of their interviews without making assumptions based on demographic information which I felt added no value to my research questions.

My research questions were:

– How do Anglophone black female African, Caribbean, and American graduate students see themselves fitting into American higher education?
– What are the experiences of Anglophone black female African, Caribbean, and American graduate students attending American higher education institutions?
– How do Anglophone black female African, Caribbean, and American graduate students perceive other black women in American higher education?

Context

Cultural competence has become an important issue in American Higher Education. Diversity in age, culture, ethnicity, and gender presents challenges to college students, faculty, and staff alike. Understanding differences and recognizing the interrelation of these cultures is one way of meeting these challenges head on (Demenchonok, 2005; Strasser & Seplocha, 2005).

It is often the case that black African, Caribbean, and American women are categorized and stereotyped as being the same, with little consideration to the differences in their cultural background. While it is quite possible that there is a common thread in motivations, feelings, concerns, and thoughts of Black women in higher education it is important that generalizations not be made. Explorative research in this area is necessary to understanding the diversity that lives in American Higher Education.

One such theory that lends credence to a better understanding of the nuances associated with different cultural backgrounds is socio-cultural theory. A higher education system that embraces this theoretical perspective is a system that values the cultural capital of all students even when that capital is not representative of the dominant culture (Fay, 2001). Exploring the experiences of Black women in American Higher Education and distinguishing the differences in experiences based on cultural backgrounds (i.e. African American, African, and Afro-Caribbean) supports the socio- cultural perspective. The premise being that the cultural worlds in which individuals have grown and developed in are directly related to how individuals interpret who they are in relation to others, and how they learn to process, interpret, and encode their world (Perez, 1998).

Socio-cultural theory is also very accepting of past learned experiences of individuals. It embraces the idea that individuals construct their own knowledge and meaning according to what they already know about the social, historical and linguistic dimensions of their world. In order to fully understand the educational experiences of black women in American higher education it is imperative that the culture and discourse communities within which individuals interact and learn be recognized not just as a credible and viable mode of differentiating but also as a mode of recognizing the value of interrelatedness (Alfred, 2003; Demenchonok, 2005).

Although differences are expected between the lived educational experiences of these three groups of black women based on their unique cultural backgrounds, there is another school of thought that promotes the concept of diaspora culture. The diasporaconcept suggests that once a people have historically shared values, cultural heritage, and racial/ethnic identities, if dispersed into an antagonistic environment and faced with an alien and/or dominant society around them, an identifiable culture which retains vestiges of the original traditions materializes (Wilentz, 1992).

The Diaspora explored in this study the African Diaspora, was constructed as an umbrella term to identify Africans and people of African descent. According to Gordon & Anderson (1999), it was a racial identifier purported through the Pan-African ideologies of Delaney, Blyden, Garvey, Dubois, and others. The original intent of the term African Diaspora was not to identify specific locations across the globe. The term was used to describe the experiences of Blacks who were marginalized based on internationally held racist ideologies of Black inferiority (Gordon & Anderson, 1999). These ideologies depicted Blacks as uncivilized people without culture, history, or national or territorial connections (Gordon & Anderson, 1999). While one would hope that such marginalization does not exist in American Higher Education today women who fit into this group often describe their experiences as those of disempowerment, alienation, and discrimination (Meera, 2002; Alfred, 2003; James, 2006). In my view, the theories of Diaspora culture and socio-cultural theory do not contradict each other but provide a window into the potential complexities inherent in the lived experiences of Black female graduate students studying in American Higher Education. The findings and analysis resulting from my three interviews with these women follows and represents an example of storytelling and poetry as viable modes of inquiry.

STORYTELLING AND POETRY: FINDINGS AND ANALYSIS

*The knowing which lives in our experiences is a dictator
in the politics of our perceptions of Self and Other*

Sisters of the Diaspora

Our mother bore many children, but Sarah, Sarah was our big sister, our protector. Mother was always busy taking care of the other children, particularly the boys. They always seemed to be in a state of confusion. But our big sister Sarah took care of us, her three younger sisters. In many ways she was our mother and I, Lily, her second in command, knew she had a special knowledge and understanding of our thoughts and feelings.

Sarah told me I had the greatest gift of all the sisters, the gift of storytelling. She told me, long ago, it was a gift passed down to very few in our tribe and only to those who showed great wisdom. Sarah told me storytelling was how we knew of our past and learned how to shape our future. She was my big sister, ten years my senior, and as a child I thought her the wisest woman alive. And so I continue to shape my world by storytelling. The story that follows tells of the journey of my three sisters and me.

It happened one night nearly four centuries ago. All four of us were stripped naked and touched inappropriately by his hands. Sarah was older and stronger and she was able to resist him and chase him away from her room. But she couldn't protect us. He took the three of us with him and left Sarah behind. Sarah mourned the night he took us and cried at her inability to help us. She later told us her tears dried quickly because she knew the strength of our hearts. She missed us nevertheless and feared for us as we journeyed into the unknown.

The three of us that were captured that night would never forget the journey that followed. Our captor told us, in an unrecognizable tongue, soon to be our own, that we were journeying to the New World. He grew tired of me first and left me on the most easterly islands in the New World. He left Olivia next, our baby sister, with his French cousins in the West Indies. He kept Chloe though. At the time I couldn't understand why. Chloe was younger than I was and didn't appear as strong. That later proved far from the truth. Chloe was stronger than we ever imagined. Compared to us she survived the longest and most arduous of the three journeys. He took her to the capital of the New World in the North. Our journey to these three points was written in our hearts and we tried to pass our story on to as many of our relatives as we could but much of these details are lost. Our captor had refused to document them, other than in the pounds and pence of accounting.

Even though Sarah had stayed at home she had not remained safe. He had left some of his relatives behind to "civilize" Sarah and all the others that remained. Sarah knew we would meet again but she didn't know where and when. She knew she had remained at the Source but she could still feel the three of us. Now that the three of us were so far away from our truth she could feel our confusion and our lost knowledge of home. She understood our search but what hurt her most was the burning sensation in her skin whenever the three of us, her younger sisters, tore our flesh from scratching at what we thought was our unAfricanness.

Over the years Sarah had heard many stories from her village. Stories of how her three sisters were taken from home. No one knew of the chant that we each said on the nights we shared the sight of the midnight sky. On those nights each of us sat at the cardinal points of the Diaspora and promised that someday we would meet again and when we did, it would be a meeting for reparation.

We knew our reparation would be slow in coming but compensation for what had occurred over the years was possible. We knew we couldn't force his hand. His system was fixed but not impenetrable. Knowing that reparation could only come through knowledge, we made the decision to meet in the North.

The irony of our decision was not lost on us. We knew Chloe had the most difficult journey of the three of us and we were now seemingly heading straight into the lion's den. We knew full well he was still in charge of Chloe's northern world more so than he was in charge of ours but he was the gatekeeper of the knowledge we sought. We made the conscientious choice as sisters to pursue knowledge and wisdom as the most prodigious way to reparation.

Sarah was proud of us. She saw what we had to face to get to our meeting place, especially Chloe. Sarah knew if she hadn't been successful in chasing him away that night, many years ago, she would have faced the same struggles we did. But Sarah also knew how he portrayed our home to us, her sisters. Sarah knew his people thought she and our relatives back home were ignorant. She often wondered if her own sisters thought the same.

We had all journeyed a long way and finally the day came for us to sit down together for the first time in nearly four hundred years. When that day came we almost didn't recognize each other. Each of our struggles had embittered us in so many ways. Now that we were at the same place in our journey, that bitterness from our struggles was hanging over our heads and threatening to divide us, even though we were heading in the same direction. Sarah was the first to realize that since we hadn't seen each other for so long we had made assumptions about each other, most of which were based on what others had said about us. Some of our assumptions were based on what each of us had experienced ourselves. We all hoped and prayed that there was a commonality based on our sisterhood but we needed to hear the tale of each of our journeys.

Being the eldest, Sarah took the lead in our conversation and I closed my eyes and listened to her. I thought that would help me remember our home and mother. When Sarah first spoke my eyes sharply blinked open, Sarah spoke his language. She spoke his language as her own and it angered me. Sarah had remained at home; she had chased him away. Why was she speaking his language? I thought loud enough for Sarah to hear. She said nothing. She didn't even glance at me. Sarah knew how impulsive I was and trusted that if I were given a minute I would come to my senses.

I thought through my feelings and I knew obviously Sarah hadn't chased him away soon enough and I resigned to knowing in my heart we, the sisterhood of the Diaspora, had all learned submission in one way or another. So I closed my eyes again and I listened to Sarah once more. I listened to the tone of her voice and the spirit of home that lay in the flavor of her accent. His language was forgotten and the meaning of her words spoke to me as she asked Olivia to go first, just as it was when we were children. Olivia went first because she was the youngest. And Olivia told us she always knew she was the baby and that made her feel more different than special, more isolated than part of the whole but then, in feathery tones, she told us:

Olivia

"I came here to meet you my sisters
But I also came here to master the art of hearing
But no one listened

I came here to master the art of hearing
But no one listened
As I first moved in whispers of naiveté
And scrambled in the confusion
of Franco..... aummm
of Anglo......aummm
of Afro........aummm
I don't know

I came here to master the art of hearing
But no one listened
As I left the culture of before so sure in promise
But I soon learned to ration my trust

I came here to master the art of hearing
But no one listened
To me, never minding to clue them in
Since they doubt me anyway

I came here to master the art of hearing
But no one listened
As I took logical steps to my goals
And my knowledge grew

I came here to master the art of hearing
But no one listened
To the sharp tones of money
And the dissonance of stereotypes

I came here to master the art of hearing
But no one listened
When he consistently questioned my intelligence
and I proudly answered him in two languages

I came here to master the art of hearing
But no one listened
When I cursed the privilege he claims he bestowed on me
When really it was my choice

I came here to master the art of hearing
But no one listened
To my prideful march to prove him wrong
Prove wrong his expectation that I will fail

I came here to master the art of hearing
But no one listened
To the high pitch tones of my loneliness
Of my isolation and depression

I came here to master the art of hearing
But no one listened
To me shiver from the coldness
That remains throughout the seasons

I came here to master the art of hearing
But no one listened
As I called on the strength of both my fathers
To shelter and feed me so I could complete this journey

I came here to master the art of hearing
And now that we are all here
I find great comfort in knowing
That you,
My sisters,
Will listen"

It was now Chloe's turn and we expected that she would have the angriest of words. Chloe had been in the Northern part of the Diaspora and we all knew her journey lasted the longest when compared to ours. We also thought her struggle to be the most strenuous. We were all surprised when Chloe said:

Chloe

"My sisters
I am most me
When I am on the inside of knowledge
And so I purposely stand on the margin
Of all the Isms of promises I made
I was wise enough
To learn from my mother's example
And now
No one is allowed to call me names

My sisters
I have been on the inside
So I know how to think in this space
How to learn in this space
How to earn in this space
I know when to show my face
When not to feel displaced

My sisters
I have long since adapted
For the most part accepted
The uncertainty that is my fate
I have been on the inside
And now my decisions
Revolve around the sacrifices
That I'm willing to make

My sisters
Like you
I sift through the subtext
Of the unspoken
At times I know I'm not heard
When painted invisible
I keep adding value
I always give me, my word

My sisters
My dream is my journey
Watching you I inhale inspiration
But I know it's all relative
This status of ours
As we all stand
On the precipice of self actualization"

I thought I was next but Sarah told me that I was the storyteller and so it was my job to listen to what they said. She said "Lily it will be your job to pass this tale on to the next generation of the Diaspora." And so I listened as Sarah said:

Sarah

"I am the Source
The Source of why
You all find yourself
Knowing
I stayed home
And struggled
With the left behind
Of our father's
own fear of failure
His need to live through
His children
It was not elementary for me

I am the Source
The Source of 4 degrees
of separation
Separation from
Being caught up in
A need to prove
My value, my worth
And now I
click
click
click
For this the final degree
The most terminal of them all
Because I am the alpha of knowing
The omega of my undoing

I am the Source
The Source of the tied
And untied
A human doing
The suicide of
My need for attention
I am fierce
And my knowledge
Has allowed me
To
Use your own weapons
Of mass instruction
Against you

I am the Source
The Source of the undefined
Of minority
The core of ebony
Cause I kept learning
When you called my sisters
Ignorant
Ignorant indeed
My seed
The Source
Of the knowledge
which now invades
"your" lands

I am the Source
The Source of all fear
Because I know you
I chased you away
So now I watch my sisters
With excitement
And pride
Because I know
Their struggle
As you smile polite
Racism glossing your lips

I am the Source
The Source of choice
As my sisters pull at roots
Buried deep in
The knowledge
I now bring
So that they know
We have arrived
Far different
From the preposition
You injected in the middle
Of their sentencing
To a life of creating
Cultures and subcultures
International and intentional
Beautiful still
And rich in the Source
Of this Afro-Diasporic sisterhood"

After listening to my sister's words I knew we were the same four sisters from nearly 400 years ago. We were no longer girls we had grown into beautiful women. I could feel my sisters' realization of where we were in our journey. I could feel our sisterhood. Even though we had been separated for so many years we still described our journey in the way of our people. We expressed our journey in the blue-black rhythms of the storyteller.

PHASE ONE DRAWS TO A CLOSE

As a novice to the qualitative research arena I intend to continue to get to know more about this community. I want to continue to learn how to creatively present findings from my research to a diverse audience. So far, moving in this direction has allowed me to see that creative writing and research can subsist. While I recognize that many in academia have not yet accepted the worth of this burgeoning analytical method in qualitative research, I think it will eventually become a fixture. After this research project I now have a window into the world of narrative and poetic inquiry as a method that can join the creative with the researcher and allow them to work effectively together as catalyst for social action and change.

While the subject under study in this research was important to my growth, the journey and process involved in getting here will continue to have a positive long-term effect on me mentally, spiritually, and intellectually. It represents an inner growth which evolves from continuous knowledge seeking and meaning making. It confirms to me the worth and value of an education. My investment in this research writing was at times so intense I was paralyzed by all of the things I wanted to say. I knew that creative writing on this particular topic was the only way that I could feel some closure and satisfaction with what I had heard from these three women. Poetry and storytelling in this instance allowed me to take what I had heard, felt, perceived, and interpreted, and express it in the most robust way that I could. I wanted to make my findings and analysis of 'self' and 'other' within the context of American Higher Education and the African Diaspora experience accessible to a diverse audience. This project allowed me to gain an intuitive understanding of my Diaspora and in so doing ensured the growth of 'self'.

I am well aware that this research is a novice's attempt at qualitative research and the room for improvement could probably hold a large audience of criticizers. My dream for 'self' is that future representations of my research through storytelling and poetry brings me closer to being described in similar terms as the ethnographer described by Reisman (2002, p. 697) as a woman who "artfully infiltrates her informants, depositing her authorial word inside others' speech to speak her truth without erasing the others' viewpoint and social language."

REFERENCES

Alfred, M. V. (2003). Sociocultural contexts and learning: Anglophone caribbean immigrant women in U.S. postsecondary education. *Adult Education Quarterly, 53*, 242–260.

Chase, S. (2005). Narrative inquiry. Multiple lenses, approaches, voices. In N. K. Denzin & Y. S. Lincoln (Eds.), *The sage handbook of qualitative research* (3rd ed., pp. 651–679). Thousand Oaks, CA: Sage.

Clarke, J., Febbraro, A., Hatzipantelis, G., & Nelson, G. (2005). Poetry and prose: Telling the stories of formerly homeless mentally ill people. *Qualitative Inquiry, 11*, 913–932.

Demenchonok, E. (2005). Intercultural discourse and African-Caribbean philosophy. *Dialogue & Universalism, 15*, 181–201.

Denzin, N. K., & Lincoln, Y. S. (2005). Methods of collecting and analyzing empirical materials. In N. K. Denzin & Y. S. Lincoln (Eds.), *The sage handbook of qualitative research* (3rd ed., pp. 641–649). Thousand Oaks, CA: Sage.

Fay, G. (2001). Uncovering sociocultural influences leads to a call for personalized learning. In D. M. McInearney & S. Van Etten (Eds.), *Research on sociocultural influences on motivation and learning* (pp. 139–157). Greenwich, CT: Information Age.

Gordon, E. T., & Anderson, M. (1999). The African diaspora. Toward an ethnography of diasporic identification. *Journal of American Folklore, 112*, 282–296.

James, G. R. (2006). *Crossing over, moving over: Personal narratives of Caribbean adult college women's struggles and strategies.* Paper presented at the 2006 Adult Education Research conference (pp. 185–189). Retrieved October 10, 2006, from http://www.adulterc.org/ Proceedings/2006/ Proceedings/James.pdf

Meera, S. (2002). Out in the cold: Surviving graduate school as a woman of colour. *Resources for Feminist Research, 29,* 135.

Perez, B. (1998). *Sociocultural contexts of language and literacy.* Mahwah, NJ: Lawrence Erlbaum.

Reisman. (2002). Analysis of personal narratives. In J. F. Gubrium & J. A. Holstein (Eds.), *Handbook of interview research: Context and method* (pp. 695–709). Thousand Oaks, CA: Sage.

Richardson, L. (1996). A sociology of responsibility. *Qualitative Sociology, 19,* 519–524.

Richardson, L. (2001a). Getting personal: Writing-stories. *Qualitative Studies in Education, 14,* 33–38.

Richardson, L. (2001b). Poetic representation of interviews. In J. F. Gubrium & J. A. Holstein (Eds.), *Handbook of interview research: Context and method* (pp. 877–891). Thousand Oaks, CA: Sage.

Schwalbe, M. (1995). The responsibility of sociological poets. *Qualitative Sociology, 18,* 393–413.

Strasser, J., & Seplocha, H. (2005). How can university professors help their students understand issues of diversity through interpersonal & intrapersonal intelligences? *Multicultural Education, 12,* 20–40.

Wilentz, G. (1992). Toward a diaspora literature: Black women writers from Africa, the Caribbean, and the United States. *College English, 54,* 385–405.

Gina Edghill
Adult, Higher, and Community Education
Ball State University
Muncie, Indiana, USA

ANN, DANITA, DEVON, JULIE, LYNN & SHELLEY

"CAN YOU IMAGINE . . . . WHAT IF WOMEN WERE SENTENCED TO EDUCATION?"

Women Speaking Out Inside the Gate[1]

When they crack the gate —
You're out you got a bus ticket
Back to where you started

This system of Crime and Punishment is obviously not working. We need to educate the country, help people see that the system is archaic, locked up (in awareness). This system has to change: we need to get rid of some of the guards, slim down the prison population, provide resources outside. We need to be dealing with the problems on the street.

I'm doing time,
I need positive things in here to do on the outs
Negative talk, shit like that,
You're stuck in the same place

      This is going to be a long process, ma'am

In prison, the entire structured system governs women. Women in prison are told what to do, how to do it, when to do it, and "you have a blue shirt standing behind you." You're here waiting to be sentenced, to start your countdown, 'til they crack the gate, to get . . . back to where you started.

You got no one
Cause of the life you made
Because of the choices you made

When they crack the gate . . .
You feel . . .
      Total anxiety
         Stress
             Happy, you get that happy feeling in your chest

M. Prendergast, C. Leggo and P. Sameshima (eds.), Poetic Inquiry: Vibrant Voices in the Social Sciences, 301–306.

Overwhelmed by the outside world
Even the cars seem like they're going too fast
The simple everyday things seem like too much

Most of the women in the prison system are uneducated, from financially challenged families who because of failures in our system wound up on the street and losing themselves in the use of drugs.

Formal Education, maybe but lots of informal education.

My pipe is my way of dealing with things

Can you ever imagine another way?
It's the only way I know
This is what I do this is what I know

The majority of women in prison are physically and mentally abused and suffer from low self-esteem. **DRUGS KILL PAIN**. *And all of us in here are core-deep suffering. We need to replace the guards with facilitators, educators, provide one-on-one counseling, not once a week, but when a woman is in need.*

We are the voice because we are living it.

Can you imagine doing one-on-one counseling?
  And then bringing up problems you've never dealt with
   And they look at their watch . . .
    And you get stressed, and punch someone out
     And they say, okay next week you can come
   back

I'm lucky my mom's all for recovery
My mom's like a blue shirt, she'll be standing right there for me
I tell my mom, I'm getting a year — she says she's missed ten years of my life, what's another year?

When I had my son I stayed clean and I stayed out of jail. My son was my drug
My son is what kept me clean

A year and two days

Who's going to help you if you relapse?

They don't have recovery houses for people who have other addictions. Most women in here are women who have gone through traumatic experiences. We're being punished for being abused. Killing the pain with drugs — the only way we know how to deal with pain. It's a band-aid.

I've broken that cycle for myself

She's broken the cycle but she still feels the pain
And she'll feel it for the rest of her life
Unless it's addressed

One-on-one
You can empty yourself to this person
Give feedback
And show you how to heal
A lot don't know how to heal.

Recovery is all about relapse
Whether you can get up and dust yourself off
Whether you can recognize the symptoms (systems)
If you get caught using
You're out you're back in jail
You're back to step one . . .

People go through N.A. (Narcotics Anonymous) treatment centers on their release, and counseling that still doesn't address the fact that after that there is still a void in Education, in the sense that a person should be able to find out what their passion is so you have the facilities to educate a person in their chosen field with a back-up of educators and counselors taken right to the point of job placement or apprenticeship, of course, with follow-up counseling to make sure that their concerns are addressed.

When I got arrested
Okay it was bad timing
I got money owed to me I'm going to collect
I'm just setting myself up to come back
Just 'cause I'm in jail it doesn't mean your debt is cleared
It was bad timing . . .

Can you imagine coming here,
        find out what your passion is,
                sentenced directly into an educational institution, counseled,
                        and put right into a job?

Lot better than sitting in jail

All jails do is institutionalize people.

We need to shut these prisons down
       and get the money out
              where it can do the most good.

If you break the law, has to be addressed.
People just waiting to get out to do it again.
Lots of people don't want to change. Welfare wouldn't support me . . .
you need to be —
              know (no) where else to go

That's a big thing, money,
That's the reason I'm in jail

You sold to a cop
That happened to me too

You go hustle
Hustle, hustle man

Given the knowledge that prison isn't working, funding could be accomplished by stopping imprisonment in the courts, and instead sentencing these people to educational facilities where they could be placed when given the choice of what they could do to make their life better. We need half way houses for provincial women. If they didn't put you in prison, you wouldn't have that record.

If you had some hope
If you could choose a direction that would heal you
If you had some support . . .

My boyfriend will keep me clean — that's my hope
He was upset when I came in

If I had some hope I could get the education I need
I could get my skipper's license
I want to start a charter business in time for the Olympics but now I'm on hold
Set a goal and get yourself there

I've got my plan
To open my own flower shop
I had my own computer, I was making payments
I pay into my son's education

I just found out I can get a grant

I want my own travel agency
Just travel for free

Fulfilling desires can take people a long way. In this way the need for so many guards and prisons could be eliminated and all that money in wages and costs of keeping inmates incarcerated could be put into places that would do the most good. Can you imagine a woman coming to jail, finding out what her real desire is, choose a career, educate, get a place . . . can you imagine a better system outside the box — imagine that!

I can imagine going back and staying clean
We can't continue our plans we've been put on hold
He's my everything, he's my support
I still got things on the outs that still need to be taken care of
If they didn't put you in prison
You wouldn't have that record

I want my place back

When they crack the gate —
You're out you got a bus ticket
Back to where you started

NOTES

[1] This article shares our learning from a participatory action research project conducted with women incarcerated in a provincial correctional centre. This project was part of an ongoing federally-funded research project investigating ways to improve the health and wellbeing of women in prison and those in transition. Four of the authors were prison inmates and members of the research team established inside the prison that consisted of prison inmates in role as peer researchers. The peer researchers worked in consultation with the correctional centre's doctor and recreational director who were members of the university research team. Two of the authors, a university researcher and a volunteer in the correctional centre, facilitated discussion around a transcript that was to be analyzed and coded. The transcript being discussed was a portion of a transcribed tape of an inaugural meeting organized by the prison doctor to initiate the participatory action research project.

The text is a compilation of fragments of conversation as the four peer researchers responded to the transcript text. The present text is entirely verbatim. The text in italics was written during lunch break by one of the peer researchers in response to our conversation. This multi-voice interpretative text is what might be called a reciprocal analysis of the original transcript and emergent discussion, with recommendations. The researcher and volunteer recorded the women's conversation, selected and rearranged the text in its current representation — a poetic response to the commitment and care and passion that the women brought to our conversation together. The final version was read and approved by all participants. All names are first names for reasons of confidentiality and so as to not privilege any individual but to recognize that in participatory action research projects, such as this one, we are all learning reciprocally within each other's presence.

We would like to acknowledge the support of the B.C. Medical Services Foundation, Vancouver Foundation, and the Canadian Institutes of Health Research (CHIR), Ottawa, Canada. The title of this research project was *Community-based participatory action research: Collaborating with women in prison to improve their health.* Our special thanks to Dr. Ruth Martin whose enthusiasm and commitment to the welfare of women in prison and those in transition continues to inspire us.

Lynn Fels
Arts Education
Simon Fraser University
British Columba, Canada

KATHLEEN GALVIN & LES TODRES

POETIC INQUIRY & PHENOMENOLOGICAL RESEARCH

The Practice of 'Embodied Interpretation'

To see one loved so much,
change in this way? . . . No!
It is so natural to refuse that this is happening; her memory can function as before.
How deep is the urge to want to stop it?
It deserves at least an angry 'No'
a great refusal
A denial in any way that is possible.
At times
it is also a sinking feeling
A 'nausea' of awareness that relentlessly breaks through.
His being sickened by her saying something over
and over
and over again
He needs to temper this: her memory loss can't be stopped
anger towards self, her, professionals.
but this is not enough
Helplessness dawns.
Saying 'no' to her memory loss heightens their struggle.
She feels pressurized
Upset
He feels remorse, such deep remorse carries a dawning
trying to deny that her memory . . .
that she is seeping away
Just does not work.

This is an example of an embodied interpretation of a phenomenological description from a study of caring for a partner with Alzheimer's. This chapter describes how we as qualitative researchers have been influenced by poetic enquiry in our work. More specifically we tell the story of developing an approach to re-presenting other peoples' experiences, rather than using primarily autobiographical sources. We have called this approach *embodied interpretation* (Todres & Galvin, 2006), and indicate how this is based on an epistemological foundation influenced by Gadamer

*M. Prendergast, C. Leggo and P. Sameshima (eds.), Poetic Inquiry: Vibrant Voices
in the Social Sciences, 307–316.*

(1975) and Gendlin (1992). The chapter finally addresses how our approach of embodied interpretation may be located within the field of poetic enquiry.

IN A NUTSHELL

We see embodied interpretation as a more poetic form of representation that follows phenomenological descriptive analysis of transcribed text (Giorgi & Giorgi 2003). Other's texts are used as a foundation for our embodied interpretations. We go back and forth between our embodied sense of the meanings conveyed in the text and a search for words that can evocatively communicate these meanings. It is a body based hermeneutics that goes back and forth between language and the felt sense of the text carried in our bodies. The importance of this felt sense is central to the practice of embodied interpretation as we want to find words that come 'from there'. The term 'felt sense' has been clarified by Eugene Gendlin (1997), and we will describe this in greater detail later. As qualitative researchers we are interested in serving public understanding by providing descriptions of peoples' experiences that reflect the 'excess' and the aliveness of what our participants have shown us. This interest in the excess and aliveness of what participants share, led us to a consideration of the kind of language that is adequate to this task, and this further led us to a more poetic sensibility in the way that we interpreted and expressed our findings.

HOW POETRY FOUND US

So what has this got to do with poetry and poetic enquiry? Our experience has been that it is a very short step from phenomenology to poetry. Heidegger took this step in his later life in engaging with the work of Hölderlin and Rilke and in how he used poetic language as a way of furthering philosophical insight (Heidegger, 1971). As phenomenological researchers we have often been 'stopped short' by how the complexity of lived experience, whether others or our own, says much more than is verbalised. We thus became increasingly sensitised to the challenge of how to represent what is implicit in others' experience. Our engagement with this 'implicit' sense raised questions for us about the limits of language and the kinds of language that can be somewhat faithful to the fullness and complexities of the lifeworld (lived experience). We remembered where we had experienced such fullness and complexity: it was in the poetry of Seamus Heaney, Rainer Maria Rilke, Pablo Neruda, Wallace Stevens and Mary Oliver. We wondered how this sensibility could be integrated with our practice of phenomenological analysis of others' experiences, and this led to an interesting dialogue with Gadamer's hermeneutics (Gadamer, 1975) and Gendlin's philosophy of 'implicit entry' (Gendlin, 1992). So poetry found us from the richness of the lifeworld and we wanted to respond in a way similar to Neruda's response to 'the street' in his poem "Poetry": Neruda opens the poem with an indication that poetry searched him out. At first he did not know how or from where it came. It was not language that called, but something deeper. What follows is a short extract from Neruda's poem as published by Housden (2003) pp. 8-9:

no, they were not voices, they were not
words, not silence,
but from a street I was summoned,

The eros of poetry spoke to a certain aesthetic motive that we found had been excessively left out in the research world to which we were socialised. But there was another reason for our interest in poetry and that has to do with how we understand its communicative tasks within communities and culture. Both qualitative research and poetry within this context function to share understanding of living and what it is like 'to be there'. We want to do the kind of qualitative research that communicates human experiences in ways that people can really feel and relate to, and this has led us to want to contribute to a more aesthetic trend within the phenomenological tradition. All of this has culminated in a felt concern with how our qualitative research can touch us, so that it can touch others. We have pursued epistemologies (Todres & Galvin, 2008) that acknowledge that there is something in such ' touched understandings' that matter more than much of the so called knowledge that is being generated in our journals.

Therefore the aesthetic concern in our work is interested in the pursuit of a language that deeply describes existential dimensions of experience in order to facilitate resonance, a sense of our common humanity with others, and an emotional homecoming. The aesthetic context for this is focused on the space between language, the lifeworld, and body-based being, knowing and living.

BRINGING THE RICHNESS OF EXPERIENCE INTO LANGUAGE

A more aesthetic phenomenology is different from traditional descriptive phenome-nology which uses a particular type of language that is concerned with summatively capturing the boundaries of the experience in a bare boned and systematic way. This summative emphasis can kill the aliveness of the experience, and as such, can replace the richness of all the implicit nuances that may get lost in a search for scientific essences (Gendlin, 1973). Our particular interest in poetic enquiry centres on what we can learn to serve the challenge of finding words that are faithful to the phenomenon in all its complexity and texture.

So what kind of language does this need? It's a kind of practice. We are trying to develop a capacity to enter into that aliveness, and represent that aliveness in ways that don't kill it, even though words cut things up. The re-presentation has to be able to connect to people in a heartfelt way and be complex enough to awaken not just a logical understanding, but also the sense of it as it lives. When it is living in this way, it is in excess of the words, and more than words can say. So aesthetically, we are learning to differentiate the kind of words that open up its aliveness and the kind of words that close it down. We want the words to provide an understanding that is both of 'head' and 'heart,' and as such, carry forward both the logical dimensions as well as the textural dimensions of experience.

THE 'FELT SENSE': THE LIVED BODY KNOWS THE ALIVENESS OF WORDS

Communicating the relationship between the lived body, live words and 'the implicit' is important but also difficult. Gendlin's (1972) philosophy of 'entry into the implicit' has provided us with both epistemological and practical guidance in this context.

Gendlin was interested in the relationship between language and the aliveness or excess of what language was trying to represent or point to. One of the ways he characterises this excess is his term, 'the more'. The 'more' refers to all the implicit meanings that are 'more than' words, but which are still related to what the words are about. In working with language and the aliveness of things, the emphasis is on an experiential practice rather than just 'a thinking about'. This is because thinking on its own cannot provide the more participative openness and contact with 'the more' that the aliveness of the lifeworld requires. It therefore needs an experiential immersion, and for Gendlin, this requires the faculty of the whole body: its senses, feelings, what's gone before, sense of possibilities, all that announces itself before we package experience into categories. Gendlin calls this the 'felt sense'.

A felt sense is carried in the lived body and is 'a play' between 'the more' of the lived world and the possibility of language. Working with the felt sense is active and experiential in that it requires an attention that is open to the excess of meanings beyond a mere 'thinking about'. The phrase 'entry into the implicit' means that the words that are formulated, 'come from' an action based on attending to the lived body's sense of *felt* context in any moment. This is a kind of back and forth movement between what is implicit as it comes to the bodily felt sense, and language. As such, this process may be named 'a body based hermeneutics'.

THE PRACTICE OF EMBODIED INTERPRETATION

In this process we identify a number of steps in a disciplined practice that attends to the productive interaction between the felt sense of 'the more' given by interview texts, and the kind of language that may evocatively re-present the felt sense in helpful ways.

The task is two-fold:
− To engage or enter others' experiences in a way that we 'are touched'
− To re-emerge into language from the 'touched understanding' so that one can share the insights in a way that is alive and has possible resonance and applicability for others.

Our form of engagement involves, firstly, a focus on the access to what is 'bodily alive', and secondly, an evocative form of expression that serves as a medium for shared understanding. It is not that we are setting out to produce poetry here. But rather, we want to access the experience of a researched phenomenon and speak evocatively 'from there'. In order to slow down and pay attention to 'the play' between the text, the felt sense and the possibility of language that comes from the felt sense, we engage in four phases that are reciprocal rather than linear. So it is a flow and a practice that keeps open the creative tension between words and the aliveness of what the words are about:

- Being present to the data
- Entry into the alive meanings
- 'Dwelling' and 'holding' so that meanings can form
- Finding words 'that work'

This process is muddy and murky but is a palpable movement between words, their felt complexity in the lived body, and what comes to language. Although we name different 'phases' in this process for the sake of communication, we would like to emphasise that these phases are intertwined and can only be differentiated as certain emphases that help the process. A metaphorical image that can be offered in this regard is that of how waves are not separate from the ocean, even though one can attend to their distinctive nuances.

Being Present to the Data

This stage requires us to pay attention to all the ways that we have had access to others' experiences in the course of our study. This includes a sensitivity to the voices of our participants, their body language, and all the other ways in which the meanings of their presentations can be experienced and understood. It also includes attention to a sense of the whole context of the presentation as well as to the details and content of specific meanings being communicated. Further, it includes a sense of ourselves as researchers remembering our interaction with the other, reading their texts a number of times as a whole, imagining more of their world, and thinking about the phenomena that are being portrayed. We also have access to some of the benefits of traditional phenomenological analysis in which others' accounts are synthesised in more essential and potentially transferable ways (Moustakas, 1994). Such traditional phenomenological analysis provides occasions of being present to the data from different perspectives—sometimes right up close, other times from the more reflective space of greater distance. All of these modes of access are however paths to the more fundamental task of 'being present' bodily as another human being who can feel all these significances as a whole.

Entry into the Alive Meanings

The 'felt sense' of all these significances are entered, and attended to for their palpable textures. This is a more intimate moment in which we allow ourselves to be bodily receptive to 'a breathing in' of the holistic, even aesthetic qualities of the alive meanings that appear to be carried (Todres, 2007). It is almost as if the room becomes a place where the presence of the phenomenon is directly living in some sense in this moment, rather than just 'back then' when interviews or other phases of the study took place. In this context then, meanings are more like presences than they are like cognitions or mere thoughts. Such entry into alive meanings is not something that can be actively constructed by effort, but rather requires the kind of receptivity of the lived body that 'lets be,' in a bodily participative way.

Dwelling' and 'Holding' so that Meanings can Form

There is a subtle and important difference of emphasis between 'entry into alive meanings' and the emphasis of 'dwelling and holding'. In the previous phase of entry into alive meanings, the palpability of 'all that' comes to visit and, as such, is felt. But it is very delicate and requires this next step of dwelling and holding if the felt presence is to become tangible enough so that its meaning, messages, and possible language can form in public spaces. Dwelling and holding requires a slowing down, a settling, an attentive bodily and emotional waiting, so that the felt meaning can form and be there, almost as if from its own 'centre of gravity'. Such alive presence can then become stronger and achieve a certain 'otherness' which can be related to for its message and meaning. A metaphorical image that can be offered in this regard is that of a comforting mother holding an insecure infant until the infant settles and can express herself more definitely.

Finding Words 'that Work'

The felt sense that has formed to some degree of strength out of its earlier pre-patterned and alive 'moreness,' can form further towards shared space through a certain kind of language. Our experience has been that language informed by a poetic sensibility appears to be most adequate when attending to a continuity between the felt sense and words that can do justice to what is felt to some degree. Finding words that work involves a bodily hermeneutic process of going back and forth between the felt sense as it has formed and words that resonate with this felt sense. As human beings we appear to have developed an aesthetic sense, an almost bodily satisfaction or knowing, when certain words 'feel right' in relation to what they are about. It is almost as if the lived body feels a 'yes' or a 'no' to different words and even more subtly a 'not quite,' or 'even better.' This kind of resonant validity is a source of ongoing discipline and editing which may need to go back and forth a number of times between words and phrases and the felt sense of what they are about. One of the features of this resonant validity is that the felt sense may become stronger in response to good words, or may open up even further towards the richness of further meanings implicit in the ground or gravity of the felt sense. A metaphorical image of the process of finding words that work is that of a dance that starts off slowly and tentatively and builds into a more definite rhythm and insistence that arises from the back and forth movement of self and other. A more poetic re-presentation of the muddiness and murkiness of the process is offered in the following poem.

The BodyKnows

How do words come?
As appetite, fatigue, like the rhythms of the seasons
awaiting an unfolding
from the calling of the 'more'
the flesh of the world

the interwoven body
Here I am
flickering sense
wells in me
just enough . . . .

The body knows
delicate murmuring
sensing of some gentle form
and then it goes.
Unformed yet felt . . . there is much more than this
much more than this
fleetingly,
vague stirrings echo words, each felt whisper,
an opening to what is known
The body knows
More than this

The process of embodied interpretation ends in a similar way to that in which the struggle to find closure in a poem or piece of prose ends. As we are qualitative researchers, our particular sense of closure is most likely to occur when there is a balance between 'telling' and 'showing'. 'Telling' involves providing enough context and commentary so that something interesting and new is understood based on our findings. 'Showing' involves providing enough evocative texture so that another reader may have some access to the aliveness and palpable presence of the shown phenomenon (Todres, 1998; 2000). And so we come back to our embodied interpretation that we offered at the beginning of this chapter. Our embodied interpretations are offered to others for their own hospitality so that they can make 'temporary homes' for such understanding.

LOCATING EMBODIED INTERPRETATION
WITHIN THE FIELD OF POETIC ENQUIRY

In developing embodied interpretation we have located ourselves in between a broadly literary tradition and a broadly human science tradition. We have been informed by both the aesthetics of poetry as well as the human scientific concerns of hermeneutics. Further we are partially influenced by our health and social science background, as well as our research background, and as such, are interested in both understanding and feeling. We are not just interested in how to evoke feelings as if they are alone, nor how to facilitate understandings as if they are alone. Our view is that a truly human form of understanding involves 'being', 'knowing' and 'acting' which reflects a unity of 'heart', 'head' and 'hand' (Galvin & Todres, 2007). We stop short of claiming that we are writing poetry as a primary concern because our evocative interests occur within the human scientific concern and a broadly hermeneutic tradition.

With this in mind we would thus like to elaborate a little further on our epistemological commitments. We have found Gadamer's (1975) contributions to philosophical hermeneutics helpful for us as qualitative researchers in that he provides some seminal insights into the nature of understanding. In this view understanding is 'a play' between context and detail, the personal and the relational, the past and the future. One of the implications of such a Gadamerian epistemology is that it provides us with a response to the following question that arises when we offer an embodied interpretation: *whose experience is this?*

Consistent with Gadamer, we would say that experience is both unique and shared, and thus can never be understood exclusively from a first person or third person position. As researchers engaged in offering embodied interpretations we wish to reflect themes that can communicate something of the uniqueness of individuals' experiences, as well as the shared intersubjective horizons within which any unique experience occurs. This frees us to a form of poetic re-presentation that does not merely stick to the same words as our interviewees, because the experience that we wish to understand and portray is neither fully another's alone, nor is it fully our own. Rather it reflects a meaningful-world-with-others. Embodied interpretation addresses itself most to the relevance of an existential level of understanding; that is a level of understanding that wishes to honour the places where commonality (community) and uniqueness (individual) meet. Such sensed understanding is an event where meaning can 'come home' to persons. This has resonance with Seamus Heaney's views about poetry in which he points to poetic understanding providing possibilities of emotional homecoming, where it touches some of the deepest roots of our common humanity (Heaney, 1995).

> Poetic form is both the ship and the anchor. It is at once a buoyancy and a holding, allowing for the simultaneous gratification of whatever is centrifugal and centripetal in mind and body. And it is by such means that Yeats' poetry work does what the necessary poetry always does, which is to touch the base of our sympathetic nature while taking in at the same time the unsympathetic reality of the world to which that nature is constantly exposed. (Heaney, pp. 466–467).

This kind of understanding may be particularly important in a world that has lost its appreciation of the 'I' in the 'thou' (Buber, 1970). Such an empathic, existential concern is further taken forward by another important epistemological influence: the philosophy of Eugene Gendlin (1972). His experiential phenomenology, together with influences from poetic enquiry have inspired us to contribute to a more aesthetic phenomenology. The crucial nuance that he adds to Gadamerian hermeneutics is that of a 'body- based' hermeneutics: 'the play' or back and forth movement between the felt sense carried in the lived body and the formative movements of language. In considering the lived body as a way of knowing, Gendlin has opened up ways of attending to the textures and excesses of the lifeworld (its plenum) and how this speaks through the body. As described in our sections on process, this requires a certain dwelling and waiting in which meanings can form from their pre-patterned presence and aliveness. Poetic enquiry may then benefit from an epistemology that is informed by a body based hermeneutics, in that it offers a contemplative attention to the 'from where' the language is born. This 'from where' is often not honoured enough as it is fuzzy and ambiguous and requires a patient waiting for the unformed to form. All this offers traditional phenomenological research a greater aesthetic direction because it wishes to use language as an artistic form rather than as a traditional scientific one that summarises information. Within this view, words are ways to show the plenum of experiences, lives and lifeworlds, and such showing, shows more, rather than less. So we are interested in the kind of words that retain their service to such 'more', and we can understand why Heidegger became most interested in poetry towards the end of his life. For a greater elaboration of the characteristics of an aesthetically inclusive understanding see Gendlin (2004), his paper entitled 'Carrying Forward'.

In saying good bye for now we would like to conclude with some holding phrases. Embodied interpretation emphasises its *holding* before its *sharing* in order to permit the phenomenon to touch us so that it can touch another. The aesthetics of embodied interpretation involves play, embodied resonance, care for the phenomenon, and its aliveness (rather than simply our own construction of it), care for the audience, a contemplative gesture of dwelling, an interest in a kind of human understanding of where things have come from and where things are going (narrative coherence), a hermeneutic human scientific concern with how parts and wholes fit together, and an existential concern for our uniqueness and commonality.

And finally, we offer another embodied interpretation derived from a study of "Caring for a loved-one with Alzheimer's : The experience of adjusting to more limited horizons:"

Renunciation

'Limit your horizons', announces the task of caring,
An insistence
His attention is called, a pull away from what was
and from dreamt futures that may have been calling
What Now!
Door bell ringing has to be answered
This has to be done
no time to befriend, no time to mourn, no time to dream, she needs this now
What now!
Door bell ringing has to be answered.
This has to be done
He is focused. Their time is shorter, their vision is narrower, this creeping stricture
is choking their possibilities.   What now?
He has to let go. Give way. Give up what was.
Find a way. Everything as it was is now different...
being together, bound together, they feel the way through, from an enclosed house
Thrown together here, and for now
And what to do?
And what can be done unfolds, moment to moment,
small openings. A way to the life that is possible.

REFERENCES

Buber, M. (1970). *I and thou* (W. Kauffman, Trans.). Edinburgh: T&T Clark.

Gadamer, H. (1975/1997). *Truth and method* (2nd Rev. ed.). New York: Continuum.

Galvin, K., & Todres, L. (2007). The creativity of 'unspecialisation': A contemplative direction for integrative scholarly practice. *Phenomenology and Practice, 1*(1). Retrieved July 3, 2008, from http://www.phandpr.org/index.php/pandp

Gendlin, E. T. (1973). Experiential phenomenology. In M. Natanson (Ed.), *Phenomenology and the social sciences* (Vol. 1, pp. 281–319). Evanston, IL: North Western University Press.

Gendlin, E. T. (1992). Thinking beyond patterns: Body, language and situations. In B. den Ouden & M. Moen (Eds.), *The presence of feeling in thought* (pp. 25–151). New York: Peter Lang.

Gendlin, E. T. (1997). *Experiencing and the creation of meaning* (2nd ed.). Evanston, IL: North West University Press.

Gendlin, E. T. (2004). The new phenomenology of carrying forward. *Continental Philosophy Review, 37*, 127–151.

Giorgi, A., & Giorgi, B. (2003). The descriptive phenomenological psychological method. In P. M. Camic, J. E. Rhodes, & L. Yardley (Eds.), *Qualitative research in psychology: Expanding perspectives in methodology and design* (pp. 243–273). Washington, DC: American Psychological Association.

Heaney, S. (1995). Crediting poetry: The nobel lecture. In S. Heaney (Ed.), *Opened ground: Poems 1966–1996* (pp. 445–467). London: Faber & Faber.

Heidegger, M. (1971). *Poetry, language and thought* (A. Hofstadter, Trans.). New York: Harper & Row.

Housden, R. (Ed.). (2003). *Risking everything*. New York: Harmony.

Moustakas, C. (1994). *Phenomenological research methods*. Thousand Oaks, CA: Sage.

Todres, L. (1998). The qualitative description of human experience: The aesthetic dimension. *Qualitative Health Research, 8*(1), 121–127.

Todres, L. (2000). Writing phenomenological-psychological description: An illustration attempting to balance texture and structure. *Auto/Biography, 3*(1&2), 41–48.

Todres, L. (2007). *Embodied inquiry: Phenomenological touchstones for research, psychotherapy and spirituality*. Basingstoke, UK: Palgrave Macmillan.

Todres, L., & Galvin, K. T. (2006). Caring for a partner with Alzheimer's disease: Intimacy, loss and the life that is possible. *International Journal of Qualitative Studies in Health and Wellbeing, 1*, 50–61.

Todres, L., & Galvin, K. (2008). Embodied interpretation: A novel way of evocatively re-presenting meanings in phenomenological research. *Qualitative Research, 8*(5), 568–583.

Kathleen Galvin
Centre for Qualitative Research
Bournemouth University
United Kingdom

Les Todres
Centre for Qualitative Research
Bournemouth University
United Kingdom

JACQUIE KIDD

FRAGILITY EXPOSED

The Impact of Nursing on Mental Health

Nurses are fragile. History and contemporary media portray us as angels, whores, handmaidens and battleaxes (Hallam, 2000; Jinks & Bradley, 2004), but neglect nurses' humanity. In an increasingly complex and ever-changing healthcare industry, nurses are under constant pressure to perform in technical, emotional, practical and educational terms (Kidd, 2008). For my doctoral research, I drew on autoethnographical accounts from my own experience and those of 18 other nurses to explore the impact of being a nurse, and doing nursing work, on nurses' mental health. In particular, I worked with the notion of hyphenated lives (Fine, 1994; McClelland & Fine, 2008; Sarin & Fine, 2007) to explicate the disconnections and alignments that occurred in my interpretation of our nursing lives.

This poem bears witness to our collective story.

Being a nurse is everything to me.
It feels like home.

> *Community expectations . . .*
> *accountability*
> *transparency*
> *responsibility*
> *Intense stress levels.*

I just broke down crying
I feel like crap.

Doing nursing work means everything to me.
I thought if I cared enough, then people would care for me.

> *Nursing expectations . . .*
> *expertise*
> *distance*
> *mastery*
> *I became very depressed and anxious,*
> *suicidal and psychotic.*

This is deeply distressing to me
It hurts too much.

M. Prendergast, C. Leggo and P. Sameshima (eds.), Poetic Inquiry: Vibrant Voices
in the Social Sciences, 317–319.

Tears, panic, fear,
hiding medication packages and wine bottles,
dread, anxiety, bruises,
comforting food, agonising purging,
isolation, isolation,
                ISOLATION.

Hyphens that join
        me to my work
        me to my image
                - indefatigable
                - caring
                - omniscient

                                The same hyphens separate
                                me from my needs
                                me from my life
                                        - vulnerable
                                        - afraid
                                        - ashamed

        Bullies dwell in the hyphens.
        Their words slice like scalpels
        into the scars in my psyche
                eviscerating
                enervating
                exposing

        In my need, I feel like
        I've done something wrong
        I'm being punished
                exhausting
                humiliating
                confusing

                Being a nurse
                doing my work and
                needing care is
                                NOT ALLOWED

Being a nurse means everything to me.
It should feel like home.
                        So

                                the pain?

                                I kept it to myself.

REFERENCES

Fine, M. (1994). Working the hyphens: Reinventing self and other in qualitative research. In N. K. Denzin & Y. S. Lincoln (Eds.), *Handbook of qualitative research* (pp. 70–82). Thousand Oaks, CA: Sage.

Hallam, J. (2000). *Nursing the image: Media, culture and professional identity*. London: Routledge.

Jinks, A. M., & Bradley, E. (2004). Angel, handmaiden, battleaxe or whore? A study which examines changes in newly recruited student nurses' attitudes to gender and nursing stereotypes. *Nurse Education Today, 24*(2), 121–127.

Kidd, J. (2008). *Aroha mai: Nurses, nursing and mental illness*. Unpublished Doctoral Thesis, University of Auckland, Auckland, New Zealand.

McClelland, S. I., & Fine, M. (2008). Writing *on* cellophane: Studying teen women's sexual desires, inventing methodological release points. In K. Gallagher (Ed.), *The methodological dilemma: Critical and creative approaches to qualitative research* (pp. 232–266). Toronto: University of Toronto Press.

Sarin, S. R., & Fine, M. (2007). Hyphenated selves: Muslim American youth negotiating identities on the fault lines of global conflict. *Applied Developmental Science, 11*(3), 151–163.

Jacquie Kidd
Nursing
University of Auckland
New Zealand

FRANCES L. RAPPORT

POETRY OF MEMOIR

"Like a Victory I Fooled Them"

So vivid in my mind
as you sitting in front of me.
I will start talking.
It's very easy.

We arrived through that famous gate.
Birkenau.
Auschwitz.
But Birkenau was the thing.

We arrived through that gate
and before we got there,
we already saw the chimneys –
the fires.

We saw the spouting chimneys
and the smoke and the fire.
"Raus, Raus"
and soldiers up and down.

"Leave all your luggage."
"Come out, come out."
And the smell, which you had never smelled before,
and which you couldn't place.

And the chimneys.
And the smoke.
And the ashes.
And the prisoners in striped pyjamas.

Somebody must have told us
"young ones on this side."

M. Prendergast, C. Leggo and P. Sameshima (eds.), Poetic Inquiry: Vibrant Voices
in the Social Sciences, 321–324.

Millions milling around,
at least a thousand people.
They separated men and women.
And when we saw this bedlam
you felt something eerie;
but you didn't know.

And this man – about my age
we knew each other all our life.
"See you after the war?"
I never saw him again.

Dr Mengele with those gloves.
Gauntlets –
in my memory they are gauntlets.
Stood there, boots shining.

"Here" and "there" – he pointed.
Doing 'this' with the gloves.
The mother had a five year-old child,
she went the to other side.

Nobody was afraid because –
because you didn't know.
Five in a row.
Proceed to the man with those gloves.

So we passed and I passed,
I was with a group of girls.
We went this way.
Never gave it a thought.

I had still my wedding rings,
amethyst set in silver.
I still had those with me,
the most precious things I possessed.

When I saw what's going on
that we had to leave our clothes
and the mud
and the shouting.
and the starting to run naked
and our hair being cut off.

I took my two rings,
and threw them in the mud.

No Germans will have it.
In the mud
in Auschwitz.
The most precious things I had.

Outside or under cover,
I don't remember.
We were shaven – afraid of something,
but we didn't know what.

So they shaved us.
Awful thing to loose your hair.
The most humiliating thing.
They didn't speak, just shaved our hair.

We went through those showers
and were given some horrible rags.
And then some shoes; old shoes,
I happened to get clogs.

If they were too small
we were wise enough not to ask.
In fifths, they led us to the barracks,
big but flimsy, with a door at one end.

The bunks were three-tiered,
Lie down like sardines.
And, "when will I see my parents?"
"You fool, they are in the chimney by now."

They thought we were mad.
We thought they were mad.
But we soon found out,
that they weren't mad.

You saw all the horror and it all fell into place.
And the smell and the fire and the smoke and the shouting
and the dogs and the mud.
Our first day in Auschwitz.

RAPPORT

We were never sent to work.
Top bunk.
Awful windows
without glass.

Much colder at the top because the wind blowing through.
I was there ten days,
I was so very lucky
it lasted only ten days.

Roll calls twice a day
and we weren't tattooed.
October '44
they needed every person to work.

The capos only shouted,
"stupid cows", and "you'll soon know".
Jewish from Slovakia.
Been there years.

We stood for those roll calls,
and they counted one, two, three,
And if somebody died
they had to keep the body there.

Ten days later and we were sent walking.
We didn't have luggage and they shaved our heads.
We were given a piece of bread and sent into cattle wagons.
We were leaving Auschwitz and we didn't stop.

All elated.
The train headed west.
October in Poland.
Like a victory I fooled them.

Frances L. Rapport
Qualitative Health Research at the School of Medicine
Swansea University
United Kingdom

RACHELLE D. WASHINGTON

TORNADOES, TRANSFORMATIONS AND TEXTURES

Twisting Poetry and Research

"The vitality of language lies in its ability to limn the actual, imagined and possible lives of its speakers, readers, writers. Although its poise is sometimes in displacing experience it is not a substitute for it. It arcs toward the place where meaning may lie."
—*Toni Morrison, Nobel Prize Acceptance Speech, 1993*

ARTFUL SCHOLARSHIP

In *The Wiz* by William Brown (1979), a violent tornado transports Dorothy to an urban landscape where she is greeted by Munchkins, meets a few witches—good and bad —befriends a scarecrow, tin man, and lion, and they travel through myriad urbanesque scenes—a perilous journey through unfamiliar territory. Like Dorothy and her fellow travelers, the Black women in this study dance with me and provide a glimpse of their dance with, and sometimes against, their academic experiences, their roadblocks, as well as their triumphs in the search for heart, courage, wit, and other armament necessary to wander through this qualitative jungle (Kvale, 1996; Wolcott, 1990).

Writers such as Giovanni (2004), Anzaldua (1983), and Richardson (1997) masterfully weave poetry into tales. The notion of speaking and writing freely is a complicated one. I am interested in Black women's lives and writing about their lives. I feel an obligation to problematize Black women's narratives beyond the celebratory. Toni Morrison's (1993) use of vibratory language reminds readers, "We do language. That may be the measure of our lives."[1] There is ambiguity and much subjective turmoil in our stories in the same way that there is much that documents transcendence and arrival. It is expressly for this reason that the interview study uses an alternative method to represent the stories of the participants. Upon reading Alice Walker's (2000) *The Way Forward Is with a Broken Heart,* there was both resonance and assurance in my desire to go forward in search of schooling and life stories related to the participants—Black women doctoral candidates. Framing the initial study within the constructs of Africanist cultural roots and traditions while simultaneously exposing issues relative to resistance, social justice, equity and humanity is the artful crafting of a womanist. As a womanist researcher, using qualitative methods, I drank from the wells,

M. Prendergast, C. Leggo and P. Sameshima (eds.), Poetic Inquiry: Vibrant Voices in the Social Sciences, 325–332.

holding delicious waters—quenching the longing for a tool that could speak my data—hence, I chose to use poetic representation.

I conducted 14 semi-structured in-depth interviews, collected demographic profile information, and used email correspondence and informal conversations. Using three layers of analysis—narrative analysis, cultural analysis, and poetic analysis—I analyzed the participants' narratives. Like Dorothy in *The Wiz* (Brown, 1979), I needed three companions to complete the journey, each with a unique perspective. I used cultural analysis and poetic analysis as tools in the service of narrative analysis. The three analytic lenses offer unique vantage points to viewing more wholly the narratives of these Black women. Importantly, the use of these kinds of analyses reveal deeper embedded textures of our life worlds. Poetic representation as an analysis tool stretches the boundaries of what has traditionally been accepted as knowledge and the way this knowledge is represented (Braidotti, 1993; Hill, 2005; Richardson, 1993). Glesne (1999) wrote, "Researchers hope for a description and analysis of its complexity that identify concepts not previously seen or fully appreciated." The commitment to exploring alternative methods of inquiry remains fertile as I continue to look at Black girls and women's lives. The following is a reflective poem about interviewing the study participants.

Into the well.
At various junctures
pauses
hesitations
gesturing and language
driving
ebb and flow
our sister moments resulted from
shared casings
holding the wells of tears
broken hearts
hurtful memories
spiritual pining—and,
  even
resplendent laughter
I tapped gingerly into these wells.

When I think of representing data in ways that speak to the richness of Black cultural landscape, I am drawn to links between art and research. According to Cahnmann (2003), Hill (2005), and Richardson (1997), poetic representation blends art and the world of qualitative research. Employing poetic representation is as much an art as it is research, especially for a researcher balancing cultural constructs with academic currency (Cahnmann-Taylor & Siegesmund, 2008; Hill, 2005). I use poetic representation (Cahnmann, 2003; Eisner, 1997; Hill, 2005) to represent the agency (Bourdieu & Passeron, 1977; hooks, 1996) of eight participants. Writing the poems is a very powerful experience for me, and brings forth the spirit of the women more fully than the segments of the interviews, as important as those are.

Thank you, Elma Lewis. Roxbury.
There I was, Suzy Snowflake, Head Snowflake,
tutu adorned, chocolate-dipped ballerina, cambré,
little chubby brown sugah leading the troupe.
We were dancers–twirling whirling
hues of deep sunkist, mocha-laced, blueberry dotted,
purple grained, high yellow shades
a soulful kaleidoscope.
Each step—determined, glissade.
I was the first deeeeep chocolate girl to lead.
What a prideful moment—landing the role
My Daddy said I was the Blackest and beautifullest snowflake
*   he had ever seen.*
Suzy Snowflake danced free.

In this study I am interested in understanding how Black girls' and women's schooling and lived experiences occur. I use this opening poem related to my agency to signify how my experiences at Miss Lewis's school are memorable because they led to loves, liberations, and embodiments reified today. Addressing my subjectivities was an essential element to this work (hooks, 1996; Patton, 2002; Peshkin, 1988). The poetic rendering above is first in this sequence to signal acknowledgement of my subjectivity. Its position answers hooks' (1992) concern that in order to "bear the burden of memory one must willingly journey to places long uninhabited, searching the debris of history for traces of the unforgettable, all knowledge of which has been suppressed" (p. 172).

Using reflection notes and fieldnotes, I captured biases and reflected upon them. Spending the time with my participants during interviews, classes, and outside gatherings provided multiple opportunities for "sufficient time" in the site, "persistent observations," and rapport building (Lincoln & Guba, 1985). I render data related to the "agency" poetically, whether it is the lack of it, the need for it, the acquisition or nurture of it—agency as a powerful construct urges us to a "widawakeness" (Greene, 1973). During analysis, I read and listened to data transcripts and audiotapes. I listened to the tapes for context and emphasis of words and/or phrases; and noted whatever was powerful or striking; I then extracted those pieces and repeated the process three times. Context and voice serve as "essential features of [poetic] portraiture" (Hill, 2005, p. 96). From the first set, I then extracted words or phrases based upon issues of salience (Alexander, 1988) or by a theme. I placed the work in progress in a separate document and continued to analyze.

The introductory narratives pointedly highlighted by italics are extractions of larger narratives on each of the participants. Here, you are introduced, albeit minimally, to four study participants, one you have met—Suzy Snowflake, the author. The renderings extracted from all data sources vary in length and emphasis.

Makesha, a thirty something, copper-toned woman with reddish brown dyed dreadlocks prides herself on staying fit and eating right. She wears designer named clothing and gear in an unpretentious manner. Makesha considers

*herself creative and artsy. Her stylish manner, casual chic, represents that
flair and an equaled ease for sharing lived experiences. Makesha's story is
filled with humorous vignettes related to schooling and social experiences.*

Makesha: *No flips*
Sad!
Wanting to flip my hair.
African garb, sandaled, copper toned, comfy.

the first day of school
standing at the office door
        "Oh my God, she's Black!"

the first day of school
sinking, just didn't know what to do
standing at the office door

Since the first day of school
hearing, schoolmates' voices
        My gardener's Black
        My driver's Black
        My housekeeper is Black

Since the first day of school
wondering, in my aloneness

        "Why can't I be white?"
        "Why am I not white?"
        "Why can't I have straight hair?"

Then Katia came to school. 6th grade.
The Blackest Black girl I had ever seen.
Culturally Black.
Physically Black.
A big old butt.
everything I had never seen before
        and
I loved her.
She, we, best friends
        For one year
about the time my mother
            pulled me out of school.
I think it's because Katia and I
were just having such a great time

In between these things,
Bearing Blackness.
Teasing. Jealousy.
Afrocentric mother.
Black History Month.
Hair, natural. *No* flips.

All these things kept me on the outside.
I couldn't be like them
    or Katia
therefore

I became totally unlike them.

> ***Clovia*** *is outspoken and lively and not easily rendered invisible. Her hairdo of dark natural twists roams her head and frames a face, carved by genes and time. She is the color of sorghum ready to be harvested. It is not uncommon to see her on campus wrapped in a profusion of color from head to toe or simply adorned in clothing of comfort, loosely draped. Even on her "farm" Clovia is as bright—in attire and personality—as the flowers blossoming on the land. Clovia wove a narrative of survival amidst battles of oppression.*

Clovia: *Coalesced*
Every time she saw me,
That teacher,
I was my momma. My auntie.
Someone who cleaned her house
    round brown unpretty girlchild
Every time they saw me
They feigned remembrance
I am unnoticed
One Black child
Like any other
    round brown unpretty girlchild
Every time they see me
I am untalented.
    round brown unpretty girlchild
I am invisible
Coalesced into one identity

But, I said hello, anyway.

> ***Mack's*** *honey-colored face was framed by gold-rimmed glasses that softened the dreaded-mane. Mack is tall, not willowy, but graceful. She is a Generation Xer who dresses in 70's and 80's retro style. It is not unusual to find her in*

anything from a Jimi Hendrix tie-dyed T-shirt (which she wore the day of the interview) along with faded black jeans (the in style) and a pair of worn white sneakers—to an outfit of an Indian Sari and silk scarf accompanied by chunky boots that elevate her height easily to over 6 feet. Mack's soft-spoken manner and louder body language unfolded her world, like a map—section by section.

Mack: *White girls don't go to this school*
From day one of school!

This li'l brown girl, I forget her name

Hecklin' real bold
white girls don't go to this school

I'm lookin' round and above my head
You know in that "who me?" sorta way.
I don't know what you're talking about,
(LOL) like what're you talking about?
Hecklin' again.
white girls don't go to this school.

*Whoa, I was like, **well** there's no **white** girl here!*
You know,
*she was like, **well** you **look** like it,*
*I'm like **well** I'm not!*
But.
I'm thinking of mom, she's real light
Granddaddy, he's real light
Granny, she's real light

But, but   I
*stand **my** ground*
kinda keep my game face on
for whatever that meant at seven.

Hiding, hurting, hating

I'm supposed to be
Deep chocolaty brown
So I told mom
we need to fix that.

Laughing. Shaping.
from dark spaces.
The taunting quiets but speaks just the same.
white girls don't go to this school

With rare exception, participants asked me questions or drew me into other levels of interactions as we signified, chanted, or for some, were simply loud, Black girls of our volition. With many, laughter was deep and hearty. Still others wore Dunbar's[2] mask in the retelling of significant events or occurrences to hide invisible, irascible, and oft times indelible scars upon worn faces "with torn and bleeding hearts we [that] smile." I wrestled often with the loud, Black girl wanting to resist the decorum of the study by tossing the tools of the academy. I thought often of Audre Lorde's (1979) master metaphor—*the master's tools will never dismantle the master's house.* The metaphor implicitly troubles assumptions about power and forced me to search for ways to conduct research on Black women that can inform readers especially those in power and outside of our zone of familiarity. Furthermore, a conscious effort to present voice and context without oppressing participants challenged me as a Black woman doing research on Black women. I want this work to expressly enact change: change in oppressors' perception, change in ways readers contextualize the issues for these specific Black women's lives, and change in ways research is disseminated about these lives. The master metaphor does not lend itself necessarily to change. As a womanist researcher, I chronicle interactions and changes of specific Black women on a journey in ways that honor their experiences, perceptions, and locations as lifelong learners. I asked participants questions related to their schooling and lived experiences, including challenges, successes, and decisions before the pursuit of a doctoral degree. A few of the questions were:

What was the message(s) stated or implied regarding education?

What do teacher educators need to know about the schooling experiences of young Black girls?

In your view, describe ways Black girls and women need support of and for their schooling and/or societal navigation.

A womanist perspective assisted me in recognizing the "lack of uniformity of experience among African American women," (Collins, 2000, p. 67).Many ideas prompt further investigation into the educational stories of Black women: Black feminist/womanist research methodology and analysis, documentation of Black female doctoral students' educational experiences, and findings of those landing at the thresholds of historically white research universities Arts based inquiry provides at least one tool, beyond the masters grasp.

Overall the experience reinforced the peer relationship we shared. All participants acknowledged ways their words can provide insight and significance in the larger society. In the end we were all dancers to a rhythm of our own, bound by our journey inside of this moment in time on our own special Yellow Brick Road...

NOTES

[1] Retrieved September 12, 2008, from http://www.americanrhetoric.com/speeches/tonimorrisonnobellecture. htm

[2] Retrieved September 12, 2008 from http://www.potw.org/archive/potw8.html)

REFERENCES

Alexander, I. E. (1988). Personality, psychological assessment, and psychobiography. In D. P. Adams & R. L. Ochberg (Eds.), *Psychobiography and life narratives* (pp. 265-294). Durham, NC: Duke University Press.

Anzaldua, G. E., & Moraga, C. L. (Eds.). (1983). *This bridge called my back: Writings by radical women of color* (2nd ed.). New York: Third Woman Press.

Bourdieu, P. & Passeron, J. C. (1977). *Reproduction in education, society and culture.* Beverly Hills: Sage.

Braidotti, R. (1993). Embodiment, sexual difference, and the nomadic subject. *Hypatia, 8*(1), 1-13.

Brown, W. F. (1979). *The Wiz:Aadapted from "The wonderful Wizard of Oz" by L. Frank Baum* (Rev. & rewritten. ed.). New York: S. French.

Cahnmann, M. (2003). The craft, practice, and possibility of poetry in educational research. *Educational Researcher, 32*(3), 29-36.

Cahnmann-Taylor, M., & Siegesmund, R. (2008). *Arts-Based Research in Education: Foundations for Practice.* London: Routledge.

Collins, P. H. (2000). *Black feminist thought: Knowledge, consciousness, and the politics of empowerment* (2nd ed.). New York: Routledge.

Eisner, E. W. (1997). The promise and perils of alternative forms of data representation. *Educational Researcher, 26*(6), 4-10.

Giovanni, N., & Johnson, C. A. (2004). *The girls in the circle.* New York: Scholastic.

Glesne, C. (1999). *Becoming qualitative researchers.* New York: Longman.

Greene, M. (1973). The matter of justice. *Teachers College Record, 75*(2), 181-191.

Hill, D. (2005). The poetry in portraiture: Seeing subjects, hearing voices, and feeling contexts. *Qualitative Inquiry, 17*(1), 95-105.

Hooks, B. (1992). *Black looks: race and representation.* Boston: South End Press.

Hooks, B. (1996). *Bone black: Memories of girlhood.* New York: Holt.

Kvale, S. (1996). *Interviews: an introduction to qualitative research interviewing.* Thousand Oaks, CA: Sage.

Lincoln, Y., & Guba, E. (1985). *Naturalistic inquiry.* Beverly Hills, CA: Sage.

Lorde, A. (1979). *The master's tools will never dismantle the master's house.* Trumansburg, NY: The Crossing Press.

Morrison, T. (1993). *Nobel Prize acceptance speech.* Stockholm, Sweden. Retrieved March 1, 2009, from http://nobelprize.org/nobel_prizes/literature/laureates/1993/morrison-lecture.html

Patton, M. Q. (2002). *Qualitative research & evaluation methods* (3rd ed.). Thousand Oaks, CA: Sage.

Peshkin, A. (1988). In search of subjectivity-one's own. *Educational Researcher, 17*(1), 17-31.

Richardson, L. (1993). Poetics, dramatics, and transgressive validity: The case of the skipped line. *Sociology Quarterly, 34*(4), 695-710.

Richardson, L. (1997). *Fields of play: Constructing an academic life.* New Brunswick, NJ: Rutgers University Press.

Vaz, K. M. (1997). *Oral narrative research with Black women.* Thousand Oaks, CA: Sage.

Walker, A. (1983). *In search of our mothers' gardens: Womanist prose* (1st ed.). San Diego, CA: Harcourt Brace Jovanovich.

Walker, A. (2000). *The way forward is with a broken heart* (1st ed.). New York: Random House.

Wolcott, H. F. (1990). *Writing up qualitative research.* Newbury Park, CA: Sage.

Rachelle D. Washington
Elementary Education
Clemson University
South Carolina, USA

DONNA WEST WITH LUKE, DORA, HARPER & MAISIE

"STRONG TOGETHER"

Poetic Representations of a Deaf-Hearing Family Narrative

Maisie told me once that she remembers before she was born.

She was a 'Deaf egg'.

INTRODUCTION

The work which forms the basis for this chapter is a narrative inquiry into Deaf-hearing family life (West, 2007). The term 'Deaf-hearing family' is used here to describe a family consisting of both hearing and Deaf members. The use of a capital 'D' in Deaf is commonly used as an indicator of a positive cultural Deaf identity; that is to say, sign-language users who identify themselves as members of a visual, cultural-linguistic, global community (Padden & Humphries, 1988; Ladd, 2003; Murray 2008). Deaf people proudly celebrate their sensory status, and use sign languages as their preferred means of communication, interaction, learning, teaching and cultural transmission (Bauman, 2002). Whilst there are many other people who are audiologically deaf (including hard of hearing and deafened), Deaf people claim cultural identity over medical condition.

The Deaf-hearing family narrative challenges medicalised notions of deafness-as-disability, which treat Deaf children as in need of normalisation and cure, and parents as in grief and denial. The stories bilingual-bicultural families tell reveal not only repositioning of threatened, misunderstood, misplaced, wrongly ascribed identities, but also the desire to repair these in terms of acceptance, understanding and embracing of sign language, and of culturally Deaf ways of being.

In the context of this inquiry, therefore, a child's medical condition of 'not being able to hear' (for example), and the stories a family might tell, are not necessarily grounded in discourses of loss, grief or deficit, but of resistance, of cultural identity and identification, of bilingualism and sign language, and of what a culturally Deaf child contributes to family life. Whereas previous studies on Deaf-hearing family

M. Prendergast, C. Leggo and P. Sameshima (eds.), Poetic Inquiry: Vibrant Voices in the Social Sciences, 333–356.

life have, to a greater or lesser extent, been shaped by medical, *phonocentric* ways of thinking about Deaf people and deafness, family life and family relationships can be viewed and shared from a position that regards the existence of Deaf people and Deaf children born to hearing families as vital for a fuller understanding of what it means to be human.

You are invited to one family's story. The family – Luke, Dora, Harper and Maisie – are bilingual (English and British Sign Language) and bicultural (Luke, Dora and Harper are hearing and Maisie is Deaf). The second half of the chapter re-presents a small selection of our co-authored, collective narrative. The choice of a poetic-prose format is based on joint decisions concerning the most persuasive, truthful and evocative ways of representing spoken and signed stories.

SIGNED AND SPOKEN STORIES

This narrative inquiry engages with two languages; English (written and spoken) and British Sign Language (BSL). BSL, recently granted status as one of the UK's official languages (Brennan, 2003), has no written form (Temple & Young, 2004). That is to say, while there are various notation and glossing systems (Stokoe, 1960; Brennan, Colville & Lawson, 1980; Sutton-Spence & Woll, 1999) that may be employed in order to commit various linguistic features to the page, BSL as a visual-spatial language can only be recorded through film or videotape.

BSL notation for the sign 'Deaf':

$\supset$ H $<\square^x$	The H hand is held with the palm facing left (if the hand were opened, the fingers would point up	The hand is held beside the ear	The tips of the extended fingers touch the ear (Brien, 1992: 391)

An example of a BSL gloss:

> STORY GIRL GIRL Index$_R$ GIRL NAME m-a-i-s-i-e
> This is a story about a girl called Maisie.

The challenge of transcribing spoken English is not to be underestimated – the act of transcription is highly selective (Riessman, 1993; Green, Franquiz & Dixon, 1997; Scheurich, 1997). It was only seeing my attempts in black and white that made me realise how much is lost, or cannot be captured. In transcribing from *sign* to text, however, I was not only concerned with two languages, but also with two modalities; auditory-linear and visual-spatial (Temple & Young, 2004). BSL, a language in its own right, and very different in its syntax, grammar and lexicon from English (Sutton-Spence & Woll, 1999) cannot simply be transcribed. It also has to be translated, like a foreign language, and yet, without direct word-for-sign equivalence, the task of translating and capturing often highly poetic, metaphorical language told on the hands and face (Ladd, 2003), with a productive lexicon far greater than its established one (Brennan, 1992), charges us to consider more creative textual strategies for capturing signs and meanings on the page. Much of the meaning in BSL (and in sign languages around the world) is conveyed not only on the hands, but through how that sign is linked to facial expression, speed and repetition of movement, placement in the signing space, orientation of the hands, direction of eyegaze and context (Sutton-Spence & Woll, 1999). For example, when Maisie signs "We're just strong together", one could annotate her utterance with descriptions of mood, facial expression, movement, speed and placement of her signs, for example:

> The context for 'we' is the four members of the family. The sign for 'strong' brings Maisie's fists up towards her heart in a slow, circular, powerful movement – accompanied by a lip-pattern for 'strong' and a single nod of the head as she makes eye contact with her sister, who is smiling at her, also nodding. The sign for 'together', with eyebrows raised, moves rapidly, twice, in an anti-clockwise circle, taking in not only Harper who is sat next to her on the sofa (i.e. a geographical reference) but also her parents, not in the room, but incorporated metaphorically into the signing space.

This represents one way to *describe*, albeit partially, sign language, by selecting particular elements in order to 'thicken' the textual representation. Below is another example of how I moved from an early transcript 'sketch' of a BSL conversation to a co-edited poetic re-presentation.

Early draft transcript from BSL conversation (excerpt)

Maisie: {to Harper} you want to go through? (photo album)
Harper: The book? Oh yes!
Harper gets the album and opens it to the first page
H: Same as you, when I open and read the first page it was **really** emotional (smiles) {to Maisie} really lovely what you wrote … And means **so much** … maybe other people don't realise how much this means … wow
Maisie and Harper both read what Maisie wrote
H: It says, "I would never want to swap you for a Deaf sister" and, I don't know, that's such big thing for us …
Donna: {to Maisie} Perhaps a difficult question, but that line really hit me … I wondered if, what you were feeling, to write that, or …
M: Er … well … knew I couldn't just give her the book without, I felt I had to write something! So scribble something rough, <that'll do>, copied in, that's it! (smiles)
D: (laughs) OK … so {to Harper} what about for you?
H: Well … I know it would be easy, comfortable for her to wish she had Deaf sister, but to know she was thinking that, to write she didn't want swap me for Deaf sister, make me feel **valued**, like
M: It's the truth!

H: Thank you [pats Maisie on the knee] and we know we had struggles, the two of us, but now the two of us, it's like 'Bring it on!'
Harper turns the page

Poetic representation of the story of the photograph album, which Maisie gave to Harper for her birthday

THE FAMILY ALBUM *by Harper & Maisie*

When I open this
And read the first page
It's really emotional
It's really lovely what you wrote
And it means so much

And maybe other people don't realise how much this means
And it says
"I would never want to swap you for a Deaf sister"
And   I don't know   That's such a big thing for us

> *Well I knew I couldn't just*
> *Give her the book without*
> *I felt I had to write*
> *something!*
> *So I scribbled something in rough*
> *That'll do*
> *And copied it in*
> *<That's it!>*

Well
I know it would be easy
     And comfortable for her
         To wish she had a Deaf sister
But to know she was thinking that
To write that she didn't want to swap me for a Deaf sister
Makes me feel so valued
Like   *It's the truth!*
Thank you
And we know that
We've had struggles   the two of us
But now   the two of us
It's like

     "Bring it on!"   *"Bring it on!"*

Ultimately, what we wished for was a way to create an evocative, persuasive text that would capture the raw emotion and performative intent in our conversations, to bring together the layers of our collective experience and draw the (Deaf/hearing) reader's attention to the power of both spoken *and* signed stories. In terms of audience, I wished to consider and respect the fact that Deaf people have an 'oral' heritage. Their culture and history are transmitted through unwritten, sign-language stories. How might words on a page enter their eyes and minds and make meaning? How might the textual resources I have to hand bring spoken words and signs back to life, and resonate with signing as well as speaking people?

We (Dora, Luke, Maisie, Harper and Donna) are not poets, but our poetic-prose style (see Borum, 2006), we hope, allows readers to enter the stories by engaging with patterns of words that contain some of the emotion and intention of the original speech, signs or thoughts. A poetic prose, or stanza format (Etherington, 2002; Speedy, 2001) presents the core texts, or nucleus stories (McAdams, 1996) that "distil the essence" (Speedy, 2001: 14) of the narrative. In addition, in the absence of conventions or dynamics for indicating tempo, or intonation (see Hernadi, 1981), we felt that this format conveyed the rhythms of speech and sign better than other conventions we had seen, or experimented with. Laurel Richardson has written that people generally speak in a form closer to poetry than to prose (Richardson, 2003). I would add to this by including Deaf people's signed narratives. As Etherington (2002) points out, a stanza format helps the reader to recognise more clearly that the text is a deliberate creation. The particular construction used for the work presented here, we feel, reflects more closely the conversations we had, allowing simultaneous voices to be heard, by using fonts to indicate narrator – similar to the ways in which sign languages do through role-shift, eye-gaze and facial expression – and by exploiting poetic structures as a way of highlighting rhetorical features of BSL such as repetition, and of English, such as incomplete sentences, pauses and emphases.

The Family Story

Luke and Dora are parents to Harper and Maisie. They live in London, UK. Harper attends her local school. Maisie spends her week at a residential school for Deaf children, coming home at weekends and holidays. Their stories of family life, which focus predominantly on their relationships with each other, and with their extended family, moved from conversations, from e-mails, from a shared history of friendship and of moving in Deaf and hearing worlds, to re-presentation as a series of poetic texts. Rather than repeating the names of whoever is speaking or signing throughout these texts, we have used different fonts and placement of voices on the page. Gestures are indicated by [square brackets], and signs that accompany/replace spoken words, or directly untranslatable BSL are <enclosed thus>. Contextual

337

information, laughs, nods and smiles are (placed within brackets). Dora, Luke and I conversed in English, while the conversation between Harper, Maisie and me was in BSL.

You are invited to read, and to think *with* (Frank, 1995) their stories, a selection of which is reproduced below, and to reflect on our collective aim; to render Deaf lives visible, to counter pathological, disablist views of deafness, to celebrate Deaf-hearing family life and to tell – through text – a persuasive, emotionally charged, bilingual-bicultural narrative.

CLEVER PERSON: Maisie & Harper

I asked mum
What was his reaction
   When they found out I was Deaf
I was always asking that
How did he feel?

And she said
   Of course
   He was shocked
But you know
Shocked
Not panic-stricken
Oh-my-god-quick-cochlear-implant-and-all-that
But very practical
Like
   What do we need to do?
I mean
It was all new to him
The same as mum really
      And I always think that
      How people react to the Deaf thing
      That's part of how we judge what they're like
      As people
      And I think if they're a good person
        A nice
        Clever person

        Then they'll understand

CAMERA! Maisie & Harper

It's really interesting
Watching old videos
Of us
And you can see me
Opening and closing my mouth
All the time
And it's because
I was trying to copy people talking
So opening and closing my mouth
All the time
Me just copying them all the time
And of course
I didn't realise
You had to use to voice to talk
I just thought you had to open your mouth!

But it was beautiful
When you started to learn to Sign
Your first birthday
Second birthday
Third birthday

Every time you see a photo
Maisie would be signing <camera!>

It's really nice to look back to
The signing

And see us so close

BRAVE SMILES: Dora & Luke

I think
I mean
A Deaf member of the family
Particularly a child
As adults
We're responsible for the children
It affects absolutely everything that we do
And not just on a superficial level either
In everything
It affects us

And then
That can make it sound simple
But it complicates life hugely
Socially
With other members of the family
        With other friends and family

When she was little
It wasn't the case
Because she was little
        And little children tend to kind of fit in and
They're much
There's much less need for them to be
Socially interactive

But as she's got older
I think probably we always knew the teenage years
Were going to be the challenging ones
Not just because teenagers
But because she's a real person now
And there was a tendency for her to be treated like
As sort of
Rather an attractive little pet
By members of the family
        "Isn't she cute?"
Yeah she is cute

                And grandparents still do

But that has carried on
You know
And   An ornament
Yeah an ornament
And they fail to see her as an emerging adult
Which is what she is

            Or even a person
            Because if you can't communicate
            You've got no idea who someone is
            So it's a bit like a nice fridge
            You can look at it, and say "nice fridge"
                And that's about it

And to them
Having her there
It's rather like the inclusive argument for schools
Having her there makes her included
        Well it sure doesn't

It actually completely excludes her in a bigger way
Than if she wasn't there
Cos you know there's like
It's just
It's there
It's the elephant sitting in the room

And people
It's very easy for people to carry on and not acknowledge
   Well she's there so she must be happy
Because she's sitting there with
A brave smile on her face

And I know
And Luke knows
That actually she's hating it
And she's feeling horrible
She's feeling really horrible

We're sitting there going
"Uh I can't relax and enjoy this"
Cos I know she's feeling horrible
And there's this kind of
Racking of your brains thinking
   "How can I work this out
   How can I make this work?"

And the answer is actually
You can't
It's something that you kind of
Carry along with you
And it's very hard to explain it to people
Because
They just think we're kind of difficult
Awkward and
Making problems where there aren't any

          Anti-social
Or making an issue out of it
   "She's fine look at her she's lovely,
   She looks perfectly normal"

         Yeah, "nice fridge"

But then that's a horrible thing because
She's so bright
That she goes

341

"I make your life difficult"

And what, what do you say to that?

> She makes it *different*
> Not *difficult*

Yeah
Maybe she can't see the distinction

> No

> She said

> "I make it more difficult"

STRONG TOGETHER: Harper & Maisie

Yes
It's special
And I think we're lucky
    Always
    The last
    The bottom line is
We played together and
We're lucky to have
Each other
I think

> I know all families have their problems
> And our family has had its fights
> But those arguments are
> Because of love

I don't know how we could cope any better
I feel really proud that we've pulled together
I feel that there are
New challenges now to face
And different situations to
Deal with
But I don't feel as if we simply
Face a challenge
Then move on to the next
We just

I don't know how to describe it
But
But I think
We face what comes our way
And deal with it

    I think it's like
    A problem comes up
    And we deal with it
    But we don't sit there
    Waiting for problems to turn up
     We just get on with things
     And if something turns up
     We just have to try and solve it
     And move on
    And you get used to it
     Just shrug and move on

      We're strong together

FAMILY OCCASIONS: Dora & Luke

She's quite an optimist Harper
And she'll go
"Oh it'll be all right
We'll make it work"

      Or to certainly try

And she'll work hard to try and make it work
But
But quite often at the end of something
She'll just
   Feel
   Be sad
She'll be sad because it hasn't worked
Or it hasn't worked despite her trying so hard
To make it work

But she's
But then she bounces
She bounces backand

I worry about that

I worry that it's all getting stuck in there
   <inside>

343

ALMOST LIKE GIVE UP: Maisie

It's like
How can I ever have a
Proper
Direct
One-to-one
Relationship
With him
If

With her
It's
All right
But not really good enough
I mean
She's learnt sign
But
I mean
I know it's not her fault
She's old
And it's difficult to learn to sign
When you're old
But with him

I just feel
[disappointed face]
How can we have a relationship?

I feel

[almost like give up]

KNOWING MAISIE: Dora & Luke

People are often kind of sympathetic
And see it as a terrible shame
And I've always railed against that
No it's not a shame
You don't have to be sorry for her
So that's trying to put the positive spin on it
Where actually *it is difficult* but
It's not a shame

It's not a shame
It's not
But it's very sad
You know you said before
That people don't know her

Y'see cos we think she's hilarious
            She's really funny

        People don't know that

            Practically no-one can know that

            WATER: Maisie & Harper

        We'd always talk under water

                So
        Goggles on Goggles on
            Ready? Ready?
            1-2-3 1-2-3
        [Deep breath] [Deep breath]
            And under And under
        Signing away Signing away

        Then heads up and breathe again

                But thinking about
        Why we did the underwater signing
            It's because you can't play
                And swim
                And sign
            It's too exhausting

        So if you go under the water
                It's easier

            And you can sign!

GLUE: Dora & Luke

I think the good stuff comes

Out of the effort to
Iron out the bumps
And the troughs
And there are good things that
Come out of it
And it isn't easy
But when things go right
I don't think we would feel as
Elated as that
If it hadn't been so bloody tough

It's really difficult
The Deaf thing
But sometimes
I think
It's the glue that's kept
       That really holds the family
       Together
So that must be a good thing
       That must be a good thing
I don't know if there would have been
Something else
If that hadn't been there

                There might be
                Something more
                Can't think of the word
                    Frivolous
                Like
                An interest in
                Tennis

Funny I was just gonna say Tennis

                We'd all go out for lots of
                Tennis lessons
                You know
                Something like that
                You know it's fine and
                It's good and
                You get fit and everything
                But it's
                Less meaningful

Much less meaningful

                You know
                "Actually, my back-hand's
                pretty good, y'know"

But you go on all the Marches
And you think **huh**!
This is important
And worthwhile
And um
Tennis isn't
You know?

OPENING UP THE WORLD: Dora & Luke

But that's the thing you see
That's what I meant about it
Opening up this world
The world was there
We just didn't see it

And it would have been very easy
To kinda go along that
Rather narrow little path
I don't know who we would have been in it
I suspect we might not
We wouldn't have been straightforward
I don't think

No but it would've been easy to do that

So Maisie's made us really stop and look at us
Look at ourselves

I don't know if she'll ever know that

I wonder if she'll ever know that

When she's older

NICE BELT: Maisie

We went to stay at
Our grandparent's house
For one night
And the next morning

Our aunt was there
And
Well
We don't get on with her that well (wry smile)

And we
<twiddle thumbs stare at each other>
It wasn't that nice to see her really
Because
Like with Harper
She's always asking her about
You know
University and
Things like that
But she never asks me
        Never asks me about College

Or

It's like she thinks I'm stupid
And
Could never do the same things as Harper
So she'll say things like

"Oh your hair looks nice"

    Or

    "That's a nice belt"

A REAL PERSON: Harper & Maisie

That thing about
"Not treating me like a real person"
It's like
Because people can't communicate with you
They don't realise how funny you are
And so then think you're just
        They miss **so** much!

And you just think
You're **so** stupid
Why don't you learn to sign!
You're missing so much!

348

I do think that sometimes

>And it's like my cousins'll
>Learn French
>>Or Spanish
>But it's not like there's anyone French
>In the family
>
>So why won't you learn BSL?
>
>It's only one more language
>
>There's this horror or panic
>But it's just another language
>And it's difficult to learn any other language
>So
>
>I don't get it
>
>I think
>>it's
>>>**Weird**

BANGING ON: Luke & Dora

So the banging on thing is very limiting
Because you
You might not wish to go into
That Area of Conversation
You might rather talk about
Rugby

>But it's also used as an identifier
>I know that people say
>"Oh-yes-you-know-Dora
>She's-got-a-Deaf-daughter"
>And they go
>"Oh yes I know who you mean"

But I mean
In
You know
In a restaurant
And
You know   you can hear people
Coming up to you in the street

Or in the shop
Every
Every transaction
                              "Oh-I've-always-wanted-to-learn-to-sign"
You know
(sigh)
"I've got something to do, thanks"

                    We got given a Braille menu at Pizza Hut

HAVE I GOT MY FAMILY RIGHT TODAY? Luke & Dora

That extra effort
If you do a twelve hour day at work
When you come back and
You spend lots of time talking about the LEAs
Or planning or
Anything else
Then
There's time to watch half an hour of crap telly and
Fall over
And so
That's a big relationship stress
There's no
Downtime
Relaxation
It's very difficult
                    You can't just carry on blindly
                    Or else it won't work
                    Something will crack
                    There'll be a crack in the family
                              And yet with all this thinking
                              And all this planning
                    And with everything that goes with it
                    I feel that an awful lot of the time
                    We're making a complete balls up of it
                              And getting it wrong

                    So I would hate to make it sound like
                    "Oh no we've got this down
                    We know what we're doing here"
                    It's not like that at all

You know
Just
The number of times you think
"Oh, why did I say that?   Why did I do it that way?
That was so insensitive   That was just so awful"
And of course that's
That's what you remember

But I think what I'm saying is
Even with all that forethought
It still doesn't go right

At the end of the day
<peer inside self>
"Have I got my family right today?"

Mmm
No
I'm a Jewish mother

It's *agony*!

THE THIRD QUESTION: Luke & Dora

But the banging on
The banging on situation is very interesting
Because if you meet somebody
Someone else
I met a colleague
At the interval at a do at Harper's school
And so
The third question
Is
"Where does your other daughter go?"
You know
"Got any other kids?"
                    "Do you have any other children?"
And   that
Changes the rest of the conversation
You can hardly say (laughs)
I suppose I could say no!
But yeah, so I say
"Yeah I've got a daughter of sixteen"
"So, is she at the same school?"

"You'll be sorry you asked me that!"

And you go
"No cos she's Deaf
She's at a residential special school"
And then
Quite a few people kinda go
<jaw drop>
And the rest go
"Ooh, so can she hear anything?"
"Got an implant?"

"Does she speak?"
"Does she speak does she lipread?"
"Does she lipread?"

And and then
If you actually answer those questions
You miss the second half
And so it's very difficult

You pick your opponent don't you?
I mean
That women we met
(The neighbours had drinks one Christmas)
Who   The third question was
"Where does your other daughter …?"
And I said
"Deaf, Deaf school"
And she said
"Ooh… who looks after her here ?"
I said   I said
"She's not ill!"

We do! We do!
          She lives with us

Fuck off!

A COMPLETE UNKNOWN: Dora & Luke

I don't know if you knew
But I had no idea at the start of
You know
When I first knew that Maisie was Deaf
I had no idea what the future was

                                        No

Not a clue

Not a clue
And I don't think I even particularly thought about it
You're so busy dealing with the day-to-day
That if anybody said
You know
      "Imagine her as a fifteen year old
          Sixteen year old
             Thirteen year old"
I couldn't do it
The picture I would have painted would not have been the reality

Would you have been able to paint a picture?

Probably not
                          No
                          No

I remember the Teacher for the Deaf
When she first came round saying
"Now, thinking about school"

And I was thinking
<holding baby>

"School?
      What are you talking about?

        This is a baby!
        She's not going to school!"

THE FAMILY ALBUM: Harper & Maisie

When I open this
And read the first page
It's really emotional
It's really lovely what you wrote
And it means so much
And maybe other people don't realise
How Much This Means
And it says
"I would never want to swap you for a Deaf sister"
And
I don't know

353

That's such a big thing for us

> Well I knew I couldn't just
> Give her the book without
> I felt I had to write something!
> So I scribbled something in rough
> That'll do
> And copied it in
> *<That's it!>*

Well
I know it would be easy
 And comfortable for her
  To wish she had a Deaf sister
But to know she was thinking that
To write that she didn't want to swap me for a Deaf sister
Makes me feel so valued
Like

It ' s the truth!

Thank you

And we know that
We've had struggles the two of us
But now the two of us
It's like

"Bring it on!" "Bring it on!"

AFTERWORD

In 2007, I made an art gallery of the family texts at the Centre for Deaf Studies in Bristol. I invited Deaf and hearing people to wander round and engage with the stories. I then asked them how they felt. One hearing friend said she read one of the texts, and got caught on a phrase – she laughed out loud, then, immediately, found herself wanting to cry. A Deaf colleague told me that as she read the texts, a memory, hidden deep in the back of her head suddenly materialised, and she was taken back to her childhood, trying to communicate with hearing members of her family. Her reading of a text triggered a forgotten memory. She told me, "Keep collecting stories".

DEAR WORLD: Dora & Luke

What you
What you've   put out there
I think I said
It's important
    It's important to keep going with this
    We can't just go
    Well it's all been said
    I think we've gotta keep saying it
And
Some people might hear it
And
Some people will never hear it
    But hopefully
    Some of those who do hear it will listen
    And some of those who listen will think
    And some of those who think will remember
    And some of those who remember will try to change
    And some of those who try and change will succeed
    in changing their world view
    And
    The more this happens
    The more the world can change

"Dear world ..."

REFERENCES

Bauman, H.-D. L. (2002). *Idea paper.* Paper presented at the Deaf Studies Think Tank, Gallaudet University, Washington, DC.

Borum, V. (2006). Reading and writing womanist poetic prose: African American mothers with deaf daughters. *Qualitative inquiry, 12*(2), 340–352.

Brennan, M., Colville, M. D., & Lawson, L. K. (1980). *Words in hand: A structural analysis of the signs of British sign language.* Edinburgh: Moray House.

Brennan, M. (1992). The visual world of British sign language: An introduction. In D. Brien (Ed.), *Dictionary of British sign language.* London: Faber & Faber.

Brennan, M. (2003). Deafness, disability and inclusion: The gap between rhetoric and practice. *Policy futures in education, 1*(4), 668–685.

Brien, D. (Ed.). (1992). *Dictionary of British sign language.* London: Faber & Faber.

Etherington, K. (2002). Narrative ideas and stories of disability. In K. Etherington (Ed.), *Rehabilitation counselling in physical and mental health.* London: Jessica Kingsley Publishers.

Frank, A. W. (1995). *The wounded storyteller: Body, illness and ethics.* Chicago: University of Chicago Press.

Green, J., Franquiz, M., & Dixon, C. (1997). The myth of the objective transcript: Transcribing as a situated act. *TESOL quarterly, 31*(1), 172–176.

Hernadi, P. (1981). Afterthoughts. In W. J. T. Mitchell (Ed.), *On narrative* (pp. 197–199). Chicago: University of Chicago Press.

Ladd, P. (2003). *Understanding deaf culture: In search of deafhood.* Clevedon: Multilingual Matters.

McAdams, D. P. (1996). Personality, modernity and the storied self: A contemporary framework for studying persons. *Psychological inquiry, 7,* 295–321.

Murray, J. (2008). Coequality and transnational studies: Understanding deaf lives. In H.-D. L. Bauman (Ed.), *Sightings: Explorations in deaf studies* (pp. 100–110). Minneapolis, MN: University of Minnesota Press.

Padden, C., & Humphries, T. (1988). *Deaf in America.* Cambridge, MA: Harvard University Press.

Richardson, L. (2003). Poetic representation of interviews. In J. F. Gubrium & J. A. Holstein (Eds.), *Postmodern interviewing* (pp. 187–202). Thousand Oaks, CA: Sage.

Riessman, C. K. (1993). *Narrative analysis.* London: Sage.

Scheurich, J. J. (1997). *Research methods in the postmodern.* London: Falmer.

Speedy, J. (2001). *Singing over the bones: A narrative inquiry into the construction of research and practice cultures and professional identities by counsellor educators at the University of Bristol and within the UK.* Unpublished PhD Thesis, University of Bristol.

Stokoe, W. (1960). Sign language structure: An outline of the visual communication system of the American deaf. *Studies in linguistics occasional paper 8,* University of Buffalo.

Sutton-Spence, R., & Woll, B. (1999). *The linguistics of British sign language: An introduction.* Cambridge: Cambridge University Press.

Temple, B., & Young, A. M. (2004). Qualitative research and translation dilemmas. *Qualitative research, 4*(2), 161–178.

West, D. (2007). *"Strong together": A narrative inquiry into deaf-hearing family life.* Unpublished MEd Dissertation, University of Bristol.

Donna West
Graduate School of Education
Centre for Deaf Studies
University of Bristol, UK

CONTRIBUTORS

Ivan Brady is Distinguished Teaching Professor Emeritus and former Chair of Anthropology at SUNY Oswego. A past President of the Society for Humanistic Anthropology, his poetry has appeared in various books and journals in several disciplines. He is the author of *The Time at Darwin's Reef: Poetic Explorations in Anthropology and History.* See also IvanBrady.com.

Lynn Butler-Kisber, a former elementary teacher, is an Associate Professor in the Faculty of Education, McGill, directs the Centre for Educational Leadership and the Graduate Certificates in Leadership, teaches language arts and qualitative research, and is founding editor of the LEARNing Landscapes journal. She conducts research/ development work locally and internationally with a particular interest in arts-based inquiry.

Melisa Cahnmann-Taylor, Associate Professor in Language and Literacy Education at the University of Georgia, addresses bilingualism and multiculturalism in her arts-based research. Her prize-winning poetry has been recognized by the Dorothy Sargent Rosenberg Foundation, the Leeway Foundation, and the Waging Peace Poetry Prize. She is co-editor of the book, *Arts-Based Research in Education: Foundations for Practice* (Routledge) and co-author of the forthcoming book, *Teachers Act Up! Performing Our Lives, Enacting Change* (Teachers College Press.

Bernadette Marie Calafell is Assistant Professor of Culture and Communication in the Department of Human Communication at the University of Denver. Her research converges around issues of performance, rhetoric, and intersectionality, particularly within Chicana/o and Latina/o communities.

Andrea Dancer is a published poet, radio documentarian, soundscape artist and doctoral candidate. Her research examines the soundscape as a social phenomenon, how it shapes the subjects' eco-values, and concepts of indigenity. She is working on a doctoral degree at UBC's Centre for Cross Faculty Inquiry. She lives in quiet places along Canada's West Coast and in the Czech Republic's Bohemian-Moravian Highlands..

Kimberly Dark is a pop-sociologist whose interest is in crafting poetry and performances for general audiences, using autoethnography and social research, on themes such as gender, poverty, sexuality and education. Further information about her work is available at www.kimberlydark.com. She also teaches sociology at California State University, San Marcos.

Gina Edghill is a doctoral student in Adult, Higher, and Community Education at Ball State University, Muncie, Indiana. Born and raised in Barbados, she pursued her undergraduate and graduate education in the USA. Her research interests include narrative, poetry, and fiction as educative, transformative, and healing tools.

Daniela Bouneva Elza is pursuing (poetically) her Ph.D. in Philosophy of Education at Simon Fraser University. Having lived on three continents, across geographic and cultural borders, Daniela is a semantic anomaly herself, a rogue scholar at heart. She dwells in chaordic spaces: imagination, language, metaphor, theory/practice, alternative methods of inquiry, creativity.

Sandra L. Faulkner is Assistant Professor of Communication at Bowling Green State University. Her research interests include effective sexual talk and the role of culture and identities in close relationships, and the uses and criteria for poetic inquiry.

Lynn Fels et al. [Ann, Danita, Devon, Julie, Lynn & Shelley]: All six women—four prison inmates, a university researcher, and a volunteer—were or are currently involved in a participatory action research project initially based in a correctional centre in British Columbia. At the time of writing, four of the women were at various stages in their sentencing. All names are first names for reasons of confidentiality and so as not to privilege but recognize that we are all learning reciprocally within each other's presence.

Kathleen Galvin PhD, is a nurse and Chair in Health Research, School of Health & Social Care, Bournemouth University, UK. As part of her work with the Centre for Qualitative Research she is using phenomenology to develop insights for caring practice and professional education, particularly applications of lifeworld theory to care. Her personal interest is in exploring potential benefits of poetry for communicating experiences deeply and how this could be used in healthcare. Together with her colleague Les Todres, she is developing 'embodied interpretation' an approach to re-presenting the findings of phenomenological research in more poetic and evocative ways.

Susanne Gannon is a Senior Lecturer in Education at the University of Western Sydney, Australia. She has pursued her interest in creative modes of writing as inquiry in poetry, drama and fiction through doctoral studies and articles in: *Qualitative Inquiry, Qualitative Studies in Education, Sex Education, Auto/Biography, Outskirts* and *LINQ*.

Diane Susan Grimes is Associate Professor of Communication and Rhetorical Studies at Syracuse University. Her research interests include critical organizational communication, diversity issues (including gender, race, whiteness) and visual culture. She is an associate editor for the journal *Gender, Work, and Organization*.

John J. Guiney Yallop is a parent, a partner, and a poet. A book of queer autoethnographic poetry and an exegesis constituted John's PhD Thesis. In 2008

John joined the Faculty in the School of Education at Acadia University. Research interests include narrative, poetic inquiry, and performative social science.

Wanda Hurren is a poetic photographer/cartographer living in Victoria, BC. Her mapwork has been featured in several exhibitions of text and image. She is a member of Crossgrains, one of the few remaining darkroom societies, and she is a faculty member in the Department of Curriculum and Instruction at the University of Victoria.

Kedrick James: Coming from a background in experimental poetics as a pedagogical source of inquiry, James's current research investigates how the cybernetic notion of *heuristic filtering*, adapted to suit individual navigational styles, is employed both in daily literacy practices and as a mode of digital creativity–including its role in *artificial creativity*.

Jacquie Kidd (PhD) is a Maori nurse from New Zealand, of the Nga Puhi tribe. She is a Senior Lecturer with the University of Auckland. Her areas of research interest include the mental health of the caring professions, adult mental health, and creative Kaupapa methodologies.

Carl Leggo is a Poet/Professor in the Department of Language and Literacy Education at the University of British Columbia. He is the author of several books including: *Growing Up Perpendicular on the Side of a Hill, View from My Mother's House, Come-By-Chance, Life Writing and Literary Métissage as an Ethos for our Times* (with Erika Hasebe-Ludt and Cynthia Chambers), and *Creative Expression, Creative Education* (with Robert Kelly).

Rebecca Luce-Kapler is Professor of Language and Literacy in the Faculty of Education, Queen's University. Her research focuses on writing processes and technologies. She is the author of *Writing With, Through and Beyond the Text: An Ecology of Language* and a collection of poetry, *The Gardens Where She Dreams*.

Sarah K. MacKenzie is an Assistant Professor of Education at Bucknell University where she mentors student teachers and teaches courses in literacy and educational foundations. Her current research explores arts-based epistemologies and the ways and spaces in which pre-service teachers (co)write their identities as teachers.

Ronald J. Pelias, a Professor in the Department of Speech Communication at Southern Illinois University, Carbondale, works in the areas of performance and performative writing. His most recent books are *Writing Performance: Poeticizing the Researcher's Body* and *A Methodology of the Heart: Evoking Academic & Daily Life.*

Jane Piirto is Trustees' Distinguished Professor at Ashland University, Ohio. She has published 6 chapbooks and 1 book of poetry, *Saunas,* with Mayapple Press.

She has received two individual artist fellowships from the Ohio Arts Council, one in poetry and one in fiction, and is the Mensa Education and Research Foundation's 4th Lifetime Achievement Award winner. Her nonfiction books have to do with giftedness and with creativity.

Monica Prendergast is an Assistant Professor in the Graduate School of Arts and Social Sciences, Division of Creative Arts in Learning, at Lesley University in Cambridge, MA. She has published widely in journals, books and has a co-authored (with Carl Leggo) poetic inquiry contribution in *The International Handbook of Research in Arts Education* (Springer, 2007). Her book *Teaching Spectatorship: Essays and Poems on Audience in Performance* was published by Cambria Press in 2008.

Bonnie Raingruber is the Director of the Center for Health and Human Services Research and a Professor of Nursing at California State University Sacramento. She is also an Associate Professor in the Department of Hematology and Oncology and a Nurse Researcher at the University of California Davis.

Frances Rapport, a Social Scientist with a background in the Arts, is Professor of Qualitative Health Research at the School of Medicine, Swansea University, UK, Head of the Qualitative Research Unit and a Fellow of the Royal Society of Arts. Her research interests include: notions of health and illness in Holocaust survivor stories and innovative methodological approaches to qualitative health research. She writes extensively about the scope of New Qualitative Methodologies for health services research and is currently exploring health professionals' reflections on inhabited workspaces using bio-photographic methods.

Pauline Sameshima is interested in learning system designs, technology integration, eco-responsive pedagogies and creative scholarship. Her books include: *Seeing Red: A Pedagogy of Parallax* and *Climbing the Ladder with Gabriel.* She works in the College of Education at Washington State University in the Cultural Studies and Social Thought in Education Program.

Nilofar Shidmehr is a poet and PhD student at the Centre for Cross-Faculty Inquiry in Education at the University of British Columbia. She is the author of *Shirin and Salt Man* and the Farsi translator of Tony Morrison's *The Bluest Eye.* Her research is concerned with the question of how narrativity/biographicity/translation can contribute in constructing a more viable dialogical self and function as constituting spatial practices which delimit and subvert social constructed spaces and re-arrange social power relations.

Mary Stewart, Ph.D., works for LEARN, an educational foundation supported by the Québec-Canada Entente. The foundation addresses minority language education needs within the province of Quebec. Among other duties she is the Managing Editor of LEARNing Landscapes, the foundation's open access, online education journal. Mary has a keen interest in arts-informed research methodologies and has used poetry and collage in a range of research contexts.

Anne McCrary Sullivan has an MFA in Poetry and a PhD in English Education and is Professor of Education at National-Louis University. Her poems have appeared in many literary journals including *The Southern Review* and *The Gettysburg Review,* and in a full-length collection, *Ecology II: Throat Song from The Everglades.* She writes often on the epistemology of art.

Suzanne Thomas is Assistant Professor in the Faculty of Education at the University of Prince Edward Island. She is author of *earth and flesh and bones and breath: Landscapes of Embodiment and Moments of Re-enactment* (Backalong Books, 2004) and has published journal articles, book chapters, and multi-media publications in areas of integrated arts inquiry, island studies, and arts-informed research methodology. She is currently Coordinator of the Masters of Arts, Island Studies Program at the University of Prince Edward Island.

Les Todres Ph.D. is a clinical psychologist and Professor of Qualitative Research and Psychotherapy at Bournemouth University, UK. He is author of the book: Embodied Enquiry: phenomenological touchstones for research, psychotherapy and spirituality (Palgrave Macmillan, 2007) and numerous journal articles and book chapters. Together with his colleague, Kate Galvin, he is developing 'embodied interpretation', an approach to re-presenting the findings of phenomenological research in more poetic and evocative ways.

Roxanne Vandermause, a community health and certified addictions nurse, and an Assistant Professor in the College of Nursing at Washington State University. Her research in the area of women's addictions uses multiple methods, predominantly Heideggerian hermeneutical phenomenology and other interpretive forms. She teaches qualitative health research, community health nursing and other theory and clinical courses at the graduate and undergraduate level. She is committed to sustaining participatory pedagogical and research approaches to understanding complex everyday health problems.

Rachelle D. Washington is an Assistant Professor of Elementary Education at Clemson University. Her research includes inquiry on the social context of education; educational equity and social justice issues; and language and literacy development. Rachelle employs poetic representation as a tool in the service of narrative analysis.

Mary E. Weems is a poet, playwright, author, performer, and imagination-intellect theorist. Weems' books include *Poetry Power* (Silvermoon Press, 2003) and *Public Education and the Imagination-Intellect: I Speak from the Wound in My Mouth* (Peter Lang, 2003). Her latest book of poems is *An Unmistakable Shade of Red and the Obama Chronicles* (Bottom Dog Press, 2008). Weems is currently an Assistant

Professor in the Department of Education and Allied Studies at John Carroll University.

Donna West is a PhD student at the Graduate School of Education, and a Visiting Fellow at the Centre for Deaf Studies, University of Bristol, UK. She has previously worked as an Art Teacher and Teacher of Deaf Children. Her research interests include Deaf-hearing families, Deaf education, narrative inquiry and creative-poetic representation of spoken/sign language life-stories.

Breinigsville, PA USA
23 August 2009
222744BV00001B/1/P